Language Variation

Editors: John Nerbonne, Dirk Geeraerts

In this series:

1. Côté, Marie-Hélène, Remco Knooihuizen and John Nerbonne (eds.). The future of dialects.

2. Schäfer, Lea. Sprachliche Imitation: Jiddisch in der deutschsprachigen Literatur (18.–20. Jahrhundert).

3. Juskan, Marten. Sound change, priming, salience: Producing and perceiving variation in Liverpool English.

ISSN: 2366-7818

Sound change, priming, salience

Producing and perceiving variation in Liverpool English

Marten Juskan

language
science
press

Marten Juskan. 2018. *Sound change, priming, salience: Producing and perceiving variation in Liverpool English* (Language Variation 3). Berlin: Language Science Press.

This title can be downloaded at:
http://langsci-press.org/catalog/book/210
© 2018, Marten Juskan
Published under the Creative Commons Attribution 4.0 Licence (CC BY 4.0):
http://creativecommons.org/licenses/by/4.0/
ISBN: 978-3-96110-119-1 (Digital)
       978-3-96110-120-7 (Hardcover)

ISSN: 2366-7818
DOI:10.5281/zenodo.1451308
Source code available from www.github.com/langsci/210
Collaborative reading: paperhive.org/documents/remote?type=langsci&id=210

Cover and concept of design: Ulrike Harbort
Typesetting: Marten Juskan
Proofreading: Alec Shaw, Amir Ghorbanpour, Andreas Hölzl, Felix Hoberg, Havenol Schrenk, Ivica Jeđud, Jeffrey Pheiff, Jeroen van de Weijer, Kate Bellamy
Fonts: Linux Libertine, Libertinus Math, Arimo, DejaVu Sans Mono
Typesetting software: XƎLᴬTEX

Language Science Press
Unter den Linden 6
10099 Berlin, Germany
langsci-press.org

Storage and cataloguing done by FU Berlin

Freie Universität Berlin

To Daniela

Contents

Contents

Contents

Contents

Acknowledgements

This work owes a lot to the many colleagues and friends who directly or indirectly contributed to its making and I offer my sincere apologies to anyone I might have forgotten in the list below. First and foremost, I would like to thank my supervisor Bernd Kortmann, whose door was always open, and without whom I would never have got interested in Liverpool English in the first place. I am equally indebted to Peter Auer, Brigitte Halford, Patrick Honeybone, and two anonymous reviewers, whose comments were very helpful in improving this book. Thanks are also due to a plethora of other people whose help was greatly appreciated: Christian Langstrof was a tremendous source of knowledge for anything related to phonetics, Praat, and vowel normalisation. Alice Blumenthal-Dramé and Verena Haser answered numerous questions about statistics and R. As my first, invaluable, contact in Liverpool, Michael Pace-Sigge told me where best to find Scousers to interview.

Among many others, David Brazendale, Amanda Cardoso, Marije Van Hattum, Michaela Hejna, Victorina Gonzalez-Diaz, Sofia Lampropoulou, Ian McEvoy, Linda McLoughlin, Katja Roller, Erik Schleef, and Kevin Watson (in alphabetical order) all helped me to recruit participants in one way or another. My heartfelt thanks go out to everyone who took the time to give me an interview, or who spared half an hour to take part in the online test. Without the data they provided this book would not have been possible.

I am equally indebted to Danielle Turton, who – although a proud Mancunian – consented to record Scouse lenition stimuli for the perception experiment. Andrew MacFarlane also deserves a mention here, as it was his "Herr Hitler" mnemonic that set me on the most promising track to explaining parts of my perception data. My mother Gertraude and my brother Maiko have my gratitude for going through the horror of proofreading an early version of this manuscript. All remaining errors are my own.

During the four years it took me to complete this study my wife Daniela was my anchor and my sail. She shared my enthusiasm when things were going well, and provided comfort and encouragement when they were not. Her influence and support are in every word.

1 Introduction

1.1 Intentions – what this study is about

The present book is primarily interested in the impact that sociolinguistic salience can have on the perception of language. As such, it is firmly rooted within sociophonetics, but also inherently inter-disciplinary in nature due to the fact that mental representations, cognitive processing, and the influence of stereotypes are relevant in the context of the research question. A number of studies conducted in recent years have shown that perceivers integrate social information about speakers when processing linguistic material. Niedzielski (1999) and Hay, Nolan, et al. (2006) in particular provide evidence that subjects perceive one and the same acoustic stimulus differently depending on what they sub-consciously believe to know about the speaker they are listening to. Hay & Drager (2010) then went one step further and showed that even cues that are both more subtle and more indirect are capable of biasing the cognitive system towards processing or, more precisely, categorising linguistic input in a particular way. These data are not only extremely relevant for models of how humans cognitively deal with variation in language, but especially the results of Hay & Drager (2010) additionally have the potential of changing the way linguistic experiments are designed and conducted: if even small objects completely unrelated to the task can influence the outcome of an experiment by their mere presence, then it seems necessary to control for the physical surroundings of such experiments much more carefully than most of us probably have done so far.

There is, however, an aspect that has not figured prominently in previous research and that might be able to qualify the conclusions drawn from these studies: salience. In recent years, most sociophoneticians have incorporated some form of episodic memory in their theoretical frameworks, and this is also the model that is best able to explain the results derived from previous priming studies in sociolinguistics. Within this framework, salience should actually play a crucial role for priming effects because salient sensory events are believed to dominate long-term memory due to their prominence in perception (cf. Pierrehumbert 2006). It is only logical that they should then also be more prone to manipulations such as priming, which leads to the main hypothesis of this study: the strength of an exemplar priming effect is a direct function of the sociolinguistic salience of the test variable. Priming effects of the kind that Niedzielski (1999) and Hay, Nolan, et al. (2006) found would then be restricted to linguistic variables that are highly salient, possibly even to those that have reached the level of conscious awareness in the relevant speech community (*stereotypes* in Labovian terminology).

The testing ground for this hypothesis is Scouse, the variety of English spoken in the city of Liverpool and parts of its immediate surroundings in the north-west of England. There are several points which make Liverpool English a good candidate for the present study: (1) It has a number of phonological features (some more, some less salient according to the literature) that set it apart from the standard and surrounding non-standard varieties; (2) It is one of the most widely known (cf. Trudgill 1999), and (3) most heavily stigmatised varieties in the UK (cf. Montgomery 2007a). Scouse is a convenient choice of variety in the context of this study because the presence of variants that attract overt commentary is obviously a prerequisite for testing the hypothesis formulated above.

Four phonological variables (two vocalic, two consonantal) have been selected as the focus of this book: happy-tensing, velar nasal plus, the NURSE-SQUARE merger, and lenition of /k/. The first two of these are generally thought to carry very low levels of social salience in Liverpool, while the remaining two are considered to be stereotypes by many linguists. However, there are a number of reasons that advise against blindly and exclusively categorising these variables as salient or non-salient on the basis of previous research alone. The most important of these is that, for the present study, it is desirable to have a classification that is more fine-grained than the binary salient vs. non-salient one. Additionally, Liverpool English is reported to go against the general trend of dialect levelling found in many other places (Kerswill 2003). Instead, Watson (2007a: 237) found Scouse to be "getting Scouser", at least with respect to some variables. Especially against the backdrop of this ongoing change, it is therefore necessary to independently ascertain the salience of the four variables under scrutiny here first. This is done by analysing production data (collected in the form of sociolinguistic interviews) and measuring the salience of a variable with respect to the traditional indicator-marker-stereotype hierarchy introduced by Labov.

This approach provides the opportunity to address several additional questions along the way, as it were, such as whether younger Liverpudlians have stronger local accents than older speakers in *every* respect, or how these changes are related to local identity, the internal as well as external image of their city, and attitudes of speakers towards their variety. These issues are, of course, particularly interesting in the case of Liverpool, because the city has seen such a tremendous amount of physical, economic, and social change in the last 50 years, and this is likely to have at least some impact on the (socio-)linguistic behaviour of speakers. Furthermore, Liverpool English is a variety for which Watson (2007b: 351) stated in 2007 that "modern research [was] lacking", especially in the area of variation along social dimensions such as age, gender, or class. It is true that, in the 11 years since Watson's claim, a number of linguistic studies focusing on Liverpool have been published, but I would still argue that we know far more about many other varieties of English than we do about Scouse. As far as I am aware, for instance, there is still no complete descriptive account of Liverpool English except Knowles (1973), which is now quite dated and also clearly and explicitly *not* a truly variationist study of the kind Watson (2007b) refers to. I will try to narrow this gap a bit, but it should be noted that the primary purpose of analysing production data, in the present study, is to provide a sound basis for comparison for the subsequent perception test. The focus is therefore on establishing the salience of the four test variables and on discovering any differences (with respect to salience) between social groups, particularly along the age dimension.

1.2 Restrictions – what this study is not about

An a priori limitation of my study is that it is only concerned with Scouse as an accent. Local characteristics in the lexicon, (morpho-)syntax, or discourse pragmatics will remain unaddressed. It is also *not* the aim of this book to be an updated version of Knowles's 1973 study and provide a complete description of the phonological system of Scouse. Rather, it focusses (almost) exclusively on the four variables listed above and largely ignores other segmental and suprasegmental features of Liverpool English. A detailed account of the social stratification of local variants is equally beyond the scope of my study. Social differentiations of subjects (for the production data) are therefore comparatively coarse, and the size of the speaker sample does not permit much more fine-grained distinctions. It is, however, more than sufficient for assessing the *social salience* of our variables, which is the purpose it was collected for.

   This brings me to the second issue that it might be preferable to clarify from the very beginning of this book. Despite the fact that *salience* appears in the title of this work and notwithstanding that the term will turn up again and again in what is to follow, the present study is *not* a book *about* salience per se (cf. Chapter 4). There is an ongoing debate among researchers about what exactly salience is or what precisely it should refer to. My analysis will not add anything to this discussion, mostly because I am not interested – in the context of the present study – in what *makes* something salient. Instead, I intend to address the question of what salience *does* in perception, particularly when priming is involved. In other words, the spotlight is on the *effects* of salience, not on its *causes*. Essentially, social salience will be the scale used to measure the degree of awareness of, and attention paid to, a particular variable. I will then show that the level of awareness correlates with the strength of the priming effect. How and why awareness came about in the first place is irrelevant for this purpose and will not be discussed any further.

1.3 Structure of the book

Chapter 2 sketches the history of the city of Liverpool and its accent to give the reader an idea about the social changes that have taken place in this city and how they might influence the attitudes of speakers from different generations towards Scouse and questions of local identity. Chapter 3 contains a short overview of the pool of phonetic and phonological features that Liverpool English draws from, and presents the four variables that this book focusses on. Chapter 4, finally, explains how the term *salience* is used in this work, and also how it will be operationalised. Furthermore, it lays out some fundamental principles of exemplar theory and describes how the main hypothesis of this study is motivated by the theoretical framework.

Next is a a comprehensive description (Chapter 5) of how the production data were collected (interview structure, sampling), measured (parameters, semi-automatic processing), and analysed (normalisation, statistical modelling). Chapters 6 (vowels) and 7 (consonants) contain the quantitative analysis of the data gathered from the sociolinguistic interviews, while Chapter 8 presents a recapitulatory qualitative analysis of participants' explicit comments about (specific features of) their accent, local identity, and the like. In Chapter 9, both quantitative and qualitative results are summarised, discussed, and contextualised. While this part dominates in terms of the space devoted to it, this should not be taken to imply that it is also conceptually more important – it just so happens that a detailed analysis of production patterns is rather space and time consuming, even when it is a comparatively restricted one.

In the remaining chapters, this book turns to perception. Stimulus generation, recruitment of participants, presentation of test material and other methodological issues are treated in Chapter 10, while the results of the online perception test are reported in detail in Chapter 11. My interpretation of said results (Chapter

12) takes into account both the production data, on the one hand, and previous research, particularly by Hay, Nolan, et al. (2006) and Hay & Drager (2010), on the other. Chapter 13, finally, rounds off the study with a brief recapitulation of the most relevant findings and conclusions.

Most chapters end with a summary that contains the main points. Exceptions to this rule are the chapters on methodology and the ones presenting the results of the quantitative and qualitative analyses. In the former case, a summary was deemed to be rather unnecessary as the whole point of these chapters is to describe the methods employed *in detail* for reasons of replicability. The "results" chapters, on the other hand, are summarised in the discussions (Chapters 9 and 12), and therefore do not require a résumé of their own.

2 A brief history of Liverpool and Scouse

2.1 The first 600 years

At the end of the 12th century, Liverpool, in the north-west of England (cf. Figure 2.1), was nothing but a very small fishing village in a geographically rather disadvantaged location. It had neither a parish church nor a castle and its hinterland was "marginal to the economic and political life of pre-industrial England" (Kermode et al. 2006: 59). Things began to change when King John granted Liverpool borough status in 1207, an act now widely considered as the birth of the city. Liverpool was a planned town born out of the king's need for a port of embarkation for his campaigns in Ireland. The city's most long-lasting cultural connection thus originally started out as a military one (cf. Kermode et al. 2006: 59–63).

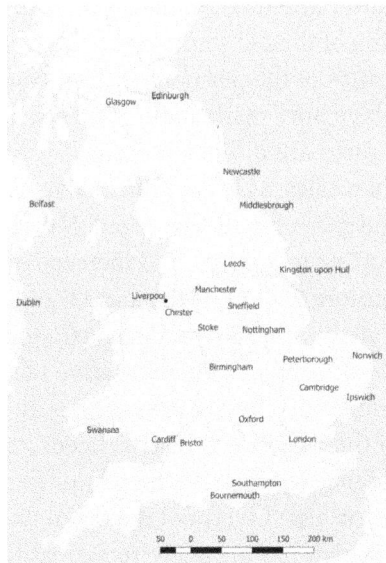

Figure 2.1: Liverpool in the UK
Created with QGIS Development Team (2016). Free vector and raster map data @ naturalearthdata.com

In the early 17th century, Liverpool had still not grown beyond its original seven streets, indicating that there was no significant population pressure. The total population of Liverpool in 1600 is estimated at around 1000 people, making it about the same size as Lancaster or Blackburn, and only between a fifth and a sixth the size of Manchester and Chester. Commercial activity was modest and remained geographically limited, although Liverpool was already used as a port for exporting Lancashire coal, timber, and textiles, and occasional trade with south-western France and northern Spain took place (cf. Kermode et al. 2006: 72–76 and 81–84). The latter part of the 17th century saw the establishment and rapid development of new routes, most notably to the West Indies and Liverpool ended up overtaking Chester, which had been the major port of the region until then (cf. Kermode et al. 2006: 107–110).

The general increase in international trade in the second half of the 17th and the first half of the 18th century stimulated growth in all European ports, and in Britain the cities facing west, for obvious reasons, prospered in particular. Liverpool became the "focal point" of a series of road and canal developments in the area, facilitating transport of Lancashire coal and Cheshire salt to the port (Longmore 2006: 129). The sugar and tobacco trade brought ever greater wealth and a constant flow of work migrants from Lancashire, Cheshire, North Wales and Ireland to the bustling port on the Mersey. Between 1700 and 1750 the population trebled to around 18,000, with the majority of the immigrants coming from Liverpool's immediate hinterland (cf. Longmore 2006: 114–119 and 169).

Right from the beginning of the 18th century, Liverpool also participated in one of the most horrible activities of the period: the slave trade. In fact, Liverpool became "Britain's leading slave port" with about 5000 voyages in a little more than 100 years. While exact figures are difficult to come by, it is estimated that in excess of 40% of Liverpool's wealth was due to the slave trade. Expansion was not halted when the slave trade was finally abolished. Merchants had already diversified their activities, resulting in a thirty-fold increase of Liverpool's tonnage in the 18th century (cf. Longmore 2006: 131–134 and 137).

It can be argued that at the time this enormous commercial success (admittedly only of a wealthy few) "provided an alternative identity for the port" since Liverpool did not have much of a medieval heritage to draw on (unlike many other provincial towns of the period, e.g. Bristol, Leeds, or Hull). Despite a rather transitory pattern of residence (even many merchant families only stayed in the city for three generations or less) Liverpool managed to create a perceived "cultural (…) distinctiveness which has arguably remained to the present day". Due to its international business contacts, the city had a "cosmopolitan outlook" and seemed to lie "outside the culture of Lancashire" (Longmore 2006: 152–154).

For Crowley (2012: 28) this is actually the point when Scouse as a distinctive variety emerged. Disagreeing with the "received" version of Scouse history that places the beginnings of Scouse in the 19th century (cf. §2.2), he claims that "given the population statistics, (…) it would make more sense to argue that if a new linguistic form was created in Liverpool, then its development surely began (and the form may have even been established) in the eighteenth century". His argument is that (in relative terms) the biggest increase in Liverpool's population occurred during this period. He does acknowledge that most of the people moving into Liverpool in the 18th century came from Lancashire but insists that "the various ports of Cheshire, North Wales and Wirral also contributed, to say nothing of those who migrated from Ireland, Scotland, America and the West Indies". Crowley seems to forget for the moment that Lancashire and Cheshire form a dialect continuum and that the ports of Cheshire and the Wirral (historically part of Cheshire anyway) would therefore not have contributed anything radically different in linguistic terms. The immediate "rural hinterland", however, provided most of the incoming population, particularly at the beginning of the 18th century (cf. Longmore 2006: 119).

Although the city did indeed continue to grow exponentially (around 77,000 inhabitants by 1800) and notwithstanding its "cosmopolitan outlook", the population of Liverpool remained rather "un-exotic". For instance, very few slaves were brought back to Liverpool and those that were sadly died "almost entirely" as "young men, young women and children". Longmore (cf. 2006: 161 and 169) further notes that, these few exceptions aside, there seems to be little evidence of a black presence at the time and the current black community therefore must have been established later. Belchem & MacRaild (2006), on the other hand, maintain that by the late 1700s a "vibrant black community" had developed. However, this community seems to have been very small – contemporary comments mention only 50 black and mixed-race children in 1787 (Belchem & MacRaild 2006: 324).

Crowley (2012) also provides some textual evidence for his claim. One of his sources is an early 19th century historian who – in Crowley's words – asserts that "the Irish presence in Liverpool not only grew [in the 18th century], it also contributed to the formation of a distinctive local culture" (2012: 30). However, the source does not mention accent or dialect in any way, but rather talks about "local manners in the town" such as "hospitality, activity and sprightliness" (Troughton 1810, cited in Crowley 2012: 30). Another piece of evidence is a play first published and performed in Liverpool in 1768. In this play a doctor from Liverpool is urged not to forget the "Lancashire dialect" when impersonating a cousin from outside the city. Crowley's point is that this should be seen as evidence for the fact that "the speech of at least some of the inhabitants of Liverpool was not the same as that of Lancastrians" (cf. Crowley 2012: 32–35).

This is hardly hot news. After all, given the language-related ideology already in place at the time – as Crowley himself points out (2012: 23) – no-one would expect a doctor, a well-respected and educated member of the middle class, to use a pronounced regional accent. The passages that Crowley quotes merely indicate that middle-class Liverpudlians were not speaking with a broad Lancashire accent, not that they had developed their own. To be fair, Crowley himself remarks on the fact that his textual evidence – just like that of the proponents of the "received version" – is rather thin. It appears even less convincing if one considers that, according to oral historians, "many working-class Liverpudlians failed to exhibit any 'scouse' (sic) characteristics (...) in their speech until well into the twentieth century" (Belchem 2006a: 43–44) – more than 100 years after the variety had been coined, if Crowley is correct.

2.2 19th century

From a linguist's point of view, the situation in Liverpool really starts to get interesting in the 19th century, but not much before – although we have seen above that there is at least one scholar who disagrees with this "received" version of the history of Scouse. It is, however, generally agreed that Liverpool English is "a relatively new variety of English" where "[a]ll the evidence" suggests emergence "from a dialect mixture" (Honeybone 2007: 113 and 121). Honeybone distinguishes three stages in the development of the "perceptually distinct Liverpool English that now exists (...)" (2007: 119):

Stage 1 Broadly pre-19th century

Stage 2 (Especially mid-) 19th century

Stage 3 Broadly post-19th century

He further states that stage 2 is the period "when the available evidence indicates that the variety came into being", at a time "when speakers of a number of dialects were mixing in the area" (Honeybone 2007: 106–107). And speakers of a number of dialects certainly did mix in Liverpool in the 19th century. From 1801 to 1901, the population increased almost nine-fold – from around 82,000 to 711,000 (GB Historical GIS 2009). This, in itself, is nothing out of the ordinary. Most major cities in Britain, as in other industrialised countries, exploded during the Victorian era. Manchester, for instance, also went from 88,000 in 1801 to 642,000 in 1901 (GB Historical GIS 2009). An additional factor is important to understand Liverpool's particular development at the time.

In urban geography, cities are often classified according to two theories, the central place model and the network model. A central place acts as an administrative and economic centre that provides "services" for its hinterland. Classical examples are medieval market towns. A network city, on the other hand, is a node in an often international system of cities and as such is less dependent on, and in less intense contact with, its hinterland compared to a central place. Important ports are prime examples of this type of city. Obviously, the two functions often overlap and many towns or cities are both central places and network cities. In the north-west, "Liverpool and Manchester divided the functions of a regional capital", with Manchester being the "summit of the array of central places" and Liverpool fulfilling the function of "gateway city linking the region to European and trans-Atlantic urban networks" (Hohenberg & Lees 1985: 188–189).

When the slave trade was finally abolished in 1807, Liverpool turned to raw materials such as timber, oils, and especially cotton. These raw materials, along with "the plethora of goods demanded by an urbanizing population" were needed by Liverpool's hinterland, "the manufacturing powerhouse that was north-west England" (Milne 2006: 258). The goods produced in Manchester and the rest of Lancashire and Cheshire were then exported through Liverpool's port to the four corners of the globe. Diversity of goods increased and Liverpool turned into one of the 19th century's only two "general cargo giants" in Britain (Milne 2006: 259). New trading contacts were established in India, China, and South America . Liverpool increasingly felt at the heart of a global maritime network. At least to a degree this was certainly justified. After all, it had become the second biggest city and the most important port in the country by 1850 (cf. Honeybone 2007: 113–114).

In addition to its importance as one of the busiest cargo ports in the world, Liverpool also acquired another function. Around 1850, the city had established itself as the principal emigration port of the Old World (especially for those bound for the United States) and acquired the nickname "the New York of Europe" (Belchem 2006c: xxvii). By way of example, Belchem (2006b: 14) notes that in 1851 alone, 455 ships sailed from Liverpool to New York, compared to 124 from Le Havre and 132 from Bremen. He goes on to explain that more than 85% of the 5.5 million Europeans that emigrated to America between 1860 and 1900 did so from or through Liverpool. These emigrants, although their presence was usually only transitory, turned Liverpool into a "diaspora space" and further enhanced its "cosmopolitan complexion" (Belchem 2006b: 14).

If contemporary commentators are to be believed, immigrants, travellers, and sailors from all around the world were generally given a friendly welcome by the locals. An anonymous source counts "[h]ospitality, social intercourse, civility to strangers, and that freedom from local prejudice which is produced by the residence of so great a proportion of strangers" among the "very favourable features in the general portrait" of Liverpool people (Anon 1812, cited in Crowley 2012: 12). Apparently, this hospitality was also extended to visitors of other races. Belchem (2006b: 13) notes that "[b]lack passengers in transit were delighted by their reception when they ventured into town, even into the established church". Belchem (2006a) also cites a contemporary comment from 1907, describing the Pier Head and the central landing-stage as the place where all of Liverpool met either for business or pleasure and that "encouraged social intermingling", having the "appearance of a democratic promenade" (Scott 1907, cited in Belchem 2006a: 45).

Due to these intensive international contacts, Knowles (1973: 15) claims that "[t]he important linguistic ties" are less with the Lancashire hinterland, and more with "Dublin and London and the whole of the English speaking world". He assumes that Scouse emerged as a distinct variety some time between 1830 and 1889, which "corresponds with the period of massive immigration from Ireland" (Knowles 1973: 18) during and after the Irish Potato Famine (1845–1852). He describes Scouse as being a still essentially north-western variety that has been heavily influenced by Irish immigrants (cf. Knowles 1973: 51). Applying Trudgill's model of new dialect formation (Trudgill 1986; 2004) to Liverpool, Honeybone (2007) provides similar dates (1841 to 1891) for the emergence of Scouse but is less categorical with respect to the Irish role in the matter. He explains that, somewhat surprisingly, there was no pronounced founder effect privileging north-western English, although clearly no *tabula rasa* situation existed in Liverpool in the 19th century. At the same time, Irish English was not simply transplanted wholesale to Liverpool (cf. Honeybone 2007: 117 and 121).

This is not to say that Irish immigrants were *not* a crucial factor in the formation of Liverpool culture and language. Their sheer number argues against such ideas. Even before the famine, many Irish emigrated to Liverpool, because it was "the obvious, indeed often unavoidable place to go from Ireland as it was the main port of Britain on the West coast, facing Ireland" (Honeybone 2007: 114). Many also originally meant to travel to the United States or other places but ended up staying in Liverpool for good (cf. Honeybone 2007: 117). As can be observed from Table 2.1 (adapted from Pooley (2006: 249)), about one in five Liverpudlians in the middle of the century had been born in Ireland. This is a sizeable proportion, and it has to be borne in mind that people with Irish ancestry but who had been born in Liverpool are not even included in this count.

Table 2.1: Selected birthplaces of Liverpudlians in the 19th century

Birthplace	1851	1871	1891
Lancashire (including Liverpool)	50.3%	58.7%	68.9%
Ireland	22.3%	15.6%	9.1%
Wales	5.4%	4.3%	3.4%
Scotland	3.7%	4.1%	3.0%
Cheshire	3.4%	3.0%	2.8%

A number of problems arise if one is to take Knowles' view and consider Irish English speakers as the dominating influence in the creation of Scouse. The Irish were a) highly concentrated – one might say ghettoised – in certain parts of the city, b) "only ever an absolute majority in few streets" (Honeybone 2007: 120), c) generally of a lower socio-economic status than people born in Liverpool, and d) for the most part Roman Catholics (cf. Belchem & MacRaild 2006: 330). These features add up to a spatially isolated and heavily stigmatised group of Liverpool society at the time. Under these circumstances, it is very difficult to argue convincingly that "their speech would swamp the dialects of inmigrants from other areas", as Honeybone (2007: 120) rightly points out. What is more, the proportion of Irish migrants was similar in other cities. Honeybone (2007: 140) cites 18.1% and 13.1% for Glasgow and Manchester in 1851 respectively, so the number of speakers alone cannot account for the particular linguistic development in Liverpool.

Table 2.1 also indicates that there was a non-negligible community of Welsh and Scots (more than 9% in 1851, again not counting second and third generation immigrants). These figures are small compared to the Irish part, but they were still large enough for Liverpool to acquire the nickname "the capital of North Wales" and to boast the second-largest Scots community in England. Neither Welsh nor Scots were spatially as concentrated as the Irish, although they did constitute what Honeybone calls "highly organised", i.e. somewhat inward-looking and self-sufficient, communities (cf. Honeybone 2007: 120–121). Unlike the Irish, these groups were associated with the skilled working population (cf. Belchem 2006d: 202–203), which makes their dialects more likely contributors to the emerging Scouse than the varieties spoken by a non-prestigious group like the Irish. To these larger minorities, one must add smaller numbers of people not represented in Table 2.1 – from all over Britain, Africa, the Caribbean, and China. All of these people have, in some way, contributed to the dialect mix in the city (cf. Honeybone 2007: 116).

Knowles and Honeybone disagree to an extent about which influences most shaped early Scouse. However, both assert, the former on the basis of somewhat cryptic comments in Ellis 1889 (cf. Knowles 1973: 18), the latter using Trudgill's new-dialect model (cf. Honeybone 2007: 118), that by the end of the 19th century a variety identifiable as 'Liverpool English' had emerged.

2.3 20th century

2.3.1 Enregisterment and the "Scouse industry"

Liverpool continued to grow in the 20th century, reaching its population pinnacle of around 855,000 in 1931 (cf. Pooley 2006: 171), despite the fact that Liverpool's economic vulnerability was dramatically revealed during the inter-war years when the world economy slumped and 30% of port-related jobs disappeared overnight. The port acquired outstanding, though short-lived, importance again during World War 2 when Liverpool was the European end point of the Allied convoys, as well as the command centre for the Battle of the Atlantic (a fact which also made it a prime target for the Luftwaffe, which wreaked considerable destruction on the city and killed thousands of people in 1940–1941) (cf. Murden 2006: 393 and 405). While immigration from all parts of the word continued (cf. Honeybone 2007: 119), attitudes towards migrants became less positive, at least in some parts of Liverpool society. At times "hysterical reaction[s]" in the local press can now be seen as precursors of the "troubled pattern of 'racialized relations'" in the latter part of the 20th century (cf. Belchem 2006b: 23).

At around the same time (the early to mid-20th century) developed what Crowley (2012: 40) calls the "Scouse industry". From the 1930s onwards, a number of articles and letters to the editors in local newspapers discussing "Liverpool" words and phrases can be found. While most of these claims were incorrect – Knowles (1973: 48) comments on "the very paucity of the material" particular to Scouse in the domain of grammar and vocabulary – they nevertheless "indicated that there was a developed sense that Liverpool as a place had a vocabulary (and a mode of pronunciation) that was part of its cultural distinctiveness within Britain" (Crowley 2012: 42). In other words, *enregisterment* was well under way, and Scouse was turning – or had already turned – into a "socially recognised register of forms" that was "differentiable within [the] language" (Agha 2003: 231). In the years following World War 2, two individuals in particular gained publicity in this domain and are still well-known today. Neither Frank Shaw nor Fritz Spiegl were linguists (Shaw worked as a customs officer, Spiegl was a flutist), but rather amateurs (in the original sense) who ran a campaign to "present Scouse as the language of Liverpool" and who tried to "popularize, celebrate and preserve aspects of the language and culture of Liverpool" (Crowley 2012: 64–65). The *Lern Yerself Scouse* series sparked off by these two in the 60s can still be found in most Liverpool book shops today. On the surface at least, these short booklets were intended as a sort of phrasebook for visitors of the city, familiarising them with vocabulary and pronunciations peculiar (in the authors' opinion) to Liverpool English. Honeybone & Watson (2013) provide a linguistic analysis of these volumes (cf. also Chapter 3).

Although the series may well be considered "the touchstone for the Scouse industry" (Crowley 2012: 79), it was clearly not its only manifestation. As early as the 1930s, the city had established for itself a "reputation for humour" that was carried on in the 1960s by comedians such as Ken Dodd and Jimmy Tarbuck, both in theatres across the country and on TV (cf. Murden 2006: 423, and Belchem 2006b: 49). Liverpool was also represented on national TV in the 1950s and 60s with series like *Z-Cars* or *The Liver Birds*, which showed characters that "often conformed to the cultural, linguistic and social representations that had been set out by the founders of the Scouse industry" (Crowley 2012: 75). Finally, numerous pop bands came out of Liverpool during the Merseybeat era, the most famous and influential of which was the Beatles. They acquired unprecedented fame for Liverpool and, at least for a couple of years, made the city the centre of the pop music world (cf. Crowley 2012: 75), while "Britain fell in love with everything connected to Liverpool" (Murden 2006: 423).

Based on his textual/literary evidence, Crowley (2012: 107) claims that the stage of "first-order (sic) indexicality with regard to Liverpool speech" was reached "in the early to mid twentieth century". His argument is that "there is clear evidence that words and sounds were postulated (often incorrectly) as belonging uniquely to Liverpool". Since these postulations stem from non-experts, however, we are at this point dealing with third-order indexicality already, since the peculiarities have started attracting explicit comment. This must be a typographical error, otherwise Crowley's claim is even more strange if we remember him arguing elsewhere that Scouse had already emerged from dialect-mixing in the 18ᵗʰ century (cf. §2.1). Based on Silverstein' 2003 orders of indexicality, Johnstone et al. (2006: 81) define first-order indexicality as "the kind of correlation between a form and a sociodemographic identity (...) that an outsider could observe", i.e. experts can identify a feature as being indicative of a particular group of speakers, possibly even while the variety is still emerging. Crucially, however, this features does not yet do social work (second-order indexicality), nor is it talked about or used in conscious performances (third-order indexicality) of local identity (cf. Johnstone et al. 2006: 83–84).

Nevertheless, Crowley correctly explains that the comments by Shaw and others, distinguishing "real Liverpudlians" from "middle-class Mossley Hill Liverpolitans", to use Shaw's phrasing, indicate (at least) second-order indexicality. Social stratification was, apparently, firmly in place with respect to Liverpool English, which is why it had already become "the index not simply of Liverpool identity, but of Liverpool working-class identity" (Crowley 2012: 107). When some features of Scouse definitely reached third-order indexicality in the 1960s, this association with the working-class was less of a problem than several decades before and might even have contributed to the "coolness" (The "Liverpool cult" – Crowley 2012: 109) of Scouse identity. As Wales (2006: 165) notes, "it became fashionable to be young, working class and urban, and the importance of this on language change in the late twentieth century should not be underestimated".

2.3.2 Decline

While Liverpool was enjoying its heyday in terms of image and popularity, it was already facing serious difficulties in other respects. After a short revival in the 1950s (cf. Murden 2006: 402), economic decline hit the city hard from the 1960s and especially the 1970s onwards. Following the 1973 oil crisis, most western countries went into recession and thousands of manufacturing jobs were lost. While new service jobs countered this loss, they usually developed in other regions (in the case of Britain, in the south of England) than those most affected by structural change (here northern England) (cf. Judd & Parkinson 1990: 16–17).

Liverpool had prospered enormously as a trading hub in the Victorian era, but the end of the British Empire, the "collapse of the colonial economic system" (Belchem 2006b: 52), and Britain's (economic) shift of focus towards Europe meant that Liverpool "found itself poorly located to take advantage of the increasing trade between the UK and mainland Europe" that now dominated (Couch 2003a: 166–167). In addition, containerisation meant that even the few ports that were able to retain their importance (Rotterdam and Hamburg alone ended up serving all of northern Europe, cf. Milne 2006: 264) no longer required thousands of workers, but just a handful of more specialised employees to operate the machinery.

Due to its container terminal in Seaforth, Liverpool's port today handles more cargo than ever before, but it does so with a workforce of only 800 (7000 in the whole maritime sector; figures for 2003, cf. Murden 2006: 477).

The central government tried to fight unemployment by encouraging private investors to open up new factories in the city, but in most cases success was short-lived. The militancy of Liverpool workers – "a myth in the making" – was often used as a pretext whenever Merseyside plants were the first to be closed again "[o]nce development aid and other short-term advantages were exhausted"(cf. Belchem 2006b: 52). Liverpool became the "beaten city" and a "'showcase' of everything that has gone wrong in Britain's major cities" (*Daily Mirror*, 11 October 1982, cited in Belchem 2006b: 52–53).

While claims concerning the militancy of Liverpudlians in general might well have been more based on stereotypes than fact, there certainly was *political* militancy in the form of Militant Tendency (a Labour "sect") in the 1980s. Until 1979, central government measures were focused on social and welfare services on the one hand and the creation of public sector jobs on the other. When Margaret Thatcher became prime minister, however, urban policy changed (cf. Judd & Parkinson 1990: 19). Public spending was to be cut back considerably. The Militant majority of Liverpool City Council disagreed and, in the eyes of some at least, tried to "force" the government into granting them additional funds and effectively "threaten[ed] to bankrupt the city if it were not given the extra resources". In 1987 the House of Lords finally disqualified 47 Labour officials of the City Council from office for failing to protect the financial interest of the city (cf. Parkinson 1990: 249–250). But the damage had been done. Liverpool's "political failure" (Parkinson 1990: 241) resulted in a "sharp decline in investor confidence" and a "deterioration in the image of the city" which lasted for many years (Couch 2003a: 172).

Economic decline was followed by physical deterioration. In the 1980s, Central Liverpool was fast losing population and jobs, the shopping centre had to yield business to retail parks in the suburbs, congestion was on the rise and environmental conditions went downhill (cf. Couch 2003b: 38). This "visual legacy of dereliction" brought with it an "air of decay" which made the area even less attractive to potential private sector investors and thereby created or at least contributed to a downward spiral of recession and decay (Fraser 2003a: 21).

Due to these economic problems (and the limited opportunities for migrants that ensued), Liverpool did not participate in the post-war mass-immigration from the Caribbean and South Asia in the same way as other major British cities did. While Liverpool was, after London, the most ethnically diverse British city in the 19th century, it is clear from Table 2.2 (data are from Office for National Statistics 2016) that this is no longer true. In fact, although minorities now make up a larger proportion of Liverpool residents than in 2001 (largely due to a recent influx of refugees and asylum seekers), it is today still one of the *least* ethnically diverse places in Britain, clearly lagging behind Manchester in this respect and a far-cry from places such as Birmingham or London (cf. Pooley 2006: 187).

Table 2.2: Ethnicity in Liverpool and other major cities (%)

	Liverpool		Manchester		Birmingham		London	
	2001	2011	2001	2011	2001	2011	2001	2011
white	94.32	88.91	80.96	66.61	70.35	57.93	71.15	59.79
black	1.22	2.64	4.51	8.64	6.12	8.98	10.92	13.32
Asian	2.27	4.16	10.44	17.09	20.04	26.62	13.20	18.49
mixed	1.80	2.52	3.23	4.60	2.86	4.44	3.15	4.96
other	0.39	1.77	0.86	3.06	0.63	2.03	1.58	3.44

In addition, Liverpool's minority population is (and always has been) highly concentrated (segregated?) in central areas of the city. Furthermore, the "most visible" minorities – especially blacks and Chinese – had to endure marginalisation and a certain degree of racial violence from the early 20th century onwards (cf. Pooley 2006: 189–191). Racial tensions and more general disappointment with the authorities culminated in the Toxteth riots of 1981, which lasted for two weeks, caused £11 million of damage, and left hundreds of people (police and civilians) injured and one dead (cf Murden 2006: 440–444).

All of this had an impact on evaluations of the primary expression of Liverpool culture, Scouse. Scouse had received poor popular ratings already in the 1970s and these results were corroborated in a 1990s survey where Scouse got an approval rating of only 6%, while at the same time frequently joining other northern accents in scoring rather highly for "friendliness" (cf. Wales 2006: 166). What is even more important than the negative *external* perceptions of Liverpool and Scouse is what Parkinson (1990: 255) calls an "internal image problem". Writing in 1990, he claims:

> Two decades of economic failure, compounded by political failure and self-destruction, have bred a degree of cynicism in the city's public life. There is clearly a cultural dimension to the city's failure that goes beyond the statistics of economic decline.

It probably goes without saying that this "cultural dimension" is highly likely to also include the linguistic domain. It would not be surprising if an "internal image problem" impacted on people's (socio-)linguistic behaviour, i.e. if at least some speakers tried to tone down their local accent a bit because they felt it to be somewhat contaminated by the negative associations attached to the city. If this was the case then it may well have helped bring about, or at least accelerate, what Knowles (1978) calls the "extensive standardisation" of Scouse in the 20th century.

2.3.3 Regeneration

Politicians in Liverpool and London did not just passively watch the city's physical decline. Post-war measures mostly focused on public housing, inner city slum clearance and relocation of the population to new housing estates on the periphery. From the beginning of the 1980s, the strategy slowly started to change. The emphasis shifted to the "potential of the city center in terms of retail, leisure, tourism, and commercial development". The city council even funded studies evaluating the tourist potential and dealing with issues such as Liverpool's negative image and city marketing (cf. Parkinson 1990: 250–253).

Decline continued all the same, and in 1993 Liverpool (and the whole region of Merseyside to be exact) had spiralled down into Objective One status – a label given by the EU to regions whose GDP per capita is 75% or less of the EU average. Belchem (2006b: 53–54) notes that "[a]lthough at the time it seemed a badge of failure" this may well turn out to have been a "decisive turning point for the city", because it gave access to considerable European funds. In its wake, the city council turned towards "urban entrepreneurialism, partnership governance and civic boosterism", which is very unlike the political style that was prevalent in the 1980s.

Economically, it had become clear, in Liverpool and elsewhere, that it was not possible to recreate the past. Instead, the future was envisaged in information technology and new (tertiary) industries, such as banking and advertising (cf. Fraser 2003a: 32). A local film industry was also successfully established in the second half of the 1980s and 1989 saw the creation of the Liverpool Film Office, the first of its kind in the UK (cf. Murden 2006: 479). First and foremost, however, Liverpool turned towards tourism and (re-)discovered its cultural heritage as an economic asset (cf. Fraser 2003a: 32–33). The city centre was physically improved through, for example, new squares, public spaces, and pedestrianised shopping areas. The waterfront, with its unused docks and warehouses, has proved particularly suitable for regeneration as a tourist and leisure area (Couch 2003a: 173–174).

Regeneration did (and does) also face problems. Just as in other places in the UK, the "private development sector" is rather powerful. As a consequence, most measures have focused on high-return investments in the city centre with an ensuing neglect of more peripheral areas, such as Vauxhall or North Liverpool, that are just as much (or even more) in need of regeneration (cf. Couch 2003b: 49). Furthermore, Liverpool is in competition with Manchester, which is now the undisputed regional capital thanks to its airport (the most important one outside London) and its more central location. As such, Manchester was (and still is) often the more obvious choice for potential investors in the north-west. While the "deep-seated social and economic problems (...) still remain acute" (Fraser 2003b: 188), it is nonetheless important to remember that "a great deal [was achieved], at least in terms of physical change" (Couch 2003b: 44).

Due to the fact that private investors were now operating on an international level, it became important for cities to emphasise their local attributes through the use of place promotion and marketing strategies. Cultural revitalisation, organisations like Liverpool Vision and prestige projects such as the Albert Dock are examples of this attempt to create and foster a new image. In addition to attracting investment, these projects can also instil pride into local people and thus "help to promote civic identity" (cf. Percy 2003: 201–203).

Pride in the city is an important aspect. Fraser (2003a: 20) explains that cities past their heyday such as Liverpool "should be vanishing as new centres [take] their place". Obviously, this is not what has happened. Rather, people try "to find a new rationale for its existence and re-creation of its former prosperity. *It is a matter of conscious choice to do so*" (my emphasis). This conscious choice not to give up is, among other things, based on "a *sense of place*, a special character or feeling in and for that place, which attracts loyalty from inhabitants" (Fraser 2003a: 23, emphasis in the original). Successful regeneration might well have filled Liverpudlians with new self-pride and self-respect. New self-respect in turn should manifest itself in (sub-)conscious reinforcement of social markers such as accent.

We might even suspect that the external image of Scouse has also improved. If Trudgill (1999: 73) and Honeybone (2007: 110) are to be believed, Scouse must have acquired some covert prestige by the late 1990s and spread not only to Birkenhead, but also to more rural areas in Merseyside. Montgomery (2007b: 176–177) even – speculatively – suggests that some people from Crewe in Cheshire might identify with Scouse. The fact that a great number of new call centres were established in Merseyside in 1998 also casts some doubt on "the usual stigma attached to Scouse" as "[t]elesales companies have apparently taken great care to locate

their call centres in regions where their workers' accents will be favourably perceived" (Foulkes & Docherty 1999: 3).

2.4 21ˢᵗ century – outlook

Regeneration continued into the new millennium with the construction of a new
big convention centre (the Echo Arena) and the transformation of RopeWalks
into a modern, trendy leisure quarter housing a media arts centre and numerous
bars, restaurants, and clubs. In the very centre of the city, about £920 million were
spent on Liverpool ONE, one of the largest open-air retail spaces in the UK, but
also comprising residential and leisure facilities. From 2004 to 2008 it completely
transformed about 42 acres of previously rather bleak land and, in passing, considerably improved access to the city centre by public transport thanks to the
new bus interchange that was part of the project (cf. Murden 2006: 478–479). An
even bigger development project, Liverpool Waters, was granted planning per-
mission in March 2013 and is supposed to create 17,000 jobs while redeveloping
the north docks.

Liverpool also continued to do well on the culture front. In 2004, parts of
the waterfront and the Cultural Quarter (the area around St. George's Hall and
the World Museum) were inscribed on UNESCO's list of World Heritage Sites, a
badge which surely further increased Liverpool's attraction as a tourist destination. Probably the most important achievement of the city in the new millennium
so far is its success in acquiring the title of European Capital of Culture in 2008
(together with Stavanger in Norway). Not only did this title provide the occasion
and the framework for a year of events and festivals, it also had a number of measurable effects. As a direct consequence of the title, around 9.7 million additional
visitors were counted in 2008, with 97% of the international tourists visiting for
the first time. More than £750 million of direct income for the city's economy was
created this way, and data collected from 2005 to 2010 indicate that the Capital
of Culture effect could be lasting (Garcia et al. 2010). In the long term, what may
be even more important is that media coverage has also changed. In the 1990s
national media largely focused on (usually negative) social issues when covering
Liverpool, while in 2008/2009 "culture and image stories" dominated. Local media also showed a pronounced increase in positive coverage in the years leading
up to 2008 as well. Positive impressions about Liverpool increased statistically
significantly in national surveys from 2005 to 2008 (cf. Garcia et al. 2010: 25 and
44–46).

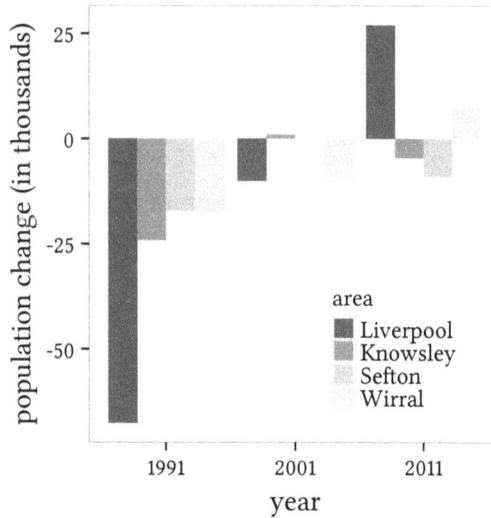

Figure 2.2: Population change in the Liverpool metropolitan area by decades (baseline 1981)

Population figures also begin to tell the story of Liverpool's revival. It is often said that the city has lost a large proportion of its population since World War 2. This statement is misleading, though, because it ignores "[t]he process of suburbanisation" which "has become a feature of prosperous and declining city regions at the same time" (Fraser 2003a: 21). It is true that the population of what is *officially* Liverpool has dropped by about 50% since 1931, but if we have a closer look at national census data (Office for National Statistics 2016), we find that the present population of Greater Liverpool is somewhere between at least 850,000 and 1.2 million (depending on where one draws the boundaries), so equal to or even well above the 1931 figure. It is equally true, however, that the central area, the one that is governed by Liverpool city council, has been losing population for decades. As Figure 2.2 illustrates, this trend has now been reversed. The graph summarises population changes in the city and the three surrounding metropolitan boroughs per decade (Office for National Statistics 2016). Data for Liverpool are visualised by the black bars on the left within each group. They show heavy population loss from 1981 to 1991, but only a fraction of that from 1991 to 2001. From 2001 to 2011, however, the population actually increased by more than double the amount that was lost in the 1990s. The central area of "official" Liverpool is thus growing again and is the only borough that has regained considerably more inhabitants from 2001 to 2011 than it had lost in the previous decade. This growth is mostly due to the city centre whose population had already quadrupled in the 1990s (cf. Belchem 2006c: xix).

Liverpool's problems have not evaporated, but much seems to be improving. The crime rate, for instance, is now "similar to that of the north-west as a whole and lower than some other cities" (Pooley 2006: 235). Economic branches other than tourism are also growing, particularly "knowledge-intensive" industries like biotechnology (cf. Percy 2003: 204) and software development. The film industry is now firmly established, with Liverpool boasting its own Film Office and studios (cf. Murden 2006: 478–480). Generally speaking, Liverpool has experienced strong (and above average) growth both in the number of jobs and in average worker earnings over the last 15 years (cf. Liverpool City Council 2016: 4). In 2013, posters in the city centre telling visitors and locals alike that Liverpool is the fastest growing economy outside London were one example of what Belchem (2006b: 54) calls "[f]orward-looking self-promotion", which "now prevails in the new 'Livercool'" (as the *Tatler* magazine called the city, cf. Murden 2006: 484).

In this climate, "certain non-standard accents" have acquired "a fashionable edge", even in "middle-class professional circles" (Belchem 2006a: 58). Helped by a new kind of (cultural) nostalgia with the 1960s, Scouse has now become "[a] fashionable accessory". As such, it is "no longer concealed", but rather "accentuated and cultivated" (Belchem 2006a: 58). There is some evidence for this claim: merchandise available in souvenir shops, the small Scouse section in the Museum of Liverpool, and the occasional poster in the city can all be considered instances of enregisterment (see Figure 2.3 for examples playing on the process of creating word forms ending in /i/ (particularly frequent in Scouse and often commented on by in-group members), or the use of the NURSE-SQUARE merger for a pun in a business name). It has to be said, however, that impressionistically at least examples of this kind seem to be comparatively rare. This book will try to add some firmer, and more direct, linguistic evidence from production data to this.

2.5 Summary

We have seen how Liverpool developed from a tiny fishing village on the Lancashire coast to a world centre of trade and commerce. In the 19th century, Scouse was formed when people from all over Britain and the Empire flocked to the city. A hundred years later, Liverpool's long decline began and accelerated after World War 2 before it finally started to recover from the 1990s onwards and became a major tourist destination. The city's external and internal image followed suit.

Figure 2.3: Examples of enregisterment in Liverpool city centre

Representations went from "Second city of the Empire" in the 19th century to the extremely popular "Beat city" in the 1960s and then via the "Beaten city" of the Thatcher era to a more positive image again linked to its year as European Capital of Culture. Among other topics, this book will investigate whether the changes in Liverpool's image during the latter half of the last century (from positive to extremely negative to more positive again) have left their mark on the linguistic behaviour of Liverpudlians.

3 Variables

3.1 General remarks

Whatever the precise details of its evolution, in Liverpool developed what Trudgill calls "an accent rather more 'modern' than that of its hinterland" (Trudgill 1999: 70) and that he describes as being "well known to most British people, and very distinctive". For instance, Montgomery (2007a) found "Scouse" to be the dialect area most often delimited and labelled by lay participants in a map drawing task. Scouse also turned out to be the most stigmatised of the language varieties mentioned by said participants (cf. Montgomery 2007a: 194 and 254). Furthermore, participants provided more linguistic characteristics for Scouse than for any other dialect area, indicating that Scouse (along with Geordie) has a higher cultural salience than most other varieties in England. Subjects commented on a wide array of (stereotypical) features, including the lexicon ('calm down'), prosody ('sing song') and phonetics (cf. Montgomery 2007b: 180–181). Crowley (2012: 15) also emphasises the salience of Scouse when he writes that "(...) in Britain and Ireland at least, Liverpool and Liverpudlians are most widely recognized by their association with a distinct form of spoken language".

Scouse is "essentially based on [the accents] of the surrounding areas and has many similarities with those of the Central Lancashire and Northwest Midlands areas (...)" (Trudgill 1999: 70). Thus, it generally belongs to the northern branch of English English, without being a prototypical specimen. Wales (2006: 18) writes that Merseyside is a "'transition' [zone] between Northern and Midland dialect speech" and Trudgill (1999: 72) claims that Scouse is in some respects as southern as it is northern. Much of its distinctiveness is due to phonetic rather than phonemic divergence from the surrounding varieties. Knowles (1973) describes Scouse as being phonologically North(west)ern but phonetically Anglo Irish (cf. also Knowles 1978: 80; but see §2.2 concerning Irish dominance in the dialect mix).

The only comprehensive description of Scouse as a whole so far is Knowles (1973), which is based on interview data from two Liverpool electoral wards – Aigburth to the south and Vauxhall to the north of Liverpool city centre. At least from the perspective of the time of writing, there are a number of difficulties with Knowles' account. Parts of his thesis are based exclusively on native speaker introspection (for instance the whole section on what he calls "setting and voice quality", cf. Knowles 1973: 102). Also, he seems to embrace some rather strange notions for a linguist, e.g. he claims that "no-one with any local knowledge would attempt to [make quantitative statements about Liverpool speech in general]" since "no sample, however unbiased, would allow one to make inferences about the Chinese and coloured communities of Liverpool 8, or of the University people of Abercromby" (Knowles 1973: 3). It is not clear whether he thinks this is because he interviewed people from only two electoral wards (which would be fairly obvious and not really worth pointing out) or because he really thinks that for some reason it is not possible to have a representative sample of Liverpool speech in general (which would be an odd thing to say, especially for a sociolinguist). Occasionally, he even slips into clearly prescriptivist vocabulary, for instance when he describes the voice quality of Scouse as being "undeniably poor and ugly, as these terms are normally understood" (Knowles 1973: 116).

That said, Knowles is aware of some of these shortcomings, calling his description of the Scouse vowel system "admittedly speculative" and "put forward extremely tentatively" (Knowles 1973: 111). He also explains that – originally having intended to apply Labovian methods in his thesis – he found it problematic to identify and analyse socially significant variables in Scouse, and, consequently, he himself does not consider his study "a contribution to socio-linguistics as such" (cf. Knowles 1973: 1). Notwithstanding these problems, his work is, as mentioned above, the most complete description of Scouse available and any study concerned with the variety of Liverpool must start out from Knowles' PhD thesis. In the general overview of Scouse characteristics that follows, this project will do the same. The four variables subjected to closer analysis in this study are discussed in more detail in §3.3.1, §3.3.2, §3.4.1, and §3.4.2 respectively.

3.2 Supragsegmentals

Knowles (1973) talks at length about Scouse intonation and indeed it is a feature which rather quickly strikes the outsider when first talking to a Liverpudlian. Several of my own participants (see §8.2.2) also mentioned "a lilt" as one of the distinguishing characteristics. Wales remarks that although "[supra-segmentals] are such readily distinctive markers of regional origin (...) they have been quite seriously under-researched" (2006: 201). This is certainly true. However, supra-segmentals are not the focus of this study either, so suffice it to say that "[t]he intonation of Liverpool speech differs notably in some respects from that in England as a whole" but that "[e]xactly how much they differ is not easy to assess" (Knowles 1973: 221) and sometimes more a matter of relative frequency than real difference (cf. Knowles 1973: 176).

According to Knowles, at least working-class intonation is "undoubtably Celtic in origin", with "Irish influence [being] much more likely than Welsh" (Knowles 1973: 221–222) and "the origin of middle class Merseyside intonation [being] more obscure" (Knowles 1973: 222–223). Just as for the segments, he claims that Liverpool intonation is, in general, "phonologically North-Western English, but largely phonetically Anglo-Irish" (Knowles 1973: 225) – a claim that has to be based on a 'phonology of intonation', which indeed he sketches in his thesis. The reader is referred to Knowles (1973: 174–226) for details.

Voicing, says Knowles, is "relatively slow to start up at the beginning of an utterance, and tends to die away just before the end" (1973: 246), meaning that voiced and voiceless sounds are mostly distinguished by the duration of the preceding sound – which is in fact the most important cue in English (cf., for instance, Hogan & Rozsypal 1980). Knowles claims that "Scouse differs markedly from the rest of North Midland English" in this respect and "is not quite the same as RP" (1973: 246), although he can only be talking about voicing starting rather late, since he – correctly – says elsewhere that RP has devoicing (in final stops) as well (cf. 1973: 114).

3.3 Consonants

The repertoire of Scouse consonants is "phonologically identical to most other varieties of English English" (Watson 2007b: 351) but the phonetic realisation is often not. Just like the Lancashire dialects it is derived from, Scouse was still rhotic in the 19th century, but it has now lost all traces of this rhoticism (cf. Knowles 1997: 149) and is just like RP in this respect. *Pre*-vocalic /r/ is often realised as a flap in broad Scouse – especially in intervocalic position, but also in onset clusters (cf. Knowles 1973: 107 and 329–330; Watson 2007b: 352). Contrary to RP, however, the realisation as [ɾ] is "a non-prestige feature in Liverpool" and therefore avoided by middle-class speakers (Knowles 1973: 329).

/θ/ and /ð/ can be both realised as "RP-type interdental fricatives [θ ð]" or as "Anglo-Irish [T, D] which can be post-dental or (apico-)alveolar stops" (Knowles 1973: 323). Knowles found the realisation as stops being "virtually restricted (…) to working class Catholics" and more frequent among men than women (Knowles 1973: 323–324). Watson's (2007b) female working-class speaker uses dental stops in all positions and, interestingly, shows no signs of TH-fronting, "despite the evidence that suggests it is diffusing throughout much of the rest of the country" (cf. Watson 2007b: 352).

3.3.1 /ŋ(g)/

Another characteristic consonantal feature of Scouse is what is often termed 'velar nasal plus'. Most varieties of English pronounce word-final <ng> clusters as [ŋ]. The original realisation – as "reflected in the spelling which we still use" (Trudgill 1999: 58) –, however, was [ŋg]. In "Central Lancashire, Merseyside, Northwest Midlands and West Midlands" (Trudgill 1999: 58) this older pronunciation prevails to this day. The area in which velar nasal plus is "a defining characteristic" (Trudgill 1999: 58) contains the cities of Birmingham, Manchester, and Liverpool. In these places, *singer* is not pronounced [sɪŋə] but [sɪŋgə], and *long* is realised as [lɒŋg] instead of [lɒŋ] (cf. Trudgill 1999: 58).

Talking about Scouse in particular, Knowles (1973: 293) describes [g] as "always optional" in <ng> clusters, provided it is not obligatory in RP (e.g. in words such as *longer* or *stronger*). He suggests that [g] is primarily realised word finally or prevocalically, and that [ŋg] "would be odd" (Knowles 1973: 293) preceding another plosive such as in *stringed*. The *ing*-forms can also be realised with an audible [g], resulting in [ɪŋg]. According to Knowles (1973: 293), "[r]eduplicated /ɪŋg/-forms as in *singing* /sɪŋgɪŋg/" are possible, but comparatively rare (cf. Knowles 1973: 293). This is probably mostly due to the fact that, just like in many other places of the English-speaking world, *-ing* is often realised as [ɪn] in Liverpool – Knowles (cf. 1973: 156) states that this is more frequently so for the present participle than the gerund.

If <ng> occurs word finally "it can be difficult to decide whether there is a final /g/ or not". In these instances, Knowles argues, the length of the preceding nasal, rather than the acoustics of the [g] itself, seems to be an essential cue for perceiving "/ŋg/ rather than /ŋ/". This leads Knowles to the somewhat strange statement that some cases of <ng> "sound like the Scouse /ŋg/ rather than the standard /ŋ/", although there is "no audible /g/" (Knowles 1973: 293). This does seem odd, since the presence of [g] is the very essence of the Scouse variant. Note, however, that Knowles 1973 is purely based on auditory analysis – in the cases described by Knowles there might very well have been some subtle acoustic cues of a "proper" [g] that would have been revealed by methods of phonetic analysis not widely available at the time.

The more or less voluntary realisation of velar nasal plus aside, Knowles (1973) also presents another theory of how [ŋg] can come about in final position. He claims that due to the "phonation pattern by which voice trails off before the end" (cf. §3.2), the (often audible) "release of the velar closure (...) sounds exactly like a weak oral [g]", because nasal resonance has stopped (cf. Knowles 1973: 294). For words such as *anything, something, nothing* (but strangely not in the simple *thing*), Knowles (cf. 1973: 156) also found the realisation [θɪŋk] , combining velar nasal plus with final devoicing (again, cf. §3.2).

Interestingly, Knowles reports that in the (mostly middle-class) district of Aighburth, the majority of the men he interviewed used [ŋ], whereas most women used [ŋg] (cf. 1973: 295) – a reversal of the familiar pattern revealed in countless sociolinguistic studies since then, according to which local forms are more common in *male* speech, whilst women tend to use more standard variants. Watson (2007b: 352) also reports velar nasal plus – including reduplicated instances as in *singing* [sɪŋgɪŋg] – as a characteristic of Liverpool English (his data are taken from the speech of a 21-year-old), so apparently it is not a feature that has disappeared since the 1970s when Knowles published his thesis.

Despite the hints in Knowles (1973) that the use of [ŋg] variants might be socially stratified in Liverpool, at least with respect to gender, velar nasal plus is not counted among the salient features of Scouse. Newbrook (1999: 98) reports the spread of [ŋg] variants into West Wirral, i.e. to the other side of the river Mersey (which is a very salient natural border for many people in the area). Realisations containing a velar plosive occurred frequently, both in intervocalic and in word-final contexts. The majority of speakers did not exhibit any style shifting with this variable (although marker patterning did occur for some of them), which "suggests limited salience" of this variable in the wider Liverpool region (Newbrook 1999: 98).

3.3.2 Lenition (of /k/)

Knowles (1973: 251) explains that in Liverpool English there is an "apparent confusion of stops, plosives, affricates [and] fricatives (...)", which he attributes to a general Scouse tendency towards "lax" articulation, resulting in incomplete blocking of the air stream during the closure phase of stops (cf. Knowles 1973: 107). The technical term is lenition, from Latin *lenis*, which describes a process of phonological "weakening" along a certain trajectory. As so often, there is some disagreement about the use of the term (cf. Watson 2002: 196). For the purposes of this study, I will adhere to Honeybone's definition as a "synchronic, variable process whereby underlying plosives are realised as affricates and fricatives in certain specific prosodic and melodic environments". He counts this process among "the clearest phonological characteristics of Modern Liverpool English" (2007:

129). All plosives can be subject to lenition in Liverpool English (cf. Honeybone 2001: 236), but most research so far has focused on /t/ and /k/ (see, e.g., Honeybone 2001; Sangster 2001; Watson 2002; 2006). According to Honeybone (2001: 236), the possible realisations (from least lenited to most lenited) are [t, tθ/ts, θ/s, h, ∅] for /t/, and [k, kx, x, h, ∅] for /k/.

In Liverpool, all of the lenited variants of /t/ that are possible actually occur (in various phonological contexts), but for /k/ only the realisations [kx] and [x] are attested (cf Honeybone 2001: 242). It should be added that the fricative realisation of /k/ is not always [x] – [ç] is also possible. The two allophones are in complementary distribution for most speakers, and phonologically conditioned: [ç] follows high front monophthongs and raising diphthongs (*week* [wiːç], *like* [laɪç]), whereas velar (or uvular) fricatives occurs in the remaining contexts (*back* [bax], *dock* [dɒχ], cf. Watson 2007b: 353). As a result of this process, words such as *matter* and *lock* can sound more like [mæsə] and [lɒkx] or [lɒx], in the last case forming a pair of homophones with the Scots word *loch* (cf. Trudgill 1999: 73). Note that Knowles (1973) talks about an *apparent* confusion, though, hinting at the fact that, while becoming more alike, a phonologically plosive sound does not usually merge completely phonetically with the respective affricate or fricative. At least as far as the alveolar plosives are concerned the three "cardinal" categories nevertheless remain distinct (cf. Knowles 1973: 327 and 252–253).

Based on his 1973 data, Knowles found that the majority of Liverpudlians used "stops with incomplete closure" at least every now and then and many apparently even realised lenited stops in rather formal speaking styles. He therefore concludes that lenition, though originally probably a working-class feature, has also taken hold in middle-class speech. He nevertheless finds that – not surprisingly – lenited variants are more frequent in working-class speech and, with respect to /t/ at least, are also more common among women. This relates back to §3.3.1 in that it represents another deviation from the common gender pattern (cf. 1973: 325–327).

The frequency of the individual variants depends mostly on the phonological environment, with, for instance, the fricatives being most frequent in "word-final and foot-medial positions", while other contexts are inhibitive to the use of lenited variants (cf. Honeybone 2007: 130; for a discussion of inhibiting environments see Honeybone 2001). Especially in intervocalic environments lenition is phonetically motivated, which is the reason why it occurs frequently in this context, both in typological terms and in Liverpool English in particular (cf. Honeybone 2001: 230 and 243).

The history of lenition is more complex than that of other features. Hickey (1996) claims that lenition was first transferred from Irish Gaelic to Irish English and then taken to Liverpool by the Irish migrants in the 19th century. The problem with this account, according to Honeybone (2007), is that the pattern-ing of Liverpool lenition is not the same as that of the 'initial mutations' in Irish Gaelic. As the name implies, the latter only occur in morpheme-initial segments, whereas lenition in Scouse – though possible and not infrequent in initial pos-ition – is much more typical word-medially and -finally. What is more, glides and nasals are also affected in Gaelic, but only stops are lenited in Liverpool Eng-lish (cf. Honeybone 2007: 131). The *t*-spirantisation attested in southern varieties of Irish English that turns /t/ into [θ] is very similar in patterning but still "dis-tinct from the affrico-spirantisation of Liverpool lenition" (Honeybone 2007: 132). Honeybone concludes that

> (...) the small amounts of plosive lenition that do exist in current forms
> of Hiberno-English provided some push towards spirantisation, along with
> the other minor affrications or spirantisations in the input dialects, and
> that these were developed, following an endogenous pathway of change,
> by those who formed Liverpool English (2007: 131).

At least parts of the lenition processes in Liverpool are thus "endogenously innovated" (Honeybone 2007: 130) and the phenomenon was not an 'off the shelf' feature readily available in one or several of the varieties that contributed to the formation of Scouse (unlike, for instance, non-rhoticity or the realisation of /θ, ð/ as 'Anglo-Irish stops'). There was clearly influence from Irish English and maybe also some other varieties such as London English which in its present form contains a certain amount of *t*-affrication and might have done so in the 19th century already (cf. Honeybone 2007: 132).

"The full patterning of Liverpool lenition", however, constitutes "a creative act", performed by "the young generations of young Liverpudlians who were forming or focusing the koine" (Honeybone 2007: 132). It was thus not the result of levelling towards one of the input varieties but "a novel, divergent develop-ment" (Honeybone 2007: 132). As a result, the Scouse type of lenition is not only special in its precise patterning, but also "unique among varieties of English in its extent" (Honeybone 2007: 132). Honeybone (2007: 130) explains that although spirantisation and affrication processes are not unknown in other forms of Eng-lish, "no other (...) variety exhibits so much" (Honeybone 2007: 130). This is cer-tainly one of the main reasons for the very high salience of the feature and its being part of the Scouse stereotype. In the case of /k/, which this book will fo-cus on, this is clearly aided by the fact that [x] is extremely rare among English varieties.

Somewhat surprisingly, /k/ lenition does not figure prominently in what Honeybone & Watson (2013) call the 'Contemporary Humorous Localised Dialect Literature' (essentially the *Lern Yerself Scouse* series). A possible explanation is that it is not a straightforward task to represent [x] with the help of the ordinary Latin alphabet. This cannot be the only reason, however, since lenition in other stops is also not represented in these booklets, despite the fact that there are orthographic representations for doing so. Honeybone & Watson (2013) hypothesise that "speakers are not very clearly aware of the existence of the phenomenon" because it is (a) a comparatively recent, and (b) a sub-phonemic feature which does not entail the collapse of categories (cf. Honeybone & Watson 2013: 329–331). Their conclusion is that /k/ lenition is "non-salient" (Honeybone & Watson 2013: 333), but it should be noted that most of the Scouse "dictionaries" date from the 1960s already. Most other studies support the idea that lenition is a highly salient feature.

For instance, lenition of /k/ had not (yet) spread to neighbouring West Wirral in 1980: Newbrook (1999: 97) recorded (heavily) fricated variants of this phoneme in only 8% of cases. In contrast to velar nasal plus, Liverpool lenition had thus not been taken over by speakers in West Wirral. The most probable explanation for the rejection of lenited variants is the stigma – which presupposes salience – attached to them (while [ŋg] variants are largely below the radar). Further evidence for the salience of lenited /k/ variants can be found in Watson & Clark 2015. The authors ran a perception experiment where subjects had to rate speech samples representing different regional accents. Since they were measuring perceivers' reactions in real-time it was possible to tease apart the impact that individual features had on the overall rating. Occurrence of /k/ lenition caused a significant drop in the status rating of the speaker, which not only corroborates that this variable is salient (i.e. it was noticed), but also that it carries social meaning (low status).

3.4 Vowels

As explained in §3.3, the Liverpool consonant system is phonologically identical to that of other Northern varieties or even English English in general. Similarly, Scouse vowels have much in common with other Northern varieties in England.

Liverpool is north of the most important and probably also best known isogloss in England and so has the same vowel in words of the STRUT and FOOT lexical sets. The most typical (and at least in working-class speech by far the most frequent) realisation is [ʊ]. Many middle-class speakers, however, tend to keep the two sets distinct. This does not necessarily mean that middle-class speakers have [ʌ] in STRUT words. Many speakers content themselves with "merely making the vowel slightly different" (Knowles 1973: 284) and actual realisations usually range from a very slightly centralised [ʊ] to [ə]. Some confusion as to which vowel should be used in which words exists, and hypercorrections and mistakes occur (Knowles 1973: 286–287 and Knowles 1978: 83).

Another issue where Scouse is in agreement with Northern English in general concerns [a] and [ɑː]. Liverpool English has [a] instead of RP [ɑː] in words like *last, grass, bath* etc. Middle-class speech again strives more towards RP but usually does not quite reach the target. Typically, the resulting vowel is a compromise between [a] and [ɑː], both in terms of quality and duration and again there is some uncertainty and inconsistency (cf. Knowles 1973: 287–289 and 1978: 83–84). Watson found that [ɑː] is generally used in START and PALM words. However, only women seem to really use the RP variant while men prefer a more fronted [aː] (cf. Watson 2007b: 358) – much like the compromise described by Knowles (1973).

Words like *book* and *look* have long [uː] instead of short [ʊ] in Liverpool. Knowles (1973) described this pronunciation as being "heard in the North Midlands from Merseyside to beyond Leeds", particularly in working-class speech (Knowles 1973: 290). Often, long [uː] is centralised or fronted. However, Watson (2007b: 358) suggests this feature is fading, a statement the author of this study can (impressionistically) corroborate. Only older speakers (roughly 60 years of age or older) seem to still have this vowel in *book*. It is also mostly this age group that makes use of [uː] as a typical accent feature in the imitation task (see §5.1).

An aspect where Scouse is different from Northern English concerns the vowels in the lexical sets FACE, PRICE, GOAT, CHOICE, and MOUTH. Unlike much of Northern England, Liverpool English has diphthongs in all these words, although PRICE is occasionally monophthongised for some speakers (cf. Watson 2007b: 358).

3.4.1 happy

This section is concerned with happy, i.e. the final vowel in words such as *city, baby, pretty*. With respect to RP, Harrington (2006: 441) writes that in the 1950s, the vowel used in this position was "phonetically closer to [ɪ] in KIT than to [iː] in FLEECE", i.e. *happy* was pronounced [hæpɪ], not [hæpi]. In the late 20th century, however, happy has undergone tensing in RP. The phonetic realisation is now [i] for most speakers, and dictionaries generally use /i/ to represent this vowel. Note that the change was purely phonetic, not phonological, as [ɪ] and [i] do not distinguish meaning in the final unstressed syllables concerned. Just like other changes in RP during this period, happy-tensing is associated with Estuary English (cf. Wells 1997). Lengthening of happy to [iː] is probably due to the fact that, (a) in English, short vowels are not permitted word-finally, and (b) happy "often occurs as the last syllable in a prosodic phrase, which is of course a primary context for synchronic lengthening (...)" (Harrington 2006: 441).

Although the standard pronunciation in modern RP is now clearly [i], some (very) conservative speakers might still adhere to the now outdated traditional ('upper-crust' in the terminology of Wells 1982) norm [ɪ] (as, e.g. Trudgill (1999) claims). However, using Christmas broadcasts over a period of about 50 years Harrington (cf. 2006: 452) found that even Queen Elizabeth II had participated in the shift to a certain degree and moved her happy vowel in the direction of the modern realisation.

Happy-tensing has now spread to most parts of England, with the exception of "[t]he Central North, Central Lancashire, Northwest Midlands and Central Midlands areas". Here, the older pronunciation [ɪ] is still retained. There are a few exceptions, though, namely the port cities Liverpool, Hull and Newcastle (cf. Trudgill 1999: 62). Liverpool, or rather the whole of Merseyside (and parts of Chester) is therefore "an 'ee'-pronouncing island surrounded by a sea of accents which do not (yet) have this feature" (Trudgill 1999: 72). In fact, it is not clear whether other areas really will follow. As a case in point, Flynn (2010) has investigated happy realisations of adolescents in Nottingham (which is part of Trudgill's 'sea of accents' without happy-tensing). Not only did he find that lax happy variants were holding their ground (although it has to be said that tense [i] variants are just as common), but also that particularly working-class females even used 'hyper-lax' [ɛ] variants in a sizeable proportion of cases, presumably because they wish to actively distance themselves from tenser happy realisations which are seen as "posh". Ultra-lax happy realisations have also been attested for Sheffield (Stoddart et al. 1999) and the Manchester area (Watts 2006).

Given the above-mentioned 'island status' of Liverpool, happy-tensing is a distinguishing feature in the (supra-)regional context. Like velar nasal plus, it had already spread across the Mersey to West Wirral by 1980. Newbrook (1999: 97 and 99) in fact found "Liverpool/general southern [i]" to dominate clearly, with rates of occurrence around 83% in informal speech registers, a change which was apparently driven by younger females, who were among the first to introduce Liverpool variants of this and several other variables.

Notwithstanding its usefulness as a feature that distinguishes Liverpool English from surrounding non-standard accents, happy-tensing seems to have low salience and is not the subject of comments about Scouse (in Liverpool itself, and also in West Wirral) – possibly because it does not diverge from the modern standard.

3.4.2 NURSE – SQUARE

As another "Merseyside feature" Trudgill (1999: 72) notes the NURSE-SQUARE merger,[1] i.e. the fact that words such as *fair* and *fur*, or *purr* and *pair* can be (near-) homophones in Liverpool English. In older, very traditional Liverpool English, this merger used to be centralised (cf. West 2015: 323), much like in the surrounding areas, but this is no longer the case. De Lyon (cf. 1981: 68 and 71) distinguishes 15 possible realisations for NURSE and 18 for SQUARE in her auditory analysis, but the most typical realisation (in a broad Scouse accent) for both vowels is [ɛː] or [eː], sometimes even reaching [ɪː] (cf. Watson 2007b: 358). Honeybone (2007: 127) mentions the same range of realisations ("central and front vowels"), but calls the front vowels in particular "very robust" and gives [skwɛː] *square* : [nɛːs] *nurse* as examples.

According to Watson (2007b: 358), De Lyon (1981) does not succeed in giving a (quantitative) description of how these variants are socially distributed (as they can be expected to be). Given his own reservations about the scope of his study (cf. §3.1), Knowles (1973) does not fare much better, but his thesis does contain a number of remarks about the subject. For example – although this is not very exciting news – he states that, generally, the working-class residents of Vauxhall do not make this distinction, whereas the middle-class speakers from Aigburth usually do, with the Aigburth women topping the list (which is, this time, in line with most research on gender differences that followed). The degree of difference between the two vowels can, however, be very subtle, to the point that "a gesture towards the prestige standard" (for the speaker), "may be for the hearer just another variant of a dialect vowel" (cf. Knowles 1973: 295–297).

At the same time he claims that the "typical middle-class vowel is /ɜ/ or the RP type /ɜ/". He reports working-class speakers as using mostly [ɛ̈] ("further forward on the axis") and explains that younger speakers have an even more fronted (and raised) [ë] (Knowles 1973: 271). He adds that /ɜ/ in particular "merits further study for various age-groups and in various parts of Merseyside" (1973: 320).

---

[1]Patrick Honeybone (p.c.) is critical of calling this feature a merger because the term either implies "speakers are actively/synchronically abandoning a contrast, or at least that this is a merger which has happened in the history of Scouse [as opposed to before the formation as a new dialect]", neither of which he considers to be true. I tend to agree, but, for reasons of convenience, have decided to follow other studies (Trudgill 1999; Watson & Clark 2013) in using the label 'merger' nonetheless.

Concerning possible sources of this merger, Honeybone (2007: 128) mentions the dialect of South Lancashire as the most obvious candidate. He attests "a similar lack of contrast" there but stresses the fact that although the same two vowels as in Liverpool are concerned, the direction of the merger is different. Where Scouse merges NURSE and SQUARE towards front vowels [ɛː] or [eː], South Lancashire English has a central vowel, "such as [əˑ: ~ ɜː] (with residual rhoticity still an option)".

Honeybone (2007) also lists a number of studies reporting similar mergers in several Irish varieties. Wells (1982), for instance, tells us that Belfast English has a merger very similar to that of Scouse, realising *fair, fir, fur* all as [fɛːɹ]. Harris (cf. 1985: 48) describes a merger comparable to the one in South Lancashire for urban speakers of Lagan Valley (in Northern Ireland). The vowel used is a central [ɜː] (his examples are [dɜːɹ] *dare*, and [stɜːɹ] *stair*). Talking about 'fashionable Dublin English' Hickey (1999) asserts that NURSE and SQUARE have the possible realisations [nəˑs] and [skwəˑ] respectively. Honeybone (2007: 128) points out that these are statements about current (or comparatively recent) stages of the respective dialects and that it is somewhat speculative to assume that "these patterns can be extrapolated to the varieties of Hiberno-English which were spoken in Liverpool at the time of koineisation". In fact, given the intense and long-lasting contacts between Liverpool and Ireland it is just as possible that the merger actually crossed the Irish Sea westwards instead of eastwards.

What these reports do show, however, is that "the pre-*r* vowels in these words are susceptible to considerable variation in Hiberno-English varieties (…) in ways which would have differed from those supplied by Welsh, Scottish and most English dialects during koineisation", which is why Irish influence does seem plausible (Honeybone 2007: 128). Honeybone (2007) still stresses the fact that the most important donor variety with regard to the NURSE-SQUARE merger must have been Lancashire English – "where there was a complete lack of contrast" – and that Irish varieties only provided a further push towards adapting this feature which was already in the pool (Honeybone 2007: 129). Just as with the Liverpool lenition pattern it has to be noted that the NURSE-SQUARE merger was not borrowed wholesale from Lancashire English or any other variety and simply carried on. Rather, it was actively selected from "the mix of dialect contact", adapted, changed, and made a part of Liverpool English (cf. Honeybone 2007: 129). As has been observed in the case of /k/ lenition, merged NURSE-SQUARE realisations were not commonly found on the other side of the Mersey in 1980. Newbrook (1999: 95) reports that 2 out of 3 speakers in his sample maintain a difference between these two vowels. At the same time both vowels seem to exhibit "surprisingly low salience" and definitely less "than elsewhere in Merseyside" (where salience must thus be higher) (Newbrook 1999: 95).

Honeybone (cf. 2007: 128) asserts that the NURSE-SQUARE merger as it is found in Liverpool is not known to exist in any other variety in England, Scotland, or Wales. This is not quite correct, though, as in Teesside "the same merger between the vowels of *hair* and *her* which is found in Liverpool (…)" is attested (Trudgill 1999: 70). While not unique to Liverpool, this merger is in any case rare enough to be generally perceived as one of the most characteristic (or even defining) and most salient features of Scouse, to the point where it is commonly picked up by comedians and the like – an early example is Ken Dodd's catchphrase "Whaire's me shairt?" (cf. Trudgill 1999: 73). The NURSE-SQUARE merger also figures prominently in the Scouse phrase books pioneered by Frank Shaw and Fritz Spiegl. In fact, these two vowels are the ones that most often occur with a non-standard spelling in the *Lern Yerself Scouse* series (cf. Honeybone & Watson 2013: 322). The particular re-spellings that are chosen for words which are minimal pairs in RP hint at "an awareness of the fact that these words in these lexical sets can be pronounced in the same way" (Honeybone & Watson 2013: 324), while the high frequency with which this is done indicates that NURSE and SQUARE "are imbued with local meaning" and constitute the "most salient" of the vocalic features the authors analysed.

Additionally, this feature is the second for which perceptual data are already available (cf. §3.3.2). Watson & Clark (2013) played recordings to subjects and asked them to rate the audio clips (again in real-time) with respect to how "posh" the speaker sounded. He naturally produced merged NURSE and SQUARE vowels with central realisations. In addition, fronted (Liverpool-like) variants were re-synthesised and participants were randomly assigned to one of two guises, which corresponded to 100% central and 100% fronted realisations, respectively (cf. Watson & Clark 2013: 305–306). Listeners from St. Helens and Liverpool reacted to non-standard realisations of both vowels (front NURSE and central SQUARE) by assigning lower status values to the speaker – at least when non-standard variants preceded standard ones in the audio clip. This corroborates that the NURSE-SQUARE merger is "a salient feature of English in north-west England" (cf. Watson & Clark 2013: 317–320).

3.5 Summary

I have tried to give a (very) short overview of the features that constitute the Liverpool accent in this chapter. Special mention has been made of the four variables whose production and perception will be the focus of the rest of this book. They are: velar nasal plus and lenition of /k/ for the consonants, and happy-tensing and the NURSE-SQUARE merger for the vowels. In the literature, velar nasal plus and happy-tensing are (implicitly) counted among the less salient features, whereas lenition and the NURSE-SQUARE merger are said to form part of the stereotype of Scouse. This received, and comparatively broad, distinction into salient and non-salient variables constitutes the starting point and the basis of the present study, and will be updated and refined in the following chapters.

4 A few words on salience and exemplar theory

This chapter contains some thoughts on the notion of salience and its role within the framework of exemplar theory. Both concepts are of prime importance for this study, and it is therefore vital that some basic assumptions pertaining to these notions be defined before we move on to the empirical results that they will help interpret and explain.

4.1 Salience

In this book, the concept of salience has already been brought up several times by now, without, however, having received a definition of any kind. Since the term is omnipresent in sociolinguistic research chances are that most readers will have a pretty good idea of what 'salience' is, but it is not at all unlikely that there will not be just one idea, but several ideas. This is because sociolinguistic salience is a notoriously vague concept that is defined in a number of different ways by different researchers. I do not intend to partake in the discussion as to which of the various definitions of salience is the most useful one, since – as I hope to make clear below – the question of what *makes* a linguistic variable salient is largely irrelevant to the present study. This study is rather interested in what salience *does*, primarily in perception. A short review of some relevant literature is nevertheless necessary in order to avoid confusion as to what exactly is meant when the term 'salience' is used in this work. However, this account will deliberately be as brief as possible; more detailed analyses of salience, its history, and use in sociolinguistics can, for example, be found in Kerswill & Williams (2002), Rácz (2013), and Auer (2014) – all three of which are also the primary sources of what is to follow below.

4.1.1 Salience and circularity

Strictly speaking, providing a basic definition of salience that all or at least the majority of researchers can agree on should be a rather straightforward and un-

controversial task. As the *Oxford English Dictionary* puts it, salience (in psychology) is the "quality or fact of being more prominent in a person's awareness or
in his memory of past experience" – in simpler terms, salience is the quality of
'sticking out' from the rest. Kerswill & Williams (2002: 81) stay very close to this
general description when they define (socio-)linguistic salience as "a property of
a linguistic item or feature that makes it in some way perceptually and cognitively prominent". While the two definitions are very similar, there is actually a
crucial difference, because Kerswill & Williams talk about salience as something
that *makes* a feature stick out, not just the simple fact that it *does*. This type of
definition can easily lead to what Auer (cf. 2014: 9) criticises as mixing *criteria*
that allow us to identify salient features with the *causes* of salience, i.e. the traits
that *make* a variable salient in the first place. He does, however, acknowledge that
criteria and causes often *are* difficult to distinguish because they can actually be
dependent on each other. His example is based on overt corrections, which are
not only evidence for the salience of the corrected feature, but which also have
their share in *making* the feature salient within the speech community.

A more serious problem ensues when *criteria* and *effects* of salience (on language change) are not strictly kept apart. This issue is addressed by Kerswill &
Williams (2002: 82) as well, who argue that when salience is used as "a potential
explanatory factor, (...) the concept all too easily lapses into circularity and mere
labelling", a point that is illustrated very well by their critique of Trudgill (1986).
According to Trudgill, salient markers can be distinguished from non-salient indicators (see §4.1.3) by the fact that, among other things, the former are stigmatised and undergoing change while the latter are not. The problem is that stigmatisation and the change that it often entails (for example, when people start
avoiding the stigmatised variant) are not only the prerequisites of marker status,
but also its outcome – people are aware of non-standard variants because they
are stigmatised, and the variants are stigmatised because people are aware of
them. This essentially boils down to saying that a variable is salient because it is
salient, which means that 'salience' loses any explanatory potential altogether.

In the present study, this would correspond to (1) hypothesising that only salient variables will create a priming effect, (2) running a perception experiment
directly, and then (3) claiming that the presence of a priming effect for some
variables but not for others is evidence for their salience, (4) which in turn explains their behaviour in the perception test. To avoid this kind of circularity it
is therefore absolutely crucial to establish the salience status of the test variables
independently, which is why the production data were collected.

Research based on the notion of salience is perhaps particularly prone to fall-ing victim to the circularity trap because "salience *attempts* to combine both structural (language-internal) factors with sociolinguistic and psychological (ex-tra-linguistic) factors in a single explanatory concept" (Kerswill & Williams 2002: 83, my emphasis), but many researchers actually focus primarily on one particu-lar aspect only. However, if salience is to have any explanatory value (which ne-cessitates avoiding circularity), "it *must* have recourse to extra-linguistic factors, which will be a combination of cognitive, social psychological or pragmatic fac-tors" (Kerswill & Williams 2002: 83, my emphasis).

4.1.2 Cognitive vs. social salience

The way it is commonly used, sociolinguistic salience is thus a concept that com-bines cognitive and social components. However, as Rácz (cf. 2013: 11) points out, it actually makes sense to distinguish cognitive and social salience. The cognit-ive aspect is at least implicitly present in the most basic definition of salience: for something to 'stick out' it needs to have some quality that makes it more promin-ent in perception, and since this is inevitably linked to processing it is part of the cognitive domain. Social salience, according to Auer (cf. 2014: 10), is based on the fact that a particular feature can be linked to a certain (social) type of speaker, who, in turn, is associated with social and emotional evaluations, which are then transferred to the linguistic feature itself. The stronger these negative or posit-ive evaluations are, the more (socially) salient the feature will be. Naturally, a feature has to be noticed first before it can be socially evaluated and judged, so cognitive salience is in fact a prerequisite of social salience. If a feature is *cognit-ively* salient it can acquire social meaning and thus become *socially* salient, too – crucially, though, it does not have to (cf. Rácz 2013: 11). Cognitive salience is thus a necessary, but not a sufficient condition for social salience.

Distinguishing cognitive from social salience can potentially help in sorting out some of the apparent confusion in salience research, because it allows to separate problems concerned with, for example, the interplay of social salience and language change, from a discussion that is more focussed on the primary causes of salience in the cognitive domain, irrespective of whether or not they result in social salience in a particular context. However, researchers are not really agreed on what makes something *cognitively* salient, either. While he does not claim that this is the only source of salience, Rácz (cf. 2013: 9) largely equates cognitive salience with surprise and operationalises it by means of transitional probabilities: a feature is surprising if it is unexpected in a particular context, i.e. when it has a low probability of occurrence.

Jaeger & Weatherholtz (cf. 2017: 37) embrace the same idea of surprisal as a function of unexpectedness, or low probability of occurrence, in a given context and equate it with informativeness – the more surprising an input, the more information is gained by processing it. They champion this operationalisation of salience not only because it is relatively easy to quantify, but also because surprisal has been found to play a role in research looking at reading times and implicit learning (cf. Jaeger & Weatherholtz 2017: 37). Crucially, Jaeger & Weatherholtz see surprisal as (one of) the cause(s) of *initial* salience, when the listener first encounters a given variant. Long-term salience, as the result of cumulative exposure, on the other hand, is based on "informativeness about social group membership" (Jaeger & Weatherholtz 2017: 38), i.e. on the association of a feature with a group of speakers, in whose speech it is usually frequent and thus not unexpected any more.

This account may well be able to explain the diverging levels of salience reported in the literature for the four variables analysed in this book. Lenition of /k/ and fronted NURSE are largely limited to Liverpool English, while velar nasal plus and happy-tensing are also found in other accents. From the point of view of the speech community as a whole, the former two have thus a lower probability of occurrence, and are also more informative with respect to their association (only) with Liverpool speakers.

Conceiving of salient features as surprising (and "informative") ones is thus in line with research in psycholinguistics and the cognitive sciences, and this approach may also go some way to explaining the salience of certain sociolinguistic variables. But at least in sociolinguistics, surprisal is by no means the only option. Many other factors have also been proposed as potential sources of cognitive salience, for example (high) frequency or phoneme status (cf. Auer 2014: 8). Furthermore, it seems quite clear that attention, as a top-down factor, interferes with the bottom-up stimulus property of unexpectedness, for example when subjects are asked to count passes in a basketball video and fail to notice a person in a weird costume (a highly surprising event) crossing the scene (cf. Zarcone et al. 2017: 8). It can thus be said that attention "weights surprisal effects from one level or another, depending on the current goals and on perceived rewards" (Zarcone et al. 2017: 8).

With regard to the effects of salience on linguistic behaviour – usually change, convergence, and divergence are the focus of interest – I agree with Auer (2014: 17) who claims that sociolinguistic salience is "hierarchically organised" in the sense that "cognitive [causes of salience] are subordinate to social ones" (my translation). He argues that cognitive aspects do contribute to the sociolinguistic salience of a variable, but much less so than social ones, and explains that this is because cognitive factors of salience are "filtered" by the social layer (cf. Auer 2014: 18). What this means in practical terms is that only certain cognitively salient features are selected for social evaluation (i.e. they receive social attention) while others do not acquire social meaning. In the first case cognitive factors merely "reinforce" sociolinguistic salience (which is nonetheless dominated by social evaluations), while in the latter (i.e. when cognitively salient features are not used to do social work), the resulting salience of the feature is "markedly" lower (cf. Auer 2014: 18). Moreover, "from a sociolinguistic perspective, the choice of features which become [sociolinguistically] salient is in large part an arbitrary one" and seems to depend primarily on "community consensus" (Llamas et al. 2017: 56), which is why I would argue that, *for a sociolinguist*, the question of what makes something cognitively salient can be considered secondary to the (descriptive) knowledge about which features the community agreed to pay attention to.

4.1.3 Salience in this study

Since the primary hypothesis of this study is that only variables having a very high degree of *sociolinguistic* salience are capable of creating priming effects in perception experiments (cf. §1.1), it follows that the focus in independently assessing the salience of the variables presented in Chapter 3 should be on social aspects. I will, therefore, only be interested in *if* a variable is sociolinguistically salient for speakers, but not in *why* it is. It is, for instance, quite possible that a variable that is found to be socially salient is so because it is more informative than others with respect to unambiguously indexing a particular speech community. Given the fact that I am interested in the *effects* of salience rather than its *causes*, however, this piece of information, while interesting, is irrelevant to the present study. For this reason, cognitive aspects of salience will largely remain unaddressed in this book.

In very general terms, the question of interest in the present study is thus simply "[w]hether a variable is recognised in any way", which means that this book is in line with many other sociolinguistic studies, where this is "what researchers (…) usually mean when they talk about *salience*" (Rácz 2013: 4, emphasis in original). In contrast to Rácz (2013), who explicitly includes his own work in the above statement, I will not, however, regard a feature as salient if it is recognised in *any* way, but only if it is "recognised" as socially meaningful. The next question, then, is of course how we know that a variable is socially meaningful for speakers. While Chapter 3 provides a rough distinction into salient and non-salient variables of Liverpool English as they are presented in the literature, these classifications are (1) primarily based on the observations of experts (dialectologists) or laypersons with a special interest in linguistic phenomena (e.g. the authors of the *Lern Yerself Scouse* series), and/or (2) grounded on databases that are often several decades old (Watson & Clark 2013 and Watson & Clark 2015 are notable exceptions to both points). An additional, up-to-date assessment of salience among the speakers of the variety themselves therefore seems desirable to make sure the conclusions drawn in the literature are still valid, and, if possible, to arrive at a more fine-grained ordering of variables on the salience scale.

Unfortunately, uncovering social attitudes towards a particular phonetic-phonological feature is seldom a straightforward task. This is because "language users are usually very much aware of particular words or intonation patterns *other* people use (...), but are much less attentive to phonetic differences" (Rácz 2013: 3, emphasis in the original). Directly asking subjects about phonetic or phonemic characteristics of an accent is still an option, but one that, for the majority of speakers, will only work in the case of the most heavily stigmatised features. A more indirect measure is required to capture the middle ground of variables that do carry some social meaning, but not enough to attract overt commentary. In this study, as in many others, this indirect measure is based on the *effects* of social salience, the most important of which include *social stratification*, *hypercorrection*, and, above all, *style shifting*.

Social stratification is based on the idea that "the normal workings of society have produced systematic differences between certain (...) people", which can be thought of in terms of status or prestige, and assumes that these social differences are mirrored in linguistic behaviour: when two people can be ranked with respect to a social status criterion, they will be ranked identically with respect to their use of a non-standard feature (Labov 1972: 44–45). What this means in practical terms is that, for instance, middle-class speakers will usually have lower frequencies of usage than working-class speakers. In this work, the term will also be extended to gender differences, but certainly not because I wish to imply a social ranking between women and men. Rather, this is because, in numerous sociolinguistic studies, women have been shown to be more sensitive to linguistic forms that are socially relevant (cf. Labov 2001: 290–291), so if women use a variant in a different way than men then this suggests that said variant has acquired at least a certain degree of social meaning.

As a general term, hypercorrection refers to the "misapplication of an imperfectly learned rule" (Labov 1972: 126). In sociolinguistics, the term is traditionally used to describe cases where a particular group of speakers (sub-)consciously tries to approximate the linguistic usage of a (prestigious) target speech community, but fails in their endeavour because the speakers actually 'overshoot the mark' and end up with realisational rates that are beyond the model set by the target group (cf. Labov 1972: 126). In the present study, the term hypercorrection will mostly be used in the more general sense, which extends its scope to any case where a given rule has been learned "imperfectly", e.g. when speakers use an even more non-standard variant in more formal speech styles (compared to spontaneous speech) or when they correct the "wrong" member of a merger. Both applications of hypercorrection imply (sub-)conscious awareness of socially meaningful variation, as both the target (in the Labovian definition) or the rule (in the more general reading) have a social component.

Style shifting, finally, is similar to social stratification (in fact, another term that is used by Labov is stylistic stratification). However, in style shifting, use of linguistic features is not correlated with social status of the speakers, but with the degree of formality of the communicative situation. A non-standard variant will thus be used most in very informal (e.g a conversation among friends), less in more formal (e.g. a job interview), and least in the most formal speaking registers (e.g. reading out a written text) – of course, the reverse is true for standard, prestigious variants. The presence of style shifting presupposes (sub-)conscious evaluation of the linguistic feature, which results in it being considered more or less appropriate in a given, socially loaded, communicative situation. In consequence, "social awareness of a given variable corresponds to the slope of style shifting" (Labov 2001: 196).

Based on social stratification, hypercorrection, and style shifting, Labov's 1972 hierarchy of *indicators*, *markers*, and *stereotypes* is a convenient way of categorising linguistic variables according to their sociolinguistic salience. An indicator is a (non-standard) linguistic feature which is shared among a particular group of speakers and can therefore act as a defining characteristic of that speech community (which it indexes, i.e. 'points to'), particularly to outsiders. The speech community itself is, however, completely unaware of the feature and uses it to the same degree in all communicative situations, so there is no style shifting. When a speech community starts to become (sub-consciously) aware of a feature it is increasingly invested with social meaning and associated with a particular degree of (non-)formality. These markers show social stratification (i.e. they are used more by some social groups and less by others) and style shifting: frequencies of non-standard realisations decrease systematically in more formal speaking styles. A *stereotype* finally, does not only exhibit social stratification and style shifting, but has actually crossed the threshold to conscious awareness, and is explicitly commented on by members of the speech community (cf. Labov 1972: 178–180). Speakers are thus completely unaware of *indicators*, only sub-consciously aware of *markers*, and fully conscious of *stereotypes*.

Originally, Labov conceived of this hierarchy as a sort of sociolinguistic life cycle that every linguistic feature invariably went through: starting out as an indicator, acquiring social meaning and turning into a marker, before finally becoming the object of stigmatisation which eventually leads to disappearance. He later on corrected this interpretation, however, after several decades of sociolinguistic research had shown that some indicators do not seem to ever turn into markers and that heavily stigmatised variants can nevertheless survive (Labov 1994), for instance when they enjoy covert prestige as markers (this time in the every day sense of the word) of a local identity. In any case, this question does not affect the usefulness of the indicator-marker-stereotype hierarchy as a means of categorising variables according to how aware speakers are of them.

Based on the work of Silverstein (cf., for instance, Silverstein 2003) Johnstone et al. (cf. 2006: 78) have introduced new terminology centred around *first-*, *second-*, and *third-order indexicality*. There is a large degree of overlap between these terms and Labov's indicator-marker-stereotype distinction, while, of course, the two frameworks are not completely identical. Notable differences can, for example, be found between stereotypes and third-order indexicality: the former is (traditionally, at least) closely linked to stigmatisation and a higher chance of disappearance of the feature, while the latter term focusses on the conscious use of these features in performances of local identity and presumes that the relevant linguistic variants are, at this stage, primarily associated with place, and less with other social categories such as class (cf. Johnstone et al. 2006: 81–84). As we will see later, features of Scouse that can be classified as Labovian stereotypes *are* actually used in accent performances, and do not seem to be disappearing either, so it might seem preferable to use Johnstone et al.'s terminology. However, with respect to a hierarchical ordering of variables according to how conscious speakers are of them, indicator, marker, and stereotype – on the one hand – and first-, second-, and third-order indexicality – on the other hand – can be regarded as synonyms. Since the degree of sociolinguistic awareness is what this study is interested in, I will therefore stick to the more traditional Labovian terminology.

Rácz (2013: 6) criticises the indicator/marker distinction as "impl[ying] a complete absence of gradience" while linguistic awareness should be conceived of as having "many levels, very few categorical". I agree with the second part of this statement, but I do not see why one would have to give up on the convenience of Labov's classification (which is indeed rather categorical in nature) just because one believes that salience is gradient. It seems to me that it is quite possible to distinguish, for example, different *degrees* of style shifting (How many styles are kept distinct? How significant are the differences?), *in addition to* a simple binary assessment of whether style shifting is present or not, and the same should hold for social stratification or hypercorrection. Such an approach should allow us to arrive at more fine-grained classifications of variables such as, for example, 'solid marker close to stereotype status' or 'indicator showing the beginnings of style-shifting'.

No matter how fine-grained the classification, however, what I intend to do is clearly what Kerswill & Williams (2002) have called using *salience* as a label, which means that it is "no more than another term for the indicator/marker distinction" (Rácz 2013: 32). This statement is certainly true with respect to the present study, but, as I hope to have made clear, the use of salience as a 'mere label' should not constitute a problem against the backdrop of what this book is interested in. I do not, in fact, *need* more than a convenient label that describes how much social meaning a particular variable carries for its users. In contrast to the argument presented by Kerswill & Williams (2002) – who mainly talk about research investigating change and contact – salience *will* nevertheless have an explanatory value in the present study when it is linked up to how sociolinguistic variables behave in priming experiments. Salience, in this book, will thus be understood as meaning the amount of (social) awareness speakers have of a sociolinguistic variable. As such, it will be measured by the presence and, if applicable, degree of social stratification, hypercorrection, style shifting, and explicit comments and evaluations.

4.2 Exemplar theory

Any linguistic study that deals with the perception of speech is faced with the theoretical problem of how listeners process the range of intra- and inter-speaker variation that is abundant in naturalistic language data. Sociophonetic studies in particular have largely turned away from traditional accounts which assume that variation in the speech signal is normalised away to make the input fit into highly abstract and idealised mental categories. Most researchers explain their results against the backdrop of exemplar theory, and the present study is no exception in this respect. I will therefore provide a short overview of the assumptions and principles of this theory before addressing the place of salience in this model. Just as in §4.1, my account (which is inspired by the one presented in Juskan 2011) must be considered nothing but a brief summary, albeit one that should be more than sufficient for the purposes of the present study. The reader is referred to Pierrehumbert 2006 for a more detailed discussion.

4.2.1 Basic principles

Exemplar theory has its origins in psychology (cf. Medin & Schaffer 1978), where it was conceived as a general theory to model how information is stored, organised, and accessed in long-term memory. The basic tenet of this model is that every stimulus, or sensory experience, leaves a memory trace in the perceiver's mind. Crucially, now, these traces, or 'exemplars', are specific in nature, so what is remembered is not a (single) abstract and idealised prototype of a category, but rather there will be a whole number of similar, but still slightly different exemplars. The information that is stored for any episodic memory is not restricted to the single feature of an exemplar that is most useful (or maybe even sufficient) to distinguish different mental categories. Instead, the memory trace is poly-dimensional and can include several characteristics (cf. Pierrehumbert 2006: 517). For a visual stimulus, for instance, this might include shape, colour, size, and others, even when only the shape is relevant in that hypothetical context. In fact, exemplars are even "indexed" with additional information that is not directly linked to physical or sensory properties of the stimulus itself, but which pertains to the situation or the circumstances under which the experience in question was made. It would, for example, be remembered that the hypothetical visual stimulus from above was encountered in an experimental setting as part of a categorisation task – and possibly also whether the stimulus was categorised correctly or not (cf. Medin & Schaffer 1978: 210–212). The outcome in long-term memory of a number of similar sensory experiences will thus be a cloud of specific exemplars which are indexed with all sorts of additional information.

This should not be taken to imply that there are no mental categories, because exemplar theory by no means denies their existence. It assumes, however, that they are created on the basis of – and in addition to – the individual exemplars that are stored in memory in full detail. Categorisation happens via the process of indexation just explained. When perceivers are confronted with stimuli as representatives of a particular category (for example that of "circle") then the concrete realisations will be remembered as detailed individual exemplars, but each of them will *also* be indexed as being a member of that category. A mental "bin" in exemplar theory thus consists not of a single idealised prototype, but rather of a cloud of individual instantiations that all share a given label.

Newly encountered input will then be perceived (and categorised) with respect to how similar it is to the traces that have already been acquired. If, for example, a perceiver has remembered a cloud of small blue triangle exemplars, which are indexed as belonging to category A, and a second cloud of big red circles (indexed as instances of category B), then a newly encountered small blue circle is likely to be categorised as a kind of A because the stimulus is more similar to the A exemplars than it is to the B exemplars (provided shape, colour, and size all have equal weighting) (cf. Medin & Schaffer 1978: 210–212). A stimulus 'activates' all remembered exemplars that are similar to it, which essentially means that they are cognitively foregrounded and therefore more "accessible" (compared to other exemplars) for help in categorising the new input. Once an exemplar is stored in memory it can also act "as a retrieval cue to access information *stored with* stimuli similar to the probe" (Medin & Schaffer 1978: 210, my emphasis). This means that a stimulus that is similar to one particular exemplar X will not only activate this one memory trace (and possibly a few others that are also extremely similar), but in fact the whole memory cloud of exemplars that share a particular label with X, for example category membership or context in which the exemplar was acquired. It will become clear in the following paragraphs that activation of exemplars via indexed information is a crucial aspect of exemplar theory for any sociolinguistic priming study.

4.2.2 Application in (socio-)linguistics

According to Pierrehumbert (cf. 2006: 517), Goldinger (1996) and Johnson (1997) were the first to interpret linguistic findings (from speech processing) with the help of exemplar theory. In traditional approaches, variation in the speech signal is normalised away to reduce different phones to idealised, essentialist forms which correspond to the abstract phoneme categories in the perceiver's mind. In an exemplar theoretic account, speech sounds enter long-term memory as phonetically detailed exemplars, so "the lowest level of description is a parametric phonetic map rather than a set of discrete categories" (Pierrehumbert 2006: 519). Phonemes do exist as mental categories, but as just explained for episodic approaches more generally, they have to be viewed as "clusters of similar experiences", whose centres of gravity are malleable and can be changed by "incremental updating" of remembered exemplars (cf. Pierrehumbert 2006: 519). A phoneme is thus a collection of phonetic variants (the memory traces) which are all indexed as being realisations of one particular phoneme (cf. Pierrehumbert 2002: 113).

Indexation is, however, not restricted to phoneme assignment, but can also extend to other bits of linguistic information such as the immediate phonetic context. And of course any exemplar can be indexed with information that is somehow related to the wider context the experience was made in (cf. §4.2.1). Sociophonetic studies usually assume that phonetically detailed exemplars are primarily indexed with social information about the speaker who uttered them, e.g. their regional origin, gender, age, etc. (cf. Hay, Nolan, et al. 2006: 370).

Activation of remembered exemplars is conceived of in the same way as in psychology. When speech sounds are perceived they activate any exemplars stored in long-term memory which are phonetically similar to the new input. The foregrounded memory traces then form the basis the input is processed and classified against. Activation can also be triggered indirectly via social information that the episodic memories are indexed with, a process which is actually very useful in dealing with variation in the speech signal.

Consider, for instance, the perception of vowels. It is a well-known fact that the formant structure of vowel realisations differs between women and men due to differences in vocal tract length. A perceiver who has been exposed to both female and male vowel articulations will therefore have two separate clouds of exemplars in long-term memory: one indexed with "female", one with "male". When this perceiver now engages in conversation with a person they have never met before a non-linguistic perception (such as a visual cue that the interlocutor is female) will activate the memory cloud indexed with the appropriate gender before the other person has uttered a single sound. Thanks to this pre-activation of potentially similar exemplars subsequent perception of new material should be easier and more successful. The two types of activation (via similarity and via indexation) can reinforce each other: In cases where perceived social information about the speaker and the phonetic shape of the input activate the same group of exemplars, full activation will be reached faster (cf. Hay, Nolan, et al. 2006: 370–371). If, however, social cues and the phonetics of the stimulus are at odds (for example when a woman has an unusually deep voice), the "wrong" exemplars will be activated via indexation and misperception becomes more likely.

Social indexation of phonetically detailed memory traces is not merely a theoretic assumption of exemplar theory but something that has been tested empirically. Strand & Johnson (1996) had participants classify synthesised vowels from a FOOT-STRUT continuum, which were presented together with photos of female and male faces. One and the same audio stimulus was classified differently depending on whether it had been accompanied by a photo of a woman or a man. This non-linguistic bit of information (gender of the speaker) was thus used in perception and biased subjects towards using "female" or "male" vowel boundaries when classifying the stimuli. The same effect could be achieved when confronting perceivers with a range of (consonantal) s-ʃ variants. These two fricatives are primarily distinguished by their central frequency, and the boundary between the two phonemes (i.e. the point where, perceptually, a /ʃ/ becomes a /s/) is typically lower for male than for female realisations. When subjects assumed a speaker to be male (because they had been shown a photo of a male) the threshold for categorising an auditory stimulus as an instantiation of /ʃ/ was lower (cf. Strand & Johnson 1996; Strand 1999).

Of course, the sex/gender distinction is a rather crucial one in language perception, as men have vocal tracts that are physiologically different from those of women, which results in markedly lower resonance frequencies for the former. Since the difference is – at least to a degree – biologically determined and thus phylogenetically precedes other social categories such as class or occupation, it could be that gender of speaker is a piece of information that enjoys a particular status in linguistic processing.

Niedzielski (1999) has shown, however, that effects of social information on the perception of linguistic material are not limited to gender. She tested perception of Canadian Raising in Detroit. Many Canadian speakers have a raised onset in the /aʊ/ diphthong, so that the realisation of this vowel is often [əʊ]. These raised variants can also be found in the speech of Detroiters, but while Canadian Raising is a firm part of the stereotypical believes people from Detroit hold about Canadians, they are completely unaware of raised onsets in their *own* speech, which they consider to be standard US English (cf. Niedzielski 1999: 63). Niedzielski played her participants recordings of a female Detroit speaker, who naturally produced Canadian raising, presented them with 6 resynthesised vowels (ranging from hyper-low to hyper-raised onsets), and asked them to indicate which one sounded most like the one they had heard in the stimulus. All perceivers listened to the same voice, but half of them had "MICHIGAN" written at the top of their answer sheet, while in the other group the corresponding label was "CANADIAN". These labels had a significant effect: although everyone received the same acoustic input, subjects who had been primed for "Canada" were significantly more likely to perceive Canadian Raising than those who had been primed for "Michigan" (cf. Niedzielski 1999: 64–68).

While Niedzielski does not do so herself, these results can be interpreted as evidence for the existence of social indexation of phonetically detailed exemplars. When the concept "Canada" is invoked (via the label on the answer sheet) participants activate memory traces that are marked ("indexed") as having been produced by speakers of Canadian English. These exemplars contain raised onsets of the /aʊ/ diphthong and, since they are cognitively foregrounded, they bias the perceptual system towards hearing these variants in the new input as well. If the prime is "Michigan", however, perceivers activate exemplars that are indexed with 'US standard English' (because Detroiters consider themselves to be speakers of standard English). The centre of gravity in this exemplar cloud is, of course, shifted towards lower onsets, so subjects are more likely to perceive non-raised variants of /aʊ/ when these memory traces bias perception (cf. Hay, Nolan, et al. 2006: 372).

Hay, Nolan, et al. (2006) later successfully replicated Niedzielski's findings. They had an essentially identical methodology, but used the New Zealand-Australia opposition to prime participants, instead of Michigan-Canada as in Niedzielski's study. Their experiment was concerned with the perception of short front vowels, particularly /ɪ/. This phoneme is often realised as a raised [i] by Australians, and as a centralised [ə] by New Zealanders. Speakers in both countries frequently comment on this feature under the label of the "fish 'n' chips" stereotype, as this is a common phrase that can be used to illustrate the differences in realisation (cf. Hay, Nolan, et al. 2006: 354). Participants were asked to match synthesised vowels to the ones they had heard in recordings of a female New Zealand speaker. The only difference between the experimental groups was once again the label at the top of the answer sheet. Results were comparable to Niedzielski 1999: subjects primed for New Zealand were more likely to perceive centralised tokens, while subjects primed for Australia were more likely to report more Australian percepts (cf. Hay, Nolan, et al. 2006: 359–363). Jannedy et al. (2011) have shown that a perceptual bias can even be generated when the priming categories are (socially and ethnically stratified) districts of one and the same city.

Whether subjects actually *believed* that the speaker was Australian turned out to be irrelevant: once exemplars indexed with "Australia" had been activated by the prime they biased perception, irrespective of conscious evaluations of the prime (cf. Hay, Nolan, et al. 2006: 374). In a follow-up study Hay & Drager (2010) furthermore demonstrated that such priming effects can be generated by much more subtle and less direct cues. Instead of an explicit label on an answer sheet they used stuffed toys commonly associated with Australia (kangaroo, koala) and New Zealand (kiwi) to prime perceivers. The toys were merely present in the room where the participant was seated, but they were not directly linked to the experiment. All the same, they generated a priming effect that was comparable to the one found in the replication of the Niedzielski study (cf. Hay & Drager 2010: 871–872 and 874–875). Previous research has thus clearly shown that information about the regional origin of speakers is part of long-term phonetic memory, and that exemplars activated on the basis of this type of extra-linguistic information can bias subjects towards perceiving variants that are typically associated with the primed group of speakers.

4.2.3 Frequency and salience in exemplar theory

My hypothesis that exemplar priming in sociolinguistics is a phenomenon that only occurs with (highly) salient variables is not a purely exploratory one. Rather, it is actually directly motivated by the framework of exemplar theory, where salience has been suggested to play a role from the very beginnings.

For one thing, salience is believed to structure long-term memory to a certain degree by "ranking" different aspects of a given exemplar. With respect to (in-dexical) information that is stored with a particular memory trace, for instance, Medin & Schaffer (cf. 1978: 210–212) already pointed out that not all bits need to be equally important, but that the different dimensions an exemplar is associated with can, in fact, be weighted. They use the example of a mannequin, a stimulus which, for almost any perceiver, will share many features with remembered ex-emplars of the category "human" (e.g. overall shape, size, proportions, number of limbs...). However, the mannequin stimulus differs from the "human" exemplars in a very 'salient' category, viz. that of animacy. As a consequence, no subject will cognitively include (i.e. 'perceive as') a mannequin among the exemplar cloud of humans, despite the large degree of overlap in features related to physical ap-pearance. In perception, the difference in a salient feature category (animacy) thus overrides more numerous similarities in less salient ones.

While interesting, this is not the effect of salience that is most important for the study at hand, because it can, by definition, only unfold in this way once a stimulus has been remembered. Salience is, however, already a crucial factor during the act of perception *before* the stimulus enters long-term memory as an exemplar. Although humans do seem to be able to store quite an impress-ive amount of information (cf. Johnson 2005, cited in Rácz 2013: 44) – meaning that our memory *could* theoretically contain all experiences ever made – we do not, in practice, remember every single stimulus we have encountered during our lifetime. Rather, exemplars fade over time if they are not activated, just like any other kind of memory, which results in "[d]ifferent exemplars hav[ing] dif-ferent strengths" (cf. Pierrehumbert 2002: 115). For this reason, exemplar theory has "frequency effects everywhere" (Pierrehumbert 2006: 524). Variants that are encountered more often than others can be memorised more often, and will dom-inate memory structure in one of two ways.

Firstly, frequent remembrance of similar stimuli results in denser memory clouds, i.e. mental categories which simply contain more exemplars than oth-ers. By their sheer numbers, these exemplars develop a "cumulative force" that biases the processing of new material: subsequent input is likely to be categorised as a member of this dense cloud as well (cf. Pierrehumbert 2006: 524). Secondly, a new experience can be so similar to an already remembered one that it will not be stored as a separate exemplar. Instead, it will "impact the same [neural] circuits", which "involves updating or strengthening" of the extremely similar exemplar already stored in memory (Pierrehumbert 2006: 525). There is thus not an increase in the number of exemplars in a category, but – at least up to a certain extent – the existing memory traces themselves enjoy a "cumulative effect of exposure" (Pierrehumbert 2006: 525), i.e. they become more prominent or foregrounded due to a higher degree of remnant activation from the last exposure.

A crucial aspect here is that we are talking about *frequency of remembrance*, and not simply *frequency of occurrence*, of a particular variant. It is therefore not sufficient to consider the frequencies of certain tokens in, say, a corpus in order to model the memory structure of subjects who are exposed to these tokens. The reason for this is that long-term memory is not a mirror image of "undifferentiated raw experience" (Pierrehumbert 2006: 525). Instead, "a process of attention, recognition, and coding which is not crudely reflective of frequency" intervenes between the physical, sensory input on the one hand, and the act of actually storing an exemplar on the other (Pierrehumbert 2006: 525). As a general rule of thumb, research in psychology has shown that perceivers seem to pay more attention to "informative" events (cf. also the discussion in Rácz 2013) and "[e]vents that are attended to are in turn more likely to be remembered" (Pierrehumbert 2006: 525). Pierrehumbert (cf. 2006: 525) stresses the fact that informative events are often infrequent. If one passes a particular shop every day, this event will soon not be informative any more and will (no longer) be attended to, resulting in an inability to remember details like specials of the day even a short time after the experience. If, however, on one occasion, there is a hot-air balloon in the car park next to the store, then this rare event will probably be remembered for a long time and in vivid detail.

Two points need to be mentioned here: (1) the tendency Pierrehumbert describes should not be taken to mean that high frequency and high informativeness are, a priori, mutually exclusive, and (2) even if they were, the general statement that events that attract attention are more likely to be remembered would still hold – and high frequency tokens could very well be attended to by perceivers for reasons other than their informativeness (particularly in terms of surprisal). The bottom line is that which (and how many) exemplars are retained in long-term memory is not simply a matter of raw frequency in the linguistic input a person receives, but rather one of "*effective* exposure", which is "a function of actual exposure as well as cognitive factors such as attention and memory" (Pierrehumbert 2006: 519, my emphasis).

It is not really surprising that Pierrehumbert (2006) discusses the whole issue under the sub-heading *Salience*, because salient features are features that stand out in perception (whatever the exact cause for this may be), which is essentially the same as saying they attract above average degrees of attention. The way salience is understood in the present study (cf. §4.1.3) ties in with this: if speakers are (sub-)consciously aware of a linguistic feature because it carries social meaning, and this awareness shows in production differences (i.e. attention paid to their own speech), then it only makes sense to assume that they also pay more attention to these features in perception.[1] If, in turn, salient variants receive more attention then it follows that they will be remembered more often, meaning that long-term memory will either contain more of these exemplars or it will be biased to a degree by salient memory traces that are cognitively more prominent. In both cases, exemplars containing salient variants should activate considerably faster and more strongly than less- or non-salient ones, and, as a consequence, the resulting priming effects should be more powerful for the former than for the latter.

Existing research in sociophonetics has, in fact, collected some evidence that hints at the possibility that exemplar priming might only work for highly salient variables. Niedzielski (cf. 1999: 69–75), for instance, found that the priming effect discovered in the perception of Canadian Raising was not statistically robust for vowels undergoing the Northern Cities Chain Shift (which served as secondary test variables). The 2006 study of Hay, Nolan, et al., in turn, produced two secondary findings which are also of considerable interest for the present study: (1) the priming effect was particularly strong for stimuli containing the word *fish* (which also occurs in the label commonly used to denote this shibboleth) (cf. Hay, Nolan, et al. 2006: 363), and (2) priming with the two secondary dependent variables /æ/ and /ɛ/ was statistically less robust or even completely non-significant (cf. Hay, Nolan, et al. 2006: 367). Both experiments have thus unearthed priming effects exclusively, or at least primarily, for linguistic variables that can be classified as sociolinguistic stereotypes.

---

[1]In fact, several studies have produced evidence for a connection between production and perception. Hay, Warren, et al. (2006), for instance, found that New Zealanders' perception of /ɪə/-/ɛə/ pairs depends on whether the listeners merge these two vowels in their own production. In another study using synthesised vowel continua, Kendall & Fridland (2017) showed that perceptual discrimination of /æ/ and /ɑ/ is influenced not by the absolute position of these vowels in US subjects' realisational spaces, but actually by the degree to which they produced a merger of the low back vowels /ɑ/ and /ɔ/ – which suggests that the link between production and perception can also have a more indirect base in the relations between vowels instead of their absolute positions.

While Hay, Nolan, et al. (2006) do hint at a possible connection between exemplar priming and the salience of the test variable, this is clearly not the primary concern of their study. Understandably, their discussion of this issue is therefore very brief and also somewhat speculative. To my knowledge, there is no study to date that has thoroughly and systematically investigated the impact that (social) salience has on the presence and strength of exemplar priming effects. It is the intention of the present study to start closing this very gap.

4.3 Summary

Salience is defined in a number of ways by different researchers and there is a particularly high degree of disagreement with respect to what causes a feature to be salient. This book does not partake in this discussion, but is merely interested in the *effects* of salience in perception, not its *causes*. Sociolinguistic salience will be understood as a scale of (sub-)conscious awareness. Features will be classified with respect to Labov's indicator-marker-stereotype hierarchy which, in turn, will be based on the presence and extent of social stratification, style shifting, and hypercorrection. For perception, exemplar theory (a model which assumes that long-term memory contains phonetically detailed exemplars indexed with social information) predicts that – thanks to the attention filter – salient features will be stored in memory more often and/or will be more prominent than non-salient ones. As a consequence, activation of salient exemplars should be easier, faster, and stronger. It is therefore to be expected that exemplar priming effects either do not occur at all or are at least considerably weaker when the test variable does not enjoy a high degree of (conscious) awareness among perceivers.

5 Interview method

Chapter 3 has introduced the four variables that this book focuses on. On the basis of previous work, it has also broadly divided them into a (comparatively) non-salient and a highly salient, even stereotyped and stigmatised group. However, this distinction was largely based on experts' judgements and evaluations, and especially external stereotypes may well "become increasingly divorced from the forms which are actually used in speech" (Labov 1972: 180). This part of the book will therefore try to corroborate the alleged salience of the variables "from the inside", as it were, and also to go beyond the simple binary distinction of salient/non-salient by ordering our four variables more precisely in relation to each other on the social salience scale.

5.1 Interview structure

Production data for the four variables of interest were obtained in the form of "classical" sociolinguistic interviews. All of these interviews were one-on-one and conducted by the author. Being an outsider to the community entails a number of disadvantages with respect to naturalness of speech of the subjects. However, this was true of all interviews in the same way, so it cannot be a factor influencing inter-group comparisons. The interviews consisted of a free speech section where subjects were asked a number of questions about the area of the city they grew up in, changes in the city, football and other sports, Liverpool's image in the UK and the rivalry with Manchester.[1] Furthermore, subjects were questioned about their use (particularly with respect to themselves) and their understanding of a number of identity labels. See appendix A for the complete questionnaire. Not all questions were asked in all interviews, but all topics were discussed or at least touched upon with every participant, with most of the time

---

[1]Although this rivalry has historical reasons (cf. Chapter 2), it is today dominated by the rivalry between the football clubs from Liverpool and Manchester in many people's minds. This does not, however, diminish its potential for bringing up questions of identity and local pride in the slightest. Indeed, as Beal (2010: 97) remarks, "[t]he football derby (...) is one of the clearest manifestations of local identity and rivalry in Britain today"

typically devoted to the areas "children's lore", "attachment to Liverpool", "identity", and "Liverpool's image".

Towards the end of the interview, participants read out a reading passage (see appendix B) and a list of keywords (appendix C). Most of the test words on the list were also contained in the reading passage for better comparability. Next, subjects were asked to read out the reading passage a second time using their strongest Scouse accent. Not all interviewees wanted to do this or explained they weren't capable of "putting it on" on demand, but the vast majority of participants completed all three reading tasks. In graphs showing register differences, the data gathered during the accent imitation task will be situated towards the informal end of the style spectrum. I am aware of the fact that the imitation style is almost certainly one where subjects are likely to pay *more* than average attention to their speech. A reviewer quite correctly points out that accent performance probably qualifies as a "frozen, ritualistic" style (Labov 1972) that, in terms of attention, should rather be placed towards the more formal end of the style continuum. However, this task should still – for obvious reasons – trigger the most 'extreme' and/or most frequent local variants, even when compared to spontaneous speech, so in that sense I would argue it is quite different from, say, a sermon or some other form of scripted public speech. A linear increase of local variants can be expected from word list through reading and free speech style to accent imitation, so it seems to me the placement of the latter towards the 'informal' end of the style spectrum is justified in that respect. Purely for reasons of convenience, accent imitation will occasionally be referred to as the 'most informal' speech style, simply because it should be the most 'vernacular' register, *not* because I believe subjects paid no attention to their speech.

Finally, subjects were asked a number of questions concerning Scouse, notably whether they thought the accent had changed in their life time and what features they considered most typical. Analysis of these statements can only be qualitative in nature and should be considered an impressionistic snapshot rather than anything close to a representative picture of the relevant groups' explicit linguistic knowledge. Usually, the interviews lasted between 50 and 60 minutes (40–45 minutes of free speech and 10–15 minutes of reading/accent imitation and metalinguistic comments). Testing took place in a number of locations: pubs and cafés in central Liverpool, cafeterias at Hope University and the University of Liverpool, people's offices and homes. Not all of these environments were equally quiet, but recording quality was at least acceptable in all cases. All interviews were recorded using a Roland Edirol R-09HR MP3/Wave recorder, and named according to the following pattern:

1. a two digit participant/interview number

2. "F" or "M" to code the participant's gender

3. "MC" or "WC" to code the participant's social class

4. two digits coding the participant's age in years at recording time

"02MWC20", for example, is the code for interview number 2 with a male, working-class subject, who was 20 years old at the time of the interview. These codes will occasionally be used in this study to refer to specific interviews or to attribute quotations to their sources.

5.2 Participants

Participants were recruited through a number of ways. Notes in pubs, cafés, football grounds, community centres, and churches were complemented by e-mail calls for participants through Hope University and the University of Liverpool mailing lists, word-of-mouth advertising and by approaching people in person (mostly students at Liverpool Hope University). Interviews were conducted during two field trips, in September/October 2012 and April/May 2013, respectively. The first 8 subjects participated for free, the remaining ones were offered £10 for their time (some declined). No selection of participants in terms of "typicality" or "strength of accent" was made (as opposed to, for example, the "new NORMs" in Honeybone 2001).

A total of 38 subjects were interviewed. All participants were born and/or had grown up in the Liverpool Urban Area since age 12 or younger. Several subjects had also lived in other cities or towns at one point or another of their life, the reason usually being either job or (university) education related. Most interviewees, however, had spent all their life in Liverpool and its suburbs. Both men and women were interviewed and a rough socio-economic distinction into working class or middle class was made. English was the first (and, with the exception of one participant who was later excluded, also the only) language for all subjects. All participants were White British. The age range was 19–85, with people being classified as belonging to one of three age groups (19–29, 30–55, and 56–85) to mirror social, economic, and cultural change in Liverpool. With the boundaries set as they are the formative years (roughly up to and including the 20s) of most of the participants in the respective group fall together with one of the three phases of the city's development in the latter half of the 20th century (cf. §2.3

and §2.4): 50s and 60s (post-war recovery and Merseybeat era) for the oldest, 70s and 80s (economic depression) for the middle-aged, and 90s and 2000s (regeneration) for the youngest speakers. For reasons of time and space, only 20 interviews could be included in the present study. Interviews entered this sub-sample in the order they had been conducted in until all cells (cf. Table 5.1) were represented by 2 informants (1 in the case of the oldest group). These subjects form what I will call the "primary sample" for the production part of this study. In total, they contributed almost 19 hours of recorded material. The secondary sample (including all 38 interviews) is the basis for some results in Chapter 8, but other than that all production analyses are exclusively based on the smaller primary sample. Table 5.1 shows how participants in this primary sample are distributed across the categories outlined above.

Table 5.1: Age, gender, and social class of subjects (production)

	19–29		30–55		56–85	
	F	M	F	M	F	M
WC	2	2	2	2	1	1
MC	2	2	2	2	1	1

Figure 5.1 – generated with the QGIS software (QGIS Development Team 2016)[2] – illustrates which part of the city/conurbation the subjects are from or, to be precise, where they currently live. As is clear from the map, most areas of the city are represented although, to be fair, some (suburban) northern parts of Liverpool are underrepresented. There is also a slight bias towards the area around Liverpool districts Aigburth, Mossley Hill and Allerton in the south end of the city (12 subjects in total are from one of these three areas). Note, however, that all age groups are more or less evenly spread across the city.

The study was not restricted to people from within the Liverpool Council boundaries (black line in the map), but also included areas which are administered by other local councils (Sefton, Knowsley, Wirral) and which are, therefore, "technically not Liverpool" as a number of subjects put it. This is indeed, however, more of a technicality since we are talking about a contiguously built up area – just like in most other urban agglomerations. It is clear that invisible lines (sometimes separating one side of a street from the other) can still

---

[2]Map tiles by Stamen Design, under CC BY 3.0. Data by OpenStreetMap, under CC BY SA. Shapefiles from CDRC 2015 OS Geodata Pack by the ESRC Consumer Data Research Centre; contains Ordnance Survey data © Crown copyright and database right 2015.

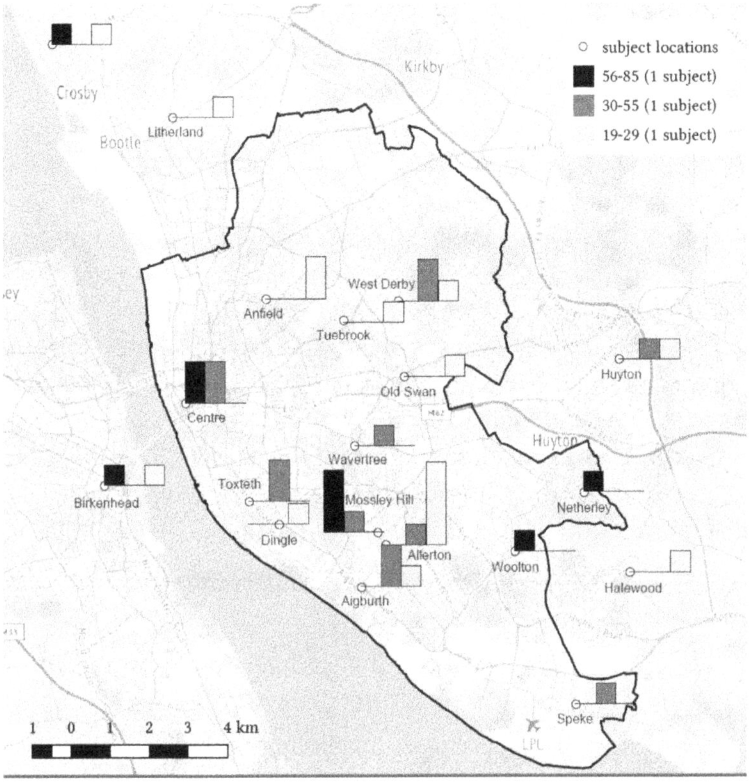

Figure 5.1: Geographical distribution of interview subjects

be important for people's identity, but all of the participants in this study self-identified as Liverpudlians or Scousers. This also held for the two subjects who were actually living on the Wirral and who had both been born in Liverpool (and in one case also lived half her life within Liverpool city boundaries). Generally speaking, people in urban areas often move around quite a bit and this might be especially true for Liverpool where many people from inner city areas were actually relocated (sometimes very reluctantly so) to new housing estates on the outskirts of the city during the slum clearances of the 50s and 60s. This is indeed what many of the older participants experienced themselves. For these reasons it was deemed unjustified to restrict the pool of subjects to those living within Liverpool city boundaries only.

5.3 Transcription

All interviews were transcribed orthographically in Praat (Boersma & Weenink 2015) by the author. Since the transcriptions' sole purpose was to serve as input for automatic measuring (cf. §5.4), pauses, intonation, stress, etc. were not marked in the transcripts. Questions and other utterances by the interviewer were also ignored. On separate tiers of the Praat TextGrid, speaking style (word "list", "reading" (passage), "free" (speech), and (accent) "imitation") and topic ("childhood", "Manchester", "identity" etc.) coded, followed by a third one where the participant's speech was segmented into chunks and transcribed. Words containing test tokens and the individual variables themselves were marked on individual tiers called "word" and "variable" respectively. Finally, a sixth tier called "aspiration" was used to mark relevant parts of the consonantal variables (cf. §5.4.1). Figure 5.2 provides an extract from a TextGrid (zoomed to word level) for purposes of illustration.

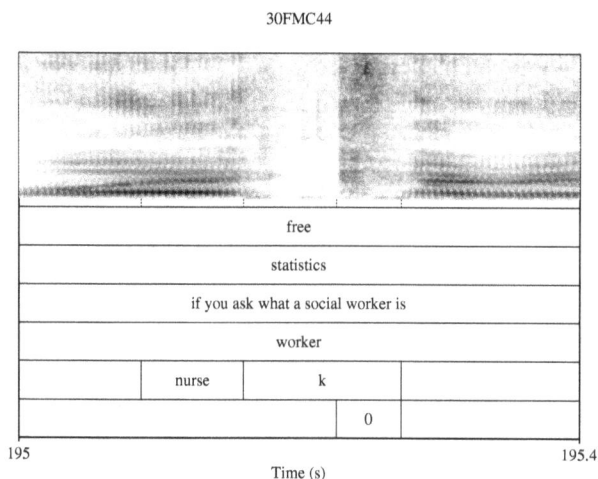

Figure 5.2: Extract of Praat TextGrid (subject 30FMC44)

5.4 Measuring

5.4.1 Consonants

The two consonantal variables were analysed both acoustically and auditorily. The method for acoustic measuring of /k/ was heavily inspired by the one used in Sangster 2001 to investigate lenition of alveolar stops. Phonetic plosives have a period of silence, or closure, followed by a burst and friction. For affricates, there is the same silence, but more friction than for plosives, and fricatives have either a very short period of silence or none at all and consist (almost) entirely of friction.

Beginning and end of the friction phase were marked in a Praat TextGrid for every /k/. A script written by the author was then used to automatically measure the duration of these segments as well as the total durations of the plosives (i.e. including the closure phase). /k/ tokens without any friction phase were registered as "unreleased" (and ignored in the analysis). Next, what Sangster calls "the proportional duration of friction" (PDF) was calculated by dividing the duration of the friction phase by the total duration of the plosive. The result is a figure between 0 (or 0%) and 1 (100%), with lower values for more plosive-like realisations and higher values for sounds that are phonetically speaking affricates or fricatives.

The same technique was applied to /ŋ(g)/. This decision might seem strange at first, because the realisational options of /ŋ(g)/ do not seem to be readily comparable to those of /k/. Closer examination, however, reveals that the standard realisation as a nasal [ŋ] involves complete oral closure – just as with [k] – and that for the typical Scouse realisation as [ŋg] this closure phase is followed by a release burst / friction. While the friction of [ŋg] will never be as long as that of a /k/ realised as a fricative, the PDF values will mean the same thing for velar nasal plus as they do for /k/: lower values (no or little friction → [ŋ]) indicate a standard-like realisation and higher scores (presence of friction → [ŋg]) mark non-standard, Scouse variants. Alveolar variants of /ŋ(g)/ were coded as "in" and later removed for the quantitative analyses for two reasons. First, [n] is a non-standard variant that is not limited to Liverpool or even a clearly bounded region, but one that is used in all varieties of English English and many others as well. It is also rather salient and commented on by many non-linguists as 'g-dropping'. However, in order to assess the impact of salience, particularly in perception, this study required a local/regional feature with little or no salience, to compare to the highly salient and local /k/ lenition. Alveolar variants of the <ng> cluster fulfil neither criterion, while [ŋg] realisations tick both boxes. The second reason concerns the method of measurement. Realising <ng> as [n] by definition excludes the presence of even a hint of a plosive, so the PDF measurement outlined above is not applicable. The difference between [ŋ] and [ŋg] (or the devoiced variant [ŋk]), on the other hand, exhibits the same kind of gradualness and, as explained above, can be measured in the same way as /k/ lenition. This parallelism is again crucial for the perception experiment, because it means the stimuli for /k/ and /ŋ(g)/ could be manipulated in a way that was phonetically similar (and thus not a confound). Since linking up data from production and perception is a major interest of this study, the focus in the production part was also exclusively on the [ŋ]-[ŋg] distinction. Figure 5.3 shows two examples and their respective marking in the TextGrid.

03MMC33_con

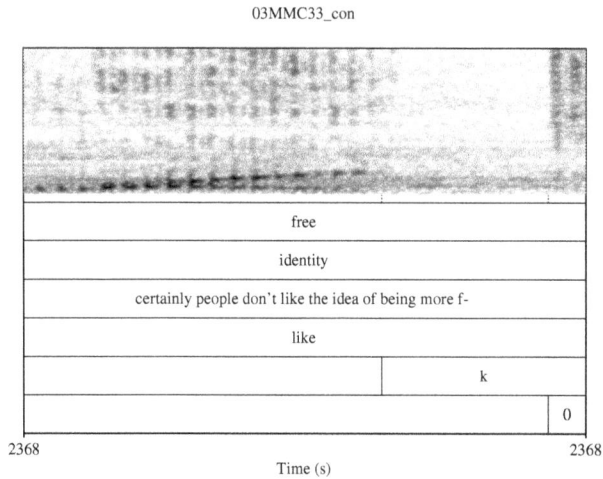

| free |
| identity |
| certainly people don't like the idea of being more f- |
| like |

| | k |
| | 0 |

2368   2368

Time (s)

(a) plosive, PDF = 18.47% (03MMC33)

36FWC20_con

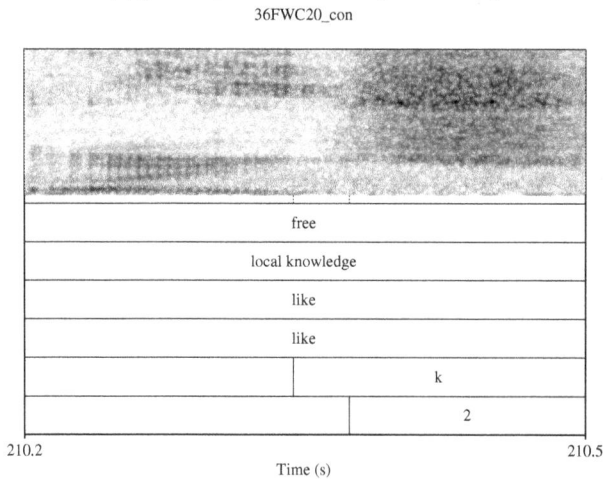

| free |
| local knowledge |
| like |
| like |

| | k |
| | 2 |

210.2   210.5

Time (s)

(b) fricative, PDF = 81.84% (36FWC20)

Figure 5.3: Spectrograms of /k/ (zoomed to word level)

This very precise method of acoustically measuring /k/ and velar nasal plus requires high quality recordings with little to no background noise. As it was unclear at the beginning whether all interviews fulfilled these criteria, the data were also analysed auditorily by the author. Coding was '0' (plosive), '1' (affricate), and '2' (fricative) for /k/, and '0' (nasal) and '1' (nasal plus burst) for /ŋ(g)/. It turned out that all interviews included in this project actually did permit an analysis based on the more precise Sangster method, so the auditory coding was not used in the analysis in the end. It is, however, still accessible for future research.

5.4.2 Vowels

For the measurement of the first two (later three) vowel formants (NURSE, SQUARE, and HAPPY) a Praat script[3] was used to automatise data collection. NURSE and SQUARE were measured first by hand and then in an automated way by the script for the first three (male) subjects. Paired t-tests were then administered to make sure the automated measurements were reliable. Neither test ([t(545) = -0.975, p = 0.330] for F1 and [t(545) = 1.768, p = 0.078] for F2) found a significant difference between hand and automated measurements, although there was a trend for the F2 values. However, the mean difference between hand and automated measurements for F2 was a mere 2.15 Hz. Scatterplots furthermore show a near-perfect correlation of hand and automated measurements, which is why the script was deemed reliable and all formant measurements used in the final analysis were taken automatically only. Clear mismeasurements were later removed from the dataset.

The script took as input pairs of sound files and TextGrids. It then went through each TextGrid and looked for vowel labels in the variable tier. When it found a relevant label it noted the start and end of the segment and measured F1, F2, and F3 at midpoint of the vowel. It then extracted information about the style, topic, carrier word, and the larger context it appeared in from the other tiers and saved all these data into a textfile. F3 was measured because it was needed for one of the normalisation algorithms that were later applied to the raw measurements (cf. §5.4.3). In addition to the three vocalic test variables happy, NURSE, and SQUARE (of which all instances were included), between 10 and 25 tokens of FLEECE and TRAP per subject were also measured. These were taken from the reading passage and word list sections of the interviews since these contexts were considered most likely to produce the most "extreme" realisations (in terms of the periphery

---

[3]Generously made available by Mietta Lennes – http://www.helsinki.fi/~lennes/praat-scripts/, last accessed 2013-01-29 – and modified by the author.

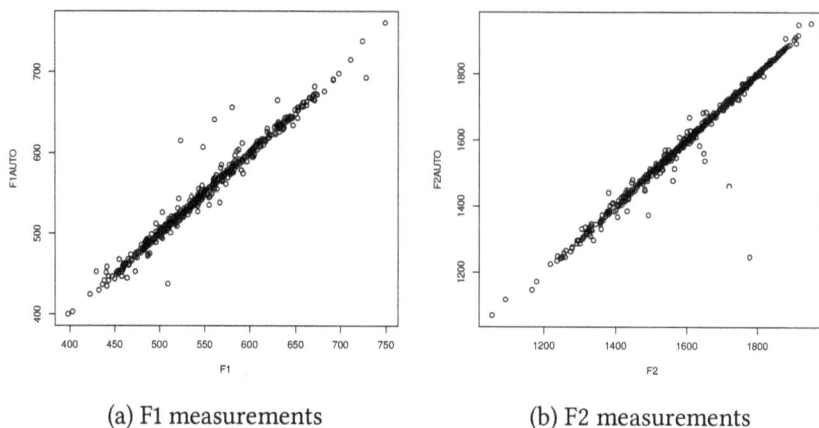

(a) F1 measurements   (b) F2 measurements

Figure 5.4: Manual (x-axis) vs. automatic (y-axis) measurements of NURSE and SQUARE

of speakers' vowel spaces). Observations of TRAP were used exclusively as input for normalisation and for comparison of the algorithms (again, cf. §5.4.3). FLEECE measurements were additionally included in the calculation of Pillai scores for happy (cf. §6.1.3).

5.4.3 Normalisation

It is a well known fact among phoneticians and phonologists that there is a huge amount of variation in the acoustic signal that is not due to linguistic or sociolingustic, but rather purely physiological reasons. Even multiple realisations of one and the same phonological sound chain produced by a single speaker in the same style will all be slightly different from one another. In addition to these intra-speaker differences, there are also inter-speaker ones. The most pronounced differences in this area are due to vocal tract length. The length of the vocal tract correlates inversely with vowel formant values. On average, therefore, children (with the shortest vocal tracts) have higher formants than women, who in turn have higher formants than men for one and the same phonological vowel. The potential effect of vocal tract maturation, i.e. changes to length and shape of the vocal tract over the course of an individuals lifetime, further complicates matters (cf. Harrington 2006: 440–441).

It is therefore not possible (or at least not advisable) to directly compare, for instance, women's and men's raw formant values, or those of younger and older speakers. This is where normalisation comes in. According to several articles on the matter (cf., for example, Fabricius et al. 2009; Clopper 2009; Disner 1980; Kendall & Thomas 2009; Thomas 2002), normalisation should ideally achieve four different goals:

1. elimination of differences that are due to physiological reasons

2. preservation of differences that are (socio-)linguistic in nature

3. preservation (or improvement) of phoneme distinctions

4. modelling the process that allows listeners to assign realisations from different speakers to one and the same phoneme

The author is well aware of the irony involved here. This study is, after all, set in an exemplar framework which suggests that listeners do *not* normalise acoustic input, at least not in the same way and to the same degree as is assumed in most other phonological theories. This is most relevant with respect to point 4 in the enumeration above. Sociolinguists, however, usually largely ignore this aspect and focus more on points 1 and 2 (cf. Clopper 2009: 1430; Fabricius et al. 2009: 414–415; Kendall & Thomas 2009), and the present study is no exception. By applying a normalisation algorithm to the data I do not mean to suggest that this procedure mirrors or approximates what happens in listeners' brains. Rather, it is simply the only option one has if the goal is to compare production data of men and women (or those of younger and older speakers) to each other instead of treating them separately.

Normalisation methods are generally categorised with respect to two dimensions: vowel-intrinsic vs. vowel-extrinsic and speaker-intrinsic vs. speaker-extrinsic (cf. Kendall & Thomas 2009). Vowel-intrinsic algorithms extract all data necessary for normalisation from the individual token. Often these methods use F0 and/or F3 to estimate vocal tract length. Vowel-extrinsic algorithms include formant measurements from more than one vowel in their formulas and achieve normalisation with the help of means over several (often all) measured vowels. Speaker-intrinsic methods differ from speaker-extrinsic ones in that the former perform normalisation for each speaker individually (i.e. only taking into account vowels produced by that speaker), whereas the latter include some sort of inter-speaker mean in their calculations (cf., for example, Labov et al.'s (2006) *grand mean*).

A number of algorithms have been proposed over the years, and the question which of those fares best in achieving the goals spelled out above has generated a series of investigations (among others: Hindle 1978; Disner 1980; Adank et al. 2004). Generally speaking, "vowel-extrinsic methods tend to perform better over-all (...) for vowel space normalization across talkers", and "vowel-intrinsic meth-ods are appealing as perceptually plausible models of human speech processing" (Clopper 2009: 1440). For this reason, two different normalisation methods were tested in this study, a vowel-intrinsic and a vowel-extrinsic one (both of them speaker-intrinsic). Both normalisations were applied to the raw data using the NORM package for R (Kendall & Thomas 2009). The first, Bark difference, was devised by Syrdal & Gopal (1986), and is a vowel-intrinsic method. Formants are, first of all, transformed into – perceptually "more accurate" (Clopper 2009: 1431–1432) – Bark values using the formula taken from Traunmüller (1990):

$$Z_i = \frac{26.81}{1 + \dfrac{1960}{F_i}} - 0.53 \tag{5.1}$$

Where F_i is the raw value of a given formant. The Bark rescaled values Z_1 and Z_2 are then substracted from Z_3 to arrive at normalised measures of height and frontness respectively. Syrdal & Gopal originally used Bark-converted F0 instead of F3 for the height dimension, but Kendall & Thomas (2009) argue that a number of things, for instance "[i]ntonation, tone, and consonantal influences affect F0" and consider it preferable to use Bark-converted F3 for both the back-front and the high-low dimension.

The most popular vowel-extrinsic normalisation method among sociolinguists is probably Lobanov (1971). This is unsurprising given the fact that it has fre-quently been found to be (one of) the most efficient algorithm(s) in reducing physiological and preserving sociolinguistic variation (cf. Clopper 2009: 1440). The main drawback of Lobanov – and many other vowel-extrinsic algorithms – is that it works best when *all* vowels of a system are measured. Constraints of time and resources made this endeavour impractical for the present study. The choice fell on Watt & Fabricius (2002) in its modified version (Fabricius et al. 2009) instead, a method which is "conceptually similar" and deemed "also successful" (Clopper 2009: 1440).

Watt & Fabricius (2002) assume a triangular vowel space with the corner vow-els [i], [a], and [u']. In RP (for which the algorithm was originally designed), these would correspond to FLEECE, TRAP, and GOOSE, but the NORM package automatically chooses the highest/most fronted and the most open vowel avail-able in the sample as [i] and [a], irrespective of their labels. Obviously, [i] and [a] should be relatively stable in the variety under scrutiny (cf. Watt & Fabricius

2002: 163). Since I am not aware of any evidence that suggests this is *not* true for FLEECE and TRAP in Scouse, these two were used as corners in this study. From these benchmark vowels, a centroid S or "centre of gravity" (Watt & Fabricius 2002: 164) is then computed as follows:

$$S(F_n) = \frac{[i]F_n + [a]F_n + [u']F_n}{3} \tag{5.2}$$

Where F_n is a mean raw formant value of the corner vowels $[i]$, $[a]$, and $[u']$. The centroid value $S(F_n)$ is computed separately for each formant, and normalised values are then expressed as the ratio of the raw measurement to the corresponding centroid: $\frac{F_n}{S(F_n)}$. Note that $[u']$ is not measured, but derived from $[i]$, assuming that $[u']F_1 = [u']F_2 = [i]F_1$. As a result, only FLEECE and TRAP have to be measured. To counter potential skewing due to the fact that TRAP might not be exactly halfway between FLEECE and GOOSE with respect to frontness, $[a]F_2$ is also derived instead of measured in the modified version of the algorithm employed in this study (cf. Fabricius et al. 2009: 420–421; Kendall & Thomas 2009).

With respect to the tests applied to assess the power of the normalisation algorithms, this study largely follows Langstrof 2006. One criterion for determining whether a normalisation process was successful is the degree to which it has reduced variance *within* categories and overlap *across* categories. In our case this would mean that phonemes should be more distinct and that scatter around phoneme means should be reduced in the normalised data. When we look at Figure 5.5b this is not immediately obvious. It should be borne in mind that with respect to NURSE and SQUARE we are talking about a merger for most speakers so we would not necessarily expect these two phonemes to appear more distinct in normalised data. The third vowel under scrutiny here, HAPPY, however, should be more distant from both NURSE and SQUARE in the normalised data. At least for the Bark-difference method, the graph does not suggest that it really is.

It does not look as if scatter for any of the variables had been reduced either. If anything, scatter around the mean seems to have increased, particularly in the front-back dimension. The scatter plot for the Watt & Fabricius normalised data looks a lot more promising. Scatter in both dimensions seems to have been (slightly) reduced, and the phonemes appear to be more distinct. But then again, we are using different scales in the three representations so a purely visual inspection is insufficient. We will thus have a look at variation coefficients next. I am well aware of the fact that the measure of dispersion most commonly used in such cases is the standard deviation. Since we have very different means in our

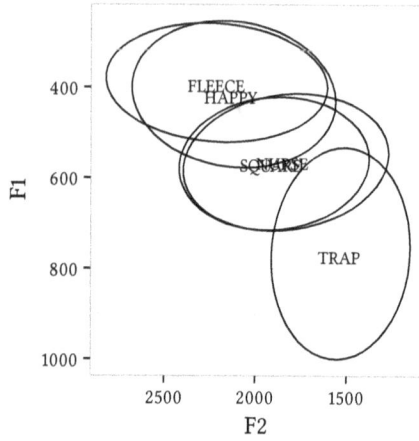

(a) raw data

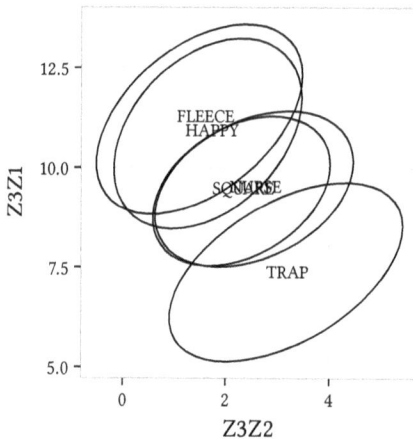

(b) Bark difference normalised

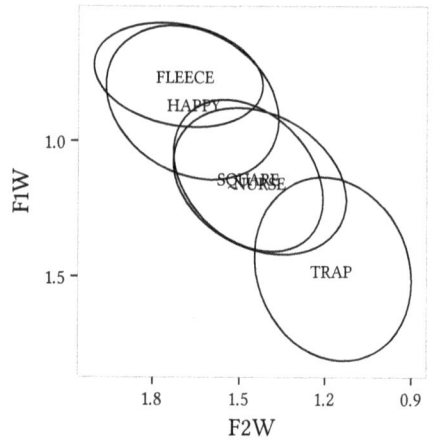

(c) Watt-Fabricius normalised

Figure 5.5: Vowel distributions (all subjects pooled)

samples due to different scales, however, comparing standard deviations would be highly misleading as they depend on the means of the samples. We will therefore use variation coefficients which normalise standard deviations by dividing them by the mean of the sample. These variation coefficients can then be meaningfully compared to each other.

Table 5.2: Variation coefficients for raw and normalised data

vowel	F1			F2		
	raw	Bark	Watt	raw	Bark	Watt
happy	0.187	0.107	0.167	0.120	0.506	0.089
NURSE	0.127	0.101	0.115	0.139	0.356	0.104
SQUARE	0.123	0.101	0.115	0.123	0.363	0.084

Table 5.2 shows a rather mixed picture. While the Bark difference algorithm was successful in reducing variance in the F1 dimension for all three vowels, it actually *increased* variance of F2 considerably for all vowels involved. We thus cannot clearly claim that the Bark difference normalisation reduced within-vowel variance overall. Watt & Fabricius fares a lot better. Reduction in variance for F1 is systematic, if only marginal and slightly less successful than Bark-difference. When we look at F2, however, we see a clear improvement. Again, the reduction in variance is not huge, but Watt & Fabricius does reduce variance systematically across all three vowels, whereas Bark-difference actually *increases* variance dramatically. On the whole, then, Watt & Fabricius seems to do a better job than Bark-difference in reducing intra-category variance.

Next, we look at Pillai scores as a measure of distance between distributions, in our case of vowel discreteness. Pillai scores were first used in a linguistic study by Hay, Warren, et al. (2006) and their usefulness for sociolinguistic investigations is discussed in Hall-Lew 2010. They are considered to be superior to simple Euclidean distance measures because a Pillai score "takes account of the degree of overlap of the entire distribution" (Hay, Warren, et al. 2006: 467). Pillai scores range between 0 and 1, with values close to 0 (and an accompanying high p-value) indicating a large degree of overlap between the distributions, and values near 1 (and a low p-value) representing distributions that are (almost) completely distinct. The pairing NURSE-SQUARE is not represented in Table 5.3 as these two vowels participate in a merger for most speakers and it can therefore not be assumed that they *should* be distinct in the first place.

Table 5.3: Pillai scores for total and female/male vowel distributions

vowel(s)	raw Pillai	raw p-value	Bark Pillai	Bark p-value	Watt Pillai	Watt p-value
happY-NURSE	0.486	< 0.001	0.460	< 0.001	0.550	< 0.001
happY-SQUARE	0.372	< 0.001	0.323	< 0.001	0.425	< 0.001
happY (female/male)	0.446	< 0.001	0.090	< 0.001	0.020	< 0.001
NURSE (female/male)	0.570	< 0.001	0.229	< 0.001	0.131	< 0.001
SQUARE (female/male)	0.659	< 0.001	0.185	< 0.001	0.115	< 0.001

Table 5.3 confirms the impression we already got from Figure 5.5: the Bark difference normalisation does not distinguish happY from both NURSE and SQUARE better. We also see, however, that it does not really fare worse. Pillai scores for raw and normalised data are very similar and p-values are close to 0 in both cases. So while the Bark difference normalisation did not make different phonemes appear more distinct, it did at least not result in significantly *less* distinct categories either. Watt & Fabricius, on the other hand, increases the distinctness of happY to both NURSE and SQUARE. Only slightly so for the former, it has to be said, but quite clearly for the latter. As is obvious from the table, p-values are extremely low for all pairings (often too small to be treated as different from zero by the R software), which is in all likelihood simply due to the fact that they are based on comparatively large datasets where even small differences will show up as (highly) significant. When we look at the three vowels individually and compare female to male realisations, we see a clear "improvement" in the normalised data. For all three vowels, female and male realisations are quite distinct in the raw data, a fact which is reflected in Pillai scores which are comparable or actually higher than those for different phonemes, and p-values that indicate highly significant differences.

All Pillai scores for the Bark difference normalised data are lower than their counterparts calculated for the raw data. Intra-category overlap has increased by 0.356 for happY, 0.34 for NURSE, and 0.474 for SQUARE. This means that female vowels are more similar to male vowels in the normalised data, which is precisely what we would expect a vowel normalisation process to achieve. Female and male distributions are still significantly different from each other in the normalised data, but, (a) again, this could simply be due to the fact that we have a comparatively large data set where even small differences will come out as significant (cf. the very low Pillai score of 0.09 for happy), and, more importantly, (b) we do not want *all* differences to be filtered out, but only the *physiological* ones.

All three vowels are test vowels in this study and we expect to see at least some gender differences which are due to sociolinguistic rather than physiological reasons. This is particularly true for the NURSE-SQUARE merger, a sociolinguistic variable which is considered to be highly salient (cf. Chapter 3) and with respect to which we would therefore not be surprised to see women and men behave differently. happy, on the other hand, is believed to be non-salient (again, cf. Chapter 3), so gender differences are less likely here. This is exactly what the figures in Table 5.3 suggest: a very low Pillai score for happy, indicating almost complete overlap of the distributions (although this small difference is still significant) and considerably larger ones for NURSE and SQUARE, meaning that women and men differ in their realisations of these vowels even *after* normalisation. It thus appears as if the Bark difference normalisation had (largely) eliminated physiological variation but maintained sociolinguistic one, which is just what we want a useful normalisation procedure to do.

The values for our other candidate, however, are even better. Watt & Fabricius increases intra-category overlap for happy by 0.426, for NURSE by 0.439, and for SQUARE by 0.545. The remaining differences between female/male distributions are also less (though still highly) significant in the Watt & Fabricius normalised data. It is possible that Watt & Fabricius has in fact eliminated some information that we are interested in, namely the assumed sociolinguistic gender difference for NURSE and SQUARE. However, the figures show that although the gender distributions are less distinct than in the Bark-difference normalised data, they are still (and by a much larger factor than in the Bark values) more distinct than the normalised female/male distributions of happy. Also, it could very well be that the smaller differences we find for NURSE and SQUARE in the Watt & Fabricius normalised data are simply the more realistic ones. Both algorithms thus create a pronounced relative difference between the female/male Pillai scores of happy and those of NURSE and SQUARE, but in addition Watt & Fabricius decreases interphoneme overlap more, so the conclusion with respect to Pillai scores is again that Watt & Fabricius seems to be the preferable choice.

Euclidean distance measures can also be used to determine the usefulness of normalisation procedures. Once again, we cannot directly compare euclidean distances because of different scales. What we can do, however is look at a ratio that is calculated as follows:

$$\frac{d_k}{d_l} = \frac{\langle\sqrt{(F_{1i} - \bar{F}_{1j})^2 + (F_{2i} - \bar{F}_{2j})^2}\rangle}{\langle\sqrt{(F_{1i} - \bar{F}_{1i})^2 + (F_{2i} - \bar{F}_{2i})^2}\rangle} \tag{5.3}$$

Where F_{1i} and F_{2i} are the F1 and F2 values of tokens in phoneme category "i", $\bar{F}_{1i}$ and $\bar{F}_{2i}$ are the mean values of category "i", and $\bar{F}_{1j}$ and $\bar{F}_{2j}$ are the mean values of category "j". d_k is then the average distance of tokens in category "i" to the mean of category "j" (e.g. happy tokens to the mean of NURSE), and d_l is the average distance of tokens in category "i" to their own mean (e.g. happy tokens to the mean of happy). This ratio should always be greater than 1, i.e. the average distance to the mean of *another* category should be bigger than the average distance to the mean *within* the category. A successful normalisation procedure would have to increase this ratio since both intra-category spread and inter-category overlap should be diminished.

Table 5.4: Euclidean distance ratios for raw and normalised data

vowels	raw	Bark	Watt
happy-NURSE	1.574	1.599	2.326
happy-SQUARE	1.429	1.533	2.187
NURSE-happy	1.694	1.741	2.320
SQUARE-happy	1.579	1.786	2.355

Table 5.4 shows that, while the difference is marginal for the pairing happy-NURSE, all euclidean distance ratios are higher for the Bark difference normalised data than for the raw data. Normalisation using this method was therefore an improvement. Yet the figures for Watt & Fabricius are, once again, even better. While the distance ratio increases on average only by about 0.096 for the Bark-difference normalised data, Watt & Fabricius produces distance ratios that are on average 0.728 higher.

With the current dataset Watt & Fabricius thus yields better results than the Bark-difference method in visual representation (scatter plots), reduction of inter-category variation coefficients, Pillai scores for inter- and intra-category (gender) comparisons, and euclidean distance ratios. Despite the fact that the Bark-difference normalisation is presumably more plausible in perceptual terms, the Watt & Fabricius algorithm will therefore be used in this study whenever normalised vowel values or plots are reported or represented.

5.5 Phonological context

In order to extract the phonological context of the variables under scrutiny ortho-graphical representations of the carrier word and the one following the carrier word were extracted from the transcripts. These orthographic representations were then automatically replaced (in R) by a phonemic transcription that was gathered from the interactive web-based CELEX lexicon database (Baayen et al. 1993). With regard to those transcriptions, CELEX allows the user to choose from four different character sets. For this study, the DISC set was selected because it represents each English phoneme with a single character (vowel length is not coded separately as this bit of information is already included in the vowel quality – in English!). This is highly useful if the transcriptions are going to be processed automatically, as diphthongs and affricates (which are regarded as single phon-emes) are represented by a single character. It is therefore impossible to misinter-pret the first element of a diphthong (or and affricate) as a simple monophthong (or plosive). This is a crucial advantage, as the software often has no straight-forward way of knowing whether it is faced with a diphthong or a sequence of monophthongs. DISC uses a set of simple ASCII characters. In Table 5.5 the char-acters that are different from IPA are listed together with their IPA equivalents.

Table 5.5: DISC characters and IPA equivalents

consonants		monophthongs		diphthongs	
IPA	DISC	IPA	DISC	IPA	DISC
ŋ	N	ɪ	I	eɪ	1
θ	T	ɛ	E	aɪ	2
ð	D	æ	{	ɔɪ	4
ʃ	S	ʌ	V	əʊ	5
ʒ	Z	ɒ	Q	aʊ	6
tʃ	J	ʊ	U	ɪə	7
dʒ	_	ə	@	ɛə	8
ŋ̩	C	iː	i	ʊə	9
m̩	F	ɑː	#		
n̩	H	ɔː	$		
l̩	P	ɜː	3		

The impact of neighbouring sounds on the test variables *will* be investigated to provide a more complete picture of how these sounds are used in Liverpool.

However, since the focus of this study is clearly on independent variables that are social in nature, this part of the analysis will be rather basic. Only the immediately preceding and the immediately following phonemes are considered. In the case of the two consonantal variables, measurements were furthermore restricted, from the start, to cases where /ŋ(g)/ and /k/ occurred either intervocalically or at the end of a word, because these contexts have been identified as the ones where lenition is most likely to occur (cf. §3.3.2). The three test vowels were only measured in content words (and, for NURSE and SQUARE, also exclusively in stressed syllables), both to keep the number of vowels that had to be measured manageable and in order to avoid introducing unnecessary noise into the dataset by including weakened vowels.

All but two measured vowels either occurred at the beginning of a stretch of speech or were preceded by a consonant. NURSE and SQUARE tokens, without exception, either were the last phoneme in a stretch of speech or were *followed* by a consonant, too. Only happy had a sizeable proportion of observations where the test vowel was followed by another vowel. The difference between happy measurements followed by a consonant and those followed by a vowel was small but significiant with respect to the normalised F1 dimension ($t(2016.295) = -13.593$, $p < 0.001$), but insignificant as far as the (sociolinguistically more important, cf. Labov 2006: 502) F2 dimension is concerned ($t(1935.124) = -1.355$, $p = 0.176$). It was therefore decided to drop happy tokens that occurred before another vowel (along with *any* observation where a test vowel was followed or preceded by silence) when fitting mixed linear effects regression models (see §5.6) because this allowed me to use the same set of phonological predictors (place and manner of preceding and following consonant) for all three vocalic test variables and thereby improved comparability of the models. Measurements of happy still accounted for the largest share of total observations, and in figures and other statistical comparisons (t-tests), the complete data set (including happy followed by another vowel) was used. Of course, this meant that it could not be investigated whether happy formants might be influenced by vowel harmony. This is an interesting question, but given the focus of the present analysis, it was considered outside of the scope of this book anyway, and will have to be addressed in a separate study in the future. Word frequencies were considered for all variables investigated, and operationalised using Zipf scores based on occurrences in SUBTLEX-UK (Van Heuven et al. 2014). See §10.1.1 for a more detailed discussion.

5.6 Statistical analysis

Mixed linear effects models have become a sort of gold standard in recent years, especially in subdisciplines like psycho- and neurolinguistics. Their biggest advantage is the possibility to include so-called random effects. The reasoning behind this is that in most common experimental designs, we have "fixed effects" and "random effects". Fixed effects are the variables the experimenter is primarily interested in and which are, as a consequence, controlled for in the experiment. They are theorised to have the same or a similar impact in the sample that is the basis for the experiment as in the total population which the sample is drawn from. Random effects, on the other hand, are responsible for variation that is not part of the experimental design, but due to the particular sample. As a result, the effects of random factors cannot be extrapolated to the population as a whole (cf. Barr et al. 2013).

In Mixed linear effects models, the impact of random factors is estimated and taken out of the data before the relevance of the fixed effects is calculated. The result is a reduction in noise since variation that is supposed to be due to chance is filtered out. As a common example, consider a hypothetical lexical decision experiment where subjects have to decide whether a particular string of sounds or letters is a word of their language. The words that are presented fall into two intrinsically different groups (e.g. different word class, length, complexity,...) and the experimenter is interested in whether reaction times for these two word groups differ. In such an example it is often found that individual words produce generally higher or lower reaction times across subjects (e.g. due to a non-controlled factor such as frequency or number of similar words in the language). The experimenter, however, is not interested in the effect of particular words but only in the general effect of the group they are part of. The actual words chosen for the experiment are, in this case, considered a random sample of the whole group ($\rightarrow$ population). The same goes for the sample of participants, as some people are generally faster or slower to respond than other subjects. Both sources of variation are "random" because re-running the experiment would (or at least *could*) involve choosing a different sample of words and a different sample of participants (cf. Barr et al. 2013: 259–260). It thus makes sense to filter out variation that is due to individual differences between subjects and test words as it is a characteristic of the sample, and not considered representative of the population.

It was thoroughly considered whether subject and carrier word – the two most straightforward options – should be entered as random factors in an analysis of the production data presented here. Especially with respect to word, this would make some sense. After all, there is no control over which words subjects use the relevant variables in (at least in the free speech part of the interviews which makes up the vast majority of observations). Treating carrier word as a random factor was still deemed problematic, however. This is because the frequency of the carrier word, as well as the sounds directly preceding and following the target sound are factors of theoretical interest here. While word itself could be considered a random factor in this research design, it seems likely that filtering out word effects would also eliminate a lot of *relevant* information that is coded in the variables "preceding sound", "following sound", and "word frequency", as these bits of information (among others) are included in the overall word context of the observation. In the end, the risk was considered worth taking in order to counteract a scenario where (highly frequent) individual words would otherwise unjustifiably dominate the sample, and – possibly – obscure or overlay any more general effects of frequency or phonological environment.

Treating interviewee as a random effect is even more of an issue. As explained above, the reasoning behind treating subject as a random effect in many psycholinguistic experiments is that the group of people that actually took part is a random subset of the population one wants to extrapolate the results to and that individual differences are therefore noise. This crucial assumption, however, is not met in the dataset that is analysed in this chapter. There was no active a priori selection of participants (cf. §5.2) in terms of typicality etc. Nonetheless, the participants that ended up in the sample *are* considered to be representative of their social group. We look at a comparatively small number of middle- and working-class (female/male, old/young...) speakers and analyse their speech because we believe our results *can* be generalised to the group as a whole (at least to a certain extent). This is an essential tenet of any sociolinguistic analysis and argues against treating participant as a random effect.

It is possible to calculate random effects for speaker sub-clusters, e.g. for young working-class women only. This would eliminate the theoretical problem just outlined, as the variation between, say, young working-class women and young working-class men would not be filtered out, but just the differences between individuals *within* the respective sub-groups. This course of action was still rejected, because (a) for the relevant sub-groups (divided by gender and social class) among the young and middle-aged subjects this would mean filtering out the variation between two participants only (which does not really seem worth-while), and (b) more importantly, there is only one subject each in the gender/social class subgroups for the oldest speakers, so there is no other subject to estimate any potential effect of the individual against.

In summary, there are both conceptual and practical problems if one is to consider speaker and/or carrier word as random effects in the production data under scrutiny here. The use of carrier word as a random effect seemed to be more acceptable, though, since this might, in fact, make the results somewhat more representative and comes with less severe downsides. A random intercept for carrier word was therefore included in all mixed-effects models that will be reported on. Sum coding was used for all these analyses so that main effects and interactions (instead of *simple* effects and interactions) could be identified. For the vocalic variables, the set of main predictors entered into the maximal model was: style, age group, gender, social class, frequency, vowel duration, place of articulation (preceding sound), manner of articulation (preceding sound), place of articulation (following sound), and manner of articulation (following sound). Style is the independent variable I am most interested in as the presence or absence of style shifting is taken as an indicator of salience (cf. Chapter 4). It is quite possible (and actually expected given the main hypothesis of this study) that style differences can be present in one group but lacking in another (or be present in all groups, but not to the same extent). To test for this (and other, sociolinguistically meaningful combinations), all two-way interactions of style, age group, gender, and class were included as well, along with the two three-way interactions of style, age group, and one of the other social variables gender and social class. Interactions of the phonetic-phonological factors were not considered, as these predictors are not of primary interest in this study, and adding their interactions would have unduly inflated the models.

Model structure for the two consonantal variables velar nasal plus and /k/-lenition was identical as far as the social predictors are concerned (both in terms of main effects and interactions). Frequency of the carrier word was also included, but the set of phonetic and phonological predictors had to be different. Firstly, vowel duration is not applicable to consonants (plus the timing domain is already included in the dependent variable – proportional duration of friction), so this factor was not relevant for the mixed-effects regression models that were fit to the /ŋ(g)/ and /k/ measurements. Secondly, the phonological context had been restricted to intervocalic and word-final occurrences from the start, so it was considered unnecessary to enter information in the same way as it had been done for the two vocalic variables (i.e. "spread out" over four different independent variables). Instead, phonological environment was summarised in a single predictor ("Environment" in the spreadsheet), which was to code whether the measurement had been taken in an intervocalic context (within a word) or at the end of a word. The second context was further divided with respect to whether the measurement was followed by silence (pre-pausal), or by another word, in which case the type of the first sound in the following word (vowel, affricate, liquid...) was coded.

All statistical test were performed using the R software (R Core Team 2015). Mixed linear effects models were computed with the help of lmerTest (Kuznetsova et al. 2015), an R package which builds on lme4 (Bates et al. 2015), but adds p-values calculated on the basis of F statistics, with degrees of freedom derived from Satterthwaite's approximation. Sum coding, instead of R's default treatment coding, was used for all regressions. Model selection was based on AIC scores and F-tests comparing nested models. Calculating a simple goodness-of-fit measure is not a straightforward task in the context of mixed-effects models. As a rough (!) equivalent of the R^2 value known from linear regression models this book reports the R^2 of a linear model that regresses the observed values on the fitted ones from the linear mixed-effects model (cf. r-sig-mixed-models mailing list 2015). Models were checked for collinearity using the kappa.mer and vif.mer functions written by Austin Frank.[4]

---

[4]Code downloadable from hlplab.wordpress.com/2011/02/24/diagnosing-collinearity-in-lme4/

6 Vowel production

This chapter is based on the 20 participants of the primary sample who provided 7950 data points.[1] 4565 of these are observations of happy, 1770 concern NURSE, and 882 SQUARE (the remainder are instances of TRAP and FLEECE). The majority of the data were collected during the spontaneous part of the interview (n = 5245), while the word list (n = 761), the reading passage (n = 1361), and accent performance (n = 583) account for much smaller proportions. Table 6.1 provides an overview of how many realisations of the test vowels were made in which sub-sample of speakers. Within each age group, the sample seems to be fairly balanced with respect to gender and social class. There are some exceptions (e.g. the female-male ratio among middle-aged middle-class subjects), but this is only to be expected in a dataset that consists largely of spontaneous speech, and on the whole it does not seem as if a particular sub-group dominated the sample too much in numeric terms.

Table 6.1: Vowel observations by age, gender, and social class

		old		middle		young	
		f	m	f	m	f	m
happy	mc	307	201	411	705	335	362
	wc	197	248	506	380	354	559
NURSE	mc	145	78	179	334	107	129
	wc	87	98	152	157	155	149
SQUARE	mc	75	48	92	94	65	89
	wc	50	55	63	77	90	84

The two dependent variables F1 and F2 are analysed separately, both because it is well possible that change manifests itself with respect to one dimension but not the other (cf. Harrington 2006), and because this means they can be more easily

---

[1]Early versions of this and the next chapter were presented at the 21st LIPP-Symposium in Munich and at an internal workshop at the University of Freiburg. I am very grateful to the audiences for the valuable feedback received on these occasions. All remaining shortcomings are entirely mine.

compared to the two consonantal variables /k/ and velar nasal plus, for which there are only one-dimensional measurements (cf. §5.4.1). §6.1.3 and §6.2.3 briefly look at the two dimensions in conjunction, largely on the basis of F1-F2 vowel plots which are familiar from many works on phonetics and phonology. Contrary to the sections that deal with F1 and F2 individually, the focus in §6.1.3 and §6.2.3 will be much less on social predictors of vowel realisation other than age, and more on a summary synthesis of the style shifting results and a – very general – contextualisation of happy and NURSE with FLEECE and SQUARE, respectively.

All of the figures in this chapter (except those in §6.1.3 and §6.2.3) are designed in such a way that higher values on the y-axis represent 'more Scouse' variants. For NURSE, this is not straightforward: both raising (towards [e]) or lowering (towards [ɛ]) could be interpreted as 'more Scouse' as a range of different front vowels are cited in the literature as possible local realisations. In this book, [ɛ] was chosen as it is often considered to be the most typical target of the NURSE-SQUARE merger in Liverpool. When present, p-values in the boxplots (rounded to three decimal places) correspond to t-tests comparing the oldest to the middle-aged, and the middle-aged to the youngest group. The value that is horizontally centred is always taken from the t-test comparing means in the oldest and the youngest group. Arithmetic means are marked by dots in box plots, whereas bold horizontal lines in the middle of the notches indicate the relevant median. The extent of these notches, in turn, roughly corresponds to the 95% confidence intervals of the medians. Whiskers extend to the most extreme data points that are still within 1.5 times the interquartile range. All plots were generated with "ggplot2" (Wickham 2009) and dynamically integrated into this book with "knitr" (Xie 2015). As mentioned in §5.4.3, all vowel plots and analyses are based on the Watt-Fabricius normalised F1 and F2 values (coded as "F1W" and "F2W" respectively). Whenever tests on the "raw data" (as opposed to the estimates of the regression models) are reported, it is equally these normalised F1 and F2 values that are referred to, and *not* the original, absolute measurements in Hz (which would be the 'raw data' in the narrow sense).

6.1 happy

6.1.1 F1 (happy)

6.1.1.1 Overview

The maximal model for happy F1 measurements as described in §5.6 suffered from severe collinearity ($\kappa = 40.27$). Much of this collinearity turned out to be unproblematic, though, because it held between interactions and its constituent main effects (a model without these interactions had κ = 30.62) and could therefore safely be ignored. Furthermore, separate regressions of normalised F1 values on manner and place of preceding (κ = 95.67), and following sound (κ = 18.53) showed that these factors were (moderately) collinear, too, so only manner was retained from each pair. The maximal model without the predictors place of articulation of preceding and following sound (and also, for the sake of diagnostics, without any interactions) then only exhibited a moderate and acceptable degree of collinearity (κ = 15.09). Interactions were then re-entered into the regression and the minimal adequate model shown below was arrived at based on AIC scores and F-tests comparing nested models. The minimal adequate model for F1 of happy (R^2-equivalent = 0.178) is reprinted as Table 6.2.

Table 6.2: happy (F1): mixed linear effects regression

Fixed effects:	Estimate	Std. Error	df	t value	Pr(>|t|)	
(Intercept)	0.69	0.03	178.02	24.42	< 0.001	***
STYLElist	-0.06	0.03	1901.45	-2.04	0.04	*
STYLEread	0.02	0.01	1553.02	1.33	0.18	
STYLEfree	0.05	0.01	954.42	4.72	< 0.001	***
AGE56-85	-0.01	0.00	2114.86	-2.96	< 0.01	**
AGE30-55	-0.00	0.00	2109.14	-0.33	0.74	
GENDERf	-0.02	0.00	2111.94	-5.87	< 0.001	***
CLASSmc	0.01	0.00	2115.13	4.06	< 0.001	***
ZIPF	0.01	0.01	106.00	1.73	0.09	.
DURATION	-0.00	0.00	2114.64	-2.53	0.01	*
POSTMANNERaffr	-0.05	0.02	2103.57	-3.05	< 0.01	**
POSTMANNERfric	0.01	0.01	2103.23	1.00	0.32	
POSTMANNERgli	0.00	0.01	2076.64	0.80	0.42	
POSTMANNERliq	0.01	0.01	1993.46	1.11	0.27	
POSTMANNERnas	0.04	0.01	2105.78	5.05	< 0.001	***
AGE56-85:GENDERf	-0.03	0.00	2115.77	-6.71	< 0.001	***
AGE30-55:GENDERf	0.01	0.00	2114.16	3.14	< 0.01	**
GENDERf:CLASSmc	0.01	0.00	2093.34	2.69	0.01	**

Random effects:	(number of obs: 2116, groups: WORD, 221)		
Groups	Name	Variance	Std.Dev.
WORD	(Intercept)	0.001	0.038
Residual		0.015	0.122

Style is a significant predictor, as are age, gender, and social class of participant. Gender furthermore significantly interacts with age and social class, respectively. The phonetic and phonological factors duration and (manner of) following sound also have a statistically significant effect. Frequency of carrier word was not significant at the 5% threshold, but an ANOVA revealed that removing this effect from the model nevertheless resulted in a significantly worse fit to the data. Since frequency *does* qualify as a statistical trend it was therefore kept in the model. The two phonetic predictors will be briefly discussed first.

6.1.1.2 Phonological context

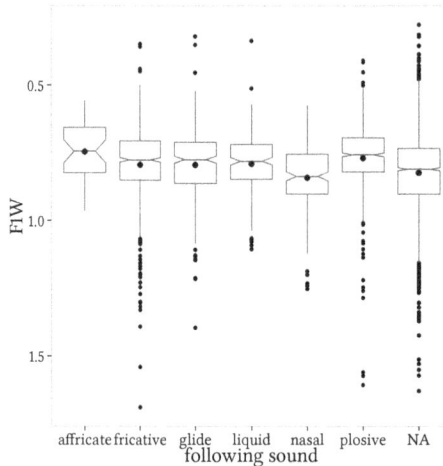

Figure 6.1: happy (F1) by following sound

Figure 6.1 shows normalised F1 values on the y-axis, and the manner of the consonant that follows the test vowel on the x-axis. Just as in the mixed-effects model, only two levels of this factor really stand out: when happy is followed by an affricate F1 values are slightly lower, i.e. the vowel is a bit higher, whereas when happy precedes a nasal, F1 is significantly higher, so the vowel is somewhat lower. All the other contexts have similar means (black dots) and medians (black horizontal bars around the middle of the boxes), and do not differ significantly from each other. It is unclear why happy should be higher when the following word (happy is, of course, always word-final) starts with an affricate, but it should be noted that the number of observations in this sub-category is rather small anyway (n = 37), so these figures might not be very representative. For nasals, on the other hand, this is less of an argument, as there are much more data in this sample (n = 194), but here the shift can potentially be explained on phonetic grounds. As an effect of regressive assimilation, it is likely that happy exhibits some degree of nasalisation when it occurs before a nasal, and nasalisation is know to shift F1 upwards (House & Stevens 1956), which explains the difference visible in the graph. Interestingly, F1 seems to be very similar in cases when happy is not directly followed by anything because it is the last sound in a stretch of speech (this context is coded as "NA" in Figure 6.1), but it is a lot less straightforward why happy should be lower before a pause.

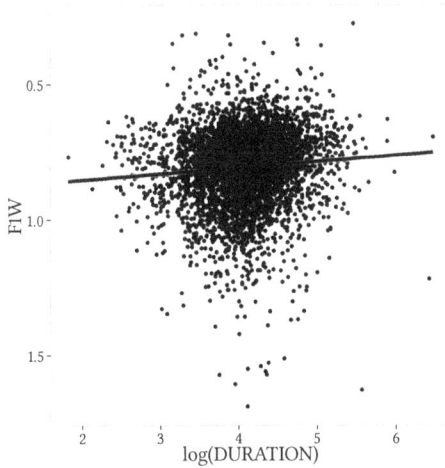

Figure 6.2: happy (F1) by duration

The effect of the other phonetic predictor, duration, seems to be more straight-forward. For this fixed effect, a negative coefficient was returned in the mixed linear effects regression, which translates into the regression line we see in Figure 6.2, with duration on the x-axis (log-transformed for better visualisation) and estimated F1 on the y-axis. The y-axis is inverted (just as in the other F1 plots of happy) because higher F1 values, i.e. lower realisations, actually indicate less Liverpool-like variants of happy. The regression line has an upward slope, which means that longer happy realisations have lower F1 values. This is hardly surpris-ing and does not call for a special explanation. Rather, it is a general phonetic principle that, all other things being equal, longer vowels will also tend to be more peripheral because there is more time for the tongue to reach its final posi-tion. Or, put another way, if a vowel is going to be short, there is *not enough* time for the tongue to move into a comparatively extreme position, so realisation of the vowel will be more central.

6.1.1.3 Frequency

Despite the fact that it is only a statistical trend we will also briefly look at the impact of frequency on F1 values in another regression plot. If one considers the

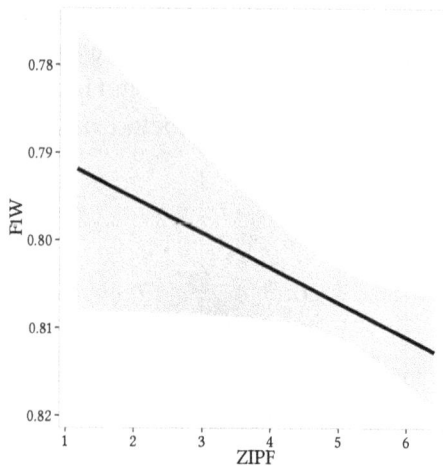

Figure 6.3: happʏ (F1) by frequency of carrier word

scales of the y-axes in Figure 6.2 and Figure 6.3 it becomes immediately obvious that both frequency and duration have only a rather small influence on F1.
Higher Zipf scores on the x-axis indicate more frequent carrier words, so the
bottom line of this graph is that the more frequent a word containing happʏ is,
the lower the realisation of happʏ will be – which is something that is also im-
plied by the positive correlation coefficient in the mixed-effects model. This is in
line with what we know about frequency effects in general, viz. that higher frequencies of use favour phonetic reduction processes. It should be borne in mind,
however, that my sample is based on spoken and relatively informal language,
and therefore consists almost exclusively of high frequency words, anyway (Zipf
scores for happʏ carrier words: mean = 5.114, first quantile = 4.57, median = 5.37,
third quantile = 5.79). Data on low frequency words are comparatively scarce,
which also shows in the larger standard deviation for these tokens (cf. the larger
dark grey area on the left-hand side of Figure 6.3). It would be interesting to see if
the tendency described above would also surface (possibly in a statistically more
robust way) in a sample that is more balanced in this respect.

6.1.1.4 Class and gender

We will now turn towards the first social predictor, class of speaker. The mixed-
effects regression model found a positive correlation coefficient for middle-class
interviewees. This highly significant correlation indicates that middle-class speakers produced lower happʏ realisations (higher F1 values) than their working-class

counterparts. This in itself is interesting (and somewhat unexpected), but instead of going into this class difference by itself, I would like to immediately include the significant interaction of social class and gender that the mixed-effects model revealed as well. Said interaction is visualised in Figure 6.4a and Figure 6.4b.

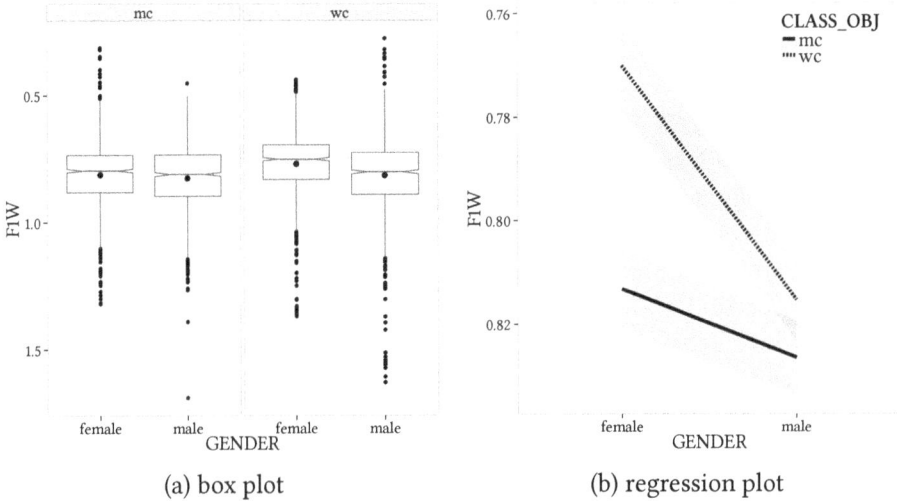

(a) box plot   (b) regression plot

Figure 6.4: happʏ (F1) by gender and class

The regression plot on the right shows estimated F1 on the y-axis and gender of subject on the x-axis. Social class is coded by line type, with dashed representing working-class, and solid marking middle-class subjects. This plot shows very nicely that the class difference seems to be mostly driven by female speakers, because, for these subjects, the two lines are comparatively far apart (estimated F1 for middle-class women is just above 0.81, whereas the value for working-class females is about 0.77), and the standard deviations are clearly distinct from one another. For males, on the other hand, the estimates are relatively similar for both social classes, and, what is more, the standard errors are not distinct (which is visualised by the grey, partially overlapping areas on the right hand side of the plot). T-tests on the raw data confirm this description: the difference between middle and working class is highly significant for female ($t(2107.847) = 7.591$, $p < 0.001$), but (just about) insignificant for male speakers ($t(2342.064) = 1.92$, $p = 0.055$). Furthermore, the steep slope of the working class line as opposed to the comparatively flat one for middle-class subjects suggests that gender differences (which were also found to be a significant main effect in the mixed-effects regression) are mostly found in the working class.

The box plots in Figure 6.4a visualise the same gender X social class interaction as Figure 6.4b, but this time the focus is on the gender, instead of the class difference. In the left panel (middle class), the two boxes for female and male participants can be seen to occupy essentially the same space. The means (black dots) and medians (horizontal bars) are very similar, although those of the males do seem to be slightly lower, and the confidence intervals of the medians (as represented by the notches) also appear to overlap to a certain extent. A t-test finds that male and female realisations of happʏ *are*, in fact, significantly different in height for middle-class speakers ($t(2249.52) = -2.437$, $p = 0.015$), but – as outlined below – it is both less significant and less pronounced than in the other group. Among working-class speakers, on the other hand, men have clearly lower realisations than women, as can be seen in the right panel of the graph. Perhaps we should rather say, that working-class *women* have significantly *higher* realisations ($t(2235.848) = -7.549$, $p < 0.001$), because it seems to be this group in particular which behaves differently. Working-class men actually have F1 values which are relatively similar to those of both middle-class men and women.

6.1.1.5 Age and gender

Before analysing the other significant interaction gender was involved in, we will first look at age of speaker as a significant main effect. Remember that one of the hypotheses that this study intends to test is that "Scouse is getting Scouser", i.e. that younger speakers have more extreme local variants and/or use these local variants more often than older speakers. Figure 6.5 plots the average F1 values of happʏ for the three groups of speakers (oldest subjects on the left, middle-aged group in the middle, youngest speakers on the right). The graph shows (a) that there is considerably less variation in the youngest group (indicated by the size of the box, and the extremeness of outliers), compared to the older speakers, and (b) that all three groups are significantly different from one another (cf. the p-values included in the figure).

Most importantly, however, it is obvious from Figure 6.5 that the hypothesis that younger speakers are, on average, more Scouse cannot be confirmed with respect to the height of happʏ. Both mean and (to a lesser extent) median values decrease "graphically" (due to the inverted y-axis; in numeric terms they of course *increase*) from left to right. Average F1 thus significantly increases from the old to the middle-aged group ($t(1838.232) = 2.257$, $p = 0.024$), and from the middle-aged to the young ($t(3609.648) = 2.949$, $p = 0.003$), meaning that happʏ systematically becomes *lower*, i.e. less Scouse, the younger the speaker. Liverpudlians between the ages of 19 and 29 are therefore actually the *least* Scouse

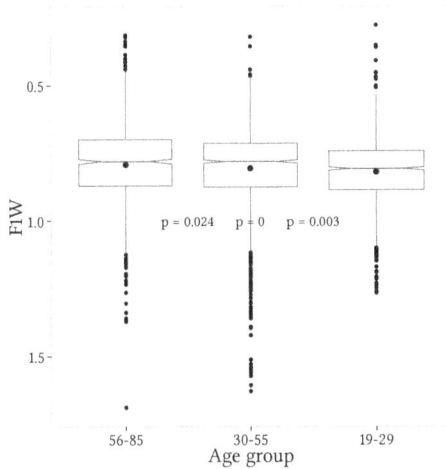

Figure 6.5: happy (F1) by age

in the sample, because they have lower realisations of happy than their parents' generation, who in turn use lower variants than the oldest speakers.

How does this predictor interact with gender, then? In Figure 6.6b, we again (cf. Figure 6.4b) see gender of participant on the x-axis and estimated F1 on the y-axis, but it is now age of participant instead of social class which is coded by line type (solid for the oldest, dotted for the middle-aged, and dashed for the youngest speakers). Just as in the corresponding graph for gender and social class, it is obvious that women seem to be behind the age differences described in the preceding paragraphs. Only for female subjects are the lines clearly distinct from one another. For male speakers, on the right-hand side, the regression lines of all age groups are either in, or at least very close to, the dark grey area which marks overlapping standard deviations. This indicates that age groups are not significantly different from one another if only the male subjects are considered. Table 6.3 shows that this is indeed the case: t-tests of all three pairings (comparing the old speakers to the middle-aged, the middle-aged to the young, and the young to the old) yield highly significant results for female, and non-significant ones for male subjects across the board.

Just as in the case of the gender X social class interaction, the differences in slope of the three regression lines (steep fall for the oldest, moderate fall for the middle-aged, and ever so slight rise in the youngest group) also suggest that, conversely, gender differences are not equally pronounced in the different age groups. Indeed, Figure 6.6a shows that there is a quite pronounced difference

Table 6.3: happʏ (F1): t-tests of age by gender

test	women			men		
	t	df	p	t	df	p
old-middle	4.062	1091.324	< 0.001	−1.368	798.429	0.172
middle-young	5.062	1596.832	< 0.001	−0.333	1999.537	0.739
young-old	8.689	888.424	< 0.001	−1.624	768.511	0.105

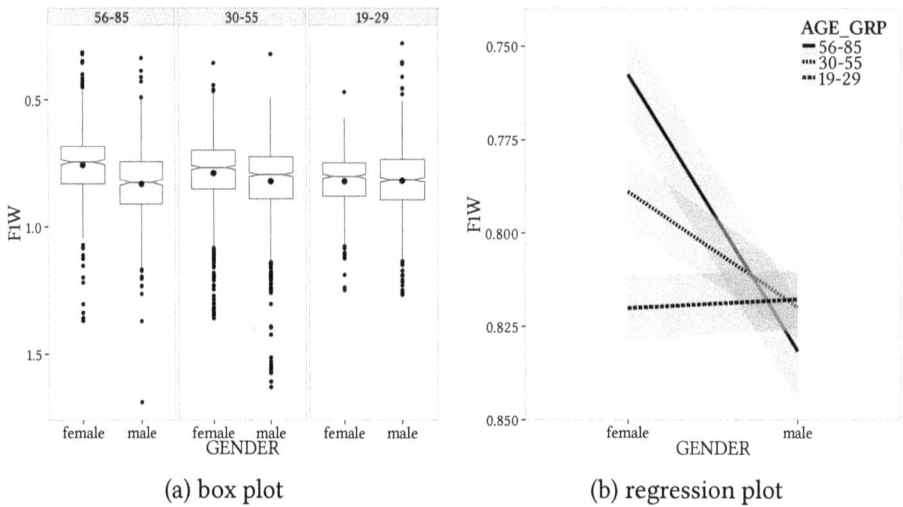

(a) box plot

(b) regression plot

Figure 6.6: happʏ (F1) by gender and age

between men and women in the oldest group, with the former having significantly lower realisations than the women ($t(896.946) = -7.773$, $p < 0.001$). This difference is still present in the middle group ($t(1955.552) = -4.707$, $p < 0.001$), although the distance has clearly decreased. For the youngest speakers, finally, there is no longer a significant difference between male and female speakers ($t(1606.076) = 0.411$, $p = 0.681$). It is interesting that men do not seem to have changed much across these three generations; their means are comparatively similar. Women, on the other hand, appear to have adapted to the men over time by lowering their originally higher happʏ realisation to one that is almost identical to that of men.

6.1.1.6 Style shifting

The last factor that turned up as a significant fixed effect in the regression model is style, the variable which this study is most interested in (though closely followed by age) because style shifting is considered as an epiphenomenon of salience. Figure 6.7 represents the style dimension along the x-axis, starting with the word list on the left and going through the reading passage and free, spontaneous speech to the accent imitation task on the right of the graph. F1 is, as usual, marked on the y-axis, while line type once again codes the three age groups of speakers. The size of the whiskers corresponds to the standard error for each register and age group.

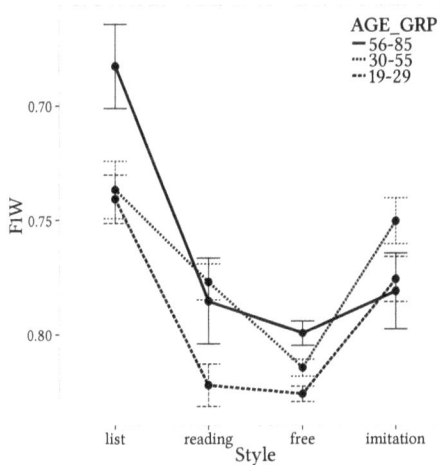

Figure 6.7: happʏ (F1) by age and style

The crucial question now is whether we are looking at style shifting or not. Productions of happʏ, across age groups, are higher in the "list" register than when subjects read out a text. These differences are visibly significant because the whiskers of the "list" and "reading" categories do not overlap for any of the age groups. From the reading passage to spontaneous speech happʏ seems to get even lower, but this is only significant in the middle-aged group. Both the whiskers attached to the solid (old speakers) and the dashed (young speakers) dots overlap for these two registers. Realisations during the accent performance are then higher again, though not as high as when reading a word list (the rise is non-significant for the oldest speakers in the sample). Older speakers thus only distinguish the word list style from the other three (which do not differ significantly), middle-aged subjects have similar realisations for the word list and the accent performance, and the youngest interviewees distinguish reading and spontaneous speech together from both imitation and the word list.

These slightly different tendencies in the three age groups are not pronounced enough to show up as a significant interaction of age group and style in the mixed linear effects regression. Judging from Figure 6.7, this is probably not too surprising because there does seem to be a similar trend across the age groups even if the differences are not all equally significant. The pattern that we see is not really one of "classical" style shifting, though. Instead of a steady decline from the most formal to the most informal speech style, a sort of U- or V-shaped pattern emerges. In this context, it seems worthwhile to consider an explanation based on phonetic aspects, more precisely on duration. Table 6.4 reports mean durations of happʏ (in milliseconds), and mean frequency scores of carrier words for each style and in each age group.

Table 6.4: happʏ: durations (ms) and frequency (Zipf scores) by style and age

| | list | | reading | | free | | imitation | |
	dur.	freq.	dur.	freq.	dur.	freq.	dur.	freq.
old	90.20	4.69	64.30	4.46	68.16	5.10	69.31	4.34
middle	90.82	4.72	62.70	4.46	62.94	5.23	62.13	4.51
young	104.07	4.69	62.72	4.41	65.36	5.37	55.94	4.43

As is to be expected, vowel durations are, on average, considerably longer when people read out a word list. Longer vowel durations, in turn, favour more peripheral happʏ realisations, as has been shown (and explained) above. At least in parts, the higher variants in the word list can thus be explained simply by the fact that they are also longer. It is clear, however, that this is only part of the story, and that some sub-conscious shifting must be involved as well, because vowel durations are comparable (and certainly not considerably longer) during accent imitation, text reading, and free speech. Higher, more Scouse realisations when performing the accent can therefore not be explained by a phonetic effect of longer vowel durations. The same seems to hold, more or less, for frequency of the carrier word as well: more frequent words, on average, are used in spontaneous speech (which could go some way to explaining lower realisations in this register), but in the other three styles frequencies are very similar, despite the fact that F1 values are not. A possible explanation that goes beyond duration and frequency will be discussed in Chapter 9.

6.1.2 F2 (happy)

6.1.2.1 Overview

Since the maximal model for happy F2 measurements was based on exactly the same dataset as the one where the dependent variable was F1, the same problems with collinearity also emerged. These were dealt with in an identical manner as has been described for the happy F1 model. In the end, interactions were likewise re-entered into the regression and model selection based on AIC scores and F-tests comparing nested models resulted in the minimal adequate model printed as Table 6.5 (R^2-equivalent = 0.268).

Table 6.5: happy (F2): mixed linear effects regression

Fixed effects:	Estimate	Std. Error	df	t value	Pr(>|t|)	
(Intercept)	1.64	0.02	656.54	75.97	< 0.001	***
STYLElist	0.10	0.05	1799.79	1.98	0.05	*
STYLEread	-0.05	0.02	1638.38	-2.55	0.01	*
STYLEfree	-0.04	0.02	1501.28	-2.09	0.04	*
AGE56-85	0.03	0.02	1959.22	1.41	0.16	
AGE30-55	0.01	0.02	1947.73	0.36	0.72	
GENDERf	0.02	0.00	2079.61	6.38	< 0.001	***
CLASSmc	-0.01	0.00	2081.99	-1.88	0.06	.
DURATION	0.00	0.00	2070.57	7.80	< 0.001	***
PREMANNERaffr	0.00	0.04	115.37	0.01	1.00	
PREMANNERfric	0.05	0.02	125.52	2.19	0.03	*
PREMANNERliq	-0.04	0.01	114.24	-3.22	< 0.01	**
PREMANNERnas	-0.02	0.02	93.43	-0.92	0.36	
POSTMANNERaffr	0.06	0.02	2071.42	3.23	< 0.01	**
POSTMANNERfric	-0.01	0.01	2077.31	-2.22	0.03	*
POSTMANNERgli	0.00	0.01	2063.14	0.32	0.75	
POSTMANNERliq	-0.05	0.01	2025.37	-5.72	< 0.001	***
POSTMANNERnas	0.01	0.01	2067.51	0.69	0.49	
STYLElist:GENDERf	0.09	0.02	1982.28	5.36	< 0.001	***
STYLEread:GENDERf	-0.03	0.01	1962.17	-3.22	< 0.01	**
AGE56-85:CLASSmc	-0.01	0.00	2080.77	-2.93	< 0.01	**
AGE30-55:CLASSmc	0.01	0.00	2070.63	3.18	< 0.01	**
STYLEread:AGE56-85:GENDERf	-0.02	0.03	1950.17	-0.54	0.59	
STYLEfree:AGE56-85:GENDERf	-0.03	0.02	1988.95	-1.22	0.22	
STYLEimit:AGE56-85:GENDERf	-0.01	0.04	1945.32	-0.34	0.74	
STYLEread:AGE30-55:GENDERf	-0.01	0.03	1945.26	-0.22	0.82	

STYLEfree:AGE30-55:GENDERf	0.01	0.02	1965.59	0.37	0.71
STYLEimit:AGE30-55:GENDERf	0.05	0.03	1944.32	1.61	0.11
STYLElist:AGE56-85:GENDERm	-0.02	0.10	2063.72	-0.19	0.85
STYLEread:AGE56-85:GENDERm	0.00	0.03	1949.44	0.07	0.95
STYLEfree:AGE56-85:GENDERm	-0.04	0.02	1978.35	-1.75	0.08 .
STYLElist:AGE30-55:GENDERm	0.10	0.07	2081.56	1.39	0.17
STYLEread:AGE30-55:GENDERm	-0.00	0.03	1942.75	-0.08	0.94
STYLEfree:AGE30-55:GENDERm	0.04	0.02	1963.18	1.75	0.08 .

Random effects:	(number of obs: 2116, groups: WORD, 221)		
Groups	Name	Variance	Std.Dev.
WORD	(Intercept)	0.002	0.043
Residual		0.015	0.124

This minimal model is very similar to the one that was reported for F1 measurements. Style and gender turn up as significant predictors again. Age is not a significant main effect for F2 of happʏ, but it does appear in a significant interaction of age and class. Social class, in turn, just about fails to reach significance as a main effect at the 5% level. The second two-way interaction that was retained in the model is that of style and gender. A three-way interaction of style, age, and gender did not reach significance, but was retained anyway because an ANOVA revealed that eliminating it resulted in a significantly worse fit to the data. With respect to the non-social predictors there are some changes as well. Vowel duration is, once more, highly significant, but frequency of the keyword does not seem to have a statistically robust impact on F2 measurements. Contrary to the regression of F1, both the following *and* the preceding consonant (or, rather, its manner of articulation) are significant fixed effects in this model. These last two predictors will be briefly analysed first.

6.1.2.2 Phonological context

Figure 6.8a is a box plot of F2 values (on the y-axis) sorted by preceding (manner of) consonant (on the x-axis). "NA" here stands for observations where no phonemic transcription was available for the carrier word and which, as a consequence, could not be coded for preceding sound (this mostly concerned proper

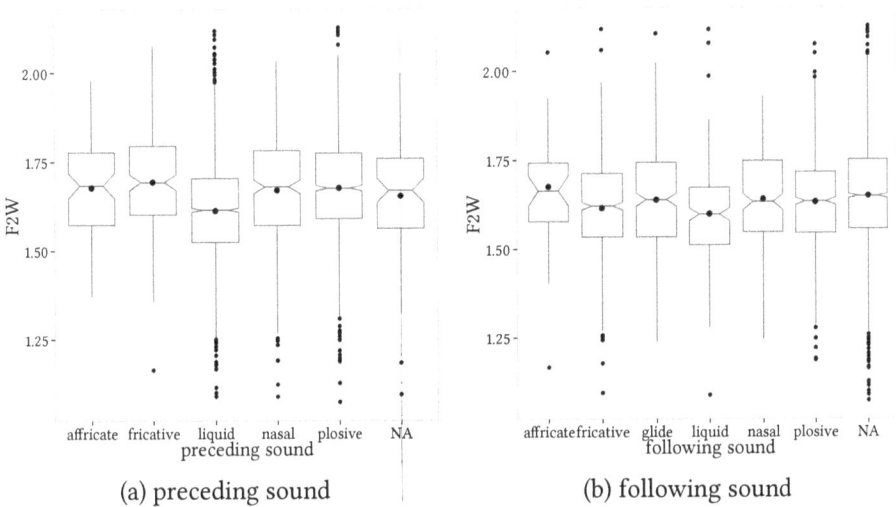

(a) preceding sound　　　　(b) following sound

Figure 6.8: happy (F2) by preceding and following sound

names, 81 observations in total). Judging from this graph, it seems as if happy measurements following liquids were the odd ones out (with lower values of F2, on average), as the remaining means are much more similar to each other and the confidence intervals of the medians (illustrated by the notches) frequently overlap. Cases where happy is preceded by a liquid were also the ones (along with, to a lesser extent, preceding fricatives) that were found to be significantly different by the mixed linear effects regression model. It should be noted that this context (preceding liquid) includes regularly formed adverbs, and therefore, by itself, accounts for the majority of happy observations (2790 out of 4565, or 61.12%), which means that the statistical basis for this phonological environment is considerably larger than for the others. Furthermore, high frequency words such as *very* or *really* are to be found in this category, so it is not unlikely that phonological context is here mixed up with other features such as duration (see below).

Interestingly, a *following* liquid (at the beginning of the next word) seems to have a very similar effect on F2 measures as a preceding one (lowering of F2 in this context has been attested before, cf. Lehiste 1964: 26). The corresponding box plot for F2 by following phoneme (Figure 6.8b) shows happy to be somewhat more central (lower F2) when a liquid follows. This is in line with the regression model (which found a negative correlation coefficient for this context). The significantly negative coefficient (in the model) for a following fricative is less obvious in this figure: while mean and median are somewhat lower, they do not appear to be significantly so (cf., for instance, the partially overlapping confidence notches of "fricative" and the neighbouring "glide"). The same holds for happy observations that are followed by an affricate. The mean in this category is higher than for other following consonants (corresponds to the positive coefficient found in the regression), but there seems to be a lot of noise in the raw data, which results in quite a large confidence interval (see the notches of the "affricate" box).

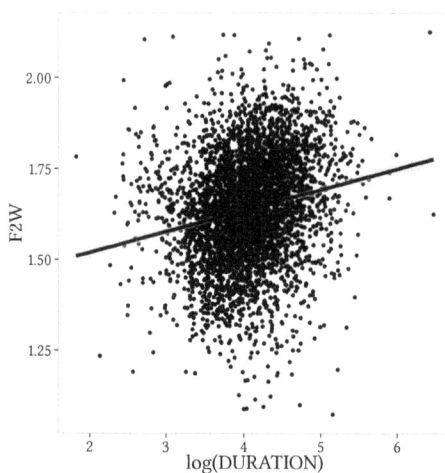

Figure 6.9: happy (F2) by duration

Let us now turn to vowel duration. The general effect is the same as for F1: longer vowel duration favours more peripheral vowel quality. In the case of F2, this translates into higher values (more advanced happy realisations). Figure 6.9 visualises the relationship in a regression plot, where log-transformed duration is marked on the x-axis and estimated F2 is found on the y-axis. While Figure 6.2 and Figure 6.9 cannot be directly compared (due to different scales), the mixed-effects models support the impression that the effect of duration on F2 is both stronger and more significant than on F1: the slope of the regression line is steeper for F2, the correlation coefficient is almost three times as big, and the p-value considerably smaller. With respect to what has been said about F2 values by preceding sound in particular, it seems worthwhile to quickly check whether vowel duration might have confounded the results reported in the preceding paragraphs.

Table 6.6 summarises mean durations of happy depending on which consonant precedes or follows. It is striking that happy realisations following liquids

Table 6.6: happy: durations by phonological environment

position	affricate	fricative	liquid	nasal	plosive	glide
preceding	79.84	70.35	62.44	62.98	70.45	NA
following	61.01	52.84	64.43	57.03	52.29	64.1

and nasals are considerably shorter, while a preceding affricate seems to have a lengthening effect. This might go some way towards explaining why happy was found to be significantly more centralised following a liquid: the effect might be due to shorter duration rather than the consonant that is found before the vowel. In this case, however, an explanation would be needed as to why a preceding nasal does not have a significant impact on F2 of happy, despite the fact that vowel duration is similar in these two contexts. Likewise, the higher duration of happy following an affricate should, but did not result in significantly fronter realisations (though this might be due to the small number of observations, cf. §6.1.1.2). When we look at the durations by following consonant, the picture becomes even messier. Before affricates happy is again slightly longer, but actually not as long as before liquids. A following affricate was found (in the regression) to be a factor favouring fronter happy realisations (in line with the duration values), but a following liquid actually has a *centralising* effect in the same model, even though happy is even longer in this environment. At least as far as the following sound is concerned, phonological environment thus does not seem to be confounded by vowel duration. At this point, no straightforward explanation presents itself as to why happy is significantly fronter in some contexts. Frequency of the keyword (as hinted at above) could be an option, but this factor was eliminated in the regression as non-significant. With respect to happy realisations in different phonological environments my account should therefore be considered more descriptive than explanatory.

6.1.2.3 Age and class

I will now turn once more towards the social predictors. Contrary to the F1 dimension, age of participant is not a significant main effect in the regression model estimating F2 of happy. The raw data, on the other hand, paint a different picture. The box plot (Figure 6.10) shows an increase in mean F2 from the oldest to the middle-aged group: happy has thus become fronter in this time frame. While the difference between groups is comparatively small, it is nonetheless highly

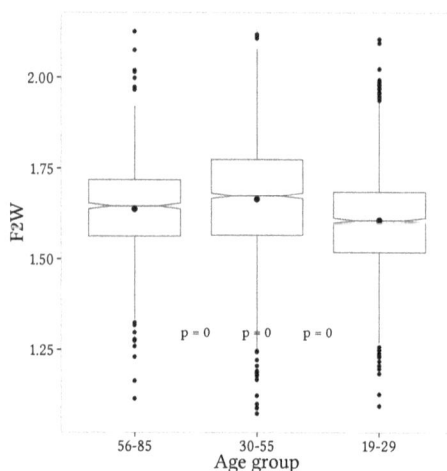

Figure 6.10: happy (F2) by age

significant (t(2321.047) = 5.117, p < 0.001). From the middle to the young group, however, the vowel does not become even more front (i.e. "more Scouse" as has been hypothesised), but rather it is centralised again. The youngest speakers in my sample do not only have happy realisations that are significantly more central than those of their parents' generation (t(3574.064) = -11.594, p < 0.001). They use, in fact, variants which are, on average, even more retracted than those of the oldest speakers, a difference which is, once again, highly significant (t(2190.006) = -5.655, p < 0.001). Just as for F1, I have to conclude that the younger the speaker, the less Scouse – in this case front – happy is. That being said, it should be kept in mind that age of participant is no longer a significant fixed effect on its own once other factors and random variation due to carrier word are considered. The same goes for class of subject, even though this factor only just about fails to cross the 5% threshold. The interaction of age and social class, however, *is* a significant fixed effect in the regression model. Figure 6.11a and Figure 6.11b illustrate the relationship.

Figure 6.11b shows separate regression lines for the three age groups, which are as usual coded by line type: solid for the oldest, dotted for the middle-aged, and dashed for the youngest speakers. Estimated F2 is marked on the y-, and social class on the x-axis. This graph shows two interesting things: (1) Class does not only have an effect that is different in degree in the three age groups, but one whose direction is completely reversed in the youngest speakers. For both the old and the middle group, working-class speakers use more advanced happy

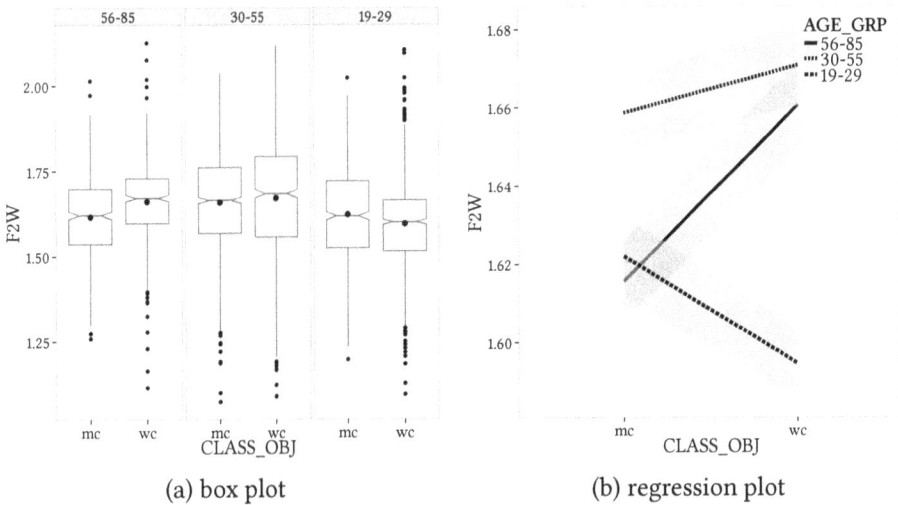

(a) box plot   (b) regression plot

Figure 6.11: happy (F2) by age and class

variants. Young working-class speakers, on the other hand, have realisations that are more retracted than those of their middle-class counterparts. (2) Which age groups are different from each other depends on which social class one looks at. In the middle class, the oldest and the youngest speakers appear as one large group, without any significant differences between them (t(1179.969) = 0.836, p = 0.403), but one which does differ greatly from the middle group – compared to young (t(1446.646) = -5.289, p < 0.001), and old group (t(1127.729) = 6.292, p < 0.001) – , where realisations are a bit more front. Among the working-class speakers, on the other hand, the old and the middle-aged participants form a group, albeit one that shows somewhat more variation (t(1192.156) = 1.219, p = 0.223), which is now significantly different from the youngest speakers – compared to middle (t(1659.468) = -10.25, p < 0.001), and old group (t(956.457) = -8.952, p < 0.001) –, who use more retracted variants of happy.

The box plot next to this regression plot (6.11a) shows the same interaction, but the focus is now more on social class. There are three panels which illustrate the differences between middle- and working-class speakers within each age group separately. On the left-hand side one can see that in the oldest age group, working-class subjects have fronter realisations of happy than the middle-class speakers of the same age group. The difference looks highly significant (the confidence interval notches do not overlap), and indeed it is (t(929.854) = -5.653, p < 0.001). In the group of participants who are between 30 and 55 years old, the mean of working-class subjects is also marginally higher, but this time there seems to be much more within-group variation and the two social classes are no longer significantly different from one another ($t(1668.574) = -1.663$, $p = 0.097$). When we look at the youngest speakers, we see again that the trend has reversed (working-class speakers in this subsample have more centralised variants of happy showing in lower F2 averages), variation – particularly among working-class subjects – has decreased and the difference between classes is once more statistically robust ($t(1443.946) = 3.878$, $p < 0.001$). There is thus no straightforward interpretation for either social class or age of participant, because their effects depend on each other not only in terms of degree, but also in direction. Notwithstanding the slightly confusing picture that these two factors create, one thing seems to be clear when we look at both the means in Figure 6.11a and the position of the dashed and dotted lines in Figure 6.11b: the youngest subjects in the sample have more retracted happy realisations than speakers of their parents' generation. They cannot be said to be more Scouse than their parents or grandparents.

6.1.2.4 Style and gender

The second significant interaction in the mixed-effects model, style X gender, is not really simpler in nature. The box plots in Figure 6.12 illustrate within-style comparisons by gender, but they also show style differences within genders. For female speakers (boxes on the left-hand side of each panel), the three styles "read-

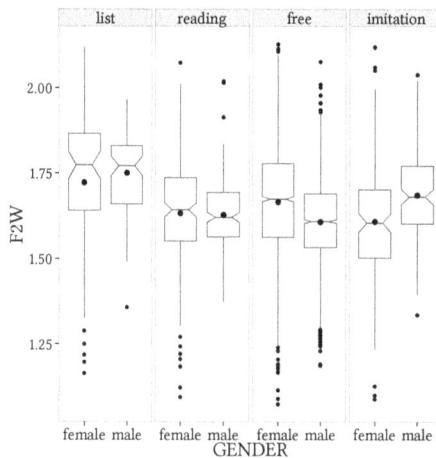

Figure 6.12: happy (F2) by style and gender

ing", "free", and 'imitation' have relatively similar realisations. This is especially true for reading and accent performance, where means are very close and notches overlap. Table 6.7 summarises t-tests on the raw data for all possible comparisons of style, separated by gender of subject. The p-value of 0.22 for reading-imitation (females) confirms that these two styles are not significantly different, whereas spontaneous speech differs from both reading (p = 0.008) and imitation (p < 0.001) in a statistically robust way. Realisations of happy elicited via the word list show slightly more variation around the mean, but are nevertheless clearly distinct from all three remaining styles as both the box plot and the t-tests (cf. Table 6.7) suggest.

Table 6.7: happy (F2): t-tests of style by gender

test	women			men		
	t	df	p	t	df	p
list-reading	3.396	113.708	< 0.001	8.343	165.401	< 0.001
list-free	2.370	79.086	0.020	11.426	94.870	< 0.001
list-imitation	3.994	141.852	< 0.001	3.984	197.933	< 0.001
reading-free	−2.661	244.712	0.008	2.362	234.779	0.019
reading-imitation	1.229	260.601	0.220	−4.279	279.877	< 0.001
free-imitation	3.482	146.933	< 0.001	−7.047	158.739	< 0.001

When we look at male speakers (right-hand boxes in Figure 6.12), accent performance and reading realisations are now clearly distinct (p < 0.001), and reading and spontaneous speech, in turn, look as if their means were comparable. A t-test on the raw data, however, does find this difference to be significant (p = 0.019), albeit slightly less so than those that hold between the other styles. The rightmost column of Table 6.7 indicates that (in the raw data!) men actually keep all four registers distinct. If we now consider gender differences within the individual registers, one thing that immediately strikes the eye is that, contrary to the other three, the difference in "reading" seems negligible, which suggests that women and men do not have different happy realisations (with respect to F2 at least) in this speaking style.

The second panel from the left visualises gender differences for the reading passage only: the larger box for the female subjects indicates that there is more variation in this subgroup, but the means of men and women (marked by black dots) are indeed almost on the same level. Furthermore, the confidence intervals (notches) of the two boxes overlap, so this difference really seems to be non-significant, a suspicion which is confirmed by a t-test (t(353.108) = 0.338, p = 0.736). Essentially the same holds true when subjects read out a word list (leftmost panel): at first glance, men seem to use fronter happy variants than women (their mean is higher than that of females). However, the medians (black horizontal bars) of both subgroups are virtually identical and the notch of the "male" box falls well within that of its "female" counterpart, both of which suggest non-significance. A t-test again corroborates this interpretation (t(113.484) = -1.07, p = 0.287).

In spontaneous speech ("free" panel), on the other hand, there is a very clear and pronounced difference between female and male speakers. Women have a considerably higher mean F2 than men, and while they also exhibit quite a bit of variation (as illustrated by the vertical extent of the box), mean and median are almost identical for both the female and the male subjects, and the confidence intervals are very small and clearly distinct. The relevant t-test provides further evidence that women really do use more advanced happy variants than men in spontaneous speech (t(3169.606) = 12.219, p < 0.001). When participants are asked to imitate or perform a strong Scouse accent, this trend reverses completely, as is obvious from the rightmost boxplot in Figure 6.12. In this register, women's mean F2 is lower, i.e. they produce more *retracted* realisations of happy than men, a difference which is highly significant (t(232.688) = -4.024, p < 0.001). Gender is thus only a significant factor in spontaneous speech and accent performance, but not for reading of a text or a word list. When it does play a role, its effect is not uniform: women are 'more Scouse' in free speech, but 'less Scouse' in the accent imitation task.

6.1.2.5 Style shifting

Before concluding this section, we will have a closer look at style and its (lacking) relation to age. I am aware of the fact that the linear mixed-effects regression did not find a significant interaction of these two predictors. Just as for the F1 dimension of happy I will print and describe the relevant plot all the same, because, (a) in this particular case, it visualises the impact of style almost as well as a plot that does not include age at all, and (b) both plots will later serve as points of reference for variables where there *is* a significant interaction. Figure 6.13 is identical in design to Figure 6.7: style is marked on the x-, and F2 on the y-axis. Age group is coded by line type, and the whiskers visualise standard deviations.

For all three age groups, there is a sharp drop from the word list to reading and the other two styles (with the exception of 'imitation' in the old group, which looks as if it might not be significantly different from the word list values in the

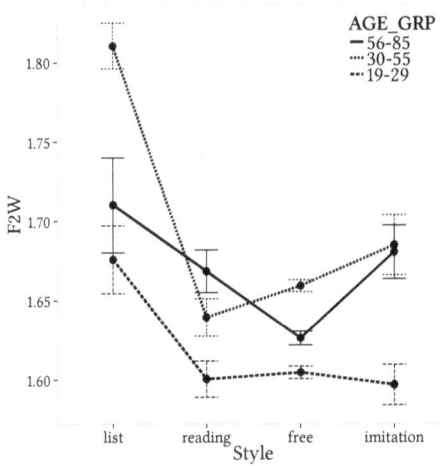

Figure 6.13: happy (F2) by age and style

same age group). This echoes what has been found for F1 of happy, and could, at least in parts, also be explained the same way: vowel duration is considerably higher when participants read out a word list (and also very similar in the other three registers; cf. Table 6.4), so the high values in this style are probably less to do with style shifting than with mere phonetic factors (although this does not explain why the difference seems to be particularly extreme for the middle age group).

One might be tempted to see some regularity in this graph (comparable to the u-shape in Figure 6.7), but the evidence is inconclusive. For the oldest speakers (where free speech marks the low point, and happy is more advanced both during reading and accent performance, which do not seem to differ significantly), a two-norms-approach might actually work pretty well: tense /i/ seems to be the target both in particularly local and particularly standard, or careful, speech. In the middle group, however, the three registers "reading", "free", and 'imitation' do not only apparently all differ significantly from one another (the standard deviations do not overlap), but happy is also more advanced in spontaneous speech than it is while reading a text – a fact, which does not go together very well with the assumption that a more formal register should pull realisations towards the tense standard, relative to a more relaxed (and therefore more central) starting point in spontaneous speech. For the youngest speakers in the sample, finally, this interpretation is completely out of the question. In this group, happy realisations are virtually identical with respect to F2 in reading, free speech, and accent performance (standard deviations for these styles completely overlap). As far as the front-back dimension of happy is concerned, the youngest speakers that were interviewed for this study are not only, once again, the least Scouse (the dashed line is below the other two in all styles), but they also show the least awareness (*if* there is any to start with) of this feature as measured by style shifting.

6.1.3 Synthesis and Pillai scores (happy)

6.1.3.1 Overview

Moving away from awareness for a moment but keeping the focus on age, we will now zoom out a bit further and consider F1 and F2 measurements of happy together. The test variable happy will also be contrasted with FLEECE. This might provide a first hint as to whether just happy is changing in the younger generation, or whether other high front vowels are moving in the same (or another) direction as well. It should be noted, though, that FLEECE vowels were only measured in the reading and word list sections of the interviews (cf. §5.4.2). For the graphs reported on the following pages, the dataset of happy observations was therefore also reduced to the ones derived from reading and word list realisations to make sure like is compared with like.

Figure 6.14 shows the spread of happy and FLEECE realisations for all three age groups separately. The three sub-plots are essentially "traditional" F1-F2 vowel plots, which means that both the x- (F2) and the y-axis (F1) are inverted, so that fronter realisations are found to the left, and closer vowels towards the top of the graph. In all three plots, FLEECE realisations are marked by dark circles, and happy observations by light triangles. The dark and light polygons[2] connect the most peripheral pronunciations of each vowel and therefore define the total realisational space that the respective phonemes occur in with respect to the sample of this study.

Looking at the oldest speakers (Figure 6.14a), the first thing that probably strikes the reader is the outlier at around (1.75, 1.70), which results in a pronounced distortion of the happy polygon towards the bottom half of the graph. When this single (and rather extreme) realisation is ignored the light polygon becomes much more similar to those found in the middle-aged and the young group, with a lower limit at around F1 values of 1.15. The other interesting aspect is that FLEECE realisations are not only all to be found within the area defined by

---

[2]The boundaries of the polygons were extracted from the dataset with the help of the R package "plyr" (Wickham 2011).

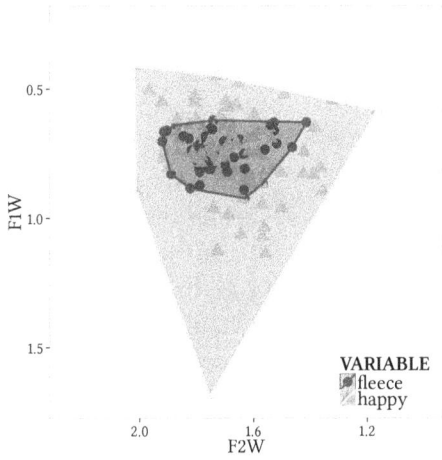

(a) old speakers

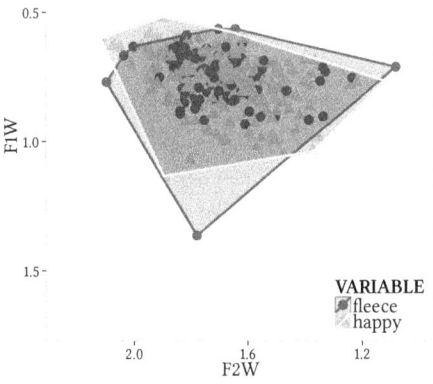

(b) middle-aged speakers

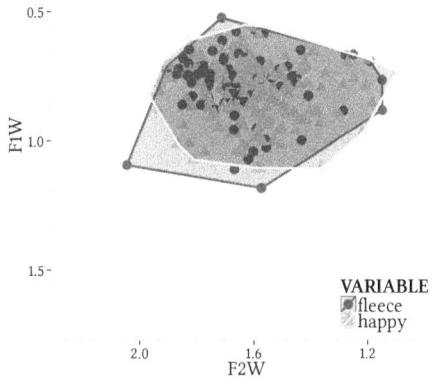

(c) young speakers

Figure 6.14: happy-FLEECE: vowel space by age

happy, but that the realisational space of FLEECE (dark polygon) is also considerably smaller than that of happy. This indicates that FLEECE realisations are much
more homogeneous among older speakers than happy pronunciations, although
it has to be said it is possible that this result is at least in part due to the fact that
there are comparatively few FLEECE observations in this age group to start with
(n = 52). Since FLEECE is – visually – entirely included within the happy distribution, it is no surprise that a MANOVA returns a Pillai score near 0 and a p-value
which clearly shows that the two vowels are (almost) completely merged (Pillai
= 0.024, F = 2.071, p = 0.129).

In the middle-aged group (Figure 6.14b) there is a similar, if somewhat less
extreme, outlier as in the sample of the old speakers: this time the dark FLEECE
area seems distorted towards higher F1 values and begs the question whether this
particular vowel should be excluded from the analysis. In any case, however, it is
clear that the (horizontal) front-back extent of the FLEECE space is considerably
larger than it was in Figure 6.14a, with or without the potential outlier. This is
equally true for the light happy space, although the difference is less pronounced
than for FLEECE. Nevertheless, it is obvious that there are happy realisations in
the middle-aged group which are either slightly more front (towards the left of
the graph) or more back (towards the right of the figure) than those found for the
older speakers; the phonetic range of happy variants is thus a bit larger in the
middle group. While the spread of FLEECE is much larger in the middle group,
the overlap of FLEECE and happy seems to be just as complete as among the
oldest speakers. A MANOVA confirms this impression by yielding very similar
values as for the old speakers, which confirm that the vowel distributions are
not significantly different from one another (Pillai = 0.003, F = 0.53, p = 0.589).

When we turn to Figure 6.14c, which represents the data collected from the
youngest speakers, the picture changes only slightly. However, both FLEECE and,
particularly, happy seem to be somewhat more retracted than in the middle-aged
or the old speakers. This is evidenced by the lack of variants that are simultaneously very front and very high – like the ones found towards the upper left
corner in Figure 6.14b and Figure 6.14a for the middle-aged and the old speakers,
respectively. Just as for the middle group, however, the distributions of happy
and FLEECE occupy essentially the same space and are not found to be significantly different by a Pillai test (Pillai = 0.015, F = 2.298, p = 0.102). The p-value of
the MANOVA is close to a statistical trend, but this should not be overinterpreted:
it is true that the difference between the two vowels is much closer to significance in the young group than in the middle-aged one, but the Pillai score is still
virtually 0 in both cases, which means that even if there was a statistically ro-

bust difference among younger speakers, the degree of overlap between vowel distributions would be extremely high.

6.1.3.2 Age means

It *does* look as if the majority of happy realisations was marginally more re-tracted than most of the FLEECE variants in the young speakers, but since the centres of gravity of the vowel clouds are difficult to establish from Figure 6.14, it makes sense to consider a plot of the mean values (Figure 6.15). This graph ignores the spread and overall distribution and only indicates where the means, i.e. the centres, of the exemplar clouds are to be found. Two pieces of informa-tion can be extracted from this figure. Firstly, age groups cluster together: both mean FLEECE and happy of the old speakers are higher than either vowel is on average in the middle-aged group. The means for the latter group are, in turn, both more front and higher than either mean FLEECE or happy of the youngest subjects in the sample. The second point of interest in this graph is that the dif-ference between the means of FLEECE and happy is smallest for the middle-aged realisations, larger for the observations pertaining to the older subjects, and most pronounced in the sub-sample of Liverpudlians aged between 19 and 29. This cor-relates with the fact that the p-value of the relevant MANOVA was largest for the middle group, smaller for the old, and close to the 0.10 threshold for the youngest

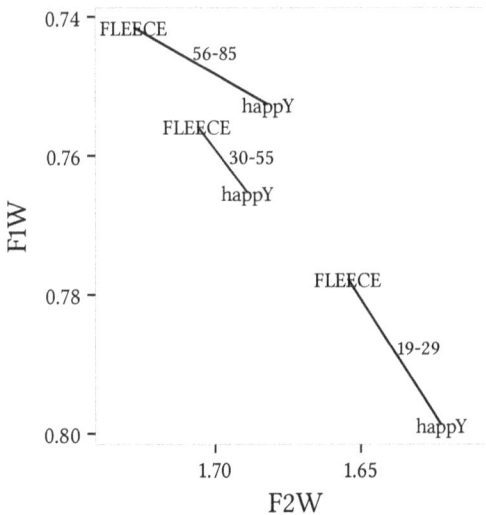

Figure 6.15: happy-FLEECE: mean vowel position by age

speakers, which indicates that mean realisations of happy and FLEECE are indeed more robustly different among the old and the young speakers.

However, two caveats should be borne in mind: (1) Figure 6.14 and Figure 6.15 do not use the same scale – the means of FLEECE and happy are not identical, but the differences visible in Figure 6.15 are actually very small. (2) The previous point is corroborated by the MANOVA results, which indicate almost perfect overlap between overall distributions (Pillai scores near 0) and no significant difference between them (all p-values > 0.5). The available statistical evidence thus clearly supports the claim that FLEECE and happy are completely merged in all three age groups investigated. Of course, this does not (directly) touch on the primary issue of change in happy across the three generations. Figure 6.15 corroborates the findings reported for F1 and F2 separately (and on the basis of mixed linear effects regressions): happy becomes lower from the old to the middle-aged, and lower and *more* central from the middle to the young speakers.

All of this only refers to rather formal realisations of these vowels, since the results in this section are exclusively based on the reading passage and the word list. It remains to be seen whether the same conclusions would hold in spontaneous speech.

6.2 NURSE

6.2.1 F1 (NURSE)

6.2.1.1 Overview

Just as with happy results, the maximal model for NURSE F1 measurements exhibited severe collinearity (κ = 38.1). Separate regression models showed that both place and manner of articulation of the following sound (κ = 34.25), and place of following consonant and frequency of the carrier word (κ = 21.22) showed troubling or at least above average degrees of collinearity. Only one of these three, manner of articulation, was therefore retained. In a second maximal model, which neither included place of articulation of preceding and following sound, nor frequency of the keyword, collinearity was acceptable (κ = 14.39). The minimal adequate model (R^2-equivalent = 0.314) that was then derived is shown below (Table 6.8).

Table 6.8: NURSE (F1): mixed linear effects regression

Fixed effects:	Estimate	Std. Error	df	t value	Pr(>|t|)	
(Intercept)	1.09	0.01	127.19	125.58	< 0.001	***
STYLElist	0.03	0.01	1078.12	3.61	< 0.001	***
STYLEread	0.00	0.01	1344.45	0.70	0.48	
STYLEfree	0.00	0.01	362.94	0.48	0.63	
AGE56-85	0.02	0.01	1475.42	3.19	< 0.01	**
AGE30-55	-0.01	0.01	1484.51	-2.86	< 0.01	**
GENDERf	-0.03	0.00	1477.09	-8.60	< 0.001	***
CLASSmc	0.05	0.00	1479.04	12.16	< 0.001	***
PREMANNERaffr	-0.05	0.02	74.59	-2.90	< 0.01	**
PREMANNERfric	-0.01	0.01	98.39	-0.82	0.42	
PREMANNERgli	0.01	0.01	65.20	0.54	0.59	
PREMANNERliq	0.02	0.02	118.12	0.82	0.41	
PREMANNERnas	0.02	0.02	377.34	0.95	0.34	
STYLElist:AGE56-85	0.02	0.01	1464.53	2.18	0.03	*
STYLEread:AGE56-85	-0.01	0.01	1465.50	-0.66	0.51	
STYLEfree:AGE56-85	0.01	0.01	1514.74	1.93	0.05	.
STYLElist:AGE30-55	-0.01	0.01	1468.34	-1.42	0.16	
STYLEread:AGE30-55	0.01	0.01	1470.78	0.80	0.42	
STYLEfree:AGE30-55	-0.01	0.01	1513.20	-0.89	0.37	
AGE56-85:GENDERf	-0.03	0.01	1475.15	-5.98	< 0.001	***
AGE30-55:GENDERf	-0.01	0.01	1475.93	-1.86	0.06	.
AGE56-85:CLASSmc	0.02	0.01	1471.18	3.15	< 0.01	**
AGE30-55:CLASSmc	-0.01	0.01	1475.87	-1.28	0.20	
GENDERf:CLASSmc	-0.01	0.00	1525.94	-2.80	0.01	**
STYLElist:AGE56-85:GENDERf	0.00	0.01	1464.29	0.25	0.80	
STYLEread:AGE56-85:GENDERf	0.02	0.01	1464.64	1.26	0.21	
STYLEfree:AGE56-85:GENDERf	0.02	0.01	1507.65	1.76	0.08	.
STYLElist:AGE30-55:GENDERf	0.00	0.01	1466.69	0.40	0.69	
STYLEread:AGE30-55:GENDERf	-0.01	0.01	1473.07	-1.07	0.28	
STYLEfree:AGE30-55:GENDERf	0.01	0.01	1506.49	1.63	0.10	
STYLElist:AGE19-29:GENDERf	0.01	0.01	1466.78	0.92	0.36	
STYLEread:AGE19-29:GENDERf	-0.00	0.01	1467.05	-0.03	0.97	
STYLEfree:AGE19-29:GENDERf	-0.02	0.01	1519.51	-2.30	0.02	*

STYLElist:AGE56-85:CLASSmc	0.01	0.01	1463.33	0.52	0.60	
STYLEread:AGE56-85:CLASSmc	-0.02	0.01	1464.04	-1.27	0.20	
STYLEfree:AGE56-85:CLASSmc	-0.02	0.01	1506.47	-1.85	0.06	.
STYLElist:AGE30-55:CLASSmc	0.02	0.01	1466.82	2.26	0.02	*
STYLEread:AGE30-55:CLASSmc	0.01	0.01	1469.86	1.27	0.20	
STYLEfree:AGE30-55:CLASSmc	-0.02	0.01	1497.92	-2.26	0.02	*
STYLElist:AGE19-29:CLASSmc	-0.00	0.01	1468.20	-0.42	0.67	
STYLEread:AGE19-29:CLASSmc	0.00	0.01	1468.92	0.19	0.85	
STYLEfree:AGE19-29:CLASSmc	0.02	0.01	1516.74	2.46	0.01	*

Random effects:	(number of obs: 1568, groups: WORD, 137)		
Groups	Name	Variance	Std.Dev.
WORD	(Intercept)	0.001	0.029
Residual		0.011	0.103

It is immediately obvious that this model contains several additional significant predictors when compared to the corresponding model of happ‌Y. Style, age group, gender, and social class are again all significant main effects. In addition, the model found significant interactions of style and age, age and class, age and gender, and gender and class. Towards the bottom of the model we see that the interaction that is of greatest interest for this study, style X age, further entered into significant three-way interactions with both gender and social class.

Non-social factors, on the other hand, seem to be less important than for happ‌Y, at least in relation to the social predictors: vowel duration, manner of following consonant, and frequency of the carrier word are all deleted as unsignificant during model reduction. The only phonological predictor that is retained is manner of articulation of the preceding consonant, and even with this one there is only one level that is significantly different: NURSE realisations are higher (i.e. more standard) when they are preceded by an affricate. However, this only concerns a small minority of observations (97 out of 1770, or 5.48%), which are relatively equally distributed across all styles, so this predictor will not be analysed any further here.

6.2.1.2 Gender and class

Instead, we will move on to the interaction of gender and class. Since the interaction is only one of degree (see below) the relevant graphs do not add much to the discussion and are therefore omitted. In the group of middle-class speakers, men have a higher mean and median than women, which means that their NURSE realisations are lower. This difference is highly significant in the raw data ($t(958.928) = -8.555$, $p < 0.001$). For working-class subjects, we have essentially the same situation: women have a lower average and median F1, indicating that they use more central variants of NURSE ($t(751.346) = -4.357$, $p < 0.001$). Technically speaking, the difference between women and men is somewhat less robust in the working class group (cf. the t-values of the two tests), but for all practical purposes the relationship is the same in both social classes as both t-tests yield p-values that are below 0.001. The degree of the effect, however, is stronger in the middle class, meaning that there is a larger distance between the means of women and men in this class.

Conversely, the effect of social class is the same for both genders, although the difference between classes is smaller for women ($t(813.931) = 7.824$, $p < 0.001$), and more pronounced in the male group ($t(941.869) = 13.469$, $p < 0.001$). Once again, however, this distinction is rather fine-grained as class differences are highly significant for both genders. What is interesting, though, is that middle-class speakers actually use lower variants of NURSE than their working-class counterparts. This, in turn, holds for both genders, even though it is ever so slightly more pronounced in the male sub-sample.

6.2.1.3 Gender and age

The interaction of gender and age is somewhat more interesting in this respect. Looking at gender differences in the oldest speakers (left panel of Figure 6.16a) we find that women have considerably lower F1 values than men. The gender effect is highly significant ($t(395.594) = -5.823$, $p < 0.001$): men realise NURSE as a lower vowel than women. The same relation holds in the middle age group. Men again have higher F1 values on average than women. Judging from the box plot, which suggests less variation (smaller boxes) and smaller median confidence intervals (width of the notches), this difference is even more significant than for the oldest speakers. A t-test supports this impression ($t(805.568) = -11.767$, $p < 0.001$), although it has to be said that (a) this could simply be due to the fact that there are less data for the oldest speakers, and (b) the difference is already highly significant in the old group. The youngest subjects in the sample differ

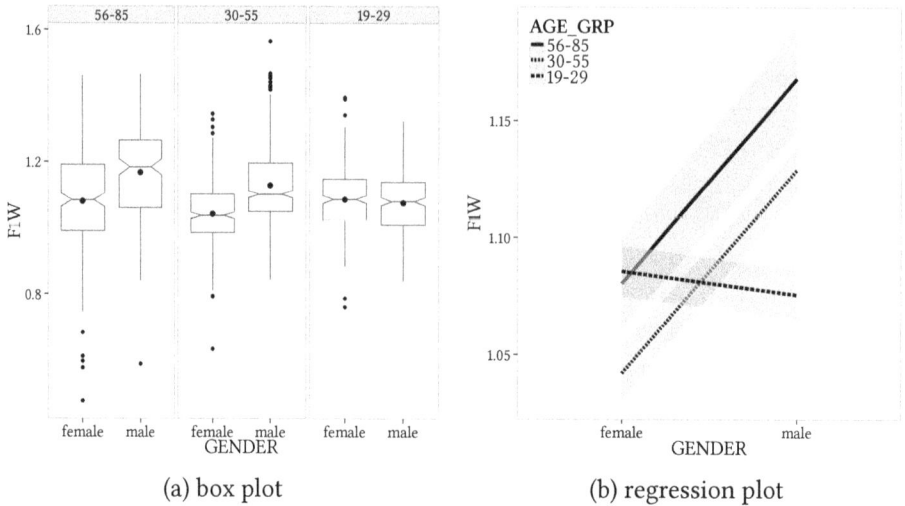

Figure 6.16: NURSE (F1) by gender and age

markedly from speakers of their parents' or grandparents' generation, because in this group there is no significant difference between male and female NURSE realisations (t(537.587) = 1.277, p = 0.202). Both means (and medians) are on a level which is almost perfectly intermediate between the means of middle-aged female and male speakers.

This non-significant difference between genders is also visible in Figure 6.16b, which has a (dashed) regression line for the youngest interviewees which is almost parallel to the x-axis of the plot. The comparatively steep positive slopes of the other two lines that stand for the old (solid) and middle-aged subjects (dotted), in turn visualise the gender difference that is already evident in Figure 6.16a. The regression plot also shows that all age groups seem to be significantly different from one another as far as the male speakers are concerned: the lines are clearly distinct and standard deviations (grey areas) do not overlap. One can reach the same conclusion based on the t-tests summarised in Table 6.9, which confirm that all three age groups are (highly) significant when the analysis is restricted to male subjects. In the female sub-sample, on the other hand, the middle age group is different from the other two, but the oldest and the youngest speakers do not differ with respect to the height of NURSE (cf. the t-tests in Table 6.9 and the standard error margins in Figure 6.16b). It looks thus as if male Scousers have constantly raised NURSE over the time period investigated here (if only to a very small extent in absolute terms), while female speakers first slightly raised NURSE from the oldest to the middle-aged speakers, only to return to the starting point again in the youngest group. Since this starting point is statistically identical to the one the youngest male speakers have arrived at, the gender difference is therefore gone in this age group.

Table 6.9: NURSE (F1): t-tests of age by gender

test	women			men		
	t	df	p	t	df	p
old-middle	−3.292	337.596	0.001	−3.242	267.935	0.001
middle-young	5.819	566.832	< 0.001	−6.908	697.042	< 0.001
young-old	0.436	352.420	0.663	−7.637	268.135	< 0.001

6.2.1.4 Age and class

When it comes to the interplay of age and social class we have again a case where one might wonder why this interaction was found to be significant in the mixed linear effects regression. There are, once more, only differences in degree so the box and regression plots are not printed here (cf. §6.2.1.2). As reported above, middle-class speakers have higher F1 values (which translate to more open, i.e. more Scouse NURSE variants) than working-class Liverpudlians. This holds across all age groups and the difference is highly significant in the old (t(403.191) = 5.927, p < 0.001), the middle (t(798.733) = 10.566, p < 0.001), *and* the young group (t(534.588) = 11.88, p < 0.001), so an interaction does not seem "necessary".[3]

Closer inspection of the figures nevertheless reveals tiny differences. The t-tests reported in Table 6.10 provide evidence that the middle-aged and the young group are not significantly different, neither in the working, nor the middle-class sub-sample. NURSE productions of the oldest speakers, on the other hand, seem to be distinct from the other two groups, both in the middle and the working-class sub-sample. In the raw data, p-values are only a bit higher for the working-class observations (but still below the 5% threshold, so NURSE variants in the oldest group *are* significantly different from the rest), but this slight deviation seems to be enough for the interaction to surface as significant in the mixed-effects model.

---

[3]A box plot based on the values predicted by the regression model (instead of the actually observed ones) was also generated to visualise the interaction once the random effects have been accounted for. This graph, however, did not look markedly different and is therefore not reprinted here either.

Table 6.10: NURSE (F1): t-tests of age by social class

test	middle class			working class		
	t	df	p	t	df	p
old-middle	−2.950	342.020	0.003	−2.064	266.401	0.040
middle-young	0.479	700.025	0.632	−0.119	610.856	0.905
young-old	−2.727	307.814	0.007	−2.133	267.448	0.034

Let us take a step back and briefly consider age of participant as a main effect before we investigate the interaction with speaking style. A box plot (Figure 6.17) clearly shows that the oldest subjects have a higher F1 for NURSE than both the middle and the young group. The difference between the old and the middle-aged group looks significant, and is indeed found to be so by a t-test on the raw data ($t(634.126) = -2.735$, $p = 0.006$). Equally significant ($t(1322.803) = -2.387$, $p = 0.017$) is the drop from the middle to the young group, even though the virtually identical medians and the notches of the boxes might suggest otherwise. Young speakers in my sample thus have a significantly more close NURSE realisation than speakers of the other age ranges.

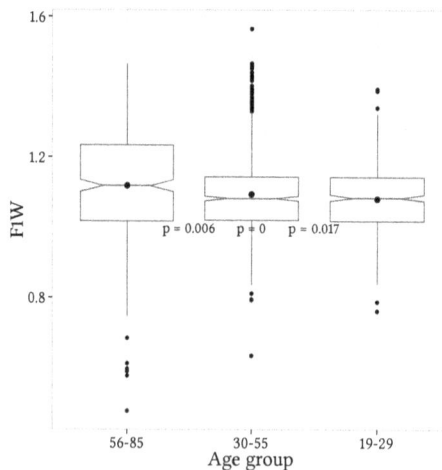

Figure 6.17: NURSE (F1) by age

6.2.1.5 Style shifting

The interaction of style and age (along with the two three-way interactions of style, age, and gender and class, respectively) are visualised by a number of line plots which are all structured similarly and were already used in §6.1.1 and §6.1.2: style is marked on the x-axis, F1 on the y-axis, and age group of participant is coded by line type.

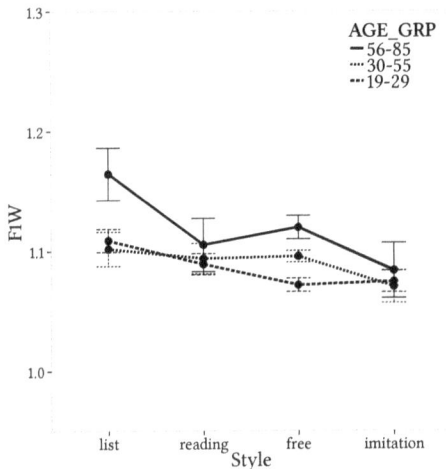

Figure 6.18: NURSE (F1) by style and age

Figure 6.18, which is based on the complete data set of NURSE observations, shows that differences between age groups are not really drastic. The young and the middle group have virtually identical values in three out of four speaking styles, only the oldest speakers are slightly more distinct. However, even that is mostly true for the word list. While reading a text and during accent performance all three groups have comparable F1 measurements. Only in spontaneous speech (which accounts for the clear majority of observations and therefore explains the results visualised in Figure 6.17) do all three groups have significantly different F1 means. No group shows systematic and significant style variation (note the often overlapping standard error bars between styles). Especially the lines of the young and middle-aged speakers look pretty level. If anything, style shifting can be found in the oldest participants, where there seems to be a more systematic downward trend from the left of the graph to the right (although the mean of "reading" is a little off in this respect). However, just as in the other groups, the line potentially has a "wrong" negative slope. If we were looking at Labovian style shifting, we would expect an *upward* slope, i.e. NURSE realisations becoming *more* Scouse from the word list to imitation, instead of the opposite.

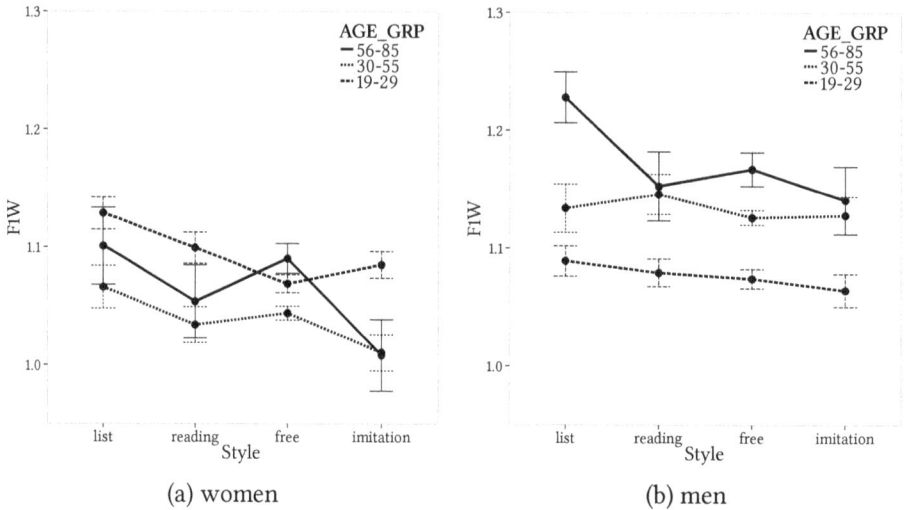

Figure 6.19: NURSE (F1) by style, age, and gender

Since the mixed linear effects regression found significant three-way interactions of style and age with both gender and social class, we should also look at the sub-samples defined by these two additional predictors. Figure 6.19a and Figure 6.19b show the same relationship of style and age as Figure 6.18, but they restrict the dataset to female or male subjects, respectively. It seems as if the slight downward trend that was visible for the oldest speakers only in Figure 6.18 can be found for females of *all* age groups (with the exception of the means in free speech, which are not really on the proposed line, but further up – for the middle and the old group – or down – for the young speakers – than they "should" be). This cannot be called more than a subtle trend, however, as styles adjacent on the formality continuum are only rarely significantly different ("reading" and "free" in the young, "free" and 'imitation' in the other two groups). Also, the near-linear development is again in the wrong direction to qualify as style shifting, because realisations of NURSE become *less* Scouse in more informal contexts. If we look at the men in Figure 6.19b even this weak trend is gone. Middle-aged and young men have lines which are, for all practical purposes, flat, and the oldest speakers distinguish only the word list from the other three styles.

The interaction of style, age, and social class presents itself as somewhat more messy. Speakers in the old group can be said to be the ones where social class seems to play the least important role with respect to style shifting. In both the middle (Figure 6.20a) and the working class (Figure 6.20b), the general tend-

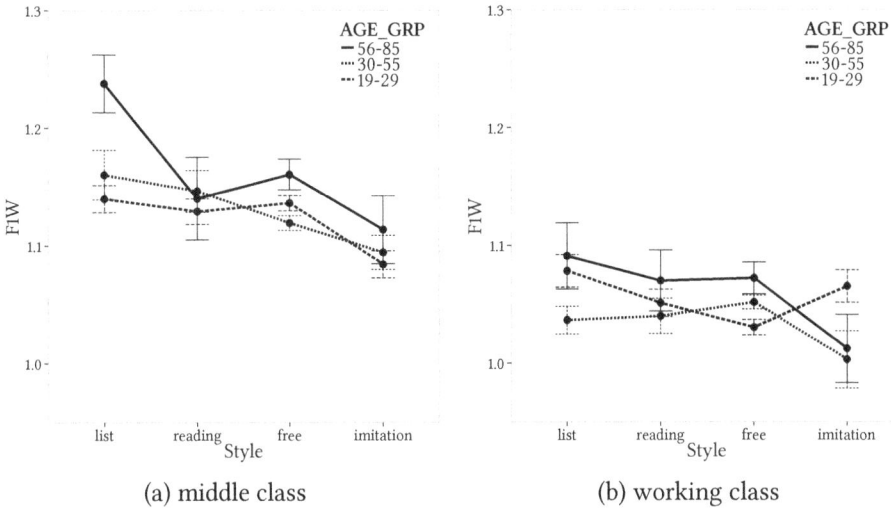

Figure 6.20: NURSE (F1) by style, age, and social class

ency for F1 values to decrease from most formal to least formal context is visible. Admittedly, vowels elicited by the word list are only (significantly) more open for old middle-class speakers, but, on the other hand, in *both* classes (a) realisations in the "reading" and "free" registers are not significantly different from each other, and (b) F1 of NURSE is (just about) significantly lower in accent performance ('imitation') than in spontaneous speech ("free").

Middle-aged subjects in the middle-class sub-sample generate the neatest version of the downward trend that should by now be familiar. First of all, F1 values for the dotted line decrease linearly, without exception, from left to right in Figure 6.20b. Second, if we lump together the word list and the reading passage (which do not seem to be different in a statistically robust way), this decrease is also significant from "reading"/"word list" to "free", and from "free" to "imitation". Working-class speakers of the same age group do not show this regular downward trend. What is more, NURSE realisations in the registers word list, reading passage, and spontaneous speech are not – statistically speaking – different. When performing Scouse, variants are significantly higher, but only when compared to free speech; the overlapping error whiskers in Figure 6.20b indicate that "list", "reading", and 'imitation' are not significantly different for subjects aged between 30 and 55.

For the youngest group of speakers it is in the *middle* class where these three styles are not significantly different from one another. Accent performance, how-

ever, is then (highly) significantly different from all other registers. Young working-class speakers echo middle-aged middle-class participants in that they have
a linear decrease in F1 from "list" to "free". In addition, both "list" and 'reading'
and "reading" and "free" are (at least marginally) significantly different. As a sort
of reversal of the pattern found for middle-aged working-class speakers, there is
then an increase towards the values found for 'imitation', a mean which is again
only significantly different from spontaneous speech, but not the reading passage or the word list. There is thus a general similarity between Figure 6.19a and
Figure 6.20a (downward trend more visible) and Figure 6.20b and Figure 6.19b
(flatter lines), which is in line with an immense body of sociolinguistic research
that has, time and again, found female speakers and those of higher socioeconomic classes to be more sensitive to sociolinguistically meaningful variables. If
we zoom in, however, it becomes obvious that the middle-aged group exhibits
a more linear pattern in the middle class (as expected), whereas the youngest
speakers actually have a flatter line in this class than in the working class.

6.2.2 F2 (NURSE)

6.2.2.1 Overview

Compared to the model reported for F1 measurements of NURSE, the mixed linear
effects regression of F2 obviously has a different dependent variable, but since
there was an F2 measurement for every corresponding observation of F1, the independent variables (and their distribution within the dataset) are the same. Collinearity was therefore reduced in exactly the same way that was described at the
beginning of §6.2.1. Model selection based on AIC scores and F-tests comparing
nested models resulted in the minimal adequate model shown below (Table 6.11,
R^2-equivalent = 0.66).

Table 6.11: NURSE (F2): mixed linear effects regression

Fixed effects:	Estimate	Std. Error	df	t value	Pr(>|t|)	
(Intercept)	1.40	0.01	347.52	103.21	< 0.001	***
STYLElist	-0.01	0.01	1514.59	-1.33	0.18	
STYLEread	-0.03	0.01	1533.43	-5.22	< 0.001	***
STYLEfree	0.01	0.01	870.58	1.20	0.23	
AGE56-85	-0.03	0.01	1432.62	-5.14	< 0.001	***
AGE30-55	0.00	0.00	1447.88	0.38	0.70	
GENDERf	0.05	0.00	1516.12	18.82	< 0.001	***
CLASSmc	-0.06	0.00	1444.81	-18.59	< 0.001	***

DURATION	0.00	0.00	1506.54	3.16	< 0.01	**
PREMANNERaffr	0.07	0.02	71.47	3.44	< 0.001	***
PREMANNERfric	0.00	0.01	86.50	0.41	0.68	
PREMANNERgli	-0.07	0.01	62.72	-4.53	< 0.001	***
PREMANNERliq	-0.03	0.03	91.59	-1.07	0.29	
PREMANNERnas	0.01	0.02	159.94	0.57	0.57	
STYLElist:AGE56-85	-0.05	0.01	1425.23	-4.97	< 0.001	***
STYLEread:AGE56-85	-0.01	0.01	1419.97	-1.33	0.18	
STYLEfree:AGE56-85	-0.02	0.01	1493.50	-3.29	< 0.01	**
STYLElist:AGE30-55	0.02	0.01	1426.13	2.37	0.02	*
STYLEread:AGE30-55	0.02	0.01	1430.56	2.05	0.04	*
STYLEfree:AGE30-55	0.01	0.01	1493.35	2.63	0.01	**
STYLElist:CLASSmc	-0.02	0.01	1424.03	-3.49	< 0.001	***
STYLEread:CLASSmc	0.01	0.01	1425.34	0.99	0.32	
STYLEfree:CLASSmc	-0.01	0.00	1495.02	-2.31	0.02	*
AGE56-85:GENDERf	-0.02	0.00	1518.78	-5.49	< 0.001	***
AGE30-55:GENDERf	0.07	0.00	1512.01	22.03	< 0.001	***
AGE56-85:CLASSmc	-0.05	0.01	1431.94	-10.02	< 0.001	***
AGE30-55:CLASSmc	0.02	0.00	1449.85	4.97	< 0.001	***
GENDERf:CLASSmc	-0.02	0.00	1517.33	-8.76	< 0.001	***
STYLElist:AGE56-85:CLASSmc	0.04	0.01	1426.89	4.02	< 0.001	***
STYLEread:AGE56-85:CLASSmc	0.00	0.01	1419.93	0.52	0.61	
STYLEfree:AGE56-85:CLASSmc	-0.00	0.01	1481.98	-0.41	0.68	
STYLElist:AGE30-55:CLASSmc	-0.02	0.01	1427.41	-2.22	0.03	*
STYLEread:AGE30-55:CLASSmc	-0.01	0.01	1430.06	-1.78	0.08	.
STYLEfree:AGE30-55:CLASSmc	-0.01	0.01	1487.18	-1.03	0.30	

Random effects:	(number of obs: 1568, groups: WORD, 137)		
Groups	Name	Variance	Std.Dev.
WORD	(Intercept)	0.002	0.044
Residual		0.008	0.091

This model contains all the social factors as significant fixed effects which were already found to be signifiant predictors when modelling the F1 values of NURSE. The only exception to this is the three-way interaction of style, age, and gender which does not reach statistical significance in the regression of F2. Age, gender, and social class of participant, however, are all significant main effects. So is speaking style, which further acts as a predictor of F2 in two-way interactions with age and social class. Gender of speaker also interacts with social class and age each. Age, finally, furthermore appears both in a significant two-way interaction with social class and a three-way interaction of style, age group, and social class. In addition to the social categories, phonetic and phonological predictors are more important than they were for the height dimension of NURSE: both the preceding consonant and the duration of the observed vowel have a significant impact on F2 values of NURSE. It is these two factors which we will look at first.

6.2.2.2 Phonological context

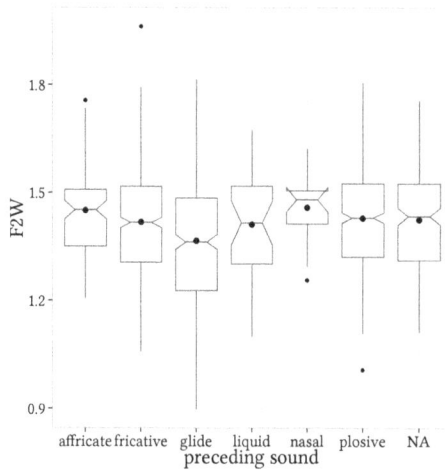

Figure 6.21: NURSE (F2) by preceding sound

The mixed linear effects regression found two levels of the factor (manner of) preceding consonant in particular to have a significant impact on F2 of NURSE. A positive correlation coefficient was calculated for cases where NURSE is preceded by an affricate (indicating that this phonological context favours fronter, more Scouse, realisations), whereas a negative coefficient (more central NURSE variants) was found for preceding glides. Realisations of NURSE that are preceded by a glide have, in fact, the lowest means in the raw data as Figure 6.21 shows. Measurements taken after an affricate have a mean that is higher than those of most other categories (with the exception of NURSE following a nasal). It is unclear why a preceding affricate should pull NURSE more to the front, but as has already been explained in §6.2.1, only a very small number of NURSE observations was made following an affricate anyway. This might mean that the result is somewhat shaky, but on the other hand it is striking that this phonological context pops up as significant again and again in this study.

Table 6.12: NURSE: durations by preceding consonant

affricate	fricative	liquid	nasal	plosive	glide
178.45	156.32	210.14	145.86	164.47	111.73

As far as F2 of NURSE is concerned, vowel durations, which are reported in Table 6.12, could give at least a hint about what might be going on, namely that the influence of the preceding sound is in fact confounded with duration. Some of the evidence is in conflict with this claim, but it is nonetheless striking that contexts where NURSE is preceded by an affricate have the second highest average duration in the sample, whereas NURSE is (by far) shortest when it follows a glide.

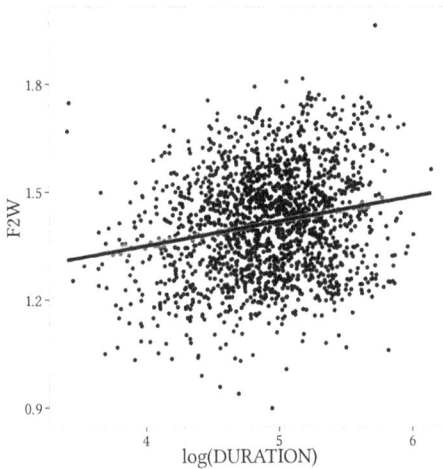

Figure 6.22: NURSE (F2) by duration

Figure 6.22 plots the log-transformed duration of NURSE on the x- and the F2 values on the y-axis. Just as with HAPPY, longer vowel duration favours more peripheral realisations. It is therefore possible that the effect found for different preceding consonants is really due to duration. A further hint in that direction is provided by a regression of F2 on manner of preceding consonant and duration of the vowel only, which expressed medium collinearity (κ = 10.48), a fact that indicates these two predictors are not completely orthogonal and explain, if only to a small degree, the same part of the variation in F2. At least to a certain extent, the phonological effect of the preceding consonant in this sample can thus be seen as an artefact of a phonetic one, and, for this reason, will not be discussed here any further.

6.2.2.3 Gender and class

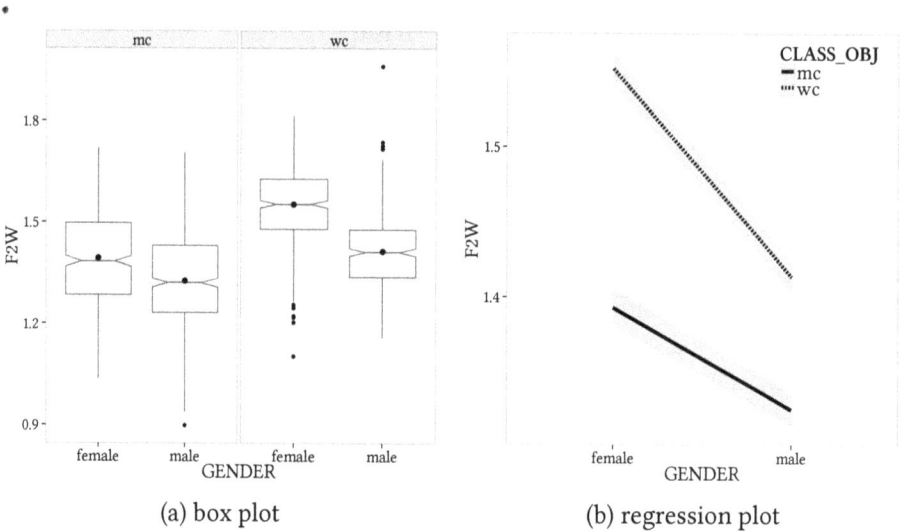

(a) box plot   (b) regression plot

Figure 6.23: NURSE (F2) by gender and class

The first interaction we will look at is that of gender and social class of participant, which is illustrated in Figure 6.23a and Figure 6.23b. The two box plots show the difference between the two genders in the middle and the working class, respectively. Male speakers have a lower mean F2 than women in both classes. This is a surprising result because lower F2 values mean more central realisations and more central variants of NURSE are *less* Scouse variants of NURSE. In most sociolinguistic studies, however, men have been found to be *more* likely than women to use local variants of socially meaningful variables. Judging from the plot, the difference between genders is already highly significant in the middle-class sample (left panel) because not only are the means of women and men clearly distinct, but they are also virtually identical to the medians of the same category (which argues for normally distributed data), and the confidence intervals do not occupy the same space at all. A t-test confirms this interpretation ($t(901.122) = 7.779$, $p < 0.001$). It is also obvious, however, that the difference between women and men is much more prounounced in the working class (right panel): (a) The distance between the means is considerably greater, and (b) even the interquartile ranges (visualised through the size and position of the boxes) hardly overlap, let alone the confidence intervals ($t(791.427) = 17.513$, $p < 0.001$).

The fact that gender has a more drastic effect in the working class than in the middle class is also illustrated by the regression plot in Figure 6.23b, where gender is to be found on the x-, and estimated F2 on the y-axis. A greater effect of gender should, in this graph, translate to a steeper slope of the regression line from "female" to "male", and this is precisely what we find when we compare the dotted (working class) to the solid (middle class) line. What we can also see is that middle-class speakers have lower F2 values than their working-class counterparts (the solid line is below the dotted one). This is not surprising because it means that middle-class speakers use less Scouse variants than working-class Liverpudlians, which is true for both female ($t(815.432) = -18.076$, $p < 0.001$) and male subjects ($t(933.018) = -11.305$, $p < 0.001$). Social classes are less distinct when we focus on male subjects only (the vertical distance between the regression lines is smaller), but it should be noted that this is a highly relative statement as the difference is statistically extremely robust for this sub-group of speakers, too. The significant interaction in the mixed-effects regression is thus not due to there being an effect in different directions in the sub-samples, but it is "merely" an expression of the fact that the effect of gender (class) is stronger for working-class (female) subjects.

6.2.2.4 Gender and age

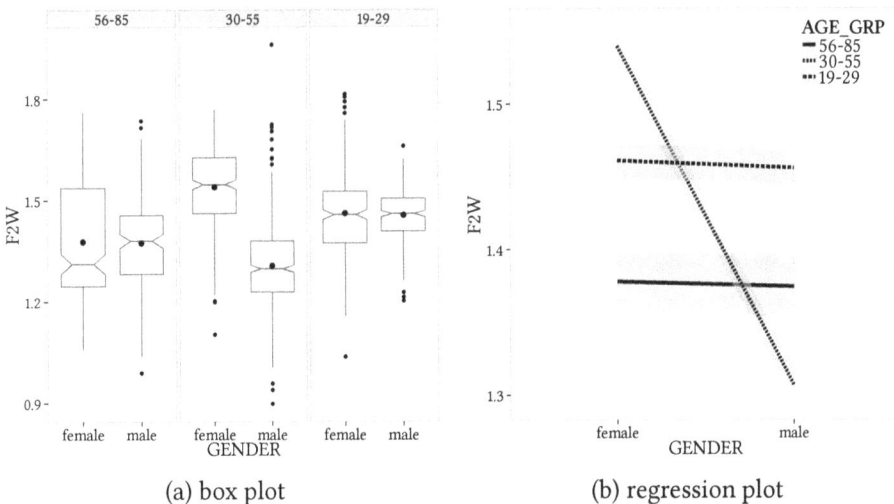

(a) box plot

(b) regression plot

Figure 6.24: NURSE (F2) by gender and age

In the interaction with age, on the other hand, the effect of gender is clearly not the same in the different sub-samples. If we focus on the gender difference in the oldest subjects (left panel in Figure 6.24a), the medians (and the notches that go with them) might suggest at first glance that male speakers have higher F2 than women, because the notches signal that the medians of the two groups are significantly different. The means, however, are virtually on the same level, because the female sub-sample is skewed towards the upper end of the scale (the arithmetic mean is considerably higher than the median due to comparatively extreme values between the second and third quartile). There is also quite a bit of variation in the female sub-sample (the box is almost twice as big as that of the old men). Indeed, a t-test reveals that NURSE productions of the oldest women and men in the sample are not significantly different from one another (t(405.995) = 0.254, p = 0.8). The same is true for the youngest speakers. Here, even the box plot does not suggest otherwise, because the data are more normally distributed for both genders (means and medians are very close to each other). The relevant t-test confirmed that, statistically speaking, NURSE is as front in the young women as it is in the young men (t(440.579) = 0.6, p = 0.549). In the middle-aged group, however, realisations are just as clearly distinct as they are identical for the other two age groups. Women aged between 30 and 55 use NURSE variants which are, on average, very noticeably fronter than those used by men of the same age group. The box plot shows that there is no overlap at all between the interquartile ranges, so the middle 50% of the data occupy completely separate areas on the scale for men and women. It is therefore not at all surprising that a t-test finds this difference to be highly significant (t(710.778) = 26.419, p < 0.001).

Table 6.13: NURSE (F2): t-tests of age by gender

test	women			men		
	t	df	p	t	df	p
old-middle	12.723	407.845	< 0.001	−6.203	308.955	< 0.001
middle-young	−7.794	567.234	< 0.001	20.528	760.911	< 0.001
young-old	6.378	419.726	< 0.001	7.804	260.802	< 0.001

In Figure 6.24b, the non-significance of gender in the oldest and the youngest speakers is expressed by the fact that both the solid and the dashed lines are essentially flat and parallel to the x-axis. The dotted line that stands for the middle-aged speakers, on the other hand, has a very pronounced negative slope, echoing that women in this group (surprisingly) use fronter NURSE variants than men. The other piece of information that can be extracted from this figure is that gender does not impact on which age groups are significantly different from one another. Both for female and male subjects regression lines are quite clearly separate and there is not even a hint of overlap for the grey standard error bands. Table 6.13 provides the data yielded by t-tests on the raw data, which found differences that were statistically robust for all combinations of age groups and within both genders, so this aspect is not influenced by gender. What *is* different for women and men is the positioning of age groups on the 'Scouseness scale': while for female speakers the middle group is the most Scouse, followed by the young and then by the old subjects, male middle-aged speakers have the most central NURSE variants, old speakers are in the middle, and the youngest men in the sample have the most advanced and therefore also the most Scouse realisations of NURSE.

6.2.2.5 Style and social class

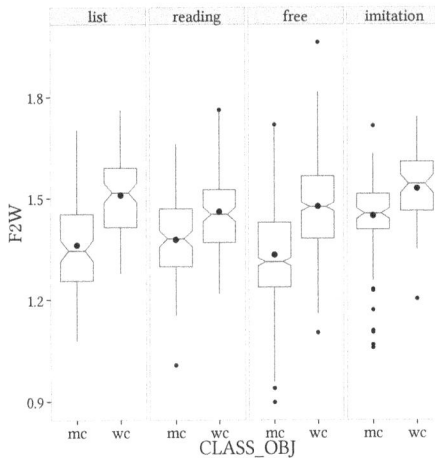

Figure 6.25: NURSE (F2) by style and social class

The interaction of style and social class is again one where we are looking at differences in degree more than in nature. If one examines the boxplots in Figure 6.25, which are sorted from most formal register (word list) on the left to least formal one (accent performance) on the right, it is clear that the pattern is pretty much the same in all of them. Boxes that visualise the data collected from middle-class interviewees (always the left one in each panel) are consistently lower than the corresponding ones for working-class speakers, which illustrates once again that working-class speakers have more Scouse NURSE variants than middle-class Liverpudlians (cf. Figure 6.23b). T-tests confirm for the means what the notches in the box plots do for the medians: the class difference is statistically significant for the word list (t(188.089) = -8.096, p < 0.001), the reading passage (t(255.085) =

-5.524, p < 0.001), spontaneous speech (t(1087.269) = -17.359, p < 0.001), and accent imitation (t(153.537) = -4.744, p < 0.001).

Table 6.14: NURSE (F2): t-tests of style by social class

test	middle class			working class		
	t	df	p	t	df	p
list-reading	−0.923	189.641	0.357	3.019	210.158	0.003
list-free	1.971	130.746	0.051	2.473	147.930	0.015
list-imitation	−4.894	192.492	< 0.001	−1.107	153.071	0.270
reading-free	3.870	209.460	< 0.001	−1.254	216.848	0.211
reading-imitation	−4.684	233.144	< 0.001	−4.039	157.841	< 0.001
free-imitation	−9.346	172.419	< 0.001	−3.684	101.284	< 0.001

Figure 6.25 also shows that while the class effect is generally the same for all styles, it is more pronounced in the reading list and free speech registers, than when people read out a text or put on a particularly strong Scouse accent. Both classes have the most Scouse realisations in the accent performance, but apart from that the order of styles is different (cf. Table 6.14 for tests of significance). For middle-class speakers 'imitation' is significantly more Scouse than "reading", which is in second place and followed by the word list (which does not differ significantly from "reading"). The most central (least Scouse) variants are found in spontaneous speech, which is very close to forming a statistically robust contrast with the word list. When we look at working-class subjects, the order from most Scouse to least Scouse is: "imitation", "list", "free", and "reading". The first and the last two of these four are not significantly different from each other, so that statistically speaking we have a more Scouse block 'imitation/list', and a less Scouse pair 'free/reading'. None of these orders corresponds to what would have been expected based on the traditional formality scale.

6.2.2.6 Age and social class

In addition to style, social class also interacts significantly with age group, but before we turn to this interaction we will first have a quick look at age as a main effect, where a very clear and simple picture emerges (Figure 6.26). F2 values increase significantly from the oldest to the middle-aged group (t(914.871) = 2.558, p = 0.011), and continue to rise from the middle to the youngest speakers (t(1347.58) = 7.955, p < 0.001). Middle-aged speakers have thus a fronter NURSE than the old-

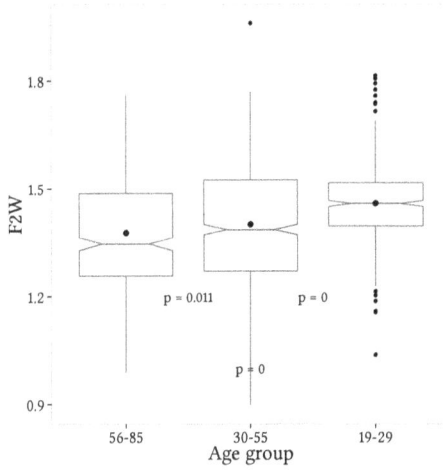

Figure 6.26: NURSE (F2) by age

est subjects in this sample, and speakers in the youngest group have, in turn, a significantly fronter vowel than Liverpudlians of their parents' generation. However, things are slightly more complicated, as an analysis of the age X social class interaction reveals.

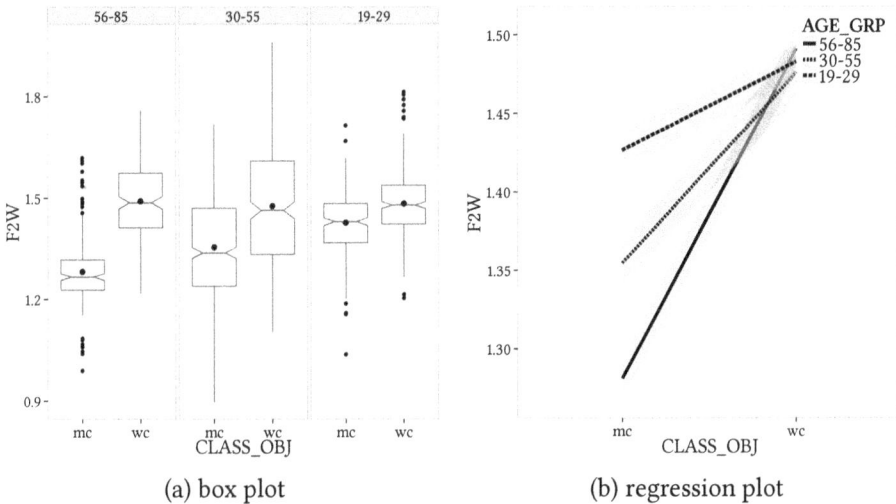

(a) box plot

(b) regression plot

Figure 6.27: NURSE (F2) by age and class

When we look at class differences in the three age groups separately, we arrive at the picture represented by the box plots in Figure 6.27a. In all three groups, the means of middle-class speakers are lower than that of the working-class interviewees. For the oldest speakers (left panel) the difference is particularly pronounced. Both means and medians are different in a statistically robust way: the interquartile ranges of the two boxes do not overlap, and a t-test also finds this difference to be significant (t(362.001) = -19.881, p < 0.001). In the middle group there is a greater amount of variation (both boxes are larger) and both means and medians are closer to each other. As a consequence, the interquartile ranges do overlap, but middle-class and working-class speakers do all the same differ in a highly significant way in this age group as well (t(615.171) = -10.466, p < 0.001). When the dataset is restricted to the youngest speakers the difference between social classes is further reduced. At the same time values are more homogeneous in this age group – visually represented by the vertical extent of the boxes, which is smaller than in the middle group and comparable to the one found for the oldest speakers. While less pronounced, the difference between middle and working-class speakers is therefore just as significant for the youngest subjects as it is in the other groups (t(521.157) = -6.815, p < 0.001).

Table 6.15: NURSE (F2): t-tests of age by social class

test	middle class			working class		
	t	df	p	t	df	p
old-middle	7.842	645.309	< 0.001	−1.189	482.408	0.235
middle-young	7.920	698.035	< 0.001	0.638	507.159	0.524
young-old	16.507	452.539	< 0.001	−0.784	349.296	0.434

Figure 6.27a also shows that it is due to the middle-class speakers that the social class difference decreases linearly from the oldest to the youngest speakers. Working-class realisations are, in fact, remarkably stable over the three generations investigated here. For middle-class speakers, on the other hand, NURSE variants become consistently fronter from the oldest to the youngest speakers. In Figure 6.27b, the decreasing distance between social classes is visible in the slopes of the regression lines, which become flatter from the old (solid) to the middle-aged (dotted) and young speakers (dashed). This graph also provides support for the other point made above. For middle-class speakers (on the left-hand side of Figure 6.27b), all three age groups are different from each other (cf. the three relevant t-tests in Table 6.15, which all yielded significant results). In the

working-class sub-sample, all regression lines occupy essentially the same place, and all standard deviations overlap (dark grey area). T-tests on the raw data (cf. again Table 6.15) also confirm the claim voiced above that age differences only exist in the working, but not the middle class.

6.2.2.7 Style shifting

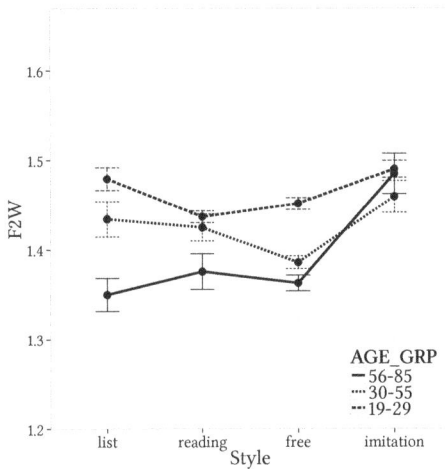

Figure 6.28: NURSE (F2) by style and age

The last combinations of predictors that can shed light on the (change in) salience of NURSE are the two-way interaction of style and age, and the three-way interaction of style, age, and social class. The relationship of style and age of participant is visualised in Figure 6.28. For the oldest group (solid line) there seems to be some movement from the word list to the reading passage to spontaneous speech, but in fact the standard error whiskers indicate that, statistically speaking, these three styles have identical NURSE realisations. Only the extreme rise when actively performing Scouse results in a mean that is significantly different from the other three registers. This sharp increase in F2 values from free speech to accent imitation is also present (and just as significant) in the middle-aged group. Spontaneous realisations in this age group are also significantly different from the "reading" register, but, interestingly, NURSE is *fronter* – more Scouse – in this more formal register. The same goes for the word list, a register which is not significantly different from reading for these subjects. F2 values in the middle age group thus strongly hint at hypercorrection (cf. §6.2.3). Speakers in the young group, finally, exhibit a pattern which is closest to what we would expect if we assume there to be style shifting: F2 increases from reading a text to free speech and from spontaneous speech to accent imitation; both these increases are (just about in the former case) statistically robust. The only thing that does not fit into this frame is that realisations when reading out the word list are actually just as front as when these speakers imitate a particularly strong Scouse accent (no significant difference). In the most formal register young speakers' behaviour is therefore opposite to what would be expected.

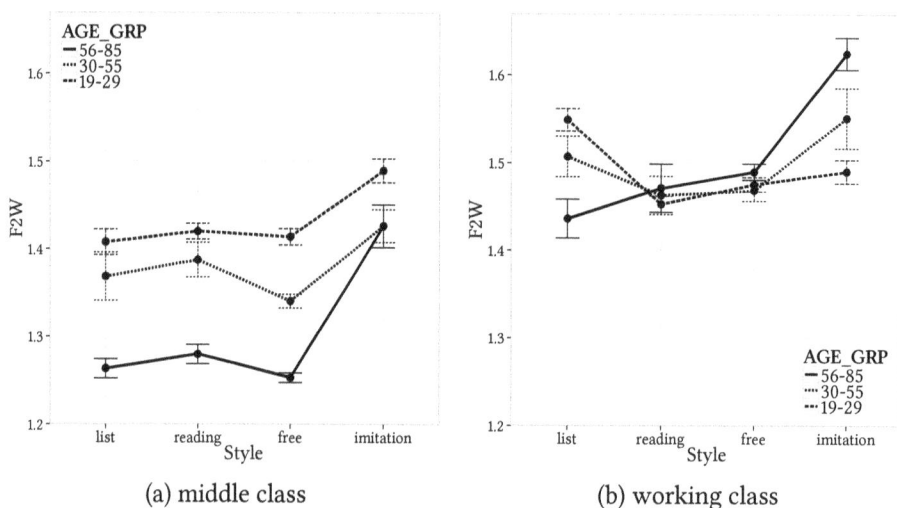

(a) middle class   (b) working class

Figure 6.29: NURSE (F2) by style, age, and social class

Since the mixed linear effects regression also found a three-way interaction of style, age, and social class of participant, we will end this section with an analysis of two figures that illustrate the interaction of style and age for middle-class (Figure 6.29a) and working-class subjects (Figure 6.29b), respectively. Class seems to play the least important role for the oldest interviewees in the sample. Middle-class speakers in this age group have an almost flat line for the first three registers: there *is* a slight but significant drop from "reading" to "free", but word list realisations are neither significantly different from those in the reading passage, nor from the variants that are found in spontaneous speech. Accent imitation is significantly (and drastically) fronter than the other three registers. The solid line in Figure 6.29b suggests a more steady increase of F2, but "list" is not significantly different from "reading", which in turn is not significantly different from "free" ("list" and "free", however, are) – statistically speaking, this line can be thought of as flat for the first three styles, just as in Figure 6.29a.

The dotted line (middle-aged subjects) in Figure 6.29a is very similar to the one found for the entire dataset in Figure 6.28. Word list and reading passage are not significantly different, F2 drops significantly in free speech, and rises significantly again in accent performance. Working-class speakers in this age group, on the other hand, have statistically identical NURSE variants in free speech and while reading a text. NURSE is again fronter when people imitate a strong Scouse accent, but the vowel is actually just as advanced in the word list, the register which was supposed to elicit more standard pronunciations.

For the youngest speakers in the sample the class distinction is most interesting. Middle-class speakers exhibit a statistically completely level line for the first three styles, followed by the same rise in F2 for 'imitation' as in the old and the middle-aged subjects. Working-class speakers, on the other hand, do not significantly distinguish free speech from accent performance. They do, however, have significantly more retracted variants when reading out a text (as compared to spontaneous pronunciations in connected speech). Furthermore, when reading out a word list young working-class speakers actually have more advanced (more Scouse) NURSE realisations than in any other register. The shifting found in Figure 6.28 for the youngest speakers thus seems to be a true combination of these two diametrically opposed patterns: The significant fronting of NURSE during accent performance is due to middle-class speakers, whereas their working-class counterparts contribute the fronting in the most formal word list style (and also drive the rise in F2 from "reading" to "free").

6.2.3 Synthesis and Pillai scores (NURSE)

6.2.3.1 Overview

Up until now, the analysis has exclusively focused on the realisation of NURSE, despite the fact that we are dealing with a vowel *merger* here. Since (near-standard) SQUARE is generally considered to be the target of this merger in Liverpool, said focus on NURSE does not seem unjustified, since it is mostly in the latter one that variation is to be expected. Nevertheless, the other member of the pair should not totally be neglected. After all, it could well be that both NURSE and SQUARE are, for example, fronted by a particular group of speakers. This *might* still make them sound more Scouse (because NURSE would be moving further away from the standard), but not necessarily so because it is primarily the merger of these two vowels that is considered a characteristic feature of the accent. While constraints of space do not permit a detailed analysis of SQUARE (such as the one provided for NURSE in §6.2.1 and §6.2.2), the remainder of this chapter will at least have a brief look at the realisational spaces of both NURSE *and* SQUARE in the different age groups, and it will also consider Pillai scores calculated on the basis of these distributions.

Table 6.16: NURSE-SQUARE: Pillai scores by age and style (groups)

style	old		middle		young	
	Pillai	p-value	Pillai	p-value	Pillai	p-value
word list	0.021	0.436	0.015	0.333	0.025	0.150
reading	0.026	0.315	0.017	0.208	0.034	0.051
free	0.073	< 0.001	0.050	< 0.001	0.025	0.007
imitation	0.016	0.533	0.007	0.727	0.014	0.398
total	0.046	< 0.001	0.031	< 0.001	0.013	0.004

Table 6.16 summarises the results of a number of MANOVAS, which were carried out in each age group and in each speaking style separately. The last line in this table (which reports the tests performed on all NURSE and SQUARE observations within the respective age group, pooled across style) tells us that NURSE and SQUARE distributions are (highly) significantly different in all three age groups investigated – all p-values are well below the 5% threshold. However, these values must be interpreted in connection with the Pillai scores that go with them, and which are just as homogeneous as the p-values: all of them are close to 0 (remember that Pillai scores can have values between 0 and 1), which indicates almost perfect overlap between the two (merged) vowel distributions. It is therefore more than likely that the low p-values are simply due to the large amount of data that are available when the observations are pooled across speaking styles, because in a sufficiently large dataset *any* difference will turn out to be statistically significant. We can therefore say that all three generations of speakers have completely merged NURSE and SQUARE distributions.

Judging from Table 6.16, style does not seem to make much of a difference either. It is true that some Pillai scores calculated for a particular register are almost twice (or, in the case of the youngest speakers, even thrice) as large as the total score in the last line, but even so all Pillai scores are (considerably) below 0.1, meaning they hardly differ from the total scores in absolute terms. This time, p-values support the idea that distributions are almost perfectly merged: With the exception of the ones pertaining to spontaneous speech (which accounts for the lion share of the data in each age group), no p-value is below the 5% threshold. All age groups seem to have merged vowel distributions in all four speaking styles for which data were collected.

6.2.3.2 Old speakers

It still does make sense to have a closer look at the individual distributions. Pillai scores allow statements about the degree of overlap between two distributions, but they say nothing about the exact shape, the location, or the centre of gravity of these distributions. Figure 6.30 represents the realisational spaces of NURSE and SQUARE in the different styles for the oldest speakers in the sample. Here and in Figure 6.31 and Figure 6.32 the vowel spaces that NURSE occurs in are marked

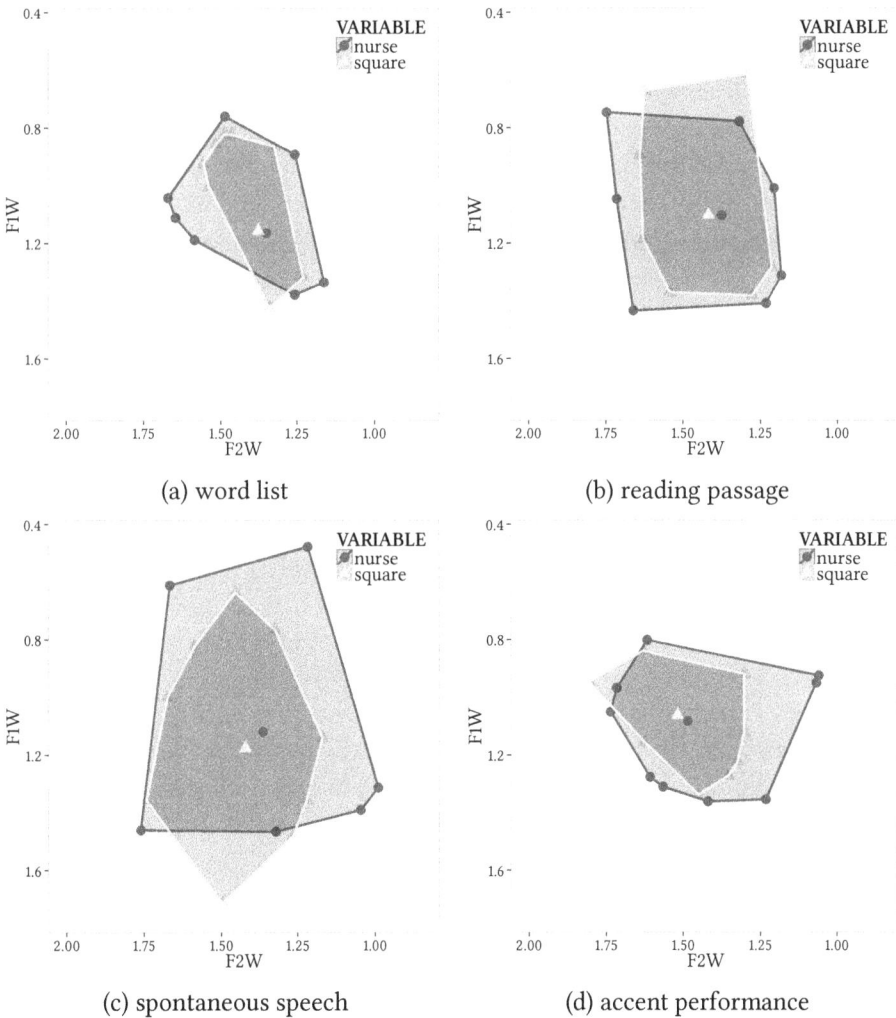

(a) word list

(b) reading passage

(c) spontaneous speech

(d) accent performance

Figure 6.30: NURSE-SQUARE: vowel space by style (old speakers)

by the dark, that of SQUARE by the light polygons. The mean realisations are represented by circles (NURSE) and triangles (SQUARE) of the respective shades.

Two aspects strike the observer when inspecting the realisational spaces of these two vowels in the old generation: (1) The range of variation (as represented by the surface area of the polygons) increases considerably from the word list to free speech, via accent imitation and the reading passage. (2) The vertical extent of the polygons is much larger than the horizontal one, which means variants of both NURSE and SQUARE are relatively stable in the front-back dimension. It is possible that the large degree of homogeneity that is found for the word list is primarily due to the smaller number of observations in this sub-sample; if more data are collected (like for the free speech style in this study) the chance of including the occasional "extreme" variant increases. It seems more likely, however, that subjects largely agree on which variants are appropriate for the more formal registers reading and word list (and, incidentally, also for the stereotype of Scouse!), but allow themselves to choose from a larger set of options in spontaneous speech. These options (in free speech and the other styles) seem to differ largely in F1, but a lot less so in F2. With the possible exception of Figure 6.30d vowel spaces are all larger in height than width, which indicates that the old speakers in my sample manipulate F1 quite considerably for these vowels, while producing all variants with a relatively stable F2.

When we look at the mean realisations of the two vowels (dark circle for NURSE, light triangle for SQUARE in the centre of the polygon) in this age group, we can, first of all, see that the distance between the centres of gravity is greatest in Figure 6.30c, which means that the higher Pillai score and lower p-value found for this sub-sample (cf. Table 6.16) is *not* only due to the larger number of observations in this style, after all. The distributions are indeed more distinct than in the other registers, if only slightly so. The relative positioning of mean vowel realisations is as would be expected: NURSE is both slightly higher and more central than SQUARE. Interestingly now, the mean of NURSE does not really move at all from spontaneous speech to the reading passage (Figure 6.30b). All the same, the average realisations of the two vowels actually become more similar (instead of more distinct, as would be expected for a more formal register), because SQUARE is both raised and centralised and thus approaches NURSE. For the word list (Figure 6.30a), both means are somewhat lowered and even closer to each other. This is, for NURSE at least, again contrary to expectations, since a move towards more standard realisations would involve raising rather than lowering. Only when we move from free speech to accent imitation (Figure 6.30c and Figure 6.30d), does the mean of NURSE change more drastically: it is considerably more front, and almost identical to SQUARE, which is fronted and raised as well.

6.2.3.3 Middle-aged speakers

When we turn to the data collected in the group of middle-aged speakers (Figure 6.31) and compare them to NURSE and SQUARE realisations of the old group, both similarities and differences emerge. For instance, NURSE is again always more variable than SQUARE, which is expected since SQUARE is supposed to be the steady target of the merger. Just as in the old group, there is also clearly

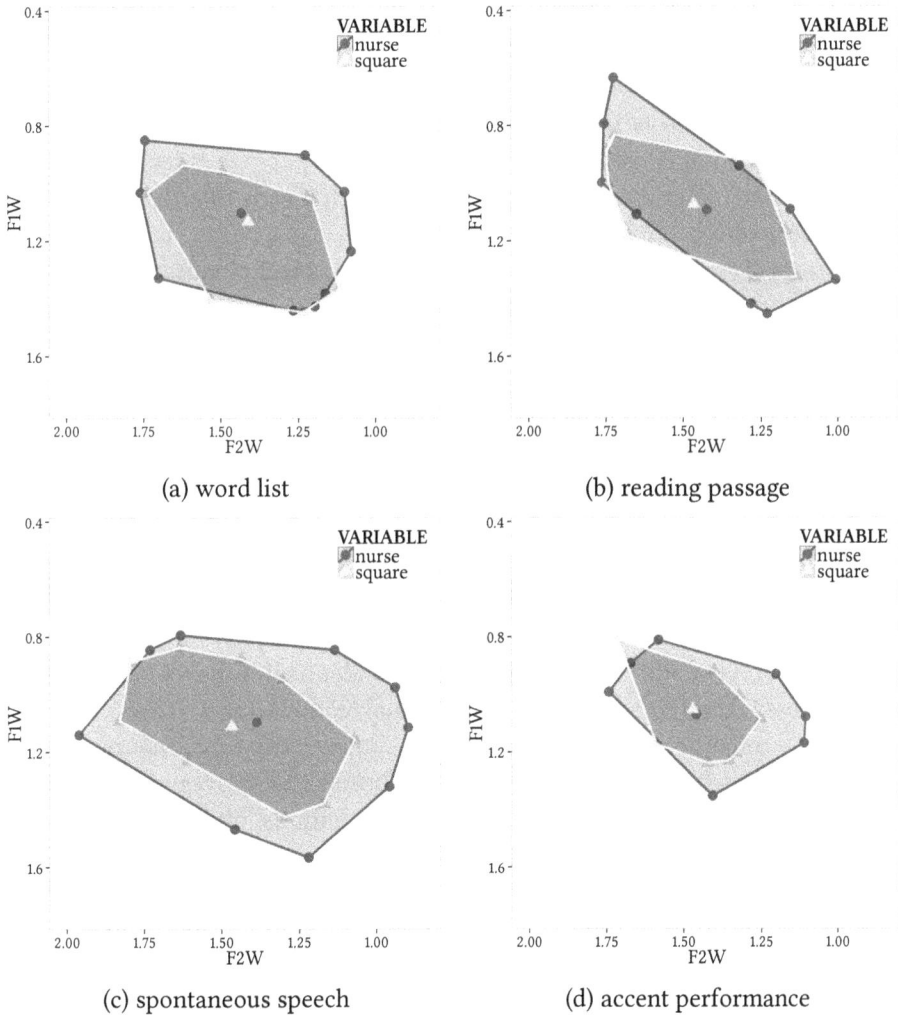

(a) word list

(b) reading passage

(c) spontaneous speech

(d) accent performance

Figure 6.31: NURSE-SQUARE: vowel space by style (middle-aged speakers)

more variation (for both vowels) in spontaneous speech than in the other speaking styles. But in contrast to the older generation, the lowest degree of variation is found for accent imitation, while the word list and reading passage seem to be roughly comparable in this respect. However, it should be noted that the realisational spaces – particularly when comparing the word list, reading, and accent performance – differ less in area in the middle-aged group, generally, which is to say that the range of variation depends less on style than in the old group. All the same, it looks as if, again, the target realisations for the more formal and the stereotype contexts are clearer, or less controversial, than in spontaneous speech, where a wider range of phonetic variants is encountered. The most pronounced difference between the old and the middle-aged speakers is that in the former most variation is found in the height dimension, whereas in the latter group the horizontal extent of the individual vowel spaces is at least as great as, and frequently greater than, the vertical one, which means that the main axis of variation seems to be F2 in this age group.

With respect to the centres of gravity of these vowel clouds, there is something going on that is even more interesting than the pattern found for the older speakers. In spontaneous speech (Figure 6.31c), the relative positioning of NURSE and SQUARE is identical to the one found for the older speakers: NURSE is both slightly higher and backer than SQUARE, which corresponds to the setup expected on the basis of the standard if the vowels are not perfectly merged yet. The means of the two distributions are also further apart from each other than in the other styles, although the difference is smaller than in the old speakers. If this register is once again taken as the benchmark, or baseline, both NURSE and SQUARE change when people are asked to put on a particularly strong Scouse accent (Figure 6.31d): The former is fronted, the latter slightly raised. As a result, mean realisations of both vowels are essentially identical. When we go the other way from less formal free speech to more formal reading (Figure 6.31b), however, mean NURSE remains almost the same, if one ignores the tiny amount of fronting that is visible. In this register it is mostly SQUARE that moves: raising takes it closer to NURSE. This results in more *merged* distributions (cf. Table 6.16), instead of the more *distinct* ones that would normally be expected in a more formal speaking style. When subjects read out a word list (Figure 6.31a) SQUARE is centralised, while NURSE is fronted at the same time. The outcome of these processes is that NURSE (dark circle) actually ends up in a position that is *more front* than that of SQUARE (light triangle), thereby completely reversing the relative positioning found in spontaneous speech, at least with respect to the F2 dimension.

6.2.3.4 Young speakers

Figure 6.32 visualises the realisational spaces of NURSE and SQUARE for Liverpudlians aged between 19 and 29. These four sub-plots look clearly different from the corresponding ones in Figure 6.30 and Figure 6.31 because the areas of all polygons are considerably smaller. Smaller areas in the figure translate to a smaller range of phonetic variants that occur in this age group. The youngest speakers in my sample can therefore be said to be markedly more homogeneous in their

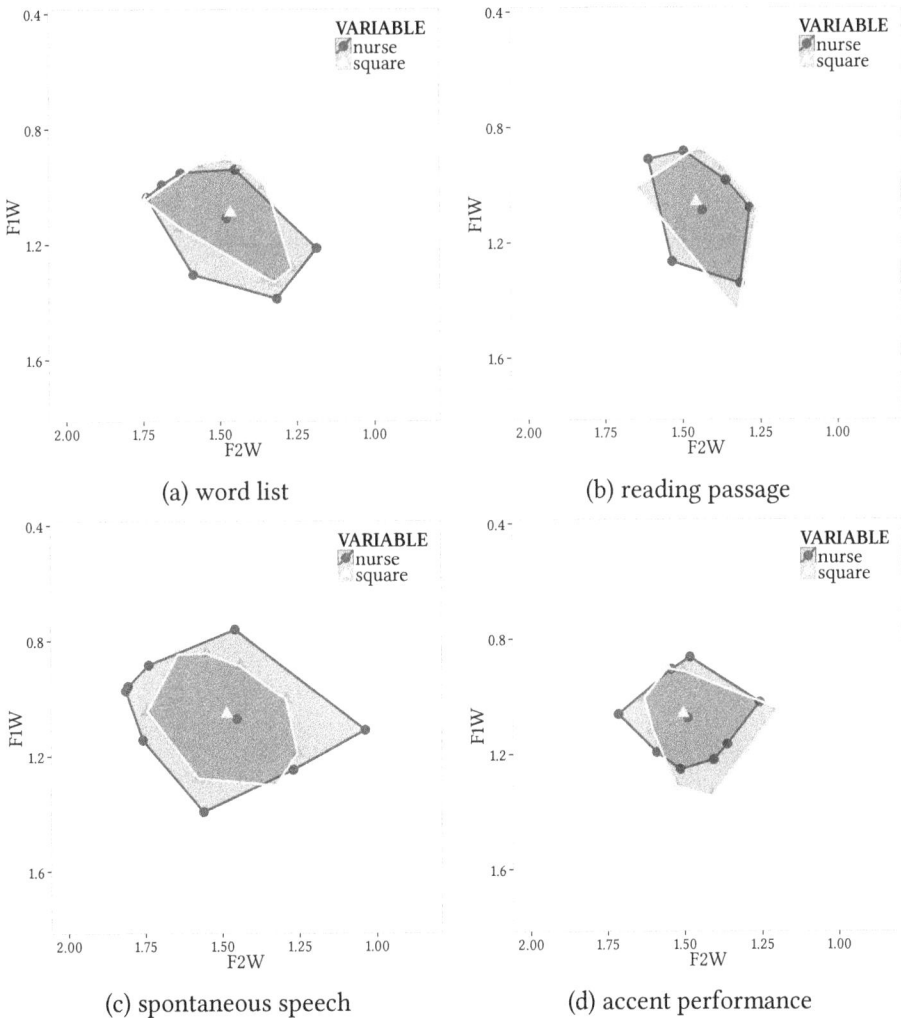

(a) word list

(b) reading passage

(c) spontaneous speech

(d) accent performance

Figure 6.32: NURSE-SQUARE: vowel space by style (young speakers)

NURSE and SQUARE productions than speakers of their parents' or grandparents' generation. Style seems to play a much less important role in this respect than it did for the other two age groups. While it is true that there is more variation in free speech (Figure 6.32c) than in the other three registers, the difference is much less pronounced than for the middle-aged and the older speakers. The plots for the word list, the reading passage, and accent imitation, in turn, do not seem to differ at all in terms of polygon area. The youngest subjects thus seem to be much more agreed on target pronunciations in *all* styles, in contrast to the old and the middle-aged speakers, who show different levels of variation in different registers. Another difference with the young speakers is that, interestingly, NURSE is only considerably more variable than SQUARE in spontaneous speech, but not in the other three styles, where the realisational spaces of both vowels have roughly equal size. Both NURSE and SQUARE seem to have about the same level of stability.

Younger Scousers also set themselves apart when it comes to the mean values of these two variables. In spontaneous speech (Figure 6.32c), mean NURSE and SQUARE are closer together than in both the middle-aged and the old group, with NURSE being just a little bit more central than SQUARE and about the same height. During accent performance (Figure 6.32d), SQUARE essentially remains in the same location, while NURSE moves forward, but only a tiny little fraction (which is not surprising, given that it is already very front in free speech). Going from spontaneous speech to reading out a text (Figure 6.32b) neither NURSE nor SQUARE change very much, although the latter *is* slightly more central. When my youngest subjects read out a word list (Figure 6.32a) SQUARE is virtually identical (to its realisation while reading), but NURSE is marginally more front and lower to the same degree. In summary, one can say that the youngest speakers in my sample do not only show less variation *within* a particular speech style, but they also show next to no change *between* styles.

6.2.3.5 Age means and individual differences

Having investigated style differences within the age groups on the previous pages, it is now time to take a step back again and briefly focus on the overall effect of age on the realisations of NURSE and SQUARE. Figure 6.33 shows the mean realisations of both vowels for all three age groups. The means plotted in Figure 6.33 summarise across the style dimension (i.e. one grand mean was calculated per age group), but of course these means are biased towards spontaneous speech realisations as they account for the large majority of observations.

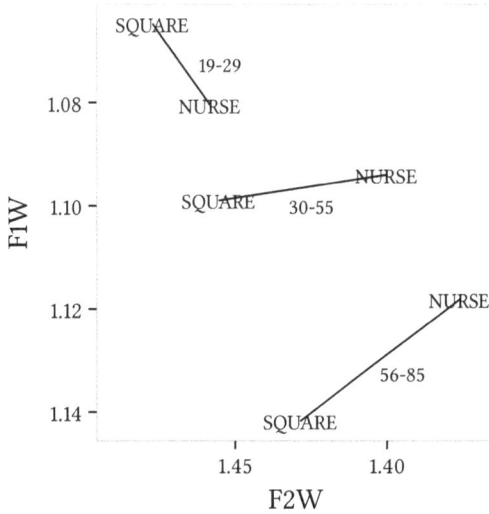

Figure 6.33: NURSE-SQUARE: mean vowel position by age

This graph essentially tells us three things: (1) In all three age groups, NURSE is (still) more central – to the right in the graph – than SQUARE. (2) The means for the old speakers are to be found in the lower right corner, the ones for the middle-aged speakers in the middle, and the averages for the young group lie in the upper left corner, which means that both NURSE and SQUARE simultaneously become fronter and higher from the oldest to the youngest speakers in my sample. While it has to be said that these differences are subtle (note the scale of the graph), they have been shown to be statistically robust in §6.2.1 and §6.2.2. (3) The decreasing distance between NURSE and SQUARE from the oldest to the youngest subjects signals that the merger becomes progressively more complete in my sample.

While a detailed analysis of individuals is beyond the scope of this study, it is important to note that all figures and tests in this section which generalise across age groups often mask considerable differences between the members of these groups. This is obvious from Figure 6.34, which plots Pillai scores of individual speakers (across all styles) on the y-, and their age on the x-axis (age groups delimited by vertical lines). The third variable represented in this graph is social class of the speaker, because it was found to be part of significant three-way interactions with style and age in §6.2.1 and §6.2.2: Pillai scores of middle-class speakers appear as black circles, those of working-class subjects as light grey ones.

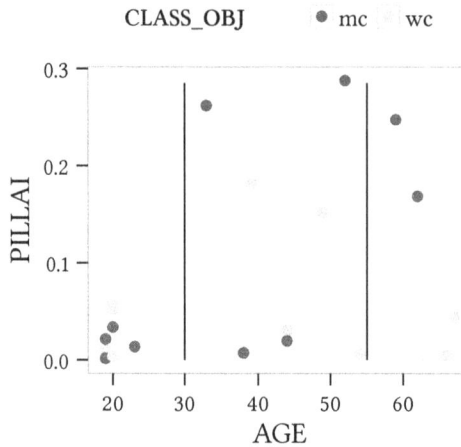

Figure 6.34: NURSE: Pillai scores by age and social class (individuals)

This setup serves to illustrate an interesting relationship between Pillai scores, age, and class. Towards the right-hand side of Figure 6.34 one can see that old working-class speakers have much lower Pillai scores than middle-class subjects of the same age, which is not surprising, given that having the merger (and thus a low Pillai score) is a non-standard feature. However, in the middle-aged group this distinction has already become a lot more fuzzy: one half of the participants in this sub-sample has Pillai scores near 0, the other half produces scores that are considerably higher (while still comparatively low in absolute terms). Crucially, these scores no longer correlate with class, because both the merged and the distinct sub-group include both middle *and* working-class speakers. In the youngest group, finally, there are only merged speakers, and social class is therefore no longer a relevant factor. Only this last age group therefore really acts like a group. The middle-aged and the old group, in contrast, are characterised by a considerable degree of individual and class-related differences between subjects.

7 Consonant production

For the two consonantal variables, the 20 participants of the primary sample provided 7569 data points (3053 for /ŋ(g)/, 4516 for /k/).[1] Once more, by far the biggest share of the data stems from free speech (n = 5733), followed by the reading passage (n = 806), accent performance (n = 640), and finally the word list (n = 390). Table 7.1 provides an overview of how the measurements are distributed across gender, age, and social class. On the whole, the sample appears to be relatively balanced, although there are a couple of "outliers" (cf. also Table 6.1). The number of /k/ observations among young working-class speakers is a particularly notable one: part of the explanation why the count of observed /k/ realisations is so high in this age group can be found in §7.2.5.

Table 7.1: Consonant observations by age, gender, and social class

		old		middle		young	
		f	m	f	m	f	m
/ŋ(g)/	mc	262	140	224	436	234	230
	wc	123	221	355	152	317	359
/k/	mc	210	129	334	542	298	430
	wc	177	267	619	224	681	605

Just as in Chapter 6, dots mark the mean values of each group in all box plots that will follow. The p-values in these graphs (if present) are the result of t-tests comparing (from left to right) the old to the middle group, the old to the young, and the middle to the young group, respectively. All plots are arranged in a way so that higher values (on the y-axis) indicate more Scouse variants.[2]

---

[1] A preliminary analysis based on a subset of the results discussed in this chapter was published as Juskan 2015.

[2] There are two exceptions to this rule (Figure 7.1 and Figure 7.6), which are flipped by 90 degrees for better visualisation and where more Scouse variants are found on the right, and more standard realisations on the left of the figure.

7.1 /ŋ(g)/

7.1.1 Overview

After [ɪn]-realisations (which are only possible for *ing*-forms) – but not [ŋ] or [ŋg] realisations in *ing*-forms – had been removed from the data set, a mixed linear effects model was fit to the remaining 1370 tokens (cf. §5.6 for the set of predictors). This maximal model exhibited a degree of collinearity which called for closer inspection (κ = 16.12). As it turned out, a lot of this collinearity was actually due to interactions and could therefore safely be ignored; a model which did not include the two three-way interactions of style and age with gender and social class, respectively, contained only an acceptable amount of collinearity (κ = 9.86). These three-way interactions were therefore re-entered as predictors before this maximal model was reduced based on AIC scores and F-tests comparing nested models. The resulting minimal adequate model (R^2-equivalent = 0.298) is represented in Table 7.2.

Style, age group and gender of participant are all found to be significant main effects. Social class fails to reach significance on its own, but it is present in a significant interaction with age. The second interaction that is retained in the model is that of style and gender of participant. Frequency of the carrier word was eliminated as non-significant from the model, but the other non-social predictor, phonological environment, was found to have a statistically robust impact on PDF of /ŋ(g)/.

7.1.2 Phonological context

Figure 7.1 is a box plot that visualises PDF of /ŋ(g)/ for the different phonological contexts separately. "NA" refers to instances of /ŋ(g)/ that occurred in words for which no phonemic transcription was available – mostly proper names – and which were therefore not coded for phonological environment. These (67) cases will not be discussed here any further. The remaining contexts seem to fall into three groups (cf. Table 7.3 for the exact means): (1) Comparatively high PDF (word-final, intervocalic, followed by liquids), (2) medium PDF (intervocalic across word-boundary, followed by voiceless fricatives), and (3) low PDF (followed by stops, voiced fricatives, and glides). The last group has mean PDF values that are close to 0. The box plot visualises that the median (thick vertical bar) is often 0 as well in these contexts (cf., for instance, "V_#affricate" or "V_#glide"), which means that at least 50% of observations in this category have a PDF of 0, i.e. they are realised by a (standard) [ŋ]. For phonological environments such as

Table 7.2: /ŋ(g)/: mixed linear effects regression

Fixed effects:	Estimate	Std. Error	df	t value	Pr(>|t|)	
(Intercept)	6.69	0.81	182.72	8.29	< 0.001	***
STYLElist	-0.31	0.83	335.30	-0.37	0.71	
STYLEread	1.29	0.61	938.39	2.13	0.03	*
STYLEfree	-1.43	0.62	271.83	-2.35	0.02	*
AGE56-85	-1.63	0.46	1345.23	-3.40	< 0.001	***
AGE30-55	2.30	0.40	1336.20	5.75	< 0.001	***
GENDERf	1.52	0.34	1286.05	4.54	< 0.001	***
CLASSmc	0.34	0.30	1338.34	1.17	0.24	
ENVIRV_V	4.22	1.19	94.01	3.59	< 0.001	***
ENVIRV_#V	1.48	0.84	1104.88	1.77	0.08	.
ENVIRV_#gli	-0.95	1.20	1335.59	-0.79	0.43	
ENVIRV_#	9.33	0.82	1071.55	11.31	< 0.001	***
ENVIRV_#liq	5.75	2.05	1341.73	2.81	0.01	**
ENVIRV_#nasal]	-7.98	2.86	1345.80	-2.78	0.01	**
ENVIRV_#vdfric	-5.61	1.36	1342.96	-4.13	< 0.001	***
ENVIRV_#vlfric	-0.54	1.16	836.32	-0.46	0.65	
ENVIRV_#vdplos	-3.48	1.62	1218.21	-2.15	0.03	*
ENVIRV_#vlplos	-3.37	1.17	1125.44	-2.88	< 0.01	**
STYLElist:GENDERf	-2.27	0.62	1260.35	-3.66	< 0.001	***
STYLEread:GENDERf	1.39	0.53	1267.53	2.61	0.01	**
STYLEfree:GENDERf	-0.34	0.44	1337.26	-0.78	0.44	
AGE56-85:CLASSmc	-2.08	0.46	1348.34	-4.39	< 0.001	***
AGE30-55:CLASSmc	2.26	0.41	1348.25	5.46	< 0.001	***

Random effects:	(number of obs: 1370, groups: WORD, 164)		
Groups	Name	Variance	Std.Dev.
WORD	(Intercept)	8.727	2.954
Residual		100.553	10.028

"V_#nasal" or "V_#vdfricative" no box (in the everyday sense) is generated at all, because the first, second, *and* the third quantile are 0 – the realisation as [ŋ] thus accounts for 75+% of cases in these categories.

It should be noted, however, that almost *all* environments have a median PDF of 0. The only exceptions are cases where velar nasal plus occurs intervocalically within a word or in phrase final position ("V_#"), i.e. when the variable is followed by silence. In these environments, some sort of plosive was observed in more than 75% of cases (the first quantile is greater than 0 for both categories). This clearly sets them apart from the remaining contexts, because in the former velar nasal plus seems to be the norm (at least in my sample), whereas in the latter it is an option, but not – statistically speaking – the default one. Having

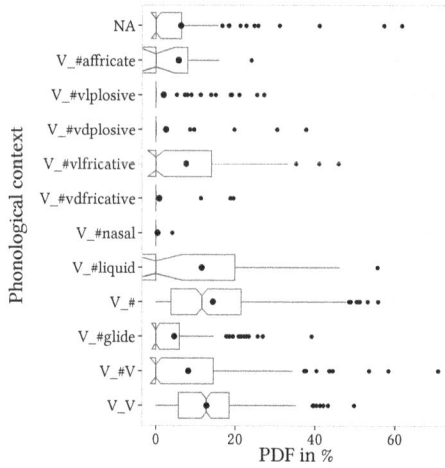

Figure 7.1: /ŋ(g)/: PDF by phonological environment (without [ɪn] real-isations)

Table 7.3: /ŋ(g)/: PDF means by phonological environment ([ɪn] ex-cluded)

environment	mean PDF	n
V_V	12.79	288
V_#V	8.19	284
V_#glide	4.62	85
V_#	14.37	360
V_#liquid	11.57	22
V_#nasal	0.38	11
V_#voiced fricative	0.84	59
V_#voiceless fricative	7.62	116
V_#voiced plosive	2.53	42
V_#voiceless plosive	1.93	100
V_#affricate	5.71	7

said that, two caveats need to be mentioned. Firstly, the amount of data that are available for each context varies greatly (cf. Table 7.3): while there is a rather sound basis for "V_V", "V_#V", and "V_#", only 11 (7) observations in the sample, for instance, represent contexts where velar nasal plus is followed by a nasal (affricate). Secondly, only the two environments 'intervocalic' (within a word) and 'word-final' (pre-pausal) occur in the word list. It is therefore possible that the high mean PDF values for these environments are at least in part due to their occurrence in the most formal speech style (the relationship between velar nasal plus and careful speech is addressed below).

This fact would constitute a problem if the present study was primarily concerned with identifying and describing the influence (on the realisation of /ŋ(g)/) of different phonological contexts. The focus, however, is on the social predictors on the one hand, and style on the other. Additionally, the intervocalic (within word) and word-final contexts are rather prominent in the sample *generally*. Together with intervocalic (across a word-boundary), an environment that is just as frequent as intervocalic (within word) and which also has a comparatively high mean PDF, these two contexts already account for 68.03% of the /ŋ(g)/ observations ([ɪn] realisations excluded). Crucially, 'V_V' and 'V_#' occur in *all* styles investigated and in roughly equal proportions (with the notable exception of the word list, as explained above). Thus, they dominate the sample by their sheer numbers, but they do not distort it by biasing it towards a particular (formal) register. It is, however, possible that PDF values calculated for the word list are higher than they would be if velar nasal plus had been elicited in more contexts in addition to the two 'plosive-favouring' ones.

7.1.3 Style and gender

Let us move on to the first interaction of social factors. In Figure 7.2 we see box plots for gender of participant, divided by speaking register. One piece of information that we can extract from this graph is that both female and male subjects use the standard [ŋ] at least 50% of the time in spontaneous speech (both medians – represented by thick horizontal bars – in the second panel from the right are 0). A t-test confirms that the difference between genders in this register is not significant ($t(683.561) = 1.06$, $p = 0.289$). The same holds true for velar nasal plus realisations observed for the word list: women and men do not differ in a statistically robust way ($t(149.982) = -1.145$, $p = 0.254$). However, mean PDF is considerably higher than in spontaneous speech. The first quantiles are to be found at just about over 10% PDF for both genders, which means that in more than 75% of tokens in this speech style a plosive was present. Additionally, subjects probably

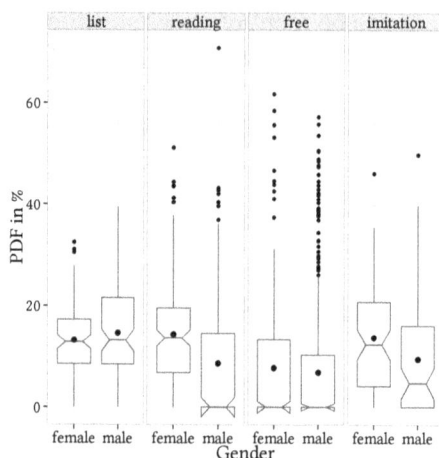

Figure 7.2: /ŋ(g)/: PDF by style and gender (without [ɪn] realisations)

used variants containing phonetically more prominent plosives (with a higher proportion of frication), which would also raise the mean. In the two remaining styles 'reading' (t(284.859) = 4.212, p < 0.001) and 'imitation' (t(140.233) = 2.228, p = 0.028), the gender difference is significant. This is due to the fact that the means of men in both registers are lower than those of women (who have comparable means for the word list, the reading passage, and accent performance).

The t-tests summarised in Table 7.4 confirm that, for female speakers, spontaneous speech is the only style that is significantly different from the other three, which have identical (and rather high) means from a statistical point of view. When we look at the male subjects, we find that 'reading', 'free', and 'imitation'

Table 7.4: /ŋ(g)/: t-tests of style by gender

test	women			men		
	t	df	p	t	df	p
list-reading	−1.039	251.857	0.300	4.060	213.270	< 0.001
list-free	5.774	283.250	< 0.001	6.569	134.510	< 0.001
list-imitation	−0.350	117.131	0.727	2.908	134.609	0.004
reading-free	6.044	321.775	< 0.001	1.502	224.352	0.135
reading-imitation	0.432	148.046	0.667	−0.482	144.108	0.630
free-imitation	−4.227	117.679	< 0.001	−1.710	90.826	0.091

are all statistically identical, 'list' is the only one that is significantly different (cf. again Table 7.4 for the details of the relevant t-tests). The interaction of gender and style can thus be summarised as follows: (1) Women have similar (relatively high) levels of velar nasal plus when reading out a word list, a text passage, or when performing a strong Scouse accent, and only reduce their usage of this feature a bit in free speech. (2) Men have comparatively low mean PDFs in accent imitation, spontaneous speech, and the reading passage; only in the word list does the use of velar nasal plus increase significantly. (3) As a result, women have a higher overall mean PDF for velar nasal plus, and can be said to favour the local, non-standard realisation [ŋg] more than men do.

7.1.4 Age and social class

Before the second interaction retained in the mixed-effects model (age X social class) is analysed further, we will have a brief look at age of participant as a main effect (Figure 7.3). The relatively high number of outliers in all groups shows that at least occasionally all speakers use variants of /ŋ(g)/ that contain a (prominent) plosive and are thus clearly Scouse. The overall rather low figures (the upper boundaries of all boxes are below 20%) are not really surprising, given the fact that even if a plosive is realised it is preceded by a nasal, so the aspiration phase will almost always be comparatively short in relation to the total duration. It is furthermore obvious that things are not the way we expected. The oldest speak-

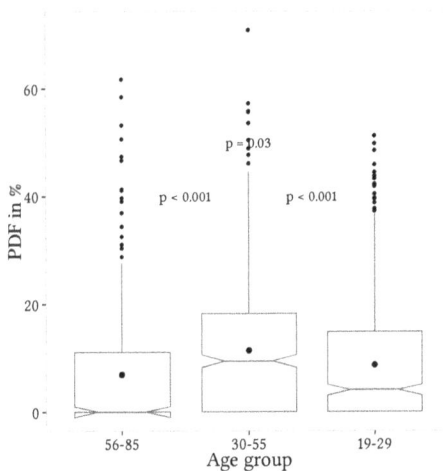

Figure 7.3: /ŋ(g)/: PDF by age ([m] excluded)

ers are the least Scouse with respect to velar nasal plus. Their average PDF is only 6.9%, while that of the middle group is, at 11.35%, almost twice as high. Furthermore, the median in the former group (again symbolised by the thick horizontal bar) is 0, so 50+% of all their /ŋ(g)/ realisations consist of a nasal only. For the middle-aged speakers, on the other hand, the median is found at a PDF of around 10% and only the first quantile is 0, so somewhere between 50 and 75% of tokens have a plosive. The increase in PDF from the oldest to the middle-aged speakers is highly significant (t(663.417) = 5.437, p < 0.001). From the middle to the young group, however, there is actually a *decrease* in PDF to 8.66%. This means that younger Liverpudlians are not getting "more Scouse" with respect to velar nasal plus, but rather they seem to be reversing the trend begun by the middle group of speakers, although not to the extent that their realisations are identical to those of their grandparents' generation. Rather, they occupy the middle ground, since both their mean and median are higher than in the older and lower than in the middle group. The youngest speakers in the sample use velar nasal plus in a significantly different way from both the old (t(630.154) = 2.178, p = 0.03), *and* the middle-aged group (t(1130.999) = -3.881, p < 0.001).

As briefly mentioned above, age is not only a significant main effect, but also enters into a significant interaction with social class of the speaker. This relationship is visualised in Figure 7.4a and Figure 7.4b. While the box plots in the three separate panels might look rather similar at first glance, they actually tell an in-

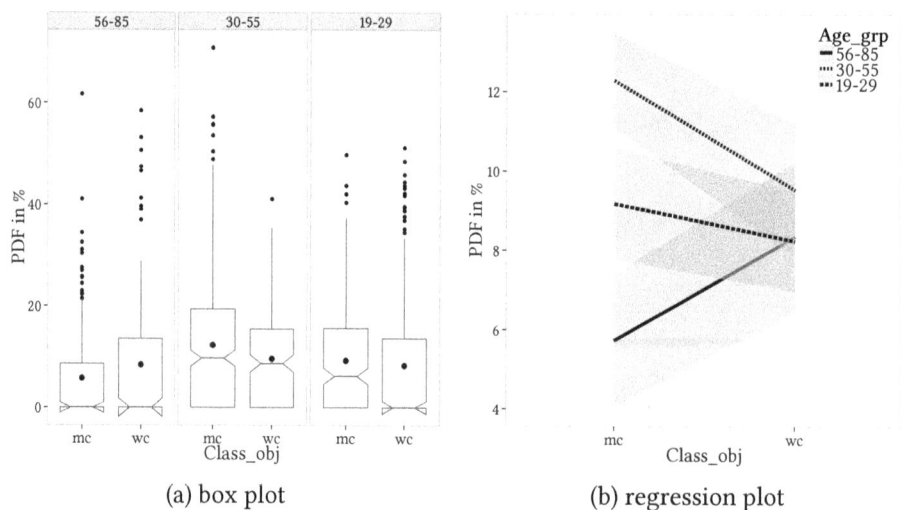

(a) box plot

(b) regression plot

Figure 7.4: /ŋ(g)/: PDF by age and class ([ɪn] excluded)

teresting story. For the oldest speakers (leftmost panel) we get the picture that we would usually expect to see for a non-standard feature: middle-class speakers have a lower PDF than working-class subjects of the same age group, i.e. the realisations of the former are less Scouse than those of the latter. Both medians are 0 (echoing that older speakers have a low PDF generally), but the means in the two classes are nonetheless significantly different (t(251.286) = -1.978, p = 0.049). When we look at Liverpudlians aged between 30 and 55, social class also seems to matter, but now it is actually the working-class speakers who use less Scouse variants than their middle-class counterparts. Despite the fact that the medians are once more statistically identical (cf. the overlapping notches), the difference between the means is now even more statistically robust (t(540.809) = 2.916, p = 0.004) – a fact which could, however, simply be due to the lower number of observations in the old group. In the youngest speakers (panel on the right), finally, the class distinction for this feature has disappeared. Even though the medians clearly are significantly different from one another (consider not only their vertical distance, but also the fact that the notches do not overlap at all), the means are not (t(515.045) = 0.975, p = 0.33).

If we approach the interaction of age and class from the other end, Figure 7.4b tells us that the age dimension is not equally important in both social classes. On the left-hand side of the graph, the estimated PDFs for middle-class speakers are plotted separately for the three age groups. All three regression lines are distinct from each other. Their error bands do not overlap, and the groups can be neatly ordered: old speakers (solid line) have a low PDF, middle-aged ones (dotted) have a high one, and the youngest speakers (dashed) are somewhere in between (cf. Figure 7.3). The differences between all three groups are statistically robust, as the relevant t-tests (cf. Table 7.5) confirm. When we move from the middle class to the working class, however, all three regression lines converge, roughly towards the value of the youngest middle-class speakers. The small differences that seem

Table 7.5: /ŋ(g)/: t-tests of age by social class

test	middle class			working class		
	t	df	p	t	df	p
old-middle	6.454	430.623	< 0.001	0.922	231.023	0.357
middle-young	−3.159	573.452	0.002	−1.406	480.721	0.160
young-old	3.319	386.920	< 0.001	−0.095	235.400	0.924

to remain between the estimates of the working-class speakers are not statistically relevant: t-tests reveal that none of the age groups is significantly different
from any of the other two when only working-class subjects are considered. It
follows that the change in the overall usage of velar nasal plus that was found for
the pooled results is not only driven by, but actually restricted to middle-class
Liverpudlians; working-class Scousers do not seem to have changed at all.

7.1.5 Style shifting

The last predictor we will look at is again the style dimension (Figure 7.5), where
we find something interesting going on. Not only is there a very clear pattern,
but this pattern is essentially identical for all three speaker groups investigated,
which is the reason why the mixed linear effects regression did not find a significant interaction of style and age. The pattern we see is not prototypical Labovian
style shifting, however. If it were, use of the local variant of /ŋ(g)/ would decrease
in more formal contexts like reading a text or a word list. Instead, the data show
that velar nasal plus is more *common* in those formal contexts. Both the oldest
and the youngest speakers in the sample have means in spontaneous speech, the
reading passage, and the word list which are all significantly different from one
another (cf. the standard error whiskers, which do not overlap between the styles

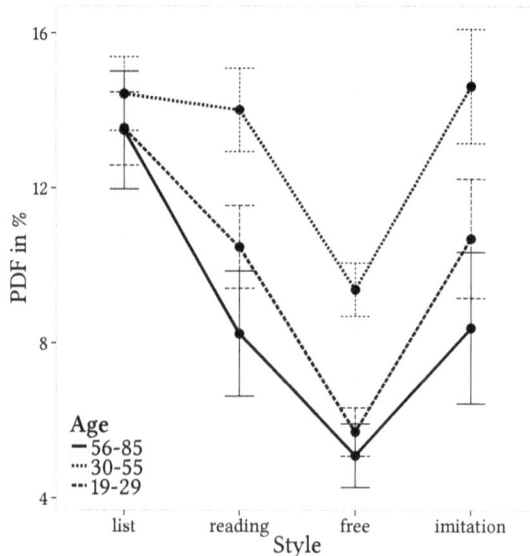

Figure 7.5: /ŋ(g)/: PDF by style ([ɪn] excluded)

and within each age group). The only difference that is found for the middle-aged speakers in this respect is that the text passage and the word lists are statistically identical, but these two formal registers are nevertheless significantly different from free speech.

On the other hand, there is an undeniable rise from spontaneous speech towards accent performance. When subjects are asked to put on a particularly strong Scouse accent they *do* make use of velar nasal plus to a certain extent. Compared to free speech, realisations during the accent imitation are clearly significantly more Scouse, irrespective of age group; PDF reaches about the same level as when people read out a text, a register which 'imitation' is not significantly different from (cf. again the (lack of) overlap in the standard error whiskers in Figure 7.5). This graph is somewhat reminiscent of the corresponding figure that was generated for F1 measurements of happy (Figure 6.7 on page 91), which also revealed more Scouse values for both the word list and accent imitation when compared to reading and spontaneous speech. It was noted earlier that observations for the register 'word list' only come from contexts that seem to favour higher PDF values generally and this could explain at least parts of the rise from 'reading' to 'word list'. It fails, however, to account for the differences between the other three styles, where these phonological contexts make up about the same proportion of tokens. Just as in the case of happy, some additional explanation is needed here (see Chapter 9).

7.2 /k/

7.2.1 Overview

Just as with velar nasal plus, a mixed linear effects model was fit to the data for /k/. Unreleased /k/'s were not included in the model, because these realisations are probably more phonologically than socially conditioned, meaning that, compared to the plosive-fricative continuum, speakers do not have the same degree of choice when to use this variant. The maximal model contained more collinearity than is generally deemed acceptable ($\kappa = 18.8$), but once again much of it was unproblematic because it was only caused by the two three-way interactions, as a separate model without these revealed ($\kappa = 12.25$). The original maximal model (including the interactions) was therefore retained and served as the point of departure for model selection based on AIC scores and F-tests comparing nested models. The final, reduced model (based on 2862 observations) is reprinted below (Table 7.6, R^2-equivalent = 0.37).

Table 7.6: /k/: mixed linear effects regression

Fixed effects:	Estimate	Std. Error	df	t value	Pr(>|t|)	
(Intercept)	58.07	1.49	142.04	39.13	< 0.001	***
STYLElist	-11.44	1.70	884.38	-6.57	< 0.001	***
STYLEread	-2.27	1.28	1729.76	-1.71	0.09	.
STYLEfree	-3.79	1.10	470.85	-3.21	< 0.01	**
AGE56-85	0.74	1.13	2761.75	0.36	0.72	
AGE30-55	-0.21	0.95	2758.04	-0.08	0.94	
GENDERf	-5.53	0.71	2742.23	-7.78	< 0.001	***
CLASSmc	-4.83	0.71	2749.02	-6.58	< 0.001	***
ENVIRV_V	18.76	1.73	124.75	10.62	< 0.001	***
ENVIRV_#V	8.22	1.31	1982.48	6.30	< 0.001	***
ENVIRV_#gli	9.64	2.21	2699.98	4.34	< 0.001	***
ENVIRV_#	10.24	1.29	1339.82	7.87	< 0.001	***
ENVIRV_#liq	6.53	3.95	2798.38	1.78	0.08	.
ENVIRV_#nas	10.43	3.05	2745.07	3.43	< 0.001	***
ENVIRV_#vdfric	-13.69	2.14	2706.45	-6.38	< 0.001	***
ENVIRV_#vlfric	-15.04	2.06	2581.56	-7.23	< 0.001	***
ENVIRV_#vdplos	-2.29	2.85	2737.97	-0.81	0.42	
ENVIRV_#vlplos	-13.86	2.60	2372.19	-5.33	< 0.001	***
STYLElist:AGE56-85	0.83	2.21	2723.94	0.53	0.59	
STYLEread:AGE56-85	-1.26	1.85	2734.49	-0.49	0.62	
STYLEfree:AGE56-85	-2.86	1.33	2815.49	-1.93	0.05	.
STYLElist:AGE30-55	4.17	1.92	2721.76	2.10	0.04	*
STYLEread:AGE30-55	0.31	1.56	2735.38	0.11	0.91	
STYLEfree:AGE30-55	-0.74	1.09	2796.95	-0.90	0.37	
STYLElist:GENDERf	-3.39	1.42	2718.38	-2.36	0.02	*
STYLEread:GENDERf	-2.14	1.17	2731.10	-1.81	0.07	.
STYLEfree:GENDERf	0.47	0.86	2804.23	0.46	0.64	
STYLElist:CLASSmc	-0.50	1.43	2721.77	-0.47	0.64	
STYLEread:CLASSmc	-1.15	1.18	2734.34	-1.12	0.26	
STYLEfree:CLASSmc	-2.16	0.85	2807.04	-2.77	0.01	**
AGE56-85:GENDERf	-4.76	1.11	2735.66	-4.25	< 0.001	***
AGE30-55:GENDERf	5.24	0.98	2749.75	5.34	< 0.001	***
AGE56-85:CLASSmc	6.00	1.12	2754.82	5.70	< 0.001	***
AGE30-55:CLASSmc	-1.72	0.99	2752.61	-1.94	0.05	.
GENDERf:CLASSmc	-2.66	0.51	2826.51	-5.31	< 0.001	***
STYLElist:AGE56-85:GENDERf	-0.80	2.22	2718.25	-0.37	0.71	
STYLEread:AGE56-85:GENDERf	-6.89	1.85	2725.93	-3.73	< 0.001	***
STYLEfree:AGE56-85:GENDERf	-0.91	1.35	2800.05	-0.64	0.53	

STYLElist:AGE30-55:GENDERf	-1.14	1.95	2722.26	-0.58	0.56	
STYLEread:AGE30-55:GENDERf	8.13	1.58	2731.42	5.16	< 0.001	***
STYLEfree:AGE30-55:GENDERf	0.99	1.14	2802.97	0.84	0.40	
STYLElist:AGE56-85:CLASSmc	2.39	2.22	2722.27	0.92	0.36	
STYLEread:AGE56-85:CLASSmc	2.48	1.85	2731.52	1.16	0.25	
STYLEfree:AGE56-85:CLASSmc	1.71	1.37	2811.58	1.03	0.30	
STYLElist:AGE30-55:CLASSmc	-5.56	1.95	2723.95	-2.75	0.01	**
STYLEread:AGE30-55:CLASSmc	-1.18	1.58	2732.59	-0.63	0.53	
STYLEfree:AGE30-55:CLASSmc	4.35	1.16	2801.01	3.85	< 0.001	***

Random effects:	(number of obs: 2862, groups: WORD, 217)		
Groups	Name	Variance	Std.Dev.
WORD	(Intercept)	39.400	6.277
Residual		551.900	23.493

This model is (by far, in most cases) the one that contains the greatest number of significant predictors in this study. In fact, only one factor was eliminated as non-significant, namely frequency of the keyword. Age of the speaker does not reach significance as a main effect (but see §7.2.5 for some thoughts on this), but it does appear in numerous interactions which do and was therefore retained. All the other extralinguistic factors (as well as phonological environment of the dependent variable) are found to be significant main effects. In addition, every single one of the two- and three-way interactions mentioned in §5.6 is found to have a statistically robust impact on PDF measurements of /k/ in this sample.

7.2.2 Phonological context

I will start once more by describing the effect of phonological environment, which is illustrated in Figure 7.6 (again flipped for better representation, cf. Figure 7.1). 'NA' refers to cases where /k/ was observed in proper names and other carrier words for which it was not possible to retrieve a phonemic transcription automatically. The phonological contexts present in my data can be roughly divided into two large groups: (1) Environments which come with comparatively low mean PDF values, and (2) environments for which we find a rather high

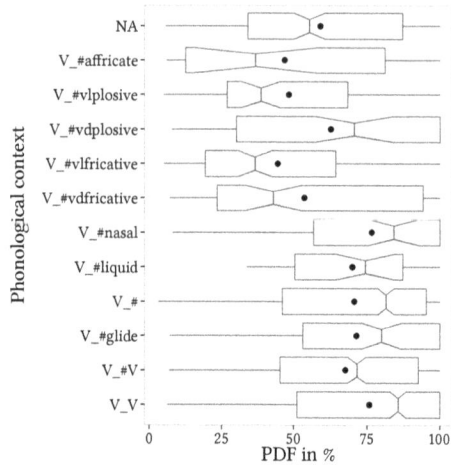

Figure 7.6: /k/: PDF by phonological environment (released only)

mean PDF. The former include cases where /k/ is followed by a word boundary and then either an affricate, a plosive, or a fricative. These contexts are found in the upper half of Figure 7.6. The latter group is made up of environments where /k/ precedes either a sonorant (a nasal, liquid, glide, or a vowel – the last one either within a word or across a word boundary) or silence at the end of a phrase.

Table 7.7 lists the exact means and the number of observations that were collected for each environment (note that this table is inverted relative to Figure 7.6,

Table 7.7: /k/: PDF means by phonological environment (released only)

environment	mean PDF	n
V_V	75.81	840
V_#V	67.66	578
V_#glide	71.43	121
V_#	70.67	775
V_#liquid	70.06	34
V_#nasal	76.59	61
V_#voiced fricative	53.63	132
V_#voiceless fricative	44.50	143
V_#voiced plosive	62.73	69
V_#voiceless plosive	48.34	95
V_#affricate	46.86	26

so contexts favouring lenition are now found at the top). The high PDF values in word-final and intervocalic (within word) environments should not really come as a surprise. These environments have consistently been found to favour lenition in previous research on Liverpool English (cf. §3.3.2), so it was only to be expected that results in this study would be similar. Lenition in intervocalic positions is also a common process from a typological point of view, and can be explained primarily on phonetic grounds. Vowels and plosives constitute the extremes of a continuum, because the former are produced with a virtually unobstructed vocal tract and the latter are defined by a (temporary) complete blockage of the airstream. Realising the phonological plosive intervocalically as a fricative (produced with a narrow, but not blocked vocal tract) can therefore be seen as an (extreme) connected speech phenomenon motivated by articulatory economy. As such it might attract less social attention than in other positions. Since word boundaries are often non-existent in phonetic terms (i.e. two adjacent words are commonly articulated as one stretch of connected speech, without any silence in between), it is no wonder that high PDF values are also found for V_#V and V_#glide environments, because phonetically speaking these contexts are largely identical to intervocalic occurrences of /k/ *within* a word (glides, or semi-vowels, are, after all, really vowels in phonetic terms). Table 7.7 also shows that, just as for velar nasal plus, the two intervocalic (within or across words) and the word-final environments are the most important in terms of absolute numbers (76.62% of released observations).

V_V and V_# are again the only two phonological contexts where observations in relevant numbers are available for all styles, but this fact was considered unproblematic for the same reasons that were outlined in §7.1.2. Once we account for the fact that there are fewer observations for the oldest group of speakers across the board (cf. §5.2), the proportional importance of these phonological environments is also found to be comparable in all three age groups. This means that phonological environment does not act as a confound in this respect (as it would have done if these lenition-favouring contexts were more common in one or two of the age groups). With respect to the cases where /k/ is followed by a word boundary and then a liquid or nasal (which are also categories where PDF was found to be high), the situation is slightly different. For the latter, the oldest speakers contribute only 5 observations (against 25 for the middle-aged, and 31 for the youngest speakers). This means that the average PDF in this context is strongly biased towards realisations by middle-aged and young speakers, who exhibit higher PDF values *generally* (see §7.2.5). V_#liquid is a less extreme case in point, but similar. It is therefore not unlikely that these two phonological contexts do not favour higher PDF rates by themselves but just *appear* to do so in my sample because they are partially confounded with age group.

7.2.3 Style and gender

We will start the analysis of social predictors by looking at the interaction of gender and style, which is visualised by Figure 7.7. One thing that can be gleaned from the box plots is that there is a substantial amount of variation when it comes to the realisation of /k/. With the exception of accent imitation (in the rightmost panel), all boxes have a relatively large vertical extent. As the lower and upper bounds of the boxes mark the first and third quantiles, respectively, large boxes indicate that there is a comparatively large spread of data around the mean. In the case at hand, this means that a wide range of realisations can be found in sizeable numbers (and not just as individual outliers) in the recordings, going from more standard variants (with PDFs of around 30) to clearly Scouse pronunciations (with PDFs of 75+). This large amount of variation seems to be characteristic of /k/ realisations in my sample: it was already present in Figure 7.6, and it will be visible in most of the other graphs that will follow in the remainder of this section.

When we look at the gender difference in the three styles word list, reading passage, and spontaneous speech (first three panels from the left in Figure 7.7), a very clear (and expected) pattern emerges: women have lower PDF values than men, i.e. they use less (or fewer) lenited variants of /k/. The notches in the graph

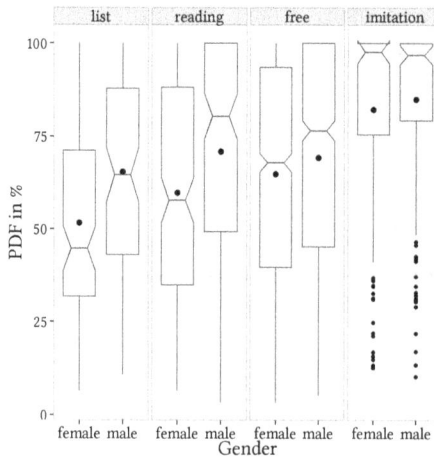

Figure 7.7: /k/: PDF by style and gender (released only)

(no overlap) suggest that the medians of women and men are significantly different in all three styles, and t-tests confirm that the same is true for the means. There is thus a statistically robust gender difference for the word list (t(198.97) = -3.554, p < 0.001), the reading passage (t(360.608) = -3.589, p < 0.001), and free speech (t(2201.103) = -3.594, p < 0.001). When subjects are asked to put on a particularly strong Scouse accent, however, /k/ realisations of women and men are no longer significantly different from one another (t(312.112) = -1.044, p = 0.297). Both genders use strongly lenited variants with PDFs of 75 and higher more than 75% of the time (cf. the position of the first quantiles in the rightmost panel of Figure 7.7).

If we focus on the style dimension within the two gender subgroups separately, differences emerge as well. The graph shows that accent imitation is clearly separate from the other three styles (the means are much higher than in any of the other registers). This holds true for both women and men, but when the analysis is restricted to female speakers, the styles word list, reading passage, and free speech are also distinguishable from each other. Medians seem to be distinct, and t-tests on the raw data (cf. Table 7.8) show that the differences in means are also statistically robust. For men, on the other hand, means are closer together and there is some overlap between the confidence intervals of the medians as well. T-tests confirm that men have statistically identical /k/ realisations in free speech, the reading, and the word list task; only accent performance is significantly different from these three (cf. again Table 7.8). In my sample, style is therefore less important for men than it is for women.

Table 7.8: /k/: t-tests of style by gender

test	women			men		
	t	df	p	t	df	p
list-reading	−2.293	226.274	0.023	−1.583	210.281	0.115
list-free	−4.500	126.152	< 0.001	−1.378	114.832	0.171
list-imitation	−8.881	205.652	< 0.001	−6.201	170.062	< 0.001
reading-free	−2.186	262.723	0.030	0.676	224.321	0.500
reading-imitation	−7.637	354.391	< 0.001	−5.052	313.565	< 0.001
free-imitation	−8.009	217.296	< 0.001	−8.152	262.352	< 0.001

7.2.4 Style and social class

The box plot visualising the interaction of style and social class of the speaker (Figure 7.8) reminds one very much of the one just discussed. Just as with style and gender, there is a clear difference between middle and working class in the registers word list (t(186.279) = -3.576, p < 0.001), reading passage (t(363.849) = -5.048, p < 0.001), and spontaneous speech (t(1794.172) = -15.7, p < 0.001). When we look at accent imitation, however, the class difference is no longer significant (t(301.161) = 0.351, p = 0.726), very much like the gender difference, which also disappeared in this speaking style. All the same, there is a subtle difference: In linguistic terms, the class distinction is slightly more pronounced than the gender one. Middle-class /k/ realisations are even more standard than female ones, and working-class speakers, as a group, are even more Scouse in this respect than males.

Using social class as the 'base' category and investigating the impact of style for middle- and working-class subjects separately also yields similar, but not quite identical results as in the case of the style X gender interaction. We can see that, again, the accent performance task produces /k/ realisations which are extremely Scouse and clearly separate from free speech, reading, and the word list. These last three, however, are very close together and have largely overlapping median confidence intervals within each social class. For middle-class subjects, t-tests on the raw data (cf. Table 7.9) confirm that all of them are significantly different from 'imitation', but none of them is significantly different from the other

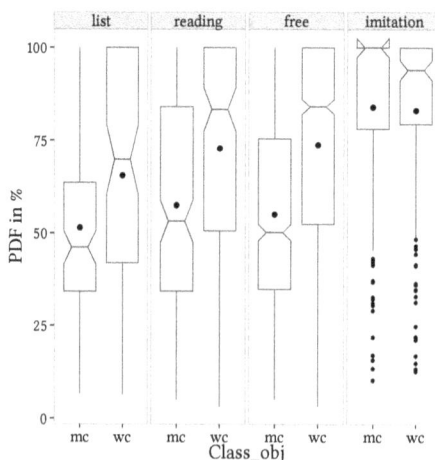

Figure 7.8: /k/: PDF by style and social class (released only)

Table 7.9: /k/: t-tests of style by social class

test	middle class			working class		
	t	df	p	t	df	p
list-reading	−1.829	246.259	0.069	−1.971	185.920	0.050
list-free	−1.340	137.888	0.182	−2.675	104.601	0.009
list-imitation	−10.750	204.745	< 0.001	−4.830	172.248	< 0.001
reading-free	1.044	268.949	0.297	−0.444	217.617	0.658
reading-imitation	−9.651	357.991	< 0.001	−3.468	317.741	< 0.001
free-imitation	−14.745	292.559	< 0.001	−4.290	185.533	< 0.001

two. When we focus on working-class speakers, observations made during free speech and the reading passage are even a bit closer than for middle-class subjects (and a t-test does indeed find that they are statistically identical), but on the other hand the distance between those two and the word list is slightly greater. Median confidence intervals still overlap a bit (cf. the notches of the 'wc' boxes for 'reading' and 'list'), but t-tests on the raw data suggest that with the exception of 'reading' and 'free' all styles are significantly different from one another in the working-class sub-sample.

Working-class speakers thus have a three-way style distinction for /k/: word list, reading/free speech, and accent performance. Middle-class interviewees, on the other hand, have statistically identical /k/ pronunciations for all three 'traditional' styles, and only distinguish accent imitation from these. It might seem strange that middle-class speakers show fewer style differences than their working-class counterparts, especially for a dependent variable that is supposed to be socially salient. It should be noted, however, that this is due to the fact that middle-class speakers have very low PDF values (comparable to the one found for female subjects in the word list in Figure 7.7) in all but the most informal register. In other words, they are more reluctant to use (pronounced) /k/ lenition even in more informal contexts, unless they are specifically[3] asked to do so (see the value for the accent imitation).

7.2.5 Age and gender

Since the age dimension is one of the primary concerns of this study, we will first look at this factor in isolation. This might seem unnecessary, because the

---

[3]In a manner of speaking. Subjects were not asked to specifically use /k/ lenition.

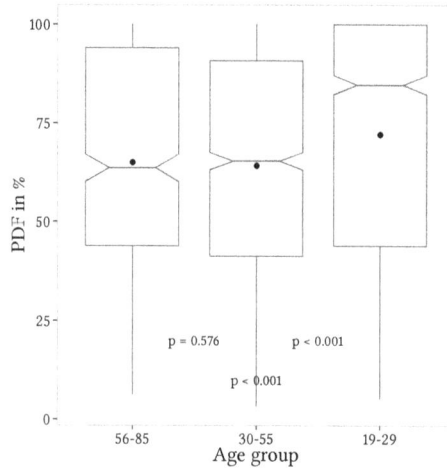

Figure 7.9: /k/: PDF by age (released only)

mixed-effects model does not list age group among the significant main effects for predicting PDF of /k/. If we consider a plot of the raw data (Figure 7.9), however, the picture changes. First of all, we can see that the upper and lower boundaries of all boxes are around or above 40 and 90%, respectively. This means that (a) there is a lot of variance in all three groups of speakers, and (b) all speakers frequently produce /k/ with quite a bit of aspiration, i.e. at least a Scouse "touch". We also see, however, that the mean (black dots) and median values (thick bars between the notches) remain constant from the old to the middle speakers (t(968.66) = -0.56, p = 0.576), but rise considerably from the middle to the young group (t(2606.825) = 6.886, p < 0.001). In contrast to the mixed-effects model, t-tests on the raw data thus do find a statistically significant age difference, at least between the middle and the young group. The cause for these incompatible results is the word *like*. Due to its role as a fashionable quotative particle, *like* is much more frequent in free speech of the young group (57.89% of /k/ tokens) than in the middle and old group (39.38 and 26.18%, respectively).

Young Liverpudlians in this study furthermore realise *like* with a very high average PDF of 71.85% (59.45% for the middle, 55.59% for the old group), which contributes considerably to their overall mean visualised in Figure 7.9 and explains part of the interaction of style and age group in the mixed-effects model as well (cf. Figure 7.13), since it is only in free speech that the preference of young speakers to use *like* (often with a Scouse pronunciation) can fully manifest itself. If we take out *like* completely, the difference between the oldest and the middle-aged speakers is still not significant (t(900.655) = -0.393, p = 0.694), but that between the middle-aged and the young is (t(1468.008) = 3.999, p < 0.001). In light of this, I feel justified in claiming that Watson's (2007a) finding has been corroborated and that with respect to /k/, Scouse is indeed "getting Scouser".

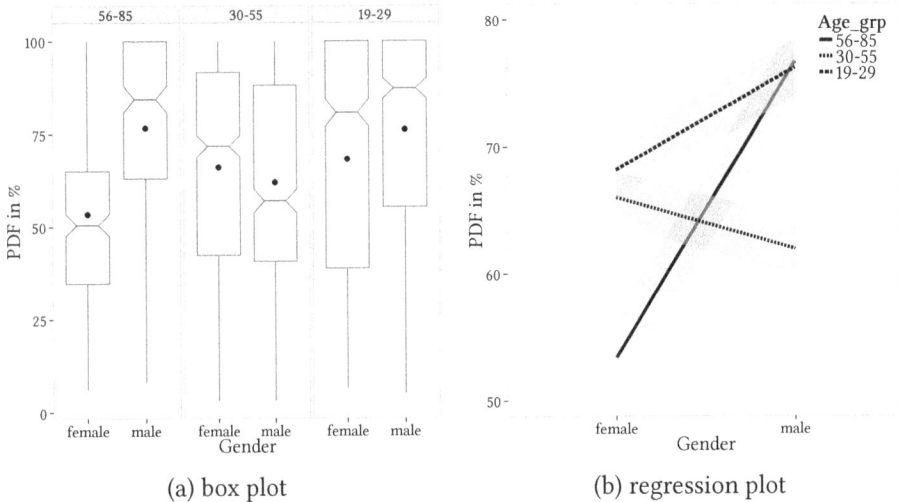

(a) box plot   (b) regression plot

Figure 7.10: /k/: PDF by age and gender (released only)

At least this is true if we pool the data for all subjects and only focus on the age dimension. However, the mixed linear effects regression found significant inter-actions of age with gender and social class as well, so a more detailed account of the impact of the predictor age is necessary. In Figure 7.10a the gender difference in the individual age groups is visualised in three separate box plots. The oldest speakers (left panel) show a very pronounced gender difference in the expected direction: women have both a lower mean and median than men, i.e. the former use less lenition than the latter. Both groups also show comparatively little vari-ation around the mean, and in consequence there is only a very small overlap of the interquartile ranges (vertical extent of the boxes). It is therefore not surprising that a t-test finds the gender difference to be highly significant in this age group (t(515.826) = -10.356, p < 0.001). For middle-aged speakers (panel in the middle), things seem to be a lot less clear. Women and men have clearly distinct medi-ans in this age group (no overlapping notches), but it is now the men who have lower PDF values than the women. The same goes for the mean, which is also lower for men than for women. However, it should be noted that the two genders are somewhat less distinct in this sub-sample due to increased variation in both groups (the interquartile ranges occupy virtually the same space). Nevertheless this difference is still statistically significant (t(1198.637) = 2.543, p = 0.011). When we focus on the youngest speakers in the sample, we find that (a) the gender distinction has become (even) more statistically robust again (t(1339.877) = -4.982, p < 0.001), and (b) it is now once more the female speakers who are less Scouse than their male counterparts (cf. the old group).

If regression lines for these three age groups are plotted with gender on the x- and estimated PDF on the y-axis (Figure 7.10b), it becomes obvious that the picture suggested by Figure 7.9 is simplistic. When women and men are analysed separately, we cannot say that there has been no change in /k/ lenition from the oldest to the middle-aged speakers. Instead, for women (left-hand side of the graph) the increase in PDF has taken place between these two very groups: older women (solid line) have a much lower PDF than those who are aged between 30 and 55 (dotted line); this difference is highly significant (cf. Table 7.10). Young women (dashed line), then, do not have a PDF that is significantly higher than that of the middle-aged group (cf. the overlapping error bands in Figure 7.10b and the relevant t-test in Table 7.10). Men, on the other hand, have a considerably higher PDF for both the youngest and the *oldest* speakers, two groups which a t-test found not to differ in a statistically robust way. Male speakers aged between 30 and 55, however, have a PDF which is significantly lower than both those of their young and old counterparts (cf. once more Table 7.10). We can thus say that for women, lenition of /k/ has already increased from the old to the middle-aged generation and has then remained on that level. In opposition to that, male Liverpudlians exhibit a kind of 'back-to-the-roots' pattern: The (rather high) PDF drops about as much from the old to the middle-aged speakers as it rises for the women in the same period, only to return to virtually the same level again for the youngest speakers in the sample.

Table 7.10: /k/: t-tests of age by gender

test	women			men		
	t	df	p	t	df	p
old-middle	6.537	502.217	< 0.001	−7.473	551.684	< 0.001
middle-young	1.363	1382.189	0.173	8.881	1169.913	< 0.001
young-old	7.397	558.982	< 0.001	−0.239	514.761	0.811

7.2.6 Age and social class

A much more linear development is visible in the interaction of age and social class as it is represented in Figure 7.11a and Figure 7.11b. If we look at the class distinction and restrict ourselves to the oldest speakers in the sample (rightmost panel of Figure 7.11a) we find that, even though the medians seem to be just about significantly different from each other (cf. the notches), the means (black dots) are virtually identical. A t-test on the raw data confirms that the difference in /k/ realisation between middle- and working-class speakers is not statistically robust in the age group 56–85 (t(515.679) = 0.608, p = 0.544). In the next generation (middle panel), things have already changed. There is now a wider gap between both the medians (cf. the notches) and the means of the two classes. Additionally, the interquartile ranges as visualised by the vertical extent of the boxes now overlap (slightly) less. For this age group, working-class speakers have a significantly higher PDF (and thus more Scouse /k/ realisations) than middle-class Liverpudlians (t(1253.101) = -6.982, p < 0.001). This difference does not only persist, but actually becomes larger and even more pronounced for the youngest speakers: the gap between middle and workings class subjects widens (t(698.451) = -13.959, p < 0.001). In terms of social class, the development that has taken place from the oldest to the youngest speakers investigated in this study can thus be described as one of divergence: Middle-class speakers become consistently *less* Scouse (PDF drops), whereas working-class speakers just as consistently become *more* Scouse (PDF rises) across three generations.

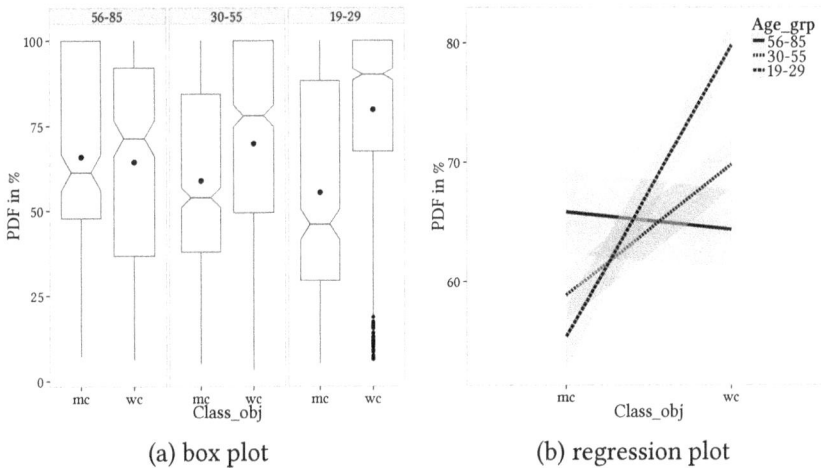

(a) box plot   (b) regression plot

Figure 7.11: /k/: PDF by age and social class (released only)

Table 7.11: /k/: t-tests of age by social class

test	middle class			working class		
	t	df	p	t	df	p
old-middle	−3.530	458.418	< 0.001	2.550	499.045	0.011
middle-young	−1.863	817.297	0.063	7.025	1243.562	< 0.001
young-old	−4.641	585.844	< 0.001	7.719	403.276	< 0.001

This divergence can also be seen in Figure 7.11b, where the solid regression line (old speakers) is essentially flat, the dotted one (middle-aged) has a moderate positive slope (which indicates a rise in PDF going from the middle to the working-class speakers), and the dashed line (young subjects) has a very steep positive slope – suggesting that the class effect is in the same direction but more pronounced than in the middle group. If we zoom in on the middle-class speakers, we find that PDF is actually highest in the old group, and decreases towards the middle and the young interviewees. The last two groups are not significantly different from one another as the overlapping standard deviations in the regression plot (dark grey areas) suggest and the t-test reported in Table 7.11 ("middle-young") confirms. In this social class, speakers have thus become less Scouse from the oldest to the middle-aged speakers, and then remained on that level. For working-class Liverpudlians, on the other hand, the order of age groups is completely reversed: Old speakers have a comparatively low estimated PDF, subjects aged 30–55 are in the middle, and the youngest participants have a very high estimated PDF of around 80. T-tests on the raw data find all three age groups to be significantly different from one another (cf. Table 7.11), which means that, with respect to /k/, old working-class speakers are less Scouse than the middle-aged, who in turn use less lenition than the youngest speakers.

7.2.7 Social class and gender

Compared to the last two interactions (age X gender, and age X social class), the one of class and gender, albeit highly significant, is a lot less interesting. Box plots (Figure 7.12a) show that gender has roughly the same impact in both classes: men use more lenition than women. This difference is significant in both the middle ($t(1293.269) = -8.004$, $p < 0.001$), and the working class ($t(1709.667) = -4.196$, $p < 0.001$), although the distance between women and men is smaller in the latter case. If we take the opposite stance and look at class differences in the two

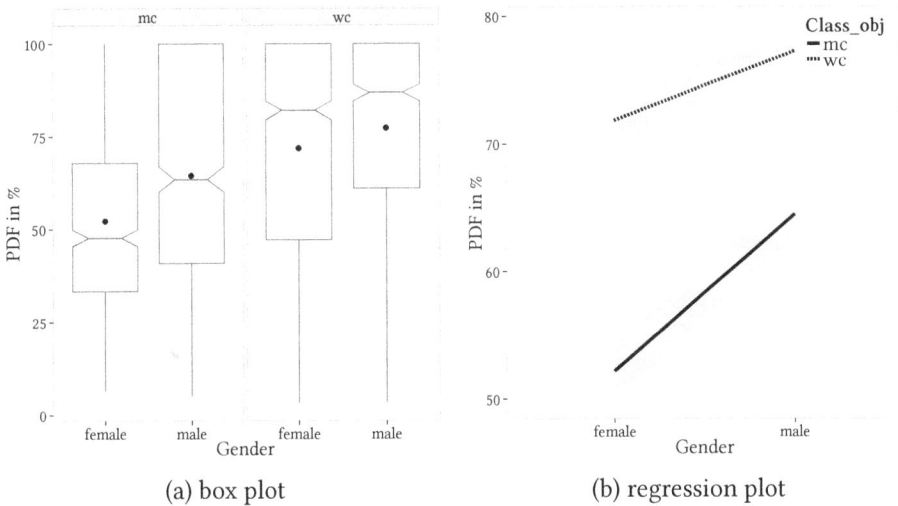

(a) box plot (b) regression plot

Figure 7.12: /k/: PDF by gender and social class (released only)

genders separately, we end up with a very similar result. The vertical distance of the regression lines shows that the difference in estimated PDF between middle (solid line) and working class (dotted) is greater for female than for male speakers. However, the effect is in the same direction (working-class speakers use more lenition than middle-class speakers), and it is highly significant for both women (t(1311.495) = -13.984, p < 0.001) *and* men (t(1431.826) = -8.893, p < 0.001). The nature of the class (gender) effect is thus essentially the same for both genders (social classes); there is only a difference in degree.

7.2.8 Style shifting

The last two-way interaction that was found to be significant in the mixed linear effects regression is the one between speaking style and age group of speaker. Just as for the other three test variables, this relationship (as well as the two three-way interactions of style, age, and gender/social class) will be visualised by a line plot (Figure 7.13), which shows register on the x-, and average PDF on the y-axis. Line type codes age of the participants, while the whiskers above and below the means mark the standard errors. The lines representing the old (solid) and the middle-aged speakers (dotted) are remarkably similar, not to say identical. There is no style shifting at all for the first three styles (word list, reading passage and free speech). The means are slightly different, but the error whiskers of any style overlap with those of the other two, which indicates that these subtle

165

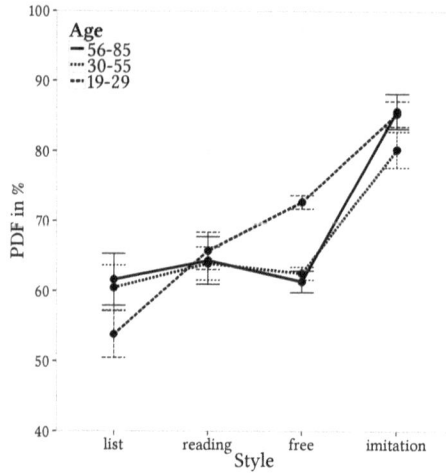

Figure 7.13: /k/: PDF by style and age (released only)

differences are not statistically significant. Only when we get to accent imitation do we see a real change: PDF values increase dramatically in both age groups. This suggests that there has to be some (sub-conscious) awareness of the variable in these groups, but it must be very limited – otherwise we would expect differences between the other styles as well.

When we look at the dashed line, which represents data collected from the youngest speakers, however, we are faced with a virtually perfect textbook case of Labovian style shifting. In this age group, average PDF of /k/ increases in an almost straight line from most formal to most informal context. When reading out a word list, these speakers use significantly less lenition than both subjects of their parents' or grandparents' generation. For the reading passage, all three groups are on the same level, but in free speech, /k/ realisations of the youngest speakers are significantly (and considerably!) more Scouse than those of the other two groups (cf. §7.2.5). During accent performance, Scousers aged between 19 and 29 reach the same level of lenition as the oldest interviewees. For the youngest speakers, every register is significantly different from the other three (no overlap between the dashed whiskers). We have thus consistent and significant style shifting for /k/-lenition in this age group.

Since the mixed linear effects regression model found significant three-way interactions of style and age group with gender and social class, respectively, we will look at both of these as well before closing this section. Figure 7.14a and Figure 7.14b visualise the style X age interaction for women and men separately. If we focus on the old speakers, women show much more systematic style shift-

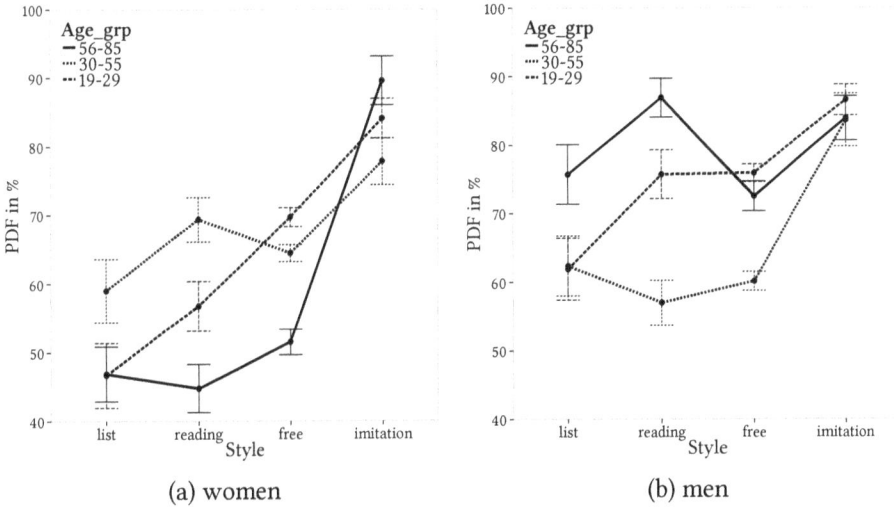

Figure 7.14: /k/: PDF by style, age group, and gender (released only)

ing than men. Provided we ignore the word list, there is actually a near linear (and significant) rise from the text passage to spontaneous speech to accent performance. This rather clear picture is only spoilt by the fact that the word list is not significantly different from the reading passage, or from observations made during spontaneous speech (although in the latter case the difference is close to significance, error whiskers only just overlap). Old men, on the other hand, show a zigzag pattern, which does not look at all like Labovian style shifting. Mean PDF is high in all registers, but there are still significant differences between the two blocks list/free and reading/imitation: /k/ realisations are even more lenited in the latter case than in the former.

In the middle aged group (dotted line) differences are smaller. Women exhibit a trend towards the typical style shifting pattern (increasing PDF from left to right), although some curious results were obtained for the registers 'reading' and 'free' – women actually use (slightly, but significantly) more Scouse realisations in the more formal text reading task than in spontaneous speech. Men, on the other hand, have the same mean PDF, statistically speaking, in the three 'natural' styles word list, reading passage, and free speech. This is followed by a steep rise into accent performance on the right-hand side of the graph, which is similar to the one found for women of this age group. All in all, the pattern found for middle-aged men looks very much like the one revealed in Figure 7.13 for the entire age group.

For the youngest speakers (dashed) we find systematic style shifting in both genders. Women in particular have a virtually perfect straight line, running from the bottom-left to the top-right corner of Figure 7.14a, just like we would expect for a socially salient variable. Each mean in this sub-sample is (highly) significantly different from each of the other three. Young men also show a general trend for PDF to raise from the more formal registers on the left to the less formal ones on the right of the graph. Two things need to be mentioned, though: (1) Means in the three styles 'list', 'reading', and 'free' are all higher than those of women in these registers, so the rise is less extreme, and (2) the reading passage and free speech do not differ in a statistically robust way, so men only have a three-way style distinction: word list, reading/spontaneous, accent performance. On the whole, however, I would consider these differences in degree, not in nature. Both men and women aged between 19 and 29 can be said to style-shift.

In Figure 7.15a and Figure 7.15b the style-age interaction is shown with respect to how it is influenced by social class of the speaker. For old middle-class speakers (solid line in Figure 7.15a) we find again that there is no significant difference between the word list and the text reading task. The, by now familiar, steep rise to a very high PDF for accent imitation is also present. In between, however, /k/ variants become more standard in free speech – PDF drops. While the difference between realisations in spontaneous speech and while reading out the word list is not statistically robust, that between free speech and the text passage is. Old

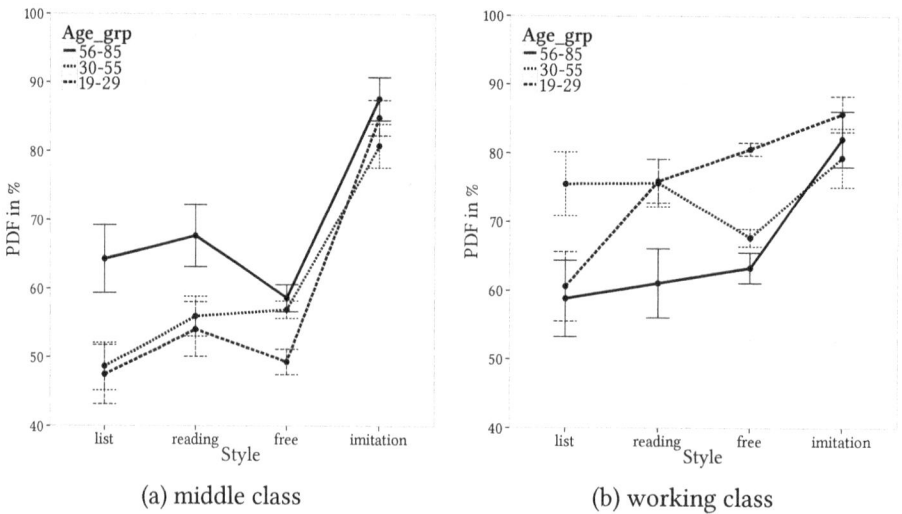

(a) middle class (b) working class

Figure 7.15: /k/: PDF by style, age group, and social class (released only) working-class speakers behave in very much the same way as the pooled age group in Figure 7.13: 'list', 'reading', and 'free' are not significantly different, but there is a steep and statistically robust increase of PDF during accent imitation.

Middle-class speakers aged between 30 and 55 show exactly the same style shifting pattern that was found for young male subjects (cf. Figure 7.14b). The reading passage and spontaneous speech are statistically identical, but apart from that, there is a steady increase in PDF from left (more formal) to right (less formal). Their working-class counterparts (dotted line in Figure 7.15b) are interesting because they echo the phenomenon just described for old middle-class speakers: 'list' and 'reading' are identical, followed by a significant drop in PDF towards spontaneous speech, and then by a significant rise for accent imitation. The only difference is that for middle-aged working-class speakers /k/ realisations in the word list and the reading passage are just as Scouse as when people put on a particularly strong Liverpool accent.

Young middle-class participants, finally, exhibit a style pattern which looks like an attenuated version of the one revealed for old middle-class speakers. In this age group, however, the drop in PDF from 'reading' to 'free' is not significant. As a result, the three styles word list, reading passage, and spontaneous speech are all identical, statistically speaking. The following increase in PDF during accent performance is then even (slightly) more extreme than for the other two age groups. Somewhat surprisingly, working-class speakers (dashed line in Figure 7.15b) do distinguish all four styles. Not only is each of them significantly different from each of the other three, but there is also a steady increase in PDF from left to right – just as one would expect for a socially salient variable that people are aware of to a certain degree. We are thus faced with the interesting situation that, among the youngest subjects, it is actually the working-class speakers who exhibit more pronounced and more systematic style shifting. It should be noted, however, that this might just be due to the fact that young middle-class speakers have considerably lower PDF values than working-class Liverpudlians of the same age in the first three styles; young middle-class speakers might just try not to use /k/ lenition at all (as far as they are able to do so, cf. §8.2.3.2), irrespective of speaking style, unless they are told to do so.

8 Awareness, comments, evaluation

Up to now, the focus of this study has been exclusively on *how* subjects say things. In what is to follow I will present a short summary of *what* the people in my sample have to say *about* Scouse, zooming in on the opinions expressed and the comments made in the interview sections on (local) identity and language. This analysis can only be qualitative in nature due to the fact that the number of interviewees is far too small to permit meaningful quantitative comparisons. It should also be considered recapitulatory, as constraints of time and space do not allow me to provide a comprehensive analysis of all the material that was collected at this point. Figure 8.1 and Figure 8.2 are based on data extracted from all 38 interviews that have been conducted (the "secondary sample"), but the more detailed description on the following pages focuses on the same 20 participants that provided the data for the quantitative analyses reported in Chapters 6 and 7 (the "primary sample", cf. §5.2). Quotes are attributed to the relevant interviews using the participant codes explained in §5.1. For reasons of readability, hesitations and repetitions in these quotes have been eliminated.

8.1 Scouse and "Liverpoolness"

8.1.1 Accent and identity

It is not really surprising that the question of identity is intertwined with the question of language (variety) for many people. Nevertheless, it is interesting how strongly these two concepts are linked up by many subjects in my sample. The most explicit comment on this issue probably stems from a male, middle-class speaker who states: "We got our identity, haven't we. We talk different" (01MMC52). A female who is some 30 years younger made a statement whose gist is very similar:

(1) I'd call meself a Scouser 'cause I always called meself that. I don't know why. (...) We've got a Scouse accent, we're labelled as Scousers. (37FWC20)

Having a Scouse accent thus seems to be, for her, essentially the same thing as *being* a Scouser. While many subjects consider the terms "Liverpudlian" and "Scouser" to be synonyms, broadly speaking, there are still quite a few for who these terms carry somewhat different connotations. The speaker quoted at the beginning of this paragraph, for instance, says that, although he "wouldn't be offended if someone said [he] was a Scouser", he nevertheless prefers the term "Liverpudlian" to refer to himself, because he "just sound[s] a Liverpudlian" (01MMC52).

While this subject does not go on to explain what distinguishes a Liverpudlian from a Scouser in terms of "sound", a young female speaker in the sample is more explicit on the issue.

(2) I'd never call myself [a Scouser] 'cause I don't sound very Scouse compared to others. So I think it's to do with the sort of, how strong your accent is. (06FMC20)

Another female of the same age group voices essentially the same idea by explaining that "people tend to think of Scousers, you know with the really strong accent" (07FMC23), and that, since she didn't have a strong accent, she was reluctant to refer to herself as a Scouser. It should be noted, however, that the issue is more complicated than that for at least some people from Liverpool. A not insignificant proportion of interviewees explained that the term "Liverpudlian" was ambiguous for them, because it could either mean (1) "someone from Liverpool", or (2) "someone supporting Liverpool Football Club". Since the football allegiance is quite important for many people in Liverpool, "Evertonians" (supporters of Everton, the other premier league football club in the city) often rejected the label "Liverpudlian" and would go for "Scouser" instead, simply because they wanted to avoid being "misunderstood".

8.1.2 Distinctness, geographical spread, and "plastic" Scousers

Despite these minor terminological issues, subjects in different age groups express the thought that a Liverpool accent might be particularly closely linked to a Liverpool identity because it is so distinctive. A 20-year old working-class male, for instance, claims that Scousers were "instantly recognisable" because of the "distinctive accent" (02MWC20), and a 44-year-old female (talking about people from Manchester in particular) says that "the minute they hear you talk (...) you see a little light go on in there" (13FWC44). Another subject from the middle-aged group hypothesises about whether Liverpool as a city might be stigmatised because "you can pick a Scouser a mile off" thanks to the distinctive accent. He even goes on to compare Scouse as a city accent to that of Lancashire as a regional one, arguing that Manchester, as a city, does not have its own accent in the same way that Liverpool does:

(3)   Someone from Manchester may sound as if they were from any number of towns (...) They're gonna be lumped together, (...) but there's a relatively small number of people who are Liverpudlian or sound Liverpudlian and so (...) maybe it's the distinctiveness which is what makes it an easy target. (03MMC33)

The same speaker also claims, that – in his opinion – the accents of places such as London or Newcastle "sound (...) a lot more similar than Liverpudlian does to anything else" (03MMC33). This seems like a rather drastic interpretation of the distinctness of Scouse, and I cannot say whether this idea is embraced by a majority of Liverpudlians, but one of the younger subjects even went one step further and admitted to feeling "a sense of detachment sometimes", supposedly "'cause the accent's so different from the rest of England" (02MWC20).

While many speakers in my sample are quite happy about, and take some pride in, the fact that their accent is (considered as) rather distinct, both the 33-year-old middle-class speaker and the 20-year-old working-class interviewee just quoted also see this distinctness as somewhat ambivalent. The older one refers to potentially negative effects indirectly when he says that the distinctness of the accent makes Liverpool "an easy target". The younger speaker, on the other hand, explicitly laments that "sometimes" outsiders linked the accent to "the negative stereotype[s]" about Liverpool, a fact which he considers as somewhat unfair because the city has "kind of evolved over the last (...), like, 20 years" and was "certainly a modern place now" (02MWC20).

Notwithstanding that most speakers in the sample consider Scouse to be so characteristic of the city, Liverpudlians of all age groups are also aware of the fact that speakers of Scouse can be found outside of the city limits. However, these people are often thought of as "fake", or "plastic" Scousers in the local terminology (cf. *crossing* as defined by Rampton 1995). Definitions vary as to where exactly plastic Scousers are to be found. For some people they "live in Birkenhead and Wallasey" (06FMC20), i.e. on the Wirral peninsula to the west of Liverpool. A person from there might have a way of speaking that is "classed [as] a Scouse accent", but they are still "not a real Scouser" because they live "over the water" (06FMC20). For many Liverpudlians this is true even though many of the plastic Scousers actually have rather strong Liverpudlian accents as one speaker explained, who first talked about a (Liverpudlian) acquaintance with "a really thick accent" and then went on to explain that "you find people of the other side of the river talk like him" (01MMC52). Also frequently labelled as plastic Scousers are people who live to the north or east of Liverpool "proper": they are not separated from the city by the natural border of the Mersey estuary, but they nevertheless live outside the administrative boundaries of the city itself. Sometimes this even refers to people who live within the contiguously built-up area of the Liverpool city region (such as in Halewood or Huyton). For most subjects, however, plastic Scousers are to be found a bit further away from the centre. For instance, a 38-year-old woman in my sample included people from "St. Helens or Skelmersdale or (...) Warrington" (around 22km, 41km, and 28km from Liverpool, respectively) in this category and gave "Mel C of the Spice Girls" and the comedian John Bishop as celebrity examples (33FMC38). Incidentally, she also thinks that the latter's accent is "the worst", which serves to illustrate another aspect often connected with the term plastic Scouser, namely the idea that "they put it on too much", i.e. that they perform an inauthentic and exaggerated Scouse accent (33FMC38).

8.1.3 In the north, but not of it?

There is thus wide-spread awareness both of the distinctness of Scouse and its close connection with the city of Liverpool. All the same, neither the ideas about the distinctness of Scouse, nor the views expressed about so-called plastic Scousers should be taken to mean that Liverpudlians across the board necessarily think that their city is absolutely unique and not part of any larger cultural region. To assess subjects' attitudes and opinions in this respect they were asked whether they would describe themselves as northerners and they were confronted with the phrase Liverpool is "in the north but not of it" (Belchem 2006d: xxx). Reactions were quite diverse.

Older speakers in my sample seem to be most willing to embrace the idea that Liverpool is separate and not really part of northern England in the same way that other cities such as Manchester, Leeds, or Sheffield are. One of the older males, for instance, does concede that he "[is] northern", but then adds that it was really "too broad a term for someone from Liverpool" and that it might better "suit someone from Lancashire or Yorkshire", whereas people from Liverpool were (primarily) Scousers (08MMC62). To be fair, this person also points out that, in his opinion, the claim that Liverpool is separate from the rest of the north was "less true" today, but that "it certainly was very true at one point, 'cause Liverpool just had a different attitude to the rest of the country". Now, however, he would not strongly object to Liverpool being called a "northern" city anymore (08MMC62). Another male speaker of about the same age is more categorical and insists that Liverpool is "distinct", "not like, say, Manchester", and "nothing like Birmingham", even though the former is "just a hop, skip, and a jump down the road" (05MWC66). Interestingly, he even provides some historical justification for his opinion, arguing that Liverpool is characterised by (1) a "mix of Welsh, Irish, some Scottish, and (...) Lancashire", (2) its peripheral geographical position in the country ("it's physically just that big way out"), and (3) "that seafaring thing", i.e. the tradition as an important port which meant that the orientation of Liverpool was "always outwards" (05MWC66).

The two women in the old group seem to have somewhat more "moderate" views in this respect, but since the sample is so small it is unclear whether this is a true gender difference that could be generalised to the majority of Liverpudlians. The working-class subject, for instance, claims that she has "always been northern" in addition to her Liverpool identity. She does not deny that the "Liverpudlian bit [comes] first", and that the northern identity is secondary, but she does think that Liverpool is "part of northern England" (18FWC67). The other older female in the sample, like many others, does attribute a "bit of a stand alone quality maybe to Liverpool", but she is also very aware of "that north-south divide" and explains that, on a recent trip to Oxfordshire, she had "really felt very northern" (28FMC59). While she also feels "there is a difference" between Liverpool and other places in the north of England, this does not keep her from including Liverpool in the north. Interestingly, she also suggests that the idea of uniqueness is an important aspect of Liverpool's identity:

(4) No, I don't think Liverpool's separate. I think Liverpool likes to *think* it's separate to the (...) rest of the north (...). I don't feel it is. (28FMC59, emphasis in the original)

In the middle age group, one also finds people who believe that Liverpool is "more unique" than other places in northern England, but they usually put this into perspective by saying something like "but I wouldn't necessarily say it was separate" (33FMC38): Liverpool is thus considered somewhat special, but special *within* the group of northern English cities and towns. Other speakers even consider Liverpool to be a prototypical northern city which "absolutely shows what (...) a northerner should be" (13FWC44). A male interviewee states he knows people who consider their city to be separate from everything else, but he adds it would be "such a shame if Liverpool wasn't able to relate to the rest of Lancashire" and "other places in northern England", and explains that he himself is "happy being of the north" (03MMC33).

The youngest speakers are again slightly more homogeneous when it comes to the issue of northernness. One of them limits Liverpool's association with the north to a purely geographical one ("we are in the north") and does not see any cultural similarities between Liverpudlians and northerners who "dress different" and "walk different" (37FWC20). Liverpool is considered to be "different from northern cities" and "sort of unique", with its own "different way of life, really" (37FWC20). A male working-class speaker of the same age group reverses the argument presented by one of the older speakers, and explains that "in the 80s and such [Liverpool] was definitely a part of the north, like a solid part of the north", whereas nowadays the city was "so detached from northern places" that he had "never thought of [himself] as [a] northerner" (02MWC20). The accent issue is brought up again by one of the young women, who believes that typical "northern people" are thought of as having "quite broad northern accent[s]", which are more likely to be found in places "like Leeds or Yorkshire, or somewhere like that maybe" (07FMC23). The intermediate position is also found, where Liverpool is special, but not too different from other places to be included in the "northern" category, especially against the backdrop of the north-south divide:

(5)   Our culture isn't the same as a lot of the other northern cities, but it's not exactly the same as the south. It's a very unique city, I suppose (…). I think it is northern, but in a rather distinct way. (04MWC19)

Generally speaking, though, most younger Liverpudlians in my sample are quite happy with a secondary identity as a northerner – especially those that have travelled more, or have family in other parts of the country (north and south). One working-class female, for example, does not even see a "drastic difference between Liverpool and Manchester", the two historical "arch-enemies" in the north-west, whereas the difference "between the north and south" is much more important to her (36FWC20). She explains that she has been to "other places" in northern England that just "remind[ed] [her] of Liverpool" instead of making her feel like she was "miles and miles away from home because the culture's so different" (36FWC20). Other subjects in this age group express similar thoughts, explicitly rejecting the idea of Liverpool's separateness as "false" and "just silly", and adding that they would most certainly "call [themselves] a northerner" (06FMC20). Context does play a crucial role here. A male middle-class Liverpudlian can serve as a typical example when he specifies that "in Liverpool" he would naturally call himself "a Scouser", but if he was "talking to (…) someone from the south of (…) England, [he]'d call [himself] a northerner" (25MMC19). "Northerner" is thus clearly a *secondary* identity, but nonetheless one that is still acceptable to (and often even readily embraced by) the youngest Liverpool speakers in the sample as a means of distancing themselves from the southern part of the country and associating with the northern one at the same time.

8.2 Features of Scouse

8.2.1 Geographical variation

Upon being asked for typical features of the Scouse accent, many subjects in my sample start out by stressing a point which an older working-class male makes very concisely when he says:

(6)   There's no such thing as a single Scouse accent. There're several Scouse accents. (05MWC66)

Most interviewees simply refer to the fact that "stronger" and "lighter" accents can be heard in the city, without necessarily being aware of any system that might be distinguishable with respect to who uses one or the other. The speaker who provided the last quote, however, goes on to specify that Scouse "varies from age to age, and area to area" and that "some people say there's a (…) very general division north and south", with the accent arguably being "softer in the south of the city rather than the north" (05MWC66). Another male speaker from the same age group also thinks that he is often able to distinguish whether someone comes "from North Liverpool or South Liverpool" (08MMC62). He adds that this was particularly true "if they're older, because South Liverpool had a much softer accent" (08MMC62). This conditional and the past tense that follows it suggest that he believes this distinction is less important or pronounced these days. It still plays a role in some people's minds, however, as a quote from an older female shows. She explains that "if you listen to (…) the boys and girls from the north end of the city, there's a real difference how they (…) speak compared to here" (28FMC59), where "here" refers to Aigburth, a middle-class suburb in the south of Liverpool. Some speakers seem to hold very similar beliefs without actually verbalising them in such a direct manner. As an example, consider the following quote:

(7)   The guy behind the bar, he's got a really strong accent. I think he's from Anfield. (01MMC52)

This speaker does not explicitly talk about different accents in different parts of Liverpool during his interview, but he nevertheless clearly makes a connection between a strong accent and a particular (northern) district of the city, Anfield, which is evidence that he does, in fact, believe that certain districts of Liverpool can be linked to stronger accents (at least in some cases).

As an aside, it should be mentioned that my subjects are probably right when they assume stronger accents to be more prevalent in northern parts of (inner-city) Liverpool. Contrary to what many of my subjects probably think, however, this is little to do with pure geography. Rather, many northern districts of the city are traditional working-class neighbourhoods (Vauxhall, Everton, Anfield), whereas the "south end" is dominated by more middle-class areas (Aigburth, Mossley Hill, Allerton). This reasoning was already behind Knowles's choice of Vauxhall and Aigburth as two electoral wards that would provide "a fairly good cross-section of Liverpool society"(Knowles 1973: 2). Recent figures confirm that the most deprived districts of Liverpool are still mostly concentrated in the northern part of the city (cf. Liverpool City Council 2010: iii). The linguistic north-south divide, if it exists, is thus likely to be a *social* distinction that just happens to coincide with a geographical split, due to the fact that social segregation has been present in Liverpool for a long time already.

8.2.2 Suprasegmentals

8.2.2.1 Voice quality

There are some more comments in the data which can be classified as rather general and unspecific statements. One subject, for example, says that "the main (...) aspect of the actual accent is just the tinge" (02MWC20), but it remains entirely unclear what this "tinge" consists of. Essentially, the speaker is just saying that Scouse somehow sounds different from other accents. This *could* also be the case for two other interviewees, who talk about "a sort of (...) twang" (04MWC19) "in our voice" (13FWC44). It is possible that *twang* in this context is a synonym for *tinge*, and that people are just referring to the fact that there is a distinct overall sound to Scouse. It should be remembered, however, that there is also the received idea of Scouse having a nasal quality to it, which is traditionally (and erroneously) linked to air pollution and the alleged omnipresence of catarrh in Liverpool in the early 20th century. While this is an opinion generated among laypersons, rather than a scientific finding based on a sound database of linguistic material, the quotes reported above might be considered as evidence that the idea is still around.

8.2.2.2 Intonation

A suprasegmental linguistic feature that *is* mentioned explicitly and unambiguously is intonation. Speakers in the middle-aged and the young group talk about this subject in similar ways. A male in his thirties mentions that there is "a lilt" in Liverpool English which makes it a bit "sing-songish" (03MMC33). Another one, who is about twenty years older, says that, at least "in the 70's", Scouse was "quite lyrical" and "singy-songy" (01MMC52). This is echoed by a 20-year-old female who describes Liverpool English as "quite melodic", and specifies that Scouse intonation is characterised by "rises and falls" which are "just on a scale of [their] own" due to "the way the melodies are in people's [Scouse] accents" compared to other varieties of English (06FMC20). It is striking that intonation seems to be such an important aspect of Scouse for at least some Liverpudlians. Together with the fact that Knowles (1973) already found it necessary to devise a "phonology" of Scouse intonation, this clearly indicates that the prosodic features of Liverpool English would merit a detailed and up-to-date analysis which could not be embarked upon in the context of the present study.

With respect to intonation, two young female subjects in the sample also mention another aspect, namely that of supposedly "high pitch as well sometimes" (07FMC23) in Liverpool English. It should be noted, however, that the interviewee does not phrase this issue in very general terms, but provides just a single example as anecdotal evidence, arguing that the footballer Jamie Carragher was "very high pitched" (07FMC23). The second subject to bring up this feature is more categorical in this respect and mentions "high pitchness, for men" generally as a characteristic of (male) Scouse (36FWC20). A caveat is in order all the same, because she further explains that she herself might just be "oblivious to it" because she "hear[s] it every day", but she argues that "there's a very high pitch" when Scousers are "being impersonated" (36FWC20). As an example she names "The Scousers" from *Harry Enfield's Television Programme*, a 90's BBC comedy show, where a group of three stereotype working-class Liverpudlians with "black curly wigs" say "calm down, calm down" and are "like, really high pitched" (36FWC20). Despite the fact that she considers this one of the "main (...) characteristics of the accent" (36FWC20), it is therefore an open question whether high pitch is something that the subject has really experienced as a typical feature of Scouse herself, or whether she is just reiterating external stereotypes that might or might not be appropriate. Again, future research would be necessary to assess whether there is an empirical base to such claims.

8.2.3 Phonological variables

Conscious awareness of phonological features of Scouse is very limited, which is not too surprising. One older female speaker who is a retired teacher and has received elocution lessons earlier in her life mentions that "[Liverpudlians] often drop the aitch" and that there was "the broad 'o', (...) we would never say [pʌb], or [kʌp]" (28FMC59). Neither h-dropping (which is a non-regional feature of colloquial, urban British English, and is found in bigger cities all over the UK), nor the FOOT-STRUT merger (which is presumably what the subject refers to as "broad 'o'") are distinctive traits of Scouse. Possibly, this subject also hinted at lenition of alveolar plosives, but this is highly speculative as she did mention contexts where "there's a double 't', as in *motto* [or] (...) *matter*" (28FMC59), but then she failed to explain what happened in these contexts and went on to talk about something else. Apart from the NURSE-SQUARE merger and lenition of /k/ (which are both discussed below in more detail), no other phonetic or phonological features were listed as characteristic of Scouse in the 20 interviews that provided the data for the quantitative analyses in Chapters 6 and 7. Neither velar nasal plus, nor happy-tensing were mentioned even once by any of the 38 participants that were originally interviewed for this study.

8.2.3.1 NURSE-SQUARE merger

The NURSE-SQUARE merger is occasionally singled out as a characteristic feature of Liverpool English by speakers of all three age groups investigated. Naturally, the descriptions that are given are often somewhat lacking in precision. For example, an older woman mentioned that (in her opinion mostly younger) Liverpudlians "keep [their] teeth together" in words like *square* (18FWC67). While it is not clear what exactly she means by "keeping their teeth together", we do at least know that she is aware of something going on with that particular vowel. Other descriptions are quite exact. A case in point is the female speaker cited in the preceding paragraph. She says about "that ur sound" that "Liverpool people have always had (...) a difficulty with pronouncing words like *church, care, air*" and that words such as "*bird* and *bear*" were "often the same thing, really" (28FMC59). In the middle-aged group, comments are not quite as precise, but there are quite a few instances of people explaining that one can tell someone is a Scouser by how they say words like "church, you know" (03MMC33); and they do so using a vowel which is much closer to [ɛ] than the typical realisation they have been using in the rest of the spontaneous speech part of their interview.

The youngest subjects in the sample rarely comment on the NURSE-SQUARE merger. Some speakers might actually be trying to refer to this variable, but their explanations are so vague that they just cannot be reliably linked to this vowel. For instance, a 19-year-old working-class male said that it was a typical feature of Scouse to "stress the (...) 'u' sound" (04MWC19). NURSE is often represented by <ur> in the orthography, so he *might* be talking about this vowel, but since he does not give an example he could just as well be trying to refer to something completely different (e.g. an actual "u"-like vowel, such as the /ʊ/ in *book*, which is – in traditional Scouse, at least – often realised as [uː]). However, we do occasionally find rather precise descriptions of the merger in this age group as well, although it has to be said that they are comparatively rare. As an example, consider this quote taken from a 20-year-old male who explains how to identify a Scouse accent:

(8)   Especially on certain words you'll notice it a lot more than others: like *church* (…) and *nurse* as well. Like, I say [nɛːs] (…) where it's actually [nɜːs]. (02MWC20)

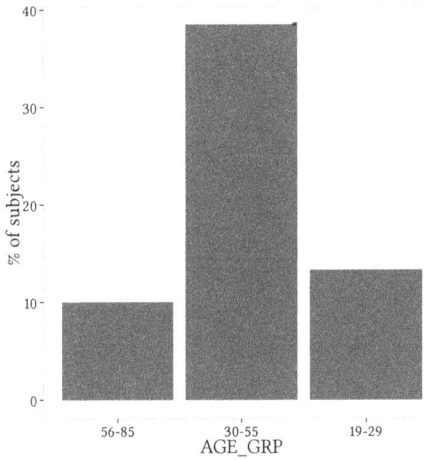

Figure 8.1: Awareness of NURSE by age

Figure 8.1 summarises awareness of the NURSE-SQUARE merger in the three age groups under scrutiny in this study. As explained at the beginning of this chapter, the database for this bar plot is not restricted to the 20 interviews used for the quantitative analyses, but includes information extracted from all 38 interviews that have been conducted by the author. The height of the bars represent the percentages of subjects in the relevant age groups who showed some sort of conscious awareness of the NURSE-SQUARE merger, i.e. they either gave an explicit explanation of the feature or they at least provided relevant examples. As is obvious from the left-most bar, only 10% of the speakers in the oldest group mentioned this feature, so we can say that the variable is virtually unknown in this age group. In the middle-aged group (bar in the middle), 38.46% mentioned the feature. While this means that people who are not consciously aware of this variable are still in the majority, awareness *has* increased considerably and the feature does seem to have acquired a certain degree of salience within this group. When we look at the youngest speakers, however, this trend has apparently not been maintained: the percentage of subjects who explicitly commented on the NURSE-SQUARE merger has not increased further, but actually dropped again to 13.33%, a value which is comparable to that of the oldest Liverpudlians in the sample. With respect to this vowel, therefore, salience seems to have decreased in the 19–29 year olds, only a small minority knows that fronted NURSE variants are a characteristic feature of Liverpool English.

8.2.3.2 Lenition of /k/

As far as lenition is concerned, it is first of all interesting to note that none of the 4 old speakers in the primary sample of this study talk about this feature at all. The retired teacher quoted at the beginning of §8.2.3 *might* constitute an exception, but even if one is willing to accept her statement as referring to lenition, it would clearly relate to lenition of *alveolar* plosives, not *velar* ones, which are the focus of this research.

In the group of subjects aged between 30 and 55, however, we do find a number of quotes that directly and explicitly refer to the way Scousers realise the phoneme /k/. Just as with the NURSE-SQUARE merger, some of these comments are comparatively vague and essentially just consist of an example word containing the relevant variable. A female working-class speaker in this sub-sample, for instance, explained that one could identify someone from Liverpool based on "how people say *chicken* and all that" (13FWC44). Other speakers explicitly generalise and talk about the variable instead of just single words ("we pronounce 'k's quite strongly at the end of words, (...) or within words" – 33FMC38), although these more general descriptions are also often backed up with concrete examples ("people used to always ask me to say *chicken*" – 33FMC38). What is more, people often additionally single out the relevant variable ("it's like /x/" – 33FMC38) and describe the place of articulation, phonetically correctly, as "like, (quite) guttural, isn't it" (33FMC38 and 01MMC52).

If we focus on the youngest Liverpudlians that have been interviewed, explicit comments on lenition of /k/ actually abound – each of the 8 subjects in this age group that were included in the quantitative analysis mentioned this variable. Again, there are some rather vague explanations, such as one 19-year-old middle-class male referring to lenition of velar plosives as Liverpudlians "put[ting] an emphasis on 'k's'" (31MMC19). Most other comments in this age group, however, are very much to the point. One speaker mentions the variable ("definitely the "k"), provides examples ("if I was to say (...) *cook* [kʊx], *back* [bax]"), contrasts the standard realisation with the Scouse one, and even talks about his difficulties in producing the former:

(9)   It's really hard for me to say [tʊk] rather than [tʊx]. (02MWC20)

These speakers are also aware of the fact that the "/x/ at the back of your throat" is particularly frequent in "some of the strong accents" and "quite distinctive" as well (04MWC19). Another subject in this age group even declares lenition of velar plosives to be a shibboleth. When asked to name sounds that distinguish Liverpool English from other accents he says:

(10) Of course you can tell (…) if people have the /x/ sound (…) when they speak. So it's easy to tell who's a Scouser, and who's not a Scouser. (25MMC19)

Other Liverpudlians between the ages of 19 and 29 also count "the /x/ sound" among the "main, like, characteristics of the accent" (36FWC20). This does not necessarily mean that they like this feature, though. For example, a middle-class female who talks about the "throaty /x/" in words like *chicken* and *bucket* also explains that she finds this pronunciation "really annoying" (06FMC20).

It is not unlikely that younger Scousers are particularly aware of this variable because it is not just a shibboleth for Liverpudlians, but also for outsiders. Two speakers in the sample mention lenition of /k/ as a typical feature of Scouse and reveal that their judgement is not exclusively influenced by their own observations, but, at least in part, by external perceptions of Liverpool English as well. Both are working-class women and 20 years old. The first one names "the /x/ sound" as a typical Scouse pronunciation variant and adds that this statement is "based on what [she's] been skitted on in the past" (36FWC20), so she is especially conscious of the feature because other people (who are, presumably, not from Liverpool) have used it to make fun of her. The second speaker also provides a personal mini-narrative when she recounts that "people say 'say chicken', 'cause we say [tʃɪxən]", and that ever since she entered university she had frequently been asked "do you want some chicken?" by people who wanted to "imitate [her]" (37FWC20). It is well possible that many other Liverpudlians have made rather similar experiences when interacting with speakers from other areas. After all, lenition is not only classified as a highly characteristic feature of Scouse by linguists, but, impressionistically at least, it also seems to be omnipresent in all imitations of Scouse by stand-up comedians and the like.

If we again zoom out a bit further and take into account all 38 interviews, the picture sketched above solidifies. Just as for the NURSE-SQUARE merger, Figure 8.2 shows the percentage of speakers in the relevant age group that explicitly mentioned lenition of /k/ as a typical feature of Scouse. As can be seen quite clearly, the rate is, at 20%, quite low in the oldest group of speakers, which is represen-

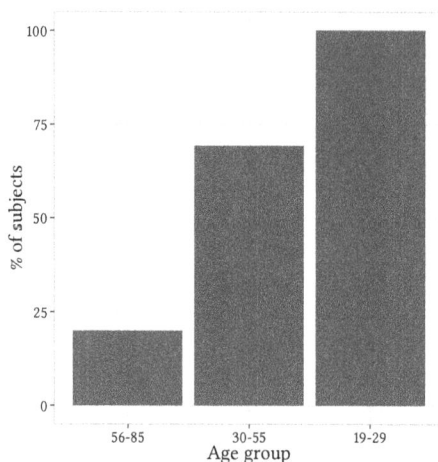

Figure 8.2: Awareness of /k/ lenition by age

ted by the bar on the left of the graph. Only one in five speakers aged 56 and older commented on lenition. In the middle-aged group, this rate has risen quite considerably: almost three out of four subjects (69.23%) are now aware of lenited /k/ variants. When we finally get to the youngest speakers investigated in this study, the bar (on the right) in the plot actually reaches the 100% threshold, which means that *every single* participant under 30 explicitly mentioned lenition of velar plosives as a typical feature of Scouse and commented on it. Awareness of lenition thus increases in a near-linear fashion from the oldest to the youngest participants: it starts out as a feature which only a handful of Liverpudlians are aware of, gains dramatically in prominence in the middle group, and finally reaches a state of full conscious awareness in the youngest generation of speakers interviewed.

Having said all that, it should be noted that it is quite possible that Scousers are *generally* aware of the variable but not, for some reason, of its presence *in their own speech*. There is some anecdotal evidence in my data that supports this idea. One subject (female, working-class, 20 years old) explicitly said that she didn't like lenition and therefore didn't use it:

(11)   I can't even do it because I've spent that long, trying to, like, train me mouth not to do it. (36FWC20)

However, she has a mean PDF of 81.87%. So in actual fact, she *can* do it quite well, and uses the fricative realisation almost categorically. Very similar things could probably be said about a number of other subjects who proclaimed not to have a strong Scouse accent or who said they did not like lenited /k/ variants, but who nevertheless quite frequently *use* these variants.

8.3 Evolution and evaluation of Scouse

8.3.1 Old speakers

8.3.1.1 Increase of "slovenly Scouse"

All four older subjects in the primary sample in one way or another express the idea that Scouse has "really changed in the younger generation" (28FMC59). Two of them make reference to the Beatles, whose "Liverpool accent" was allegedly "different (...) because (...) it's become very guttural now" (08MMC62). One might be tempted to interpret this statement as referring to increased usage of the "guttural" /k/ lenition (cf. §7.2.5), and this might very well be what the speaker is talking about. However, the same term is also used by a female subject of about the same age when she says that "it used to be (...) quite guttural, the way *we* spoke" (28FMC59, my emphasis). It follows that, for her, Scouse has thus become *less* "guttural". This could either mean she has not noticed that younger Liverpudlians use more lenition, or that she thinks of something completely different when she says "guttural". In any case, she seems to think that Liverpool English has become more distinct from the surrounding area in her life time, because she explains that in the accent she "grew up with in the sixties, that everybody recognised through the Beatles", one encountered "Lancashire expressions very often" (28FMC59). She believes "the older accent" can still be heard in "[her] generation and the older people", whereas her sons could "perfectly mimic young Scouse men talking now" which apparently sounds "just bizarre" and "strange" because the accent has "really, really changed" (28FMC59).

Another speaker has the impression that "the percentage of people that speak really slovenly Scouse has increased" (05MWC66). This change is, in his opinion, primarily driven by "the poorer people", but he also finds that "it's mostly young people that talk like that", presumably because "as they get older (...) [their accent] gets a bit rounded off (05MWC66). If we follow this line of argumentation, the increase of "slovenly Scouse" would only be temporary on the level of the individual and restricted to speakers of a certain age (the same at any point in time!) at the level of the speech community. In opposition to this, another speaker states that the present generation "has got it's own language" in much the same way as "[her] generation had a language that was different from our parents'", so she seems to find it quite natural that "each generation just create[s] their own language completely" (18FWC67) – without suggesting that this is something that people necessarily do away with later in their life.

While this is a rather liberal stance on language change, it does not completely keep her from seeing something special in the most recent changes that she does not seem to be too happy about. According to her, "there are youngsters that will (...) not say the words properly and they will put (...) the Scouse accent on" (18FWC67). While it is not quite clear what exactly she means by "not saying the words properly", it is probably uncontroversial to assume she is referring to non-standard pronunciation, coupled with the fact that this seems to happen in a non-natural, inauthentic way, as the second part of the quote suggests. This "putting it on" is something she observes in her own family ("grandson can do it very well"), and which, apparently, can start with children that are "only nine" (18FWC67). Not only does she believe that the variety that younger Liverpudlians use is "totally different from the language [she] had, and [her] daughter had", but she even maintains that her two grandsons differed in linguistic behaviour, despite the fact that "there's only two years between the two of them" (18FWC67). Both, however, seem to be using varieties of English that are considerably different from her own because she reports frequently having to ask both of them to repeat utterances she did not understand.

This subject and the other woman in the group of older speakers hint at a possible reason why the accents of young Liverpudlians seem particularly strong to this generation. When (presumably) talking about the NURSE-SQUARE merger (cf. §8.2.3) she does not only mention that younger Scousers "keep their teeth together" but she also adds that speakers of her generation "weren't allowed to do that" and that they "got told off" if they spoke with a markedly non-standard accent (18FWC67). The newly-retired teacher gives a slightly more detailed account and explains that her accent is now "modified (...), probably 'cause we had elocution at school" (28FMC59). Further research would be required to analyse if this is an experience that is rather particular to this individual speaker because she was "educated by nuns" and later became a teacher, or whether a sizeable proportion of Liverpudlians in this generation "learned to speak a more received pronunciation" (28FMC59) during their time at school.

8.3.1.2 From "amiable" to "grating"

When it comes to the evaluation of this change, the older speakers in my sample are relatively unanimous. The male working-class subject links stronger accents up not just with youth, but also with social deprivation when he says that "it's not all young people that talk like that", but especially "the poorer [ones]" among them; a fact which he does not "decry[]" but which he attributes to the influence of their peers (05MWC66). He adds that he knows he himself speaks with a Scouse accent, but – crucially – "people can understand [him]" (05MWC66). The value judgement is not explicit here, but nevertheless not too difficult to unearth: he does not object to Scouse accents in general, as long as they do not hinder communication. A mild accent that expresses where one is from is fine, a strong one which makes it difficult (for outsiders) to understand the speaker, is not. His middle-class counterpart essentially voices the same belief, but does so in a more direct way. In his opinion, the accent has "got a lot coarser" and "harder (...) amongst younger people" (08MMC62). His choice of vocabulary already clearly suggests that he considers this to be "not so good", but his main criticism is that the supposed coarseness can "make [younger Scousers] unintelligible, (...) and they don't have to be" (08MMC62). It does not take too much interpretation to arrive at the conclusion that he probably also thinks they *should* not be.

Unintelligibility is, however, not the only potential problem that this age group sees in pronounced Liverpool accents. The working-class male explains that, for him, strong Scouse accents are "normal" because he has grown up in the city, but he also finds it understandable that "the way some [Scousers] (...) talk (...) can be intimidating" to *outsiders* (05MWC66). According to him, the "very, very few" Liverpudlians who use these strong accents do not "do good for us" (05MWC66), i.e. they have a detrimental influence on the national image of Liverpool because, with their strong and "intimidating" accents, they give an impression of the city which people from outside find rather unpleasant. This speaker is not exclusively worried about external perceptions, though, but also states that he himself is not a fan of "slovenly Scouse" – as he calls it –, when he reflects about people's motivation for using these varieties:

(12)   I don't think they've consciously gone out to say "we'll speak this way so to get on everybody's nerves". The fact that it does is a bonus. (05MWC66)

So, while he does not assume that young Scousers *primarily* employ strong accents to annoy other people, he does believe that they like the idea ("a bonus") and he also acknowledges that they have this effect on him personally ("the fact that it does").

The two women in this age group seem to largely agree with this evaluation. One of them states that "the ordinary Scouse is quite amiable", but "the really (...) guttural one that they used in *Bread* (...) grates on your nerves" (18FWC67). Strong accents, such as the one that is heard in the BBC sitcom from the 80s, "grate", in her opinion, "because there's only a certain community that talks like that" (18FWC67) – presumably very deprived and poor people like the fictitious lower working-class family which *Bread* revolves around. While she does not claim that these kinds of accents are *exclusively* found among younger Liverpudlians, she does stress that particularly "some youngsters" use a kind of "plucking chicken language" (18FWC67), an attribute which can hardly be considered positive. The other older female speaker gives a very similar verdict when she says that, to her, modern Scouse accents seem "more staccato" than they used to be (28FMC59). She is not really happy about this and finds the resulting sound "not gentle" and "much more aggressive" (28FMC59) than the one she considers typical of her own youth.

8.3.2 Middle-aged speakers

8.3.2.1 Kids so Scouse it's unbelievable

In the middle-aged group, fewer subjects explicitly talk about change in Liverpool English, but when they do their gist is similar to that of the oldest speakers in the sample. A male, middle-class speaker, for instance, argues there is "no doubt about it" that Scouse "definitely has changed" and he even provides a quite precise estimate that this is something that has happened in the "last sort of 10 years" (01MMC52). He also says that "when [he] was young" the accent was allegedly more "lyrical" and "singy songy", something which, he explains, can also still be heard in the speech of "some of the older people", so this is further evidence for the fact that he believes change in Scouse to be a rather new development, "something that's recently cracked in" (01MMC52). The same speaker also brings up the issue of unintelligibility, although he does not directly link it to younger Liverpudlians. He refers to an acquaintance who has "a really thick accent" and who, on a particular occasion, spoke in a way which made it impossible for a friend from Staffordshire to "understand him at all" (01MMC52). He goes on to explain that this was, in his opinion, mostly due to lenition of velar plosives ("he does /x/") and that he also believes that "he embellishes [his accent]" and "lay[s] it on a lot" (01MMC52), so a very strong accent that is unintelligible (to outsiders) is once more associated with inauthenticity.

Other speakers in this age group connect these kinds of accents more directly and explicitly with young Scousers. A 49-year-old working-class male,[1] for instance, claimed that the accent was getting stronger and "rougher" with younger speakers, while not bringing up the subject of unintelligibility. One of his female counterparts, however, does just that in the following statement:

---

[1]During the interview of this subject the recording equipment failed. As a result, the last 2 minutes or so of his interview were not recorded. The above reproduction of his relevant statements is based on notes taken directly after the interview.

(13)   The kids, you know, they're so Scouse it's unbelievable. (...) I have
        difficulty understanding some of them. (13FWC44)

Here, the matter of change and unintelligibility is taken one step further. For this
particular speaker, it is no longer just an issue of young Scousers being unintelligible to people who are not familiar with Liverpool accents. When she says that
she herself sometimes has to "ask [her nieces and nephews] twice what they're
saying" (13FWC44) she acknowledges that even middle-aged insiders occasionally run into difficulties when talking to young Liverpudlians with pronounced
local accents. Interestingly, she also hypothesises about whether this might be
a temporary issue, i.e. whether younger speakers might change their pronunciation to a more standard-like (or at least less local) accent later in their life (cf.
§8.3.1). Her argument for this idea is based on pragmatic and presumably also
economic and social reasons, because she explains that "as you get older and
you're getting to work (...), you have to tone [the accent] down", and adds that
this is particularly true "when you're dealing with the public" (13FWC44) – in
cases where the speaker is in an exposed position where both intelligibility and
social appropriateness are an issue.

8.3.2.2 From "down-to earth" to "thick"

Middle-aged speakers evaluate Scouse and the perceived change in the accent in
a very similar way as the oldest subjects do (cf. §8.3.1.2). There is only one speaker
in this age group who has exclusively positive things to say about Scouse. This
woman explains that "[she] quite like[s] the accent", because for her "it sounds
friendly" and "down to earth" (33FMC38). She also says that it does not sound
"stuck up" (33FMC38), thereby implying that other varieties do, but without spe-
cifying which ones precisely she is comparing Scouse to. Other speakers focus
more on negative aspects: the working-class male who classified the accents of
younger Scousers as being "rougher", for instance, also explained that he found
these accents "unpleasant" (17MWC49), a judgement which is already implicit in
a term like "rough".

     This speaker, and some others likewise, only explicitly talk about aspects of
Scouse that they find disagreeable, but by expressly limiting their statements to
particular sub-variants of Scouse (i.e. "strong" ones) they also imply that they
evaluate other ("lighter") accents differently. For instance, the 52-year-old male
in the sample is only talking about particularly strong Scouse accents as they
are, in his opinion often found in younger speakers when he says: "I don't like it,
no. I just kind of think it's a bit put on" (01MMC52). It should be noted that the

dislike is, once more, connected with the fact that these accents are perceived as inauthentic and "false" (01MMC52).

Some subjects in this age group do, however, explicitly contrast different varieties of Scouse and make clear that they also judge them differently. One working-class woman, for example, says that she "[doesn't] like the *broad* Scouse" because "it can sound thick, like somebody's not all together there", whereas speaking "with a little twang is alright" (13FWC44, my emphasis). In this particular case, "sounding thick" seems to be somewhat intermingled with communicative problems, because the subject immediately follows up the above statement with (another) short narrative of her nephew who apparently often talks in a way that "you just can't understand a word he's saying", so "he certainly couldn't communicate with an adult" but only "with his mates" and should therefore "tone it down a bit" (13FWC44). It is possible that this line of thought is limited to this one individual, but it would not be surprising if "being unintelligible" and "sounding unintelligent" turned out to be related concepts for many other speakers as well.

The following quote from a 33-year-old middle-class male probably quite nicely sums up attitudes towards Scouse in this age group:

(14)   I think a natural sounding Liverpool accent that's not affected in any way sounds very nice, you know. I think, unfortunately, these days, there is an element of affectation. I think, again, probably that's just young people generally, you know. (...) I like the lilt, too [of the unaffected accent]. I like the (...) character that it brings. I don't like the over-emphasis of certain traits within the accent. (03MMC33)

Softer accents bring character and are perceived as nice, pleasant, and agreeable. Very pronounced accents, however, are not. The distinction into stronger and lighter accents is not expressly made in this quote, but it is paraphrased as "over-emphasis", on the one hand, and "unaffected" and "natural", on the other. It seems to me that this is a mental connection which is real for most speakers in this age group, and the old subjects as well. Strong Scouse accents are not only less acceptable because they can make a speaker unintelligible (although this does seem to be an important aspect), but also (and maybe even primarily) because middle-aged speakers perceive them as artificial, "affected", and "false". From the point of view of my subjects, these accents do make use of features that are recognised as being "to an extent a part of the accent" but, crucially, they are "overplayed" (03MMC33), which results in something that is perceived as a stereotypical accent performance and therefore rejected. While not limited to young Liverpudlians, this group of speakers seems to be the one that my middle-aged subjects primarily associate these "false" accents with.

8.3.3 Young speakers

8.3.3.1 A matter of personal experience

The speakers aged between 19 and 29 are considerably less homogeneous as a group when it comes to the question of whether Scouse has changed or is currently changing. Some of them, like a 19-year-old working-class male, claim that they have "not noticed any change" and/or have "never heard anyone comment the fact the accent's changing at all", but acknowledge that this might simply be due to their young age and that, for instance, their parents "might notice differences" that they themselves do not (04MWC19). Interestingly however, this speaker then goes on to explain that he would be reluctant to say his own parents "speak with a Liverpool accent in actual fact", and that his mother in particular uses "a softer (...) [and] slightly more refined" accent (04MWC19). His personal experience would thus seem to contradict his statement that he has not noticed any change in the accent, but apparently he is unwilling to extrapolate the differences within his family to a larger part of the population, for some reason.

The two young middle-class women in the primary sample are very similar in this respect. When directly asked whether she believes Scouse is changing the first one flatly rejects this idea with the words: "no, it's about the same" (06FMC20). Earlier in her interview, however, when the subject of (local) identity was discussed, she explained that she would not use the label "Scouser" for herself, but that she would "call [her] mum and dad Scousers, 'cause their accent is significantly stronger than what [hers] is" (06FMC20). We have thus, again, a young speaker who has personal experience of apparent time change (though in the opposite direction of what most older subjects report), but does not seem to consider it representative of the more general situation in Liverpool.

The other female middle-class speaker likewise says that she has not "noticed [Scouse] changing", but then immediately goes on to talk about her parents, who "don't really have a strong Liverpool accent *anymore*" (my emphasis), despite the fact that they have grown up in the Dingle and Toxteth, respectively, which are both traditional working-class districts that the subject herself describes as "quite rough areas of Liverpool", at least when her parents were young (07FMC23). Her explanation for the "softer" accents of her parents is that they later moved "out of the centre" to a northern suburb and "lost their accent, if they had one" (07FMC23). To be fair, the second part of this statement ("if they had one") indicates that she is aware of the fact that her parents might never have had such a strong accent as is nowadays typical for speakers from these districts (which would be evidence for accent change), but she does not know and apparently prefers the hypothesis that her parents changed, instead of the accent itself. It is possible that this focus on the individual is due to the fact that she has observed changes in her own use of language in her recent past. She speculates that she might have had "a stronger accent" before she went to university where she "lived with quite a lot of people from down south (...) and [her] accent just became really weird", whereas now that she has been living and working in Liverpool again for a number of years, friends and acquaintances from outside the city tell her that she has "got more Scouse" again, though she herself "can't tell" (07FMC23).

Most of the subjects that do believe Scouse is changing or has changed also base their opinion on evidence collected in their family context. There is one male middle-class speaker in my sample who believes, and explicitly verbalises, that Liverpool English is "getting less distinguished", based on the evidence that in the generation of his grand parents "they've got really strong accents" (25MMC19), although it is unclear whether he is primarily referring to his own grand parents or to this age group more generally. The remainder of the young Scousers, however, agree with the majority of the old and middle-aged speakers in saying that (a) "the accent itself has changed, definitely" (02MWC20), and that (b) the "Scouse accent's become stronger" (31MMC19). Younger speakers apparently often realise this first when they compare their own speech with that of other family members, like the middle-class male just quoted, who explains:

(15)   I talk a bit different to me mum or the rest of me family, but me and me brother talk the same, like, as each other or me mates. (31MMC19)

Some speakers are also conscious of the fact that there is probably an interaction of age and other social factors like the socioeconomic background of speakers in certain areas of the city. One interviewee, for instance, says that, in general, Scouse has "become thicker in a lot of terms" and adds that this is particularly true in "deprived areas" of Liverpool, "to the point where people (...) have actually asked (...): 'Are you from Liverpool?'", despite the fact that he himself has "a much more heavier accent" than both his parents (02MWC20). Another participant provides examples for this claim when she says that "if you grew up in Anfield or Kensington [inner city working-class districts], you're gonna sound Scouser than someone who grew up in Childwall [a more affluent suburb]" (36FWC20). She does, however, also believe that Liverpool English, as a whole, is different today than it was "a few decades ago" when it was presumably "closer to the Manchester accent" (36FWC20). Her point of reference seems to be the 60s because she mentions that in "clips of the Beatles, if you listen to John Lennon speak, he doesn't sound Scouse" although he was, which is evidence for her that the accent has "definitely changed since then, it's obviously evolved" (36FWC20).

8.3.3.2 "Unpleasant but friendly"

With respect to evaluating the perceived change of Scouse and its current form, there is again a wide range of different comments and attitudes among the youngest speakers in my sample. Few people directly comment the change itself, and when they do they do not express very strong opinions about it. A male working-class speaker, for instance, says that he "wouldn't really have a bad or positive comment on the change, to be honest" because for him it is just something that "happens" (02MWC20). A female of the same age explains that she is not sure "if [she] prefer[s], like, John Lennon's accent to [the modern one]" or the other way round (36FWC20). In general, subjects are much more willing to provide evaluations of (varieties of) modern Scouse, rather than on the process of accent change. Often, these judgements are similarly ambiguous as the ones expressed by the old and the middle-aged speakers. For instance, Scouse can be described as "unpleasant but (...) friendly at the same time" because Scousers are both "so loud and confident" (31MMC19). Another speaker explains that, to him as an insider, "it sounds friendly, but [he doesn't] know what it sounds, like, from outside looking in" and he can well imagine that, in the latter case, "it could be a bit intimidating sometimes" (25MMC19) – which is particularly interesting because it is an almost word-by-word repetition of something another Liverpudlians said who is more than 45 years older and from a different social class (cf. §8.3.1.2).

Just like speakers of their parents' and grand parents' generation, the youngest subjects in my sample also often evaluate Scouse differently depending on whether it is considered to be a stronger or a lighter variant. This is exemplified by statements such as "if it's a soft Scouse accent (...) I haven't got a problem with it", provided people "speak correctly" and "as long as I can understand them" (06FMC20), which is evidence for the fact that (un)intelligibility is as much of an issue and a relevant factor for evaluation among the youngest Scousers as it is in the middle-aged and the old group. Not every kind of Scouse accent is seen as somewhat problematic, but "the really, really thick accent where you can't understand what they're saying" is very frequently, albeit not always, considered as "very annoying" (04MWC19). The same holds true for the whole matter of authenticity. Consider the following quote:

(16)   [Scouse] does sound quite friendly and I quite like it, unless it's incredibly thick. I mean, I like the light accent, and my accent, most Liverpudlian

accent[s]. But when you get over the top with it then it's just plain ridiculous. I mean, there's no reason to go /x/ all the time. (04MWC19)

'Thick" accents are judged just as negatively as inauthentic ones where people "go over the top with it". The "plain ridiculous" accent of this kind is interpreted as the result of a (perhaps semi-)conscious process, not as something that is just naturally there from the start: The speaker believes there is no compelling "reason" to use the stigmatised fricative realisation of the velar plosive "all the time"; it is a decision people make instead of something they cannot help.

A different male working-class speaker talks about the same issue – "plastic" Scouse accents – in the context of the media (where conscious accent performances are much more likely to occur than in "real life"). He mentions that he "cannot stand [Scouse]" on television because it "sounds either really harsh or really blunt", and that "there's nothing worse than a person who has a really weird thick Scouse accent" (02MWC20). Why those accents are not just "thick", but also "weird" is also explained by this interviewee: "You know, like, most of us don't speak like what you actually see on the TV" (02MWC20). He feels he can tell "if someone's really putting it on", i.e. if they are a plastic Scouser, and finds this kind of thing "very annoying" (02MWC20). This speaker is also rather explicit on the fact that a "thick" accent is not *necessarily* also a "plastic" one, so the two concepts have to be kept separate. He stresses that there are "Scousers that (...) have a perfectly reasonable (...) tinge and (...) perfectly fine TV accent"; one of his examples is the comedian John Bishop who, as the participant notes himself "has quite a strong Liverpudlian accent", but nevertheless one that appears to be acceptable because it is not perceived as inauthentic (02MWC20). Interestingly (but probably not too surprisingly), a speaker from the middle-aged group used John Bishop as a prime example of a plastic Scouser, so it is presumably controversial among Liverpudlians where exactly the "plastic" line is to be drawn.

Negative comments and evaluations are, however, not exclusively limited to "plastic" accents, as has been shown above. In particular, three female subjects in my sample can be said to be primarily critical of Scouse, as is obvious from the fact that they almost exclusively express negative feelings towards their accent. For example, they describe the perceived change in the accent as Scouse having "gone more common" (36FWC20) or "harsher" (37FWC20), although it has to be said that this does not keep Liverpool English from also carrying connotations of home and familiarity for these speakers (e.g. when hearing Scouse accents on holiday – 37FWC20). Nevertheless, they remark that Scouse is "not [their] favourite accent", an attitude which is likely to be influenced by the awareness that, from an external point of view, the Liverpool accent is among "the most hated in England" (07FMC23). In a very similar vein, a different speaker mentions that she sometimes asks her brother to "speak properly" because his natural accent is "stronger than ours" and "sounds scallyish" (36FWC20) – *scally* being a term commonly used to refer to the stereotype of the self-assured, boisterous, and criminal (male) working-class Scouser.

The subject acknowledges that many speakers are not able to consciously control their pronunciation very well when she says that "most of the time people can't help the way they speak". All the same she insists that "just because you're from Liverpool, you don't need to speak like you were drugged", which is a rather harsh judgement, especially when considered against the backdrop that this is apparently also "how [her own] voice sounds when [she's] not thinking about the way words come out" (36FWC20). As has been reported earlier this speaker has apparently indeed tried hard to eliminate stereotyped features like lenition from her speech, but while she believes to have succeeded, the data collected for this study tell a different story (cf. §8.2.3). The fact alone that she tries, however, says a lot about her attitudes towards Scouse. Her motivation lies in the fact that she has internalised some of the negative stereotypes about Scouse, although this causes her some distress because it is her "home" accent, after all. She seems to be rather aware of this whole process and provides a comparatively detailed description:

(17)   If I thought it was a beautiful sound, if I thought it was educated, and a
       proper way to speak – then (...) I wouldn't try and think about the way
       I'm saying things. (...) No, I do think it can sound uneducated and I wish
       it didn't, but...(36FWC20)

It should be noted, however, that these extreme attitudes (which border on dissociation) are clearly the exception – most younger subjects express much more moderate views, especially when they voice negative thoughts about Liverpool English.

9 Discussion (production)

This chapter will provide a summary and interpretation of the (most important) results reported in Chapters 6, 7, and 8. In line with the primary interest of this study, the focus will be on what patterns of usage, distributions across social groups, and explicit comments and attitudes tell us about the status of the variables under scrutiny here: That is to say whether they can best be classified as indicators, markers, or stereotypes.

9.1 happy: Indicator (of northernness)

9.1.1 Overall age differences

F1-F2 plots of happy have shown that this vowel is not stable across the three generations of speakers investigated in this study, neither in terms of height nor with respect to frontness (though change in the latter is only significant in the raw data, but not once the random effects of individuals and carrier words have been eliminated by a mixed linear effects model). Rather, realisations of this vowel become simultaneously lower and more central from the old to the middle-aged, and from the middle-aged to the young speakers in my sample. Nevertheless, Pillai scores show that happy and FLEECE are completely merged for *all* speakers. Given that the vowels could only be compared in the two (formal) reading tasks this might be expected, because, in such contexts, happy is more likely to be tense due to phonetic factors such as duration. It turns out, however, that happy and FLEECE are actually moving together: *both* vowels are more central in the middle and the young group. At the same time, though, the distance between mean realisations of FLEECE and happy is increasing in the younger participants, which means that the two vowels are actually becoming more distinct due to happy being more strongly centralised than FLEECE – thus, while both vowels are moving, it does appear to be primarily happy that is changing. A general caveat is still in order, because all the differences between age groups are in fact very subtle. Impressionistically at least, almost all happy realisations are still acoustically tense, even in the youngest speakers.

Nonetheless, there is a measurable and statistically robust trend for younger speakers to have laxer and therefore less Scouse realisations of happy. Since these speakers were actually expected to have more *local* pronunciation, an explanation is warranted. Flynn (2010) found young speakers from Nottingham to employ ultra-lax variants of happy in an attempt to further distance themselves from the south of England and to emphasise their identities as (working-class) northerners. I suspect that young Scousers use laxer happy variants for the same reason. Qualitative analysis of comments about identity (cf. §8.1.3) revealed that older subjects often consider Liverpool to be "unique" or 'distinct' from the rest of England, both north and south. In the middle and particularly the young group, however, having a secondary identity as a northerner seems perfectly acceptable and even normal to the majority of subjects. Younger Scousers often readily embrace a northern identity as a means of setting themselves apart from the south and, at the same time, associating with other northern cities that they perceive as (more) similar to Liverpool.

As mentioned above, change in happy is subtle, but it *is* a movement *away* from both the traditional local norm and the modern standard pronunciation (both of which are tense), and *towards* the variant that is typical for the majority of speakers in the linguistic north of England (the only exceptions being Liverpool and Newcastle). Centralising happy can be seen as a way of linguistically expressing solidarity with other northern cities and keeping one's distance from 'the south', a region that many Liverpudlians consider to be both geographically and culturally distant.

9.1.2 Gender and class

The more detailed analysis of happy in §6.1.1 and §6.1.2 showed that both gender and social class also play a role in how this vowel is realised. For instance, it turns out that the age difference discussed above is exclusively driven by female speakers. The men in my sample actually all have comparatively low happy variants, regardless of their age. Women seem to have been adapting to the men in this respect for quite a while and have now done so to the point that there is no significant gender difference in the youngest generation of speakers any more, which could actually indicate that this variable is slightly more salient in the older two generations.

With respect to the front-back dimension women only have happy variants that are statistically different from those of men when they speak freely and when they imitate a particularly strong Scouse accent. In the former case, women's realisations are fronter, in the latter they are more retracted. It is not

really surprising for women to have fronter happʏ variants than men in spontaneous speech, because these fronter realisations are actually closer to the (modern)
standard, and numerous sociolinguistic studies have shown that women generally tend to use more standard variants than men. It does seem strange, however,
that they would use more retracted vowels than male speakers when performing
Liverpool English, given that stereotypical Scouse should have *tense* happʏ. This
could be a hint that women are at least sub-consciously aware of the fact that men
actually have more central variants than they themselves in spontaneous speech.
If we assume that the typical Scouser people think of when they are asked to perform the accent is male (which does not seem too far-fetched, given the negative
stereotypes associated with Liverpool), then one can interpret women's happʏ
realisation during accent imitation as more "realistic" than "stereotypical". This
argument is rather speculative, but it is striking that women's mean and median
F2 during accent performance are virtually identical to the values that men have
in spontaneous speech (cf. Figure 6.12 on page 100).

Providing a coherent and unifying interpretation of social class is even more
difficult, because it interacts with gender when trying to predict F1, and age when
the focus is on F2. Women actually use higher happʏ variants than men in both
the working and the middle class, but in the former the difference is more pronounced than in the latter. In fact, it is mostly working-class women that stick
out. Middle-class women, middle-class men, and working-class men all have comparatively similar mean F1 values, whereas happʏ realisations of working-class
women are considerably higher and thus more Scouse (cf. Figure 6.4a on page
87). This result is diametrically opposed to Flynn's (2010) finding, because in his
study (young) working-class women were the ones that drove the change towards ultra-lax happʏ variants, whereas in my data, these speakers seem to be
the ones that have the most tense variants. The impact of social class on F2, as
mentioned above, depends on the age of the participant: in the old and the middle-
aged group, working-class speakers have fronter vowels, but among the youngest speakers the effect is reversed and working-class Scousers actually have more
central variants.

Women having more standard-like realisations is in line with what many sociolinguists have found in many different contexts, but it is unclear why working-
class women in particular would have more standard realisations than their middle-class counterparts – unless they were hypercorrecting, which is not particularly likely for a largely non-salient (see below) variable. What is more, being
working-class favours tenser pronunciations with respect to F1 for all age groups,
but as far as F2 is concerned, this is only true for old and middle-aged speakers.

For the youngest speakers, however, the effect is reversed, and working-class speakers now *dis*favour tense happʏ realisations. The evidence regarding gender and class thus presents itself as rather inconclusive and difficult to interpret.

9.1.3 Style shifting and awareness

When it comes to style shifting the three generations of speakers do not show any significant differences: All speakers use higher and fronter variants of happʏ when they read out a word list and also when they perform a stereotypical Scouse accent (for F2 style differences are statistically less robust). This is not the pattern that is commonly associated with Labovian style shifting, but register does have an impact on how happʏ is realised, so an explanation is called for.

The lower F1 and higher F2 values in the word list readings could be explained phonetically (slower and clearer articulation, resulting in more peripheral vowels generally), but this is difficult for accent performance, where the same trend (of more peripheral realisations) was observed. People seem to believe, as explicit comments revealed, that speaking *fast* is a typical feature of Scouse, so provided they incorporate this aspect into their stereotype performance it would rather favour *laxer* realisations of happʏ instead of tenser ones. In fact, vowel durations were somewhat shorter during imitation only for the youngest speakers in the sample, the rest had happʏ pronunciations of similar length in text reading, spontaneous speech, and accent imitation (cf. Table 6.4). In none of the three age groups can vowel duration thus be part of the explanation why happʏ realisations are tenser during performance of a strong Scouse accent – for the youngest speakers durations would even pull in the opposite direction.

Another interpretation of the U-shaped line in the two relevant graphs is that two different and, in a way, conflicting, speech norms are at work here. When people read through the list, they converge towards the standard pronunciation, which is /iː/, nowadays, whereas when they do the hyper-Scouse pronunciations, they tend to use more /i/-like vowels because that is what distinguishes Scouse from the directly surrounding accents. In the "reading" and "free" styles, articulation is a bit more relaxed (with respect to *both* norms) and happʏ tends to be lower, possibly simply for reasons of economy. The approach of two conflicting norms that pull in the same direction might seem slightly unsatisfying, but some sort of very vague sub-conscious awareness of happʏ as a feature of Liverpool English must be assumed if the increase in height and frontness in the imitation register is to be explained.

Interestingly, Newbrook (1999: 102) also found "anomalous stylistic patterning" in West Wirral and adds that (a) "there was a major issue in respect to *norms*" (my emphasis), and that (b) "[t]his applie[d] in particular to happy" (New-brook 1999: 102). Part of the problem is certainly that "the dialectological facts are complex and the interpretation of responses is often debatable", and also that many subjects seemed to be confused "as to what the RP form might actually be", which is his explanation for the fact that the majority of his participants endorsed [i] despite the fact that this was still a non-standard variant in 1980 when he collected his data (Newbrook 1999: 101). On the basis of my data at least, *conscious* awareness is out of the question: Not a single participant mentioned happy-tensing as a typical feature of Liverpool English, or otherwise commented on it.

9.1.4 Classification

The analysis of happy realisations has unearthed a number of features which hint at a certain degree of salience: there is some very basic social stratification, and there is a certain impact of register. However, both are less robust for F2, the vowel dimension that usually does most of the sociolinguistic work (cf. Labov 2006: 502). Furthermore, social factors are clearly much less important as predictors of formant values (irrespective of whether we are talking about F1 or F2) than they are for NURSE (cf. §9.2), which indicates lower relative salience and strongly suggests that the centralisation of happy is a change from below (cf. Labov 1994: 78). No prototypical style shifting is found for happy, but style differences are clearly not random either. Since the (somewhat confusing) impact of style is the same in all age groups and can be interpreted as showing at least the beginnings of some sort of awareness, it seems therefore justified to conclude that happy is somewhere in between an indicator and a marker for all speakers investigated – with the aside that it might actually be on its way to returning firmly to the status of an indicator with the youngest speakers, given that gender no longer plays a role.

9.2 NURSE: Marker to stereotype and back again

9.2.1 Overall age differences

Traditional vowel plots of mean NURSE and SQUARE realisations (pooled across different speaking styles) revealed that the former is (still) more central than the latter for all speakers investigated. Both vowels do however become higher and fronter from the youngest to the oldest subjects (which means that NURSE, in particular, is becoming more Scouse, but only with respect to F2). At the same time the distance between the means decreases, which means that for young Liverpudlians NURSE and SQUARE are considerably less distinct than for middle-aged and old Scousers. Just as for HAPPY and FLEECE, a caveat is in order here, because, once again, the differences between the two vowels are minute in absolute terms (especially as far as the F1 dimension is concerned), even for the oldest speakers where the distance is greatest. This idea is corroborated by Pillai scores that are universally near 0 and show NURSE and SQUARE to be almost perfectly merged in any age group and for any style.

All the same, differences between the age groups could be found, even if they were rather subtle in nature. For one thing, realisations in the old group mostly vary with respect to F1, whereas middle-aged speakers show more variation in F2. This alone can already hint at a slight increase in salience from the old to the middle-aged speakers, because a wider range of F2 values (as the sociolinguistically more important dimension) suggests a potentially higher functional load when it comes to the social meaning of the variables. Generally speaking, there is less variation in the most formal and the most informal (stereotyped) styles, which shows that speakers seem to be more agreed on the target realisations of the two vowels in these registers. Crucially, the difference between the styles decreases across the generations, particularly from the middle-aged to the young generation. The youngest speakers in the sample not only show few differences in-between speaking styles, but they also exhibit a very small degree of variation across the board, even in spontaneous speech. Both points serve as evidence for the fact that the realisations of NURSE and SQUARE seem to have largely stabilised in speakers aged between 19 and 29, which speaks for a decrease in salience, in particular from the middle to the young generation.

Plots of mean vowel realisations also revealed interesting differences between the age groups in how NURSE and SQUARE change along the style continuum. Among the oldest speakers that were interviewed both vowels move to the front during accent performance, which is the expected behaviour, particularly for NURSE.[1] In the remaining three styles, however, NURSE is remarkably stable and it is mostly SQUARE that moves – crucially, this movement is *towards* NURSE rather than away from it, which means that the two vowels are actually more instead of less merged the more formal the register. This is thus a mild case of hypercorrection, because by centralising SQUARE (which makes it *less* standard) instead of NURSE (which would become *more* standard), people are actually moving the "wrong" vowel.

---

[1]This also indicates that even for these speakers the target for a Scouse NURSE is a front vowel, not a central one as some people might suspect given the history of the merger in Liverpool; cf. §3.4.2.

Speakers of Scouse aged between 30 and 55 also behave as expected when they are asked to perform a stereotypical Scouse accent: both NURSE and SQUARE are fronter than in spontaneous speech. For the reading passage, middle-aged Liverpudlians adjust the vowels in the same way as the old generation. NURSE hardly moves at all, while SQUARE is centralised and thus approaches NURSE. When these speakers read out a word list, finally, SQUARE is even further back, while NURSE actually gets *fronted*. As a result, NURSE ends up fronter than SQUARE in this particular speech style. We have thus a situation that is characterised not only by the fact that the two vowels are more instead of less merged in more formal contexts, but also by a reversal of their relative positioning to each other. Speakers of the middle generation can therefore be said to present a textbook case of hypercorrection, because their behaviour results in the opposite of what they are presumably trying to achieve: NURSE and SQUARE pronunciations are even more non-standard in formal registers than they already are in spontaneous speech. This suggests both heightened awareness of the social meaning of this merger (hence the urge to modify usage according to communicative situation) and also a certain degree of linguistic insecurity with respect to this variable.

Among the youngest speakers style seems to be much less important. NURSE and SQUARE are about equally stable across different registers. This is true both in terms of how big the realisational space is (i.e. the range of occurring variants) and where the centres of gravity of the vowel clouds are to be found. Variation between styles is negligible, the position of both vowels largely constant. Young speakers have completely merged distributions and almost identical mean realisations in all speech styles, which strongly suggests that salience of the NURSE-SQUARE merger is very low at best in this group.

It was also shown that the (age) group Pillai scores hide a considerable degree of inter-speaker variation, at least as far as the old and the middle-aged participants are concerned. These two samples of speakers divide rather neatly into two separate sub-groups: (1) Completely merged speakers with Pillai scores near 0, and (2) speakers with comparatively high Pillai scores, who keep NURSE and SQUARE distinct. The crucial finding here is that, for the oldest speakers, higher Pillai scores correlate with higher social status, because it is the middle-class speakers who maintain a distinction and the working-class participants who are (more) merged – just as one would expect in the early phases of the social life cycle of a linguistic variable. In the middle-aged group there are both middle *and* working-class speakers among the merged and the distinct subjects, which shows that awareness has spread to at least some working-class speakers (who then try to keep the two vowels more distinct) and also that, in the middle class, speakers have started hypercorrecting, possibly because social awareness (and stigmatisation) of this variable has increased for them as well. When one looks at the young speakers class is no longer an issue at all, because everybody has merged distributions: this echoes the non-impact of style and provides further support to the idea that the merger has reached completion and simultaneously dropped completely below the radar again (at least in production).

9.2.2 Gender and social class

Zooming in on NURSE realisations in particular revealed that gender and social class interact with age of the participant (and with each other) in a number of ways. For instance, the mixed linear effects model showed that women had NURSE vowels which were significantly higher and fronter than those of men. As far as F1 is concerned, however, this effect decreases from the old to the young speakers, and is no longer significant for the latter, which is additional evidence for the claim made above that the social salience of this variable is lower in the youngest speakers. Women use higher, i.e. more standard, realisations of NURSE in all three age groups, which is what one would expect to find for a socially meaningful variable. Their values are rather stable across the generations as well, which means that the apparent time change in F1 is almost exclusively driven by men, who have raised their NURSE to converge with the women in the young group of speakers.

When we look at the front-back dimension, there is no significant gender difference, neither in the oldest nor the youngest speakers. For the middle group, however, the difference between men and women is not only highly significant, but women actually have NURSE realisations that are so much fronter (more Scouse) than those of men that the regression model still returns gender as a significant effect although it is only so in this one sub-group. It would appear strange that women should use more Scouse variants of a salient variable, but if we remember that it is precisely the middle age group that was found to hypercorrect, then this actually makes sense. If a group of speakers is aware of a non-standard feature and so eager to avoid it that they develop a tendency to modify it in the "wrong" direction then it should come as no surprise that that tendency is actually more pronounced for women, given that female speakers are generally held to be more sensitive to linguistic differences that carry social meaning.

Social class has an effect on F2 that is somewhat similar to the one that gender has on F1, albeit in a more moderate way. Middle-class speakers have more central (standard) NURSE variants across all three generations, which is in line with most previous research in sociolinguistics. However, this difference gets progressively smaller from the oldest to the youngest speakers, which can be seen as further evidence that NURSE is decreasing in salience, although it has to be said that the class difference is still statistically significant even in the youngest group. Working-class speakers have thus always (within the time frame that is the focus of this study) had very front NURSE variants, while middle-class speakers have been adapting to this model in the last 50 years or so.

Class and gender of participant interact for both F1 and F2 of NURSE, but only in terms of degree, not direction, of effects. That is to say that, for F1 for instance, the gender effect is more pronounced in the middle class (which is to say the distance between the means is greater), but it is highly significant both among middle- *and* working-class subjects. Interestingly, middle-class speakers of both genders seem to have lower, more Scouse, vowels than working-class Liverpudlians. This is unexpected, but it is not the first time this issue has come up. After all, one might ask more generally why NURSE is consistently shifted upwards throughout each generation (which makes it *less* Scouse) while simultaneously being fronted (which makes it *more* Scouse). What might be happening is that fronting of NURSE is at least a semi-conscious process due to the social importance of the F2 dimension of English vowels, whereas the raising is a change from below that is completely subconscious. If raising of NURSE was a change from below it would not be surprising, but actually *expected* to see (working-class) women in the vanguard (cf. Labov 2001: 292–293), as is the case in my sample, where NURSE realisations become lower and thus more Scouse from working-class women to working-class men, followed by middle-class women and finally middle-class men. For the front-back dimension of NURSE the gender difference is actually somewhat clearer in the working class, but again it should be noted that men and women differ significantly in *both* classes. Women's higher F2 values have been linked to hypercorrection above, and it would not be surprising if this was primarily a feature of the (upper) working class, given that their realisations are, on average, fronter to start with, which could mean that working-class females feel a greater need to "correct" their pronunciation. As a general note of caution, however, I would like to repeat that the results summarised in this paragraph pertain to rather subtle differences of degree and should not be over-interpreted.

9.2.3 Style shifting and awareness

When it comes to style shifting there are also some differences between F1 and F2. In the height dimension, there is little to no style shifting that reaches statistical significance. If anything, it can be found for the oldest speakers in the sample, but the trend is in the unexpected direction: NURSE becomes lower (more Scouse) instead of higher in the more formal styles. When style shifting is investigated for the two genders separately, it turns out that this unexpected trend is actually driven by women of *all* age groups, whereas men exhibit next to no register differences. A similarly clear distinction is found with social class: The downward trend towards less Scouse variants the more informal the communicative context is more pronounced for middle-class subjects, particularly for the middle age group. This is again in line with previous research: Female and middle-class speakers exhibiting more style shifting is just what is to be expected for a salient variable. It is true that the shift is in the unexpected direction but this issue has already been discussed above: If raising of NURSE is a change from below it *should* actually manifest itself first (and in a more pronounced way) in more informal registers.

Age groups also differ with regard to the impact of style on frontness of NURSE. The oldest speakers exhibit almost no style shifting, NURSE realisations are only significantly fronter when people imitate a strong Scouse accent – in the other three styles pronunciations are identical from a statistical point of view. In principle, this holds for both social classes, the differences in style shifting (which is to say the changes between styles, not the absolute values!) are only marginal. Both points support, once more, the idea that salience of this feature is rather low for these speakers.

In the middle-aged group, NURSE is significantly less front in free speech than in all the other three styles, which means that the vowel does not only become more Scouse during performance of a strong accent, but also when people read out a text or a word list. Again, working- and middle-class speakers behave in a rather similar fashion. If one only looked at this result in isolation it would be tempting to conclude that there is little style shifting and therefore hardly any awareness of the variable. However, we know from looking at NURSE realisations in relation to SQUARE that the middle-age group is actually very prone to hypercorrection: they do manipulate *both* vowels in a consistent way, which is just not the expected one; NURSE is progressively fronted the more formal the register. It is this process that is responsible for pronunciations that are comparable in the most formal and the most informal styles, not a lack of salience. The fact that both middle *and* working-class speakers hypercorrect underlines this by showing that awareness of, and linguistic insecurity relating to this merger seem to be universal in this age group.

The youngest speakers, finally, have steadily increasing (and significantly different) F2 values from reading out a text to free speech and accent imitation. The only part of their graph which does not look like prototypical style shifting is that NURSE is also significantly more front (and thus more Scouse) when these speakers read out a word list. It seems thus as if younger Scousers actually style-shift more consistently than older Liverpudlians, which would be in stark contrast with the evidence discussed in §9.2.1 and §9.2.2, where I argued that salience was *de*creasing for the youngest Scousers. The contradiction is only apparent, however. For one thing, the shifting pattern just described is not representative of all speakers in this age group. Middle- and working-class Scousers aged 29 and younger behave differently, and this difference is not just one of degree. Rather, working-class speakers contribute the (hypercorrect) fronting in the word list style, while the middle-class subjects are responsible for the steep rise of F2 during accent performance. The remaining three styles are not significantly different from each other in both social classes, so taken separately none of them are great style shifters. In fact, young middle-class Scousers have the flattest line in the sample, i.e. they have a smaller amount of style shifting than any other group (plus there is no significant drop of F2 in free speech due to hypercorrection in "reading" and "list").

The other aspect worth considering is that it was shown in §6.2.3 (and discussed in §9.2.1) that young Scousers have the most merged distributions and show the fewest style differences when NURSE and SQUARE are analysed *together*. It is true that NURSE is somewhat more centralised when these speakers read out a text, but so is SQUARE, which means that vowel distributions are just as merged (and therefore non-standard) as in the other registers. We can therefore say that the salience of this variable is not gone completely: Young middle-class Liverpudlians still have at least some sub-conscious awareness of fronter NURSE variants as a typical feature of Scouse (which explains the fronting during performance), while young working-class speakers still hypercorrect a bit in the most formal styles (which accounts for the fronting in the word list). All in all, however, style shifting (and therefore salience) is a lot less pronounced in this age group than the relevant line plots suggest, and the impact of style is certainly less than in the middle-aged group.

Explicit comments made by my subjects fit in rather well with people's linguistic behaviour as it has been described and interpreted in this section so far. Generally speaking, the NURSE-SQUARE merger is not very often commented on (much more rarely than lenition of /k/, for instance), but even so there are pronounced differences between speakers of different age groups. Among the oldest speakers there is hardly any conscious awareness of the feature (10% of speakers comment on it, so only 1 in 10). In the middle group the percentage of people who explicitly mention the merger rises considerably to 38.46%, only to drop to 13.33% again in the youngest speakers, a level which is comparable to that of the oldest interviewees. In contrast to lenition, no one, irrespective of their age, singled out the NURSE-SQUARE merger as being a particularly disagreeable or "annoying" feature of Scouse.

9.2.4 Classification

Realisations of NURSE are governed by a number of social factors, and particularly their interactions. The impact of these predictors is statistically more robust than for happy, which is evidenced by the fact that even differences which are very subtle in absolute terms are found to be significant. This is true even though there are many more observations of happy than of NURSE (and SQUARE) in my sample. All of this suggests a generally higher level of salience for NURSE in comparison with happy.

Data on style shifting (particularly when SQUARE realisations are also considered) and conscious awareness clearly show that the merger is not equally salient in the three age groups of speakers. For the oldest speakers it is a marker, awareness of which is only just beginning. In the middle generations, not only style shifting but also hypercorrection is widespread. Together with a steep increase in conscious awareness this shows that the feature is now, for many at least, a stereotype that speakers actively (though rather unsuccessfully) try to avoid producing. Apparently, this boost in salience seems to have been only temporary. Data collected from the youngest speakers in my sample have shown that the NURSE-SQUARE merger has been "reduced" (in terms of social salience) to a marker again in the current generation of young adults, possibly even one that might be on its way to becoming an indicator.

9.3 Velar nasal plus: Indicator with prestige option

9.3.1 Age, class, and gender

Based on accounts in the literature, velar nasal plus was assumed to be one of the less salient features of Scouse, but realisations were nevertheless found to be influenced by at least some extra-linguistic, i.e. social, factors in interesting ways. The analysis of age, for instance, revealed that there is a significant increase in the use of velar nasal plus from the old to the middle-aged speakers, which is in line with the idea that Liverpool English is getting stronger or more local. From the middle to the young group, however, there is no further increase. Rather,

PDF rates actually drop again. Compared to the oldest speakers in the sample, Scousers aged between 19 and 29 still use velar nasal plus significantly more often, but if they are judged against the generation of their parents, they cannot be said to have more local realisations of this particular consonant as their rates are actually significantly lower.

A closer look at statistical interactions showed that this age difference is actually restricted to middle-class subjects. Only for this socioeconomic class is there a statistically robust rise and subsequent decline of PDF from the old to the middle-aged to the young speakers. For the remaining subjects, on the other hand, the age differences collapse, so in the working class /ŋ(g)/ realisations are actually stable across the timespan investigated in this study. From the old (where working class and middle class are not significantly different) to the middle age group speakers with higher social status seem to have taken up this variable (i.e. they seem to have become somewhat more aware of it) and increased their usage to a value which is then significantly higher than that of their working-class counterparts before subsequently lowering it again a bit so that the classes are, again, no longer statistically distinct among younger Scousers.

Not only social class, but also the gender of participant has an impact on how velar nasal plus is used. The mixed linear effects regression revealed that female speakers have a higher PDF (10.85%), and thus more Scouse realisations, of /ŋ(g)/ than men (8.22%). With female speakers using more local variants than male ones, we have thus another result which does not seem to resonate very well with previous work in sociolinguistics, but I would like to argue further below that this is only apparently so (see §9.3.2).

Investigation of the significant gender X style interaction also showed that women and men differ with respect to the role style has to play. Females have a comparatively high PDF in the formal styles "word list" and "reading" as well as in 'imitation', and only reduce this value somewhat in spontaneous speech. Males, on the other hand, have comparatively low (and statistically identical) values for text reading, free speech, and accent performance (although there is a slight rise from "free" to 'imitation' which is close to significance), and only change their pronunciation (in the same direction as women, i.e. towards more Scouse variants) when they are asked to read out a word list. If one takes spontaneous speech (where there is no significant gender difference) as the baseline it can therefore be said that females seem to be more sensitive to this feature, because (a) they change velar nasal plus pronunciations earlier (reading passage) on the way to the formal end of the style spectrum (whereas men need to reach the most formal register before there is any linguistic reaction), and (b) they react more extremely at the other, most informal, end of the continuum (i.e. accent performance), where the rise in PDF is much less pronounced for male speakers. Both points suggest that women are rather more aware of velar nasal plus than men.

9.3.2 Style shifting and awareness

If the data are pooled across gender and social class, no difference between age groups can be found with respect to style shifting. All speakers, irrespective of their age, have relatively high PDF values (Scouse realisations containing a plosive) when they read out a word list. There is then a decrease towards "normal" reading style, and a further drop towards spontaneous speech, so from the word list to free speech realisations of velar nasal plus actually become linearly more standard. From free speech /ŋ(g)/ pronunciations then become considerably more Scouse again when subjects are asked to perform a particularly strong Liverpool accent (PDF is on about the same level as for text reading). With one negligible exception, all these differences are statistically robust.

While the linear rise from spontaneous speech to text reading to the word list is evidence for some sort of at least subconscious awareness, this is not awareness of velar nasal plus as a *local feature of Liverpool English*, because in this case the slope would be wrong. PDF should go *down* in more formal registers, because this would translate to more standard realisations. The pattern we do actually find therefore rather shows that speakers consider velar nasal plus a characteristic of *careful* speech. This is unexpected, but actually ties in nicely with the fact that, from a purely synchronic point of view, velar nasal plus is a spelling pronunciation. Due to its presence in the orthography, it would not be too surprising if speakers considered realising the plosive the "proper" way to talk, while not doing so would be a sign of informality. As outlined above, my data provide further evidence for this interpretation because they show that women have a (very slightly but nevertheless significantly) higher PDF than men, which incidentally also echoes Knowles's (1973) finding that females used velar nasal plus more frequently than males in his sample (cf. §3.3.1). These results are only compatible with many other sociolinguistic studies if we assume that people consider velar nasal plus primarily a feature of careful speech, because then it would actually be expected that women are more prone to using it. Some additional support for this interpretation can be found: In West Wirral a not insignificant number of speakers endorsed realisations containing a plosive in both word-final and particularly in intervocalic position, probably because of "sheer ignorance or confusion as to what the RP form might actually be" (Newbrook 1999: 101).

If velar nasal plus is careful speech, why does its use go up when speakers are asked to perform a strong local accent? This task was designed to elicit markedly local speech and the evidence pertaining to the other variables (particularly /k/ lenition, cf. §7.2 and §9.4.3) suggests it succeeded. But of course the accent imitation task was still a highly artificial context and speakers presumably paid a lot of attention to their speech, albeit not in the traditional Labovian sense of the phrase. All the same, getting the stereotype "right" required them to focus on how they were articulating because this stereotypical accent was not their natural one (as is evidenced by the many comments about "falseness", cf. §8.3). It is possible that the increased use of velar nasal plus during accent performance is nothing but an artefact of a setting that required subjects to focus very intensely on their pronunciation. I consider it more likely, however, that in addition to the spelling pronunciation aspect Liverpudlians have at least some awareness of velar nasal plus as a local feature as well. In this case, the style shifting pattern would again be a result of two conflicting evaluations, or norms, that just happen to pull realisations in the same direction (cf. §9.1.3).

This account involves a certain amount of speculation and, just as for happy, the issue deserves a much more detailed discussion than the present study can deliver. Suffice it to say, for the moment, that whatever awareness there is must definitely be subconscious: Not a single subject in the extended secondary dataset (all 38 interviews) mentioned velar nasal plus as a typical feature of Liverpool English.

9.3.3 Classification

Velar nasal plus was originally assumed to be a feature with a rather low amount of salience attached to it. However, its realisations are clearly influenced by social characteristics of the users. The style dimension, too, is particularly intriguing, and forbids the classification of /ŋ(g)/ as an indicator, since there are clear differences between registers. At the same time, velar nasal plus is definitely less salient than the NURSE-SQUARE merger, which shows both in the lower statistical importance of social predictors (both quantitatively and qualitatively) and the lack of overt commentary. In light of consistent, if somewhat difficult to interpret style shifting, I conclude, then, that velar nasal plus is a marker for all three age groups investigated and that younger speakers do neither provide evidence for changing salience of the feature nor do they, in fact, use the local variant more than their parents' generation.

9.4 Lenition: From indicator to stereotype

9.4.1 Age

Among the features investigated in this book, lenition of /k/ is the one that generated statistically robust differences for the widest range of social predictors and
their combinations. In fact only frequency of the carrier word was eliminated
from the mixed-effects regression model; all the other main effects, as well as all
interactions that had been entered into the model, turned out to be significant
factors in predicting PDF values of /k/ (which is why only the most important
and relevant results will be discussed here). Perhaps surprisingly, age of speaker
was not among the significant main effects in the regression model, while t-tests
on the raw data did find significant age differences, at least between the young
speakers and each of the other two groups. Scousers aged between 56 and 85 have
mean PDF values comparable to speakers who are between 30 and 55 years old,
so from a statistical point of view, and in this particular context, the two groups
can actually be considered as one. Younger Liverpudlians exhibit a significantly
higher mean PDF than both speakers of their parents' or grandparents' generation. The apparent contradiction between the raw data and the mixed-effects
regression has been shown to be mostly due to *like* (as a discourse marker and
quotative particle), because, among the youngest speakers, this word is both considerably more frequent and also realised with a higher average PDF than in the
other two groups.

This special behaviour of *like* in the young group was filtered out by the mixed-
effects model since it had a random intercept for carrier word. While this makes
sense in a way (we do not necessarily want a single lexical item to dominate
the data in such a way), it also seems somewhat unfortunate. After all, the fact
that young Liverpudlians frequently say [laɪç] (or any other words that they are
more likely to realise with a fricative than older speakers) probably does contribute considerably to many laypersons' impression that Scouse is getting stronger
since lenition is not only one of the best known but also most stigmatised features (cf. §9.4.4). Interestingly, the same differences (non-significant between old
and middle, but significant between middle and young group) also surface when
observations pertaining to *like* are removed from the dataset altogether, so *like* is
clearly not the only factor, and young Liverpudlians really do seem to be Scouser
than those of the middle-aged and old group.

Zooming in a bit reveals that this change has not happened in quite the same
way in the two genders. For women, the increase in PDF actually already happens from the old to the middle generation. From the middle-aged to the young

speakers there is then only a slight (and non-significant) further increase of PDF, so that young female Scousers do not use lenition more than their parents' generation already did. Male speakers, on the other hand, start out with very high values of lenition in the old generation, drop to a considerably and significantly lower level in the middle group, and then increase their usage of Scouse variants again from the middle-aged to the young speakers. With respect to /k/ lenition, young men in Liverpool have thus completed a sort of revival or 'back-to-the-roots' process.

9.4.2 Gender and class

Note also that the gender difference is not quite the same within the respective age groups. It should be noted that the differences are subtle, though: /k/ realisations of women and men are statistically distinct in all three generations of speakers. However, the difference is slightly less robust in the middle group, and, what is more, women have actually higher PDF values than men in this generation. Generally speaking though, females have *lower* PDF means than males, so women use less lenition than men, which is just what one would expect for a salient and stigmatised variable. The fact that women are more Scouse than men in the middle group might therefore suggest that the variable has lost salience in this generation, but additional evidence refutes this hypothesis (see §9.4.4). Women just seem to have been in the vanguard of this change (remember that their PDF has risen systematically from the old to the youngest speakers, whereas the changes in male PDF are non-linear), despite the fact that lenition is a salient non-standard feature, which one would usually rather expect women to shun. This is indeed a strange result that does not lend itself to straightforward interpretation. It would be interesting to see whether it is something that just shows up in my sample due to the particular individuals that were recruited or whether it could be replicated and really needs an explanation.

On a different note, it is interesting that the gender difference is not significant when subjects perform a strong Scouse accent (where PDF is very high in both genders), which can be seen as evidence that both women and men (subconsciously?) consider lenition as part of the Scouse stereotype. This result is very neatly mirrored when the data are divided according to social class of the speaker. The mixed linear effects regression showed that, all other things being equal, middle-class subjects have lower PDF rates and thus more standard realisations of /k/ than working-class Liverpudlians, which is the expected outcome for a salient variable. Just as with gender, the class difference is highly significant in all speaking styles except accent imitation (where PDF means are again highest), which shows that the strong association of /k/ lenition with a stereo-typical Scouse accent is not only shared among Liverpudlians of both genders, but also across different socioeconomic classes.

However, looking at how the class difference develops across the three generations of speakers investigated here is even more fascinating. For the oldest speakers, there is actually *no* significant difference in the use of lenition between working-class and middle-class Liverpudlians. In the middle group the difference is already highly significant, and for the youngest speakers this is even more true. The reason for this is that, if we take the oldest speakers as the baseline, middle-class PDF values *de*crease linearly in apparent time, whereas working-class PDF actually *in*creases with the same regularity. As far as /k/ lenition is concerned, the claim that Scouse is getting Scouser is thus only true for working-class speakers; middle-class realisations of /k/ have actually become more standard in the last few decades. This final point indicates that the salience of this variable has increased among middle-class speakers: they are more aware of lenition (and its non-standardness) and therefore try to avoid it. To explain the opposite trend in the working class one could assume that salience in this group has simultaneously decreased, but this is not what is happening (cf. §9.4.4). Rather, /k/ lenition must have acquired covert prestige as a marker of local identity. For Scousers of lower socioeconomic classes this covert prestige seems to be more important than the social stigma attached to it, whereas for middle-class speakers priorities are reversed.

9.4.3 Style shifting

Style shifting pertaining to /k/ lenition reveals highly interesting differences between the age groups, even more so than for NURSE. Old and middle-aged speakers not only have PDF values that add up to roughly the same grand mean (cf. §9.4.1), they also end up with /k/ pronunciations that are virtually identical in (almost) all individual speech styles analysed in this study. Neither group has any differences between the registers word list, text reading, and spontaneous speech. In all three styles /k/ is realised in a comparatively standard-like way. Only when it comes to accent imitation is there a steep rise of PDF towards more fricative-like local variants. These two groups of speakers thus have, at best, a two-way style distinction (stereotypical accent vs. everything else), so their awareness of the variable, while not nonexistent, seems to be limited. Young Scousers, however, presents a textbook case of style shifting as we would expect it for a socially meaningful variable: There is a steady, statistically significant, and almost perfectly linear increase of PDF from the most formal to the least formal register.

Compared to the other two groups, the youngest speakers in my sample manipulate lenition in a much more fine-grained way, which shows that awareness has reached a level in this group that is considerably higher than for older Liverpudlians.

It has already been pointed out above that women show more awareness of lenition than men do. This higher degree of sensitivity also shows in (slightly) different style shifting patterns. Female speakers exhibit more systematic and more pronounced style differences than those that are observed for male subjects, so they are not only more sensitive to /k/ lenition in general (which would just translate to lower absolute PDF values, but not necessarily different style shifting patterns). With respect to lenited variants of /k/ women also are more susceptible to the style dimension. An additional relevant point here is that when the data are split up along the gender dimension, the youngest speakers are still the ones that show the most systematic style shifting pattern, and this is true for both women *and* men, which shows that the increase in awareness along the age dimension is not limited to just one of the two genders, but is really primarily a question of age. The fact that style shifting patterns are least different in the young group is further evidence for the idea that awareness of lenition is more universal in this generation than in the other two.

The interaction of style, age, and social class is somewhat less straightforward to interpret. First of all, old middle and middle-aged working-class subjects have a significant drop in PDF from list/reading to spontaneous speech, which means that they use more Scouse variants in the more formal registers than in free speech. This looks very much like the hypercorrection that was observed for NURSE (cf. §9.3.2), but it is difficult to see why it would affect these two subgroups in particular. Generally speaking though, there is a class difference in that middle-class speakers mostly distinguish performance of a strong accent from everything else (in the young group, too), while working-class speakers show more pronounced (and, for the youngest speakers, also more systematic and fine-grained) style differences.

Such a result is unexpected because it could be taken to imply that middle-class speakers pay less attention than their working-class counterparts to how often they use stigmatised variants in a particular register. I believe, however, that this is not the case. It has to be taken into account that the mean PDF values of middle-class speakers, especially in the middle and the young generation, are relatively low across the board (accent imitation excepted), and considerably lower than even the most standard-like values measured for the working class. I believe that middle-class Liverpudlians just try to avoid lenited /k/ variants altogether, even in spontaneous speech, and that they just cannot get much more standard than they already are, even if they wanted to. They *can* produce lenited variants, but they only do so when being asked to reproduce the stereotype. In more natural speech their normal realisation is already so close to their lower (i.e. "standard") limit that there is just no room left for any further style shifting away from the local variant.

9.4.4 Awareness and attitudes

Lenition of /k/ attracts, by far, the largest number of explicit comments and evaluations in my sample, which is clear evidence for the fact that it is considerably more salient than the other three variables investigated in this book. There are, however, pronounced differences between the three generations. Among the oldest speakers, lenition is hardly mentioned at all, less than one in four subjects mention this feature. In the middle-aged group this rate has already risen considerably to around 70%, and when it comes to the youngest Scousers in the sample, each and every one of them expresses conscious awareness of lenition in velar plosives, so the variable has reached full and universal stereotype status. Many speakers (particularly in the youngest generation) are able to provide comparatively detailed accounts of the phenomenon that include fairly accurate descriptions of the place of articulation and the systematic nature of the variable (as opposed to isolated examples of individual lexical items).

It is not quite clear *why* awareness has increased in the way that it has. This might be due to the fact that, impressionistically at least, contemporary comedians frequently – and primarily – use this particular feature to imitate or make fun of the Liverpool accent. One could assume that younger speakers are more exposed to these recent performances than people in, say, their 60s, but at this point this idea is mere speculation. Furthermore, a separate study would first have to investigate whether performances in the media and on stage really *have* changed in the last decades as to which features they focus on. After all, it is in principle quite possible that /k/ lenition was already part of the external stereotype of Scouse in the 50s and 60s (it is, for instance, mentioned in the introduction to the first *Lern Yerself Scouse* volume). We could also argue that increasing awareness in younger speakers is based on the changing usage of the variable. For instance, people's awareness of non-standard variants might go up when they realise that middle-class speakers increasingly start to avoid them. However, this would lead to the chicken and egg problem commonly encountered in salience research (cf. §4.1.1): if awareness goes up because usage changes, then what triggers change in usage in the first place? Whatever the reason for the increase in conscious awareness is, explicit comments clearly show that lenition of /k/ is even more of a stereotype for younger Liverpudlians than it is for the older generations.

Why, then, do younger Liverpudlians use this feature more than their parents or grandparents despite the fact that they know about it? A different attitude towards lenition would be an option, but this is not what we find. The majority of younger and older speakers alike explained that they themselves often found very strong Scouse accents harsh, unpleasant, or intimidating. Lenition of velar plosives is strongly associated with these pronounced Liverpool accents and considered one of its most distinctive features. Across all three generations, subjects judge it rather negatively ("annoying", 'makes you unintelligible'), possibly because at least some of them have personal experience of outsiders using this variable to make fun of Liverpudlians. Higher proportions of lenited variants among younger Scousers can thus *not* be explained by a different (overt) attitude towards the feature.

Another explanation could be that young speakers just cannot help using lenition. The regular style shifting that was found, however, rather suggests that particularly younger speakers can at least sub-consciously control their usage of the local variant quite well. It is possible that some Scousers are *generally* aware of the variable but not, for some reason, of its presence *in their own speech*. There is some anecdotal evidence in my data that supports this idea, like the young female working-class speaker who reports not using lenition at all when in fact she uses fricative variants almost categorically. It has to be noted, though, that this type of linguistic insecurity, while not restricted to this one speaker, does not seem to be the rule (especially with respect to the male speakers). Just as outlined above for the class differences (cf. §9.4.2), I would therefore argue that the higher use of lenition among the younger speakers is primarily due to the covert prestige that lenited variants appear to have acquired.

9.4.5 Classification

Lenition of /k/ shows precisely the kind of social stratification that one would expect a sociolinguistically salient variable to produce. In particular, non-standard realisations are significantly less common among female and middle-class speakers. Inter-group differences in style shifting suggest that for the old and the middle-aged speakers (sub-conscious) awareness is lower than in the young group because the former show only limited style awareness, while the latter present a textbook case of Labovian style shifting, with non-standard variants getting consistently and linearly more likely the more informal the communicative context.

Data on explicit comments and judgements further showed that conscious awareness increases in a linear fashion from the oldest to the youngest Scousers. My data thus suggest that lenition of /k/ has developed from a (beginning) marker in the old group (where only a minority is consciously aware of the variable), to a consolidated marker (for the minority) or stereotype (for about three out of four speakers) in the middle generation, and then finally to a fully-fledged and universal stereotype in the young group of speakers, where not only *every* speaker knows about the feature but where style shifting is also most consistent and regular. Liverpudlians aged 29 and younger are therefore not only 'more Scouse' than their parents and grandparents with respect to this variable, but they are also the ones that are most aware of this feature of Liverpool English.

9.5 Summary

People of all age groups closely link Scouse to their local identity. Generally speaking, they are both aware and proud of its distinctness as an accent, although some subjects also see this as something that can be problematic, because they know about the negative connotations that a Scouse accent can carry, particularly for outsiders. To a degree, some of these external stereotypes (and their evaluation!) seem to have been internalised, as when Liverpudlians base their list of typical features of their own accent on stereotypical performances by outsiders. On the whole, inside evaluations are often ambivalent: "Light" accents are seen as adding an acceptable amount of local flavour and carrying positive connotations such as down-to-earthness, while extremely "strong" Scouse accents receive much less favourable judgements (this aspect is also reported in De Lyon 1981: 33, often because they appear as exaggerated, false, and inauthentic. Old and middle-aged Liverpudlians believe these "exaggerated" accents to be more common among younger speakers, but this verdict is not shared by young Scousers who appear to reject 'plastic' accents just as much as the older subjects (interestingly, one subject interviewed by De Lyon in 1979 claimed already that some Liverpudlians deliberately "exaggerated" the accent, cf. De Lyon 1981: 30).

Norms and attitudes towards Scouse therefore seem to have remained largely stable across the three generations of speakers investigated in this book. All the same, there is some evidence that middle-aged speakers seem to be particularly sensitive to the negative image of Scouse, which shows in the hypercorrection that these speakers exhibit for the two salient variables NURSE and /k/. Arguably, this is because the formative years of these speakers (the 70s and 80s) coincided with the period when the economic situation and the national image of Liverpool as a city was at its historic low. For the youngest speakers, quite the opposite is true. While the city is still among the most deprived in the country, the participants in the young group have only ever seen things improving a bit every year. They know about the negative image of their city and their accent, but at least to a certain degree they consider these attitudes to be outdated and unjustified. Pride in their city and the will to express their local identity linguistically seem to be strong enough that the covert prestige of variables such as the NURSE-SQUARE merger and /k/ lenition is at least as (and possibly more) important than the social stigma attached to them.

However, young Scousers are not more Scouse in every respect. Rather, they use (highly) salient markers and stereotypes (NURSE and /k/ lenition in my sample) more often and extensively than their parents or grandparents, because that alone is already enough to convey a strong local identity (though it has to be said that intonation - impressionistically at least - also plays a crucial role here and deserves a study of its own). Non-salient features, on the other hand, are either neglected or even sub-consciously used for other purposes: Their non-salience allows speakers to use them as a means of expression of a regional identity without noticeably deviating from their more local accent. Thus, they enable speakers "to appear outward-looking or more cosmopolitan" without signalling "disloyalty to local norms" or, in particular, "'snobbishness'" (Foulkes & Docherty 1999: 13–14). In my sample, this is precisely what seems to be happening to happy, which is becoming less instead of more Scouse (and thus more "northern") in apparent time.

While the four variables analysed in this book do not carry identical amounts of social salience in the three age groups, their relative ordering is the same, irrespective of speaker age: (1) happy is the least salient one in the set, parts of the style differences can be explained phonetically although some sub-conscious shifting must also be involved. (2) Velar nasal plus is very similar to happy, but the style differences are more pronounced, phonetic reasons are less available as explanatory factors, and some subtle gender differences can be detected, all of which indicates slightly higher social salience than for happy. (3) NURSE shows a more detailed and more robust social distribution than both happy and /ŋ(g)/, more consistent style shifting, and, most importantly, it attracts at least a small amount of explicit commentary, which is clear evidence for a considerably higher degree of sociolinguistic salience. (4) /k/ lenition, finally, is the variable which not only generates the most significant differences in usage among social groups and the most systematic style shifting patterns, but it is also the one that most subjects consciously know about (in every generation). As the feature that is clearly a stereotype and even a shibboleth for many, or even most, Liverpudlians it is without a doubt the most socially salient variable investigated in the context of this study.

10 Experiment design

Based on a detailed analysis of production data, the first part of this study has independently established the sociolinguistic salience of happy-tensing, velar nasal plus, the NURSE-SQUARE merger, and lenition of /k/. Knowing they can be ordered in this way (from least to most salient) it is now possible to test the hypothesis that salience is a crucial factor in exemplar priming experiments. Perception of these variables was analysed with the help of an online test, the detailed methodology of which is described below.

10.1 Stimuli

10.1.1 Stimuli sentences and frequency of keywords

To ensure comparability, stimuli were designed in a way similar to that of Hay, Nolan, et al. 2006 and Niedzielski 1999. Six keywords for each of the four variables were taken from the word list that had been used to elicit production data (see appendix C). In the test, the keywords appeared twice within complete sentences, once sentence-finally and once sentence-medially. This way it was possible to investigate whether having to hold the relevant sound in memory had an impact on subjects' responses (cf. Hay, Nolan, et al. 2006). Hay, Nolan, et al. (2006) noted a problem in their methodology, namely the fact that their stimuli confounded the position of the keyword and the total length of the sentence it was embedded in. Since sentences with the keyword in the middle were always (considerably) longer than the corresponding sentences with the keyword at the end there was no way of determining whether differences found were due to the fact that participants had to hold the sound in memory or that the longer sentence just contained more phonetic material, which might have activated further (or different!) exemplars.

In this study, care was therefore taken to make sure that all stimuli sentences were (roughly) equal in length (measured in words). Total duration (in seconds and milliseconds) of the final stimuli was also measured and a paired t-test revealed that stimuli sentences with the keyword in the middle were not significantly longer than sentences where the keyword was at the end ($t(23) = -0.129$, p = 0.898). For /ŋ(g)/ and /k/, a further criterion was to have an equal number of words with the variable in intervocalic and in word-final position. This was to match the most prominent phonological contexts that these variables were investigated in in production and to be able to discover any potential differences in priming related to this criterion. Occurrences of the other three test variables were avoided in the stimuli sentences of the fourth variable. An example pair is given below (see appendix D for the complete list):

1. People in that town almost never went to *church*.

2. In that town *church* was not popular with people.

Key words from the original list were selected in such a way that there was a continuum from very high to very low frequency words. Frequency categorisation was initially based on occurrences in the BNC (spoken language section only). Table 10.1 provides an overview of the keywords used. All figures are absolute occurrences in the BNC (spoken), i.e. relative occurrences per 10 million words. These figures were later replaced by frequencies based on SUBTLEX-UK, a 200+ million word corpus of subtitles collected from BBC broadcasts (taken from 9 different channels) in the years 2010–2012. SUBTLEX-UK frequencies were preferred because they have been found to explain more variance than, for example, BNC frequencies in psycholinguistic experiments focussing on things such as lexical decision reaction times (Van Heuven et al. 2014). According to Van Heuven et al. (2014), one of the most popular frequency measures, frequency per million words, comes with a number of problems, especially for low frequency words. They propose an alternative measure called the Zipf scale, the values of which are calculated as follows:

$$\text{Zipf score} = \log(n) + 3 \tag{10.1}$$

Where n is the absolute frequency in a 1 million word corpus. This logarithmic scale produces values of '1' for words that occur once in 100 million words, '2' for words that occur once in 10 million words, '3' for words that occur once in 1 million words, etc., with a range of about 1 (very low frequency words) to 6 or 7 (very high frequency words). The actual equation used in practice is slightly more complex in order to also assign Zipf scores to words that have an absolute frequency of 0 in the corpus, but this does not drastically change the interpretation of the Zipf scores as outlined just above (cf. Van Heuven et al. 2014). The Zipf scores used in this study are based on the frequencies in SUBTLEX-UK as a whole (instead of one of the two sub-corpora "CBeebies" (pre-school children) and "CBBC" (primary school audience), for which separate Zipf values are also available).

Table 10.1: BNC and SUBTLEX-UK frequencies of keywords in the perception test

| NURSE | | | happy | | |
word	BNC	Zipf	word	BNC	Zipf
turn	2572	5.45	happy	1820	5.56
word	2222	5.29	city	1486	5.40
girl	1613	5.29	pretty	1455	5.50
church	1149	5.02	baby	962	5.29
shirt	218	4.47	lazy	101	4.07
fur	40	4.03	stingy	5	3.02
/k/			/ŋg/		
like	38153	6.53	young	1890	5.51
book	2396	5.21	song	386	5.10
pack	425	4.62	gang	119	4.39
chicken	479	4.82	singer	109	4.48
snooker	71	4.25	hanger	27	3.13
hacker	3	3.88	longish	4	2.13

The author is aware of the fact that this list probably leaves much to be desired from the point of view of linguistic frequency research. Ideally, there would have been two words each in more clearly (and more consistently) defined high, middle and low frequency ranges for every variable investigated: Van Heuven et al. (2014) draw the line between low frequency and high frequency words somewhere between Zipf values 3 and 4, which would classify only 1 in 6 of the carrier words as low frequency and the remainder as high frequency. This was difficult, however, since the group of possible keywords was already restricted by the word list that had been used in the interview. It should be borne in mind, however, that frequency is only of secondary interest in this study, and the opportunity to possibly find connections between use and perception of particular words was deemed more relevant to the task at hand. The whole design of the experiment would have looked different if frequency had been of central importance. For instance, more keywords would be needed, because with only 6 words (per variable) chances are high that any effects of frequency that might be found are, at least in part, *lexical* effects of individual words rather than (generalisable) frequency effects. Anything this study might find about frequency effects should therefore be considered a bonus rather than one of the main points.

There were thus a total of 48 stimuli sentences in the perception test, with the 12 test tokens of one variable simultaneously functioning as dummies for the other three. These sentences were recorded by a phonetician in her late twenties who is originally from East Central Manchester. She used her native Mancunian accent, meaning that NURSE was realised as [ɜ:], happy as [ɪ] (phrase-internally) or [ə] (phrase-finally), velar nasal plus as [ŋg][1] and /k/ as [k].

The stimuli participants had to choose from were created in Praat. A script extracted the key word from every sentence, manipulated the relevant sound and saved the resulting four different versions of the word. This study differs from many previous studies, e.g. Hay, Nolan, et al. 2006 or Niedzielski 1999, in that participants were presented with whole words *containing* manipulated sounds instead of just individual vowels. This choice was made because (a) it made the experimental situation ever so slightly less artificial, and (b) the manipulation of /k/ was based on differing ratios of silence and friction, and therefore depended on the /k/ having some immediately preceding phonetic material. A second deviation from the seminal studies concerns the number of answer tokens. Both Niedzielski and Hay, Nolan, et al. presented their participants with a 6-step continuum, but the present study had only 4 options that listeners could choose from. This reduction was done for two reasons. Firstly, creating more than 4 different realisations that can be reliably distinguished by non-experts would have been rather challenging in the case of velar nasal plus and /k/ lenition. Since it was deemed essential to ensure comparability between the consonantal and the vocalic variables, the number of answer tokens was therefore limited to 4 for the whole experiment. Secondly (and more importantly), it is not at all clear whether non-linguists are even able to make full use of an answer continuum that consists of 6 tokens which differ only in rather fine phonetic details. Actually, Niedzielski 1999 ended up limiting her analysis to the 3 "middle" tokens of her continuum because subjects had almost never chosen one of the other 3 options (cf. Niedzielski 1999: 64–65). As far as the present study is concerned, it was therefore decided that a 4-step continuum was difficult enough, and that in inflating the amount of answer tokens one would run the risk of potentially asking too much of the

---

[1] Using velar nasal plus as a variable in a priming test where the conditions are "Liverpool" and "Manchester" is problematic, because velar nasal plus is actually present in both accents. See §12.4 for an explanation why I still think it was justified to use this variable in this priming experiment.

average participant. An even number of stimuli was chosen to "force" listeners to one side of the spectrum (more Mancunian or more Liverpudlian).

10.1.2 Vowel stimuli

Vowel stimuli were created using a script that was heavily inspired by one written by Styler (2008). First of all, the recording was downsampled to 11 kHz. The vowels in the key words were then extracted individually and run through source-filter synthesis in Praat (Boersma & Weenink 2015). An LPC (prediction order 12, window length 25 milliseconds, time step 5 milliseconds, pre-emphasis frequency 50 Hz) and a formant object (maximum number of formants 5, maximum formant frequency 5500 Hz, window length 25 milliseconds, pre-emphasis frequency 50 Hz) were created, both using the Burg algorithm. The downsampled vowel was then inverse-filtered with the LPC, which results in a "reconstruction" of the pure source sound as generated by the vocal folds of the speaker. By applying the formant filter (which simulates vocal tract shape) to this reconstructed source a vowel can be re-synthesised that is almost identical to the natural one in the recording (token 2 was created this way). If the filter (i.e. the formant structure) is manipulated, a synthesised vowel is generated that is acoustically and perceptually different from the original, but most of the time still fairly natural sounding. The re-synthesised vowel was then upsampled again and spliced back into the carrier word. F1 and F2 of NURSE and happY were manipulated using this method. The relevant values were chosen in such a way that there was roughly equal perceptual distance (auditory judgement by the author) between any two adjacent vowels.

Table 10.2: Filter settings used in vowel resynthesis (in Hz)

	NURSE		happY	
	F1	F2	F1	F2
stimulus 1	-150	-250	+100	-200
stimulus 2	0	0	0	0
stimulus 3	+100	+150	-100	+200
stimulus 4	+200	+300	-200	+300

Table 10.2 summarises the final parameters, and Figure 10.1 illustrates the result for one set of NURSE tokens. There was thus a continuum from stimulus 1 (hyper-Mancunian), to 2 (actual) and 3 (Scouse), to stimulus 4 (hyper-Scouse).

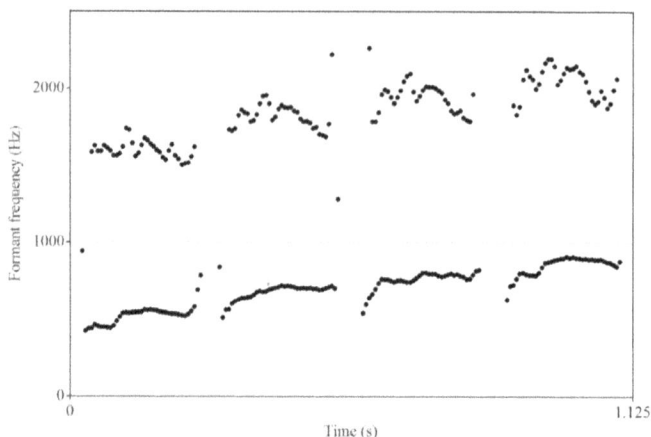

Figure 10.1: Formant tracks of *fur* tokens

The formant structure of stimulus 2 was not modified, but still re-synthesised so as not to stick out as the only completely natural recording. For NURSE stimulus 1 was thus higher and further back than the speaker's natural realisation, while stimuli 3 and 4 were both fronted and lowered to varying degrees. With respect to happy, stimulus 1 was lowered and centralised, while stimuli 3 and 4 were higher and fronter than the vowel that actually occurred in the recordings. Participants always heard the re-synthesised words in the same order (1 to 4). Unfortunately, it was not possible to synthesise stimuli of satisfactory quality from the sentences that had happy in phrase-final position (where it was typically realised as [ə], and often articulated with breathy voice). For this reason, answer tokens for these sentences were taken from the equivalent recordings where happy occurred in the middle of the sentence (and in the same carrier word). Crucially, however, the realisation of happy in the stimulus sentence itself was not altered. With hindsight, this should have been avoided as this procedure created a confound with the independent variable 'position of keyword in sentence' (cf. §11.1).

10.1.3 Consonant stimuli

An equivalent procedure was developed for the consonants /ŋ(g)/ and /k/. The link between those two in the context of this study is that the proportion of friction/aspiration is higher in the Scouse than in the standard British English variants, and this criterion was used to build a continuum similar to the one created for the two vowels. Once more, the goal was to create roughly equal perceptual distance (again checked auditorily by the author) between any two tokens, just as for the re-synthesised vowels. For every keyword a TextGrid was prepared which marked phases of aspiration, burst, and silence (for /k/) or nasality (for /ŋ(g)/) respectively (cf. Figure 10.2). For /ŋ(g)/, a script written by the author of this study then

1. cut away the aspiration for stimulus 3,

2. additionally cut away the burst for stimulus 2 (leaving only the nasal),

3. and shortened the (often rather long) nasal by 25% to arrive at a more standard-like length for stimulus 1.

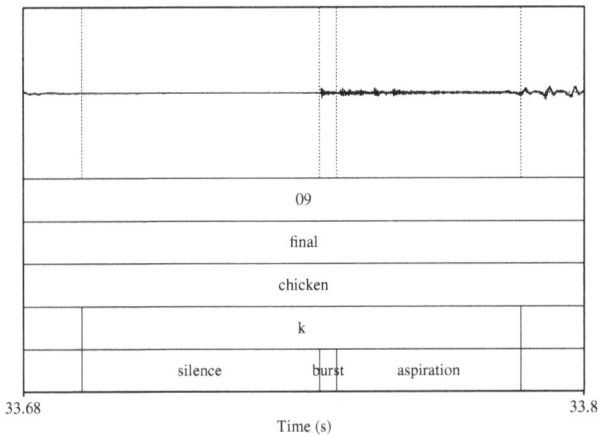

Figure 10.2: Waveform and TextGrid for *chicken* stimuli

Stimulus 4 was the full, unaltered velar nasal plus realisation [ŋg]. To make the velar nasal plus sentences comparable to those of the other variables, stimulus 2 was afterwards copied back into the sentence to replace the natural [ŋg] realisation. There was thus no voiced velar plosive present in the sentences subjects heard, and the continuum of stimuli was structured in the same way as those for the vowels and for /k/ in the sense that stimulus number 2 was the objectively most accurate choice that corresponded best to the sound actually used in the sentence.

Stimulus 2 for /k/ was the actual released plosive [k] as it occurred in the sentence recordings. The hyper-Mancunian stimulus was created from this by cutting the aspiration, but leaving in the burst. The speaker had also recorded all the /k/ sentences using the Scouse fricative variants. The frication from these variants was pasted into the place of the original aspiration to form an affricate stimulus 3 (to make the result more natural sounding half of the closure phase was also deleted). Stimulus 4, finally, had the whole plosive (silence, burst, and aspiration) replaced by the fricative by way of removing remaining silence and burst from stimulus 3.

For both /ŋ(g)/ and /k/, asymmetrical cross-fading and intensity adaptation was applied in intervocalic environments to create a smoother and less artificial transition from the nasal or the aspiration-less plosive to the following vowel in the hyper-Mancunian tokens (using a 25 milliseconds fade-in interval for the vowel and 50 milliseconds of overlap between phonemes when concatenating). Table 10.3 provides an overview of the consonantal stimuli.

Table 10.3: Structure of consonant stimuli

	/ŋg/	/k/
stimulus 1	nasal only (shortened)	plosive with burst
stimulus 2	nasal only	plosive plus burst & aspiration
stimulus 3	nasal plus burst	plosive plus burst & frication
stimulus 4	nasal plus burst & aspiration	fricative

A small pilot study was run among linguists of the English Seminar at the University of Freiburg to make sure the stimuli (both the vocalic and the consonantal ones) were (a) sufficiently natural-sounding, and (b) equally distant from one another in perceptual terms. This pilot study did not reveal any problems, so the investigation proper was carried out using these stimuli.

10.2 Presentation

10.2.1 Online platform

The actual test was administered online using *SoSciSurvey.de* (2015), a professional tool for academic online surveys and questionnaires. The platform uses flash to play audio and video files. Although declining in importance, flash is still installed on most desktop and laptop computers (though not on tablets and smartphones) so the vast majority of potential subjects should have had no technical problems related to the website. Nevertheless, participants first of all had to answer a filter question to make sure they had flash installed and activated and could actually play the sound recordings. Subjects were given the hint that they were going to hear the name of a type of bird and the questionnaire then used the flash plug-in to play a short sound file of the speaker saying *raven*. Participants then typed in the word they had heard. Wrong answers to this test question prevented the user from progressing in the questionnaire. Participants were randomly assigned to one of two groups. The control group was (correctly) told that the speaker they were going to listen to was from Manchester. The other group was led to believe that the speaker was from Liverpool (about 1 in 3 of the participants who lived outside of Liverpool actually believed this). Depending on which group subjects had been assigned to, "Manchester" or "Liverpool" was displayed at the top of every page as a reminder (cf. Figure 10.3).

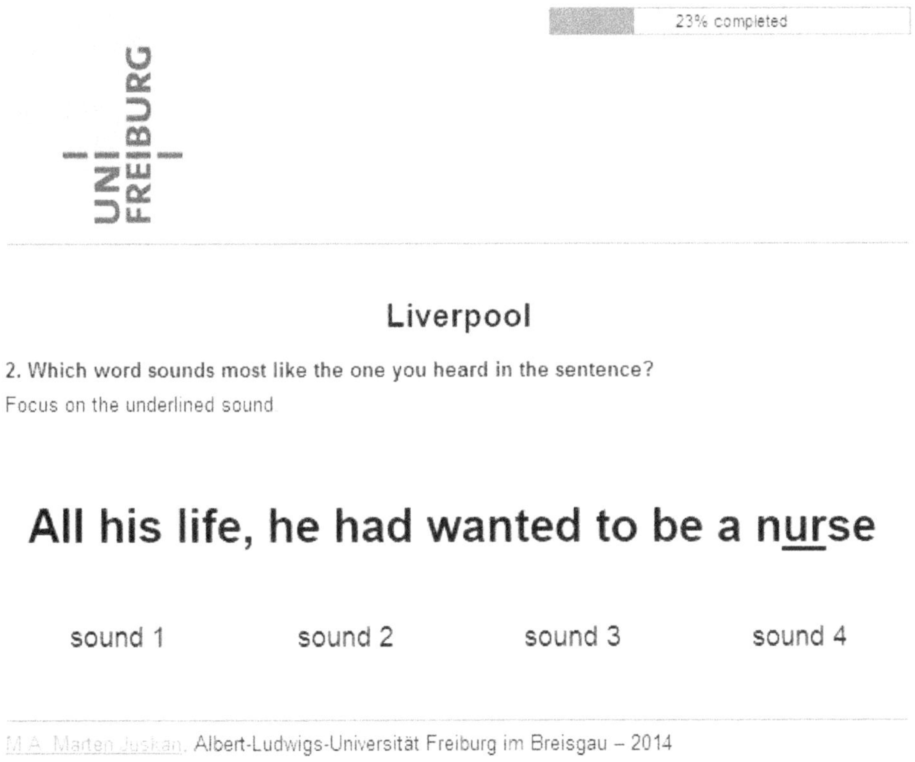

Figure 10.3: Online questionnaire - training item

After a couple of practice items (the results of which did not enter the analysis) participants were presented with 6 groups of 8 test tokens each. Both the order of the groups and the order of the items within each group was random-ised. For every sentence, subjects were asked to pay special attention to the (part of the) word that was underlined. The sound files that were played had been cre-ated using another Praat script written by the author which pasted the stimulus sentence together with the resynthesised keywords and added bits of silence in between (Figure 10.4 visualises the structure).

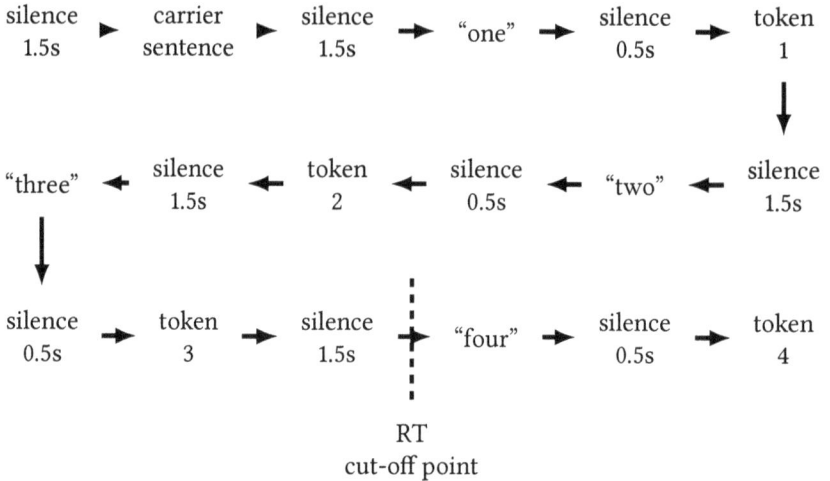

| silence 1.5s | ▶ | carrier sentence | ▶ | silence 1.5s | ➡ | "one" | ➡ | silence 0.5s | ➡ | token 1 |

↓

| "three" | ◀ | silence 1.5s | ◀ | token 2 | ◀ | silence 0.5s | ◀ | "two" | ◀ | silence 1.5s |

↓

| silence 0.5s | ➡ | token 3 | ➡ | silence 1.5s | ┇ | "four" | ➡ | silence 0.5s | ➡ | token 4 |

RT
cut-off point

Figure 10.4: Timing of perception stimuli

Each sentence was presented on a separate page of the questionnaire. Parti-cipants would see the sentence first for 1.5 seconds before the playback started automatically. After the recording of the sentence had finished playing, parti-cipants heard the four resynthesised words (introduced by "one", "two", "three", "'four" to avoid confusion[2]) with 1.5 seconds of silence in between words, and were asked to choose the one that they thought corresponded most closely to the sound in the test sentence. Participants could either choose a sound by click-ing on a button or by pressing "1", "2", "3", or "4" on their keyboard. Both the sentence and the resynthesised sounds were only played once. As soon as the subject had clicked on the button of their choice (or pressed the relevant key) the next sentence was automatically presented.

---

[2]The token numbers were recorded by a different female speaker (aged 26). This was not ideal as it is possible that the accent of the other speaker might have influenced participants. Incid-entally, however, Hay & Drager were faced with the same problem and correctly point out that any effect the second speaker *might* have had would manifest itself in identical fashion in *both* experimental conditions and should therefore not be able to confound the priming effect (cf. Hay & Drager 2010: 871 and 889).

10.2.2 Reaction times

Reaction times were also recorded. These have to be taken with a grain of salt in the context of an online survey, as a number of external factors (skill in using a mouse etc.) add a lot of variance. The potentially most important factor – speed of internet connection – can be ruled out as a confounding variable, however. This is because the platform uses JavaScript to send each subset of stimuli to the computer of the subject. Playback of the sound files does not start before all bits of the question have been downloaded. RT measurements (with an accuracy of about 10 milliseconds) are then taken locally on the participant's computer before being bundled and sent back to the server. No loading from the server takes place in between stimuli (cf. *SoSciSurvey.de* 2015). While there is still some room for variation between different hardware configurations in terms of timing accuracy and the like, there is no reason to assume that one subgroup of participants in particular would be affected in a significantly different way, so overall such unwanted effects can be hoped to cancel out. Furthermore, reaction times were not analysed as a dependent variable in its own right, but "merely" served to filter responses in the way described below.

The platform *SoSciSurvey.de* does come with some technical limitations, however, since it is not primarily designed for tests requiring RT measurements. Unfortunately, it is neither possible to define a time window outside of which participants cannot enter a response nor to specify when the reaction time clock starts. Technically speaking, RT measurements are really measurements of how long a subject spent on a particular page of the questionnaire. Measuring thus starts automatically once the page is loaded and stops when the next page is accessed (which, in this study, happened automatically once an answer had been selected). "Real" reaction times are arrived at by substracting the total duration of each audio file from the time spent on the respective page.

As a consequence of these restrictions, it was possible for subjects to make their choice at any time, including *before* the recording had actually finished even though the instructions spelled out that participants should listen to all answer options first. It would have been quite easy to filter out all of these premature answers by simply eliminating all observations with negative RTs from the dataset. This course of action was not taken for two reasons. The first one is comparability with previous research. Neither Niedzielski 1999 nor Hay, Warren, et al. 2006; Hay & Drager 2010 even recorded reaction times and responses were given on a physical answer sheet so it is quite possible that these studies were, in part, based on answers that had been given before subjects had listened to all of their options. The second, more important reason, is that it does not necessarily make sense to exclude an answer just because the subject did not listen to all resynthesised sounds first. After all, this study is interested in finding out how (stereotypical) expectations influence people's perception. The claim that at least some expectations and attitudes will prime people to perceive particular sounds *implies* that at least to a certain extent the choice is already made before subjects can really process the physical signal and this might well show in negative RTs. Many people might simply be reluctant to wait for the end of the recording if they already "know" the answer or if they have already heard the option that they think is the best match. Ignoring negative RTs might then result in involuntarily eliminating (parts of) the priming effect one is interested in from the dataset – which might be a reason why previous studies have not even bothered with reaction times in the first place.

On the other hand, it is fortunate if one is able to cleanse the dataset of nonsense answers which are particularly likely to occur in an online test where the physical presence of the researcher cannot act as an incentive to take the task at hand seriously. Responses with RTs that indicate the subject did not even listen to the carrier sentence, let alone the answer options, are clearly nothing but noise and should be eliminated from the sample. As a sort of compromise it was decided to keep all responses that were not given more than 2000 milliseconds before the end of the stimulus. This threshold ensures that the participant has listened to at least three of the four answer options (cf. Figure 10.4). Responses that were given more than 4000 milliseconds after the end of the recording were likewise eliminated.

10.3 Participants

Finding participants for the online test proved rather difficult. Subjects were recruited through a number of channels. A call for participants was distributed through Hope, Liverpool, and Manchester University. Announcements posted in Liverpool and Manchester related groups on Facebook resulted in some (but very few) responses. Some exchange students were recruited with the help of public notice boards on the campus of Freiburg University. Several friends and colleagues were kind enough to spread the word via e-mail and social media, and this friend-of-a-friend approach proved to be comparatively fruitful. Finally, personal contacts in Liverpool and Manchester and some of the people who had been interviewed about a year earlier were contacted and asked if they would like to participate. All participants were required to

1. be British

2. be native speakers of English

3. have normal hearing

The necessity of the last requirement should be obvious, as subjects were supposed to choose between audio stimuli that differed in rather subtle ways. Requirements 1 and 2 were set to make sure participants were at least likely to have some degree of experience with or knowledge of the accents of Liverpool and Manchester. After all, exemplar priming can only work if there are exemplars that can be activated by the prime. Given what Montgomery (2007a) found with respect to the status of Scouse in particular it seems not too far fetched to assume that people with British nationality (and native competence of English) have at least some exemplars indexed for "Liverpool", even if these are only derived from (stereotypical) media performances. People from, say, the U.S. or Australia, on the other hand, will probably be a lot less familiar with the British accent landscape and might not have the slightest idea of what a Scouse accent sounds like – either because they have never listened to someone from Liverpool, or because they have not done so *knowingly*, meaning that the relevant exemplars will be indexed for a more general category such as "British". In both cases, priming subjects for "Liverpool" (or "Manchester", for that matter) would not be possible.

At the end of the questionnaire, participants had to indicate their age, gender, educational level, profession (profession of parents for students), geographical origin and current town/city of residence (both via the first half of UK postcodes), and whether they self-identified as working or middle class. The occupation scale was the simplified version of the National Statistics Socio-economic Classification, which is used, for instance, by the Office for National Statistics and classifies jobs into lower, intermediate, and higher, primarily based on how much routine (at the lower end) and responsibility over others (at the upper end) is involved. Just as for the interview data, levels of occupation and education were then used to classify subjects as belonging to one of the two broad categories 'working class' or 'middle class'. Since this classification correlated strongly with the social class participants had explicitly chosen anyway, self-reported social class membership was used as a predictor for statistical modelling (see below).

On the basis of the postcodes participants provided, geographic coordinates were obtained from http://xposition.co.uk/geopostcode/, and a euclidean distance value was calculated for every subject using the following formula:

$$d = \sqrt{(lon_L - lon_s)^2 + (lat_L - lat_s)^2} \tag{10.2}$$

Where lon_L and lat_L are the longitude and latitude of central L1 (Liverpool city centre), lon_s and lat_s the (central) coordinates of the subject's postcode, and d is the resulting distance value (the higher, the further the subject lives from Liverpool). These figures are not, strictly speaking, directly comparable. This is because 1 degree of longitude translates to a different absolute distance in kilometres or miles depending on the latitude. Since the north-south extent of the UK is comparatively small, however, the amount of distortion introduced was considered negligible. Figure 10.5[3] shows the geographical distribution of participants by representing every individual with a grey dot. Two clusters are clearly visible, one in the north-west and one in the south-east of England. The first is due to the fact that recruitment initially focussed on Liverpool and Manchester, while the London bias is to a degree even representative, given that between 15 and 20% (depending on where one draws the boundaries) of the UK population live in the metropolitan area. The remaining participants seem to come more or less from all over the country, although Wales and Northern Ireland are clearly under-represented.

Figure 10.5: Geographical distribution of subjects (perception)

Subjects were given the opportunity to receive the results of the experiment after its completion and to participate in a lottery for a £100 gift card from a big online retailer. E-mail-addresses were collected for these purposes, but kept strictly separate from the questionnaire responses (using an in-built function of the online platform specifically designed for that purpose).

---

[3]Map tiles by Stamen Design, under CC BY 3.0. Data by OpenStreetMap, under CC BY SA.

In total, 67 subjects participated in the experiment and provided 2508 data points. In addition to the more detailed placement via the postcode, participants were also assigned to one of the broad geographical categories "internal" (Liverpool and Merseyside, "L" postcode area; 9 subjects) and "external" (everything else, 58 subjects). It is possible that some of subjects in the Liverpool sample had already participated in one of the sociolinguistic interviews conducted by the author, but since these interviews had taken place (at least) a year earlier it is highly unlikely that this could have a distorting effect on results in the perception test. Table 10.4 provides a more detailed overview of the "external" sub-sample (3 subjects in this group declined to indicate their gender). One thing that is immediately obvious is that the middle class is heavily over-represented, only 7 subjects were classified as belonging to the working class. Among middle class subjects, female and male participants are not really evenly distributed across priming conditions: women dominate in the group that was primed for Liverpool, while men do in the other. However, Prime and Gender are still not collinear in the dataset ($\kappa = 1.54$), and mixed-effects ordinal models regressing reported percept on Gender did not find a significant effect of the latter, neither in the "Liverpool" ($p = 0.801$) nor in the "Manchester" condition ($p = 0.597$). In other words, women and men did not behave differently in this experiment so the fact that they are unevenly distributed across conditions is unproblematic. Incidentally, Niedzielski (1999: 69 and 79–80) also found that "there was essentially no difference between what male and female respondents selected".

Table 10.4: Gender and social class distribution of subjects (perception, external)

prime	"Liverpool"		"Manchester"	
	F	M	F	M
working class	2	3	1	1
middle class	17	6	9	16

10.4 Statistical analysis

Unlike in the case of the interview data where there were fewer participants and the role of the individual subject was different (cf. §5.6), it actually does make sense to include random effects for the statistical analysis of the perception data.

However, the data collected by the experiment described above are not ratio or interval scaled. While answers are expressed in numbers (token 1, 2, 3, or 4), these are really labels for 4 distinct categories rather than measurements on a continuous scale. There is no guarantee, for instance, that the (perceptual) distance from token 1 to token 2 is identical to that between tokens 2 and 3 (although this *was* the aim when creating the tokens; cf. §10.1.2 and §10.1.3) – which is what the values suggest when they are being treated as numerical measurements. On the other hand, the data *are* ordered in a way (from most standard/Mancunian to most Liverpool), so while choosing token 4 instead of token 3 might not be the same as choosing 3 instead of 2 in terms of perceptual distance, higher values do in all cases represent a more Liverpool-like percept than lower values – much in the same way that, say, a higher RT always mean that a subject took more time to respond than another one with a lower RT. It was therefore decided not to follow Hay, Nolan, et al. 2006; Hay & Drager 2010 in treating the answers as numerical data for the purposes of statistical modelling. Instead, the R package "ordinal" (Christensen 2015) was used to calculate cumulative link mixed ordered regression models via the Laplace approximation.

Subject was entered as a random intercept (cf. §5.6), and a random by-subject slope for stimulus order was also included to counter any individual training or fatigue effects. Carrier word was not included as a random effect because frequency and, for consonants, phonological environment were of interest as fixed effects. Since there were only 6 keywords per variable filtering out any lexical effects would almost certainly also have eliminated effects of frequency and/or phonological environment. Prime was entered as a fixed factor, along with gender, social class (self-reported), age of the subject, and geographical distance from Liverpool. Furthermore, the Zipf score of the carrier word was included, as was the position of the carrier word in the stimulus sentence (sentence-medially or -finally), the position of the stimulus sentence within the experiment (when was the sentence played to the subject), and, for consonants, the phonological environment (V_V or _#). All two-way interactions of the prime with these linguistic and extra-linguistic factors were also considered. Sum coding was used for all models in order to be able to identify main effects and interactions. Model selection was based on AIC scores and F-tests comparing nested models. Collinearity was investigated applying the functions written by Austin Frank (cf. §5.6) to corresponding mixed-effects logistic regression models.

11 Perception results

Originally, the intention of this study was to focus on the perception of Scouse variants by listeners from Liverpool and Manchester (in order to have a rough equivalent of the oppositions Michigan-Ontario in Niedzielski 1999, and Australia-New Zealand in Hay, Nolan, et al. 2006). However, I only managed to recruit 9 subjects from the Liverpool/Merseyside area and 3 from Greater Manchester over the course of the 15 months that the perception test was online, despite my own best efforts and notwithstanding the fact that many people with personal contacts in Liverpool and Manchester helped to spread the word. A detailed analysis of such a small sample does not seem to make much sense. All the same, the most basic tests were carried out on the Liverpool sub-sample as well, and, crucially, almost all results are comparable to those in the rest of the sample. Mixed-effects ordinal models regressing reported percept on Area ('internal' vs. 'external') showed that the responses given by subjects from outside were not significantly different from those provided by participants from Liverpool as far as HAPPY (estimate = 0.025, se = 0.115, z value = 0.216, p = 0.829), NURSE (estimate = -0.001, se = 0.185, z value = -0.007, p = 0.994), and /k/ (estimate = 0.053, se = 0.193, z value = 0.275, p = 0.783) are concerned. This is also obvious when the relevant bar plots (not reported here) are compared with the ones generated on the basis of the "external" sample. Furthermore, whenever there is a significant priming effect in the Liverpool sub-sample, this effect is in the same (unexpected) direction as the ones reported below for perceivers from outside of the city.

For velar nasal plus, on the other hand, there is a statistical trend (estimate = -0.382, se = 0.210, z value = -1.815, p = 0.070). With respect to this variable, the difference between priming conditions is more pronounced for subjects from Liverpool, and the effect is in the opposite direction compared to the remaining participants from the rest of the country. The production data suggest that velar nasal plus carries at least some social meaning, but this result *could* indicate that it is actually even more salient in Liverpool than suspected, despite the fact that nobody comments on it. This variable could present a fruitful area of future research, but it should be borne in mind that these statements are based on a very small and unbalanced sample, which means that we might well be talking about a non-issue because the effect would disappear in a larger dataset.

In any case, /ŋ(g)/ is the only variable where results seem to diverge. With respect to the other three, perceivers from Liverpool and elsewhere do not exhibit any statistically meaningful differences in behaviour. In addition, it has been shown that impersonations and comments by outsiders have an impact on what variables Liverpudlians themselves are consciously aware of (cf. Chapter 8), so internal and external salience correlate to a degree and are not completely unrelated. For these reason I would argue that it does not appear completely unjustified to assume that most of what is described below would also hold in a larger sample of listeners from Liverpool, but this claim is in need of proper empirical confirmation in the future. All further results reported in this chapter are exclusively based on responses provided by people living outside of Liverpool.

11.1 happʏ

11.1.1 Overview

As described in §10.4, a mixed-effects ordinal regression model was fit to the data by hand. This maximal model did not contain any troubling collinearity (κ = 13.99), but for reasons of comparability (cf. §11.2, §11.3, and §11.4), the frequency of the keyword expressed in Zipf scores, as well as the interaction of Zipf score and priming condition, were removed from the model.[1] Collinearity was further

---

[1]When Zipf scores are included they show up as a significant predictor in the corresponding minimal adequate model (p < 0.001). The same is true for position of keyword (p < 0.001) and age of participant (p = 0.043). In addition, geographical distance from Liverpool almost reaches statistical significance as well (p = 0.080). Frequency and age are therefore briefly discussed below for the sake of completeness.

Table 11.1: happʏ (perception): mixed-effects ordinal regression

Fixed effects:	Estimate	Std. Error	z value	Pr(>|z|)	
POSfinal	-0.932	0.091	-10.194	<0.001	***
DISTANCE	0.169	0.093	1.811	0.070	.
Random effects:					
Groups	Name	Variance	Std.Dev.		
QUESTIONNAIRE	(Intercept)	0.162	0.402		
QUESTIONNAIRE	TOKEN	<0.001	<0.001		
(number of obs: 516, groups: QUESTIONNAIRE, 55)					

reduced this way (κ = 10.61). Model selection based on AIC scores and F-tests comparing nested models resulted in the minimal adequate model printed below. Only two factors show up as main effects (one of them not quite significant) and no statistically significant interactions could be found. Position of the stimulus (in the middle or at the end of the sentence) is a highly significant predictor. Geographical distance of the participant from Liverpool does not reach significance at the 5% level, but the p-value is low enough to qualify as a statistical trend. For this reason the factor was kept in the model.

11.1.2 Prime

Prime is not among the fixed effects. This indicates that for the happy stimuli it did not make a difference whether participants thought they were listening to a speaker from Liverpool or Manchester. Figure 11.1 visualises this fact. As with all the following bar plots in this chapter, answers from subjects who were primed for "Liverpool" are represented by black bars, those given by people who were correctly told the speaker was from Manchester are visualised by light grey bars.

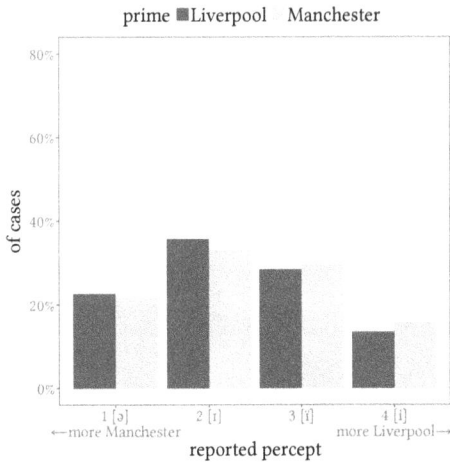

Figure 11.1: happy (perception) by prime

There is a slight preference for stimulus number 2 (the one actually present in the stimulus sentences) at around 35% of answers given, followed by the somewhat tenser (and more Liverpool-like) stimulus 3 at just below 30%. The 'hyper-Mancunian' and 'hyper-Liverpool' stimuli 1 (about 20%) and 4 (15–17%) were less frequently chosen. The crucial point, however, is that only marginal differences between the two conditions are visible, which corroborates the result of the mixed-effects model that subjects were not influenced by the prime when perceiving happy-stimuli.

11.1.3 Position of carrier word

Figure 11.2 shows the clear influence of carrier word position within the stimulus sentence that was identified as a significant predictor by the mixed-effects model. Perception of sentence-final stimuli can be said to be more objective as participants chose stimulus 2 (which actually occurred in the recording) in around 45% of cases. The hyper-centralised stimulus 1 was, at about 35%, also quite frequent, whereas the "Liverpool" stimuli 3 and 4 only account for 20% of answers, with stimulus 4 being particularly rare. When the carrier word was presented in the middle of the sentence, subjects most often reported having heard stimulus number 3, a vowel higher and fronter than in the actual recording. Stimuli 2 and 4 were both chosen around 25–30% of the time, while the hyper-Mancunian vowel was only selected in a bit more than 10% of cases. Overall then, participants were more likely to perceive a "Liverpool"-type tenser /i/ when the carrier word was presented in the middle of the sentence than when it occurred as the last word in the sentence.

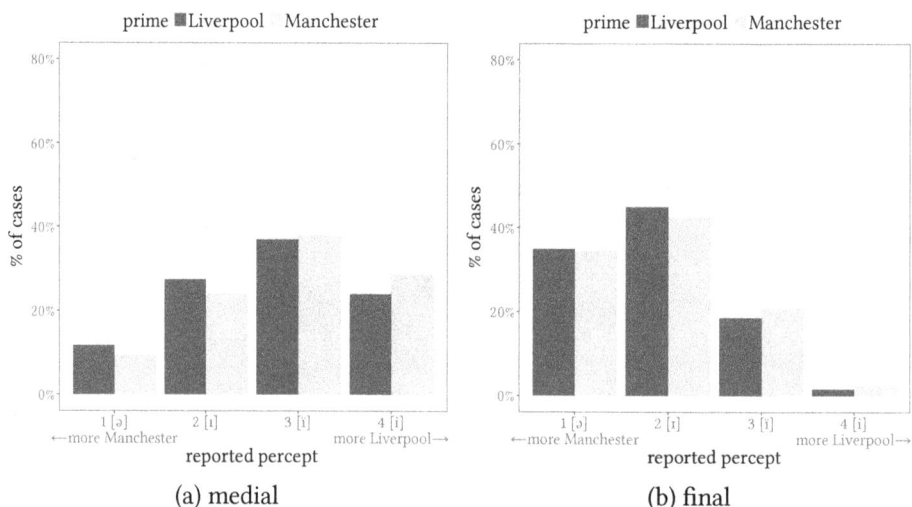

Figure 11.2: happy (perception) by position

It is dubious, however, whether this difference is due to the fact that subjects have to hold the relevant sound in memory – which would be what the different stimulus sentences were meant to test (cf. §10.1.1). It seems at least as plausible that the effect is caused by the acoustic material. In Mancunian English, happy is typically realised as [ɪ] in phrase-medial and [ə] in phrase-final position, and the stimulus sentences used in this experiment were authentic in this respect (cf. §10.1.1). The happy realisations were thus more central when the word occurred at the end of the sentence than when it appeared in the middle of it. It is possible that participants picked up on this difference in realisation and hyper-corrected by selecting one of the tenser answer options when the carrier word was sentence-medially, simply because the vowel sounded tenser than the one they encountered in the sentence-final stimuli.

Another option is that the difference due to word position is an artefact of the method of stimulus creation. Since satisfactory continua could not be resynthesised out of many phrase-final happy vowels, the continua resynthesised on the basis of the same words presented in a sentence-medial context were used as answer options instead (cf. §10.1.2). This meant that, for sentence-final happy stimuli, answer option 2 was a bit tenser than the vowel actually present in the sentence. In this interpretation then, subjects would have reacted quite similarly for both sentence-medial and sentence-final stimuli – most often choosing an answer option that was a bit tenser than the vowel they had actually heard. The only difference would then be that for phrase-final sentences stimulus 2 already fulfilled this criterion, whereas for phrase-medial sentences it was not before stimulus 3 that participants encountered a vowel that was tenser than the one contained in the carrier word.

In any case, position of the stimulus does not show up in the mixed-effects model because of priming which only occurred in one context but not in the other (if this was the case the model should have revealed a significant interaction of prime and position). This is also visible in Figure 11.2b and Figure 11.2a, neither of which shows pronounced differences between priming conditions.

11.1.4 Geographical distance

Geographical distance does not quite reach statistical significance, but qualifies as a statistical trend (p = 0.070). The regression coefficient is little greater than zero (0.169), indicating a weak correlation of distance and answer, which means that subjects who live further from Liverpool are, on average, more likely to choose one of the more Liverpool-like tokens. Inspection of Figure 11.3 reveals, however, that this effect seems to be mostly driven by participants in the priming condition "Manchester". In this graph, answer is marked on the y-axis and geographical distance on the x-axis. Priming conditions are coded by line type: solid for "Liverpool", dashed for "Manchester". The estimated percept increases

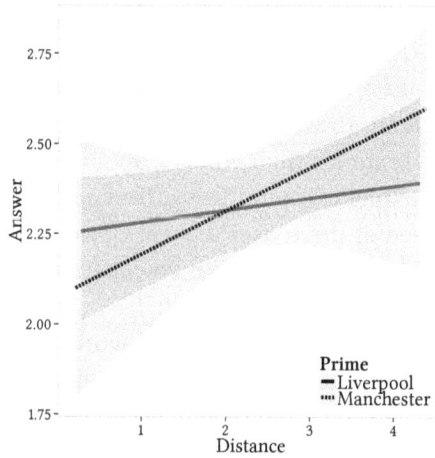

Figure 11.3: happʏ (perception) by distance

for subjects in the "Liverpool" condition as well, but only ever so slightly from 2.25 to around 2.4. In the "Manchester" condition, on the other hand, the regression line has a much steeper slope, with estimated percept rising from 2.1 to roughly 2.6. That being said, it should be borne in mind that both Figure 11.3 and the mixed effect ordinal regression model reported above make it clear that there is no statistically *significant* difference between priming conditions in relation to geographical distance. The two regression lines in Figure 11.3 lie within the overlapping standard error range of both conditions, represented by dark grey in the graph, and the minimal adequate model reported above does not contain a significant interaction of prime and geographical distance. The simple main effect of distance, however, is close to statistical significance, so it is at least worth mentioning that subjects across conditions have a certain tendency to perceive more Liverpool-like tokens the further away they live from Liverpool.

11.1.5 Frequency

For the sake of completeness we will now briefly turn to frequency and age because these two factors show up as (near-)significant in a mixed-effects model that includes the Zipf scores (see page 238). The coefficient for the factor frequency of the carrier word (0.622) is positive in the model not reported here, which means that for higher frequency carrier words higher-numbered (i.e. more Liverpool-like) answer options were more likely. This general correlation is visible in Figure 11.4, which shows Zipf scores on the x-axis and estimated percept

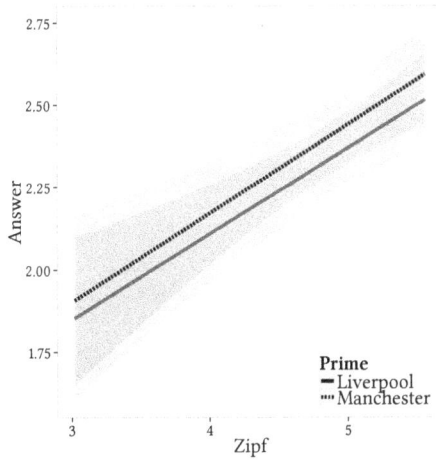

Figure 11.4: happy (perception) by Zipf score

on the y-axis; priming condition is again shown by line type (solid for Liverpool, dashed for Manchester). We can see the positive correlation suggested by the linear mixed-effects model: more centralised percepts for lower frequency items (on the left) and tenser percepts for higher frequency items (on the right). It should be borne in mind, however, that we are only looking at a very restricted set of 6 different carrier words, so the potential frequency effect we are seeing could be heavily overlaid with *lexical* effects, although the two are not unlikely to interact anyway. The direct cause for the correlation of frequency and reported percept might quite simply be that the higher frequency carrier words are realised with tenser happy in the particular stimuli used for this study. There is indeed a trend of this sort in the data: higher-frequency words in the stimuli sentence have a slightly lower F1 and simultaneously a higher F2, the difference between the most frequent and the least frequent two carrier words is about 100 Hz for F1 and about 80 Hz for F2. However, this difference is then carried into the answer tokens since they were generated individually for each sentence (cf. §10.1.1 and §10.1.2), so the effect cannot really be due to the test material. The most important point, in any case, is that, again, the figure supports the absence of a prime X Zipf score interaction in the mixed-effects ordinal regression model. While there are smaller differences between priming conditions, the general relationship between reported percept and Zipf score seems to be the same regardless of whether participants believe they are listening to a speaker from Liverpool or Manchester. Both the solid and the dashed regression line have an upward slope that is almost identical (the lines are very nearly parallel), which illustrates that the effect of frequency (if there is any) is the same in both priming conditions.

11.1.6 Age

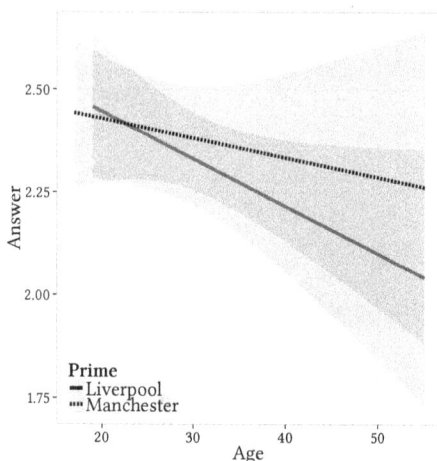

Figure 11.5: happy (perception) by age

As mentioned above, age only reaches significance as a predictor (p = 0.043) in the mixed-effects model that includes Zipf scores, but we will still have a very quick glance at this factor as it is of particular interest in the production part of this book. Figure 11.5 shows age of the participant on the x-axis and estimated percept on the y-axis, again coding priming condition by line type. The general downward trend is visible, but it is rather weak and especially in the "Manchester" condition there is a very large amount of variation in the dataset. It is not straightforward how to interpret the relationship of age and perception of happy. One might speculate that older subjects are on average more aware of lax happy variants because happy-tensing is now the norm both in standard British English and in many other accents of the British Isles. On the other hand, however, there are still large regions of England that have lax happy and there is evidence of happy becoming even more centralised in some of these areas (cf. Flynn 2010), so it is not really clear why younger subjects should expect more peripheral happy vowels across the board. Suffice it to say, in the context of this study, that once more no priming effect is visible in Figure 11.5. It does look as if priming might have more of an effect the older the participant (the distance between the regression lines grows towards the right hand side of the graph), but if this was statistically significant it should have shown in the regression models as an interaction of prime and age. This was not the case in either the mixed-effects model that was finally chosen or the one that included frequency of the keyword. Both Figure 11.4 and Figure 11.5 also visualise that there is no significant difference between priming conditions for any level of frequency or age of participant because all regression lines run fully within the dark grey area, i.e. within the standard error of the other condition.

11.2 NURSE

11.2.1 Overview

Just as for happy, a first maximal mixed-effects model including frequency as a predictor was fit to the responses relating to NURSE. While the condition number was not extremely high it did suggest more than medium collinearity ($\kappa = 21.78$) and therefore called for closer inspection of the model. Removing the Zipf scores from the group of fixed effects improved the model in this respect and made the level of collinearity drop considerably ($\kappa = 8.05$). Model selection based on AIC scores and F-tests comparing nested models was carried out on both mixed-effects ordinal regression models (the one including frequency as a predictor and the one lacking it). The minimal adequate model in both cases was identical and is printed below. It is, again, a rather simple model with just two significant main effects, prime and position. No significant interactions of prime and any of the other factors could be found.

Table 11.2: NURSE (perception): mixed-effects ordinal regression

Fixed effects:	Estimate	Std. Error	z value	Pr(>|z|)	
PRIMELiv	-0.325	0.125	-2.599	0.009	**
TOKEN	-0.011	0.007	-1.621	0.105	
POSfinal	0.395	0.098	4.031	< 0.001	***
PRIMELiv:POSfinal	0.183	0.095	1.913	0.056	.

Random effects:				
Groups	Name	Variance	Std.Dev.	
QUESTIONNAIRE	(Intercept)	0.219	0.469	
QUESTIONNAIRE	TOKEN	<0.001	0.014	
(number of obs: 547, groups: QUESTIONNAIRE, 55)				

Token was kept in the model because it just about fails to qualify as a statistical trend (p = 0.105) and is therefore still worth a quick investigation as the position of the stimulus within the experiment turned out to be a crucial factor in a previous study of the author, where a (weak) priming effect could be identified, but this effect was only temporary and disappeared in the course of the experiment (cf. Juskan 2011).

11.2.2 Prime

First of all the most interesting predictor, prime, will be investigated. Figure 11.6 shows the pooled results for NURSE. We can see that in a very clear majority of cases (between 65 and 70%) subjects reported having perceived stimulus number 2, the one that objectively corresponded most closely to the vowel in the carrier sentence.

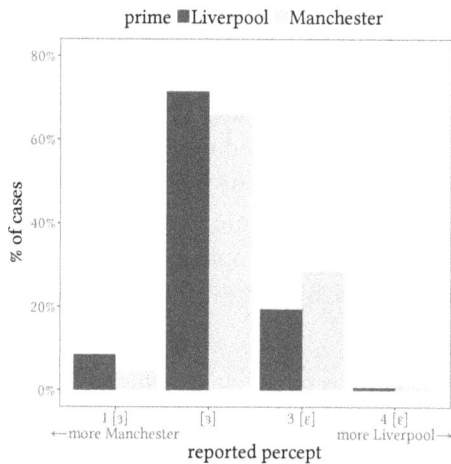

Figure 11.6: NURSE (perception) by prime

This preference for the actual token was much more pronounced for NURSE than for HAPPY stimuli. The fronted and lowered token 3 was chosen 20 (prime "Liverpool") to 30% (prime "Manchester") of the time. The ultra-central token 1 accounts for less than 10% of answers, and the ultra-Liverpool token 4 was hardly ever chosen. While the general pattern is the same, it is obvious that there are also clear differences between priming conditions. When participants are led to believe the speaker is from Liverpool they are more likely to choose tokens number 1 or 2, and less likely to report having heard the fronted and lowered tokens 3 and 4. For NURSE we thus find the priming effect that was absent for HAPPY.

This was expected and is in line with the hypothesis that only salient variables will show a priming effect. What is surprising, though, is that the priming effect is not in the expected *direction*. When participants are primed for "Liverpool" they are actually *less* likely to perceive one of the Liverpool NURSE variants 3 and 4. As is visible in Figure 11.6, token 3 accounts for about 30% of answers in the "Manchester" condition, but less than 20% in the "Liverpool" condition. Token 4 was very rarely chosen in both conditions, but again slightly more often when participants had been primed for "Manchester". Tokens 1 and 2, on the other hand, were more often chosen when subjects had been told the speaker was from Liverpool.

11.2.3 Position of carrier word

The mixed-effects ordinal regression model returned an interaction of prime and position close to a trend and also a highly significant main effect for position of the carrier word alone. Figure 11.7 shows the distribution of NURSE answers by position in the stimulus sentence.

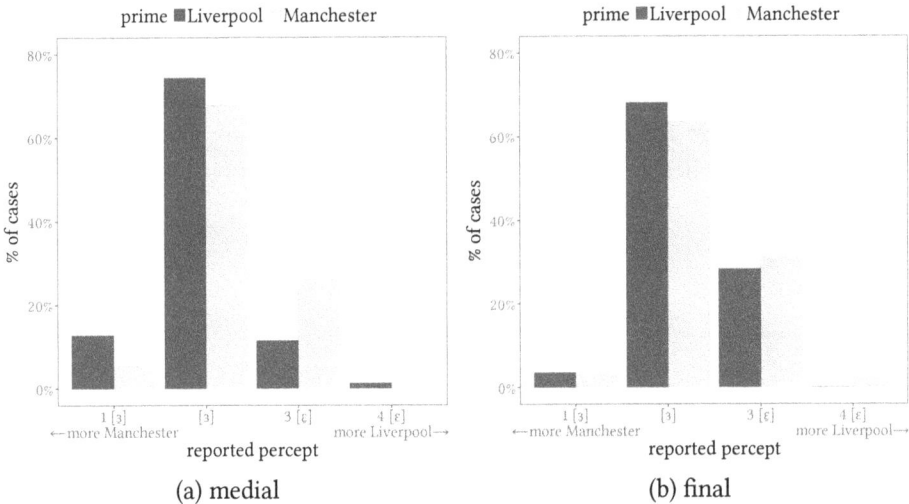

(a) medial   (b) final

Figure 11.7: NURSE (perception) by position

It is immediately obvious that Figure 11.7a and Figure 11.7b do not differ as much as Figure 11.2a and Figure 11.2b do. The general pattern of the distribution is the same as in Figure 11.6: token 2 is by far the most frequent answer, followed by 3, 1, and 4, and the Liverpool tokens 3 and 4 together are more likely in the "Manchester" condition. The differences between priming conditions, however, are more pronounced for the stimuli that presented the carrier word in the middle of the sentence. For the sentence-final stimuli we find virtually no difference between priming conditions when we look at token number 1, for example. For answer tokens 2 and 3 the difference is only about 5%. In the sentence-medial stimuli, on the other hand, there is a clear difference for token 1 as well, and for subjects primed for "Manchester" the rate of token number 3 is 14% higher than in the other group.

The graphs thus suggest that the priming effect illustrated in Figure 11.6 is mostly driven by sentence-medial stimuli. Judging from these three figures it might seem surprising that the interaction of prime and position did not quite reach significance in the mixed-effects model reported above. Probably, this is simply due to the fact that subject (coded as "Questionnaire" in R) was entered as a random factor (cf. §10.4). Since a single subject was only in one priming condition it is possible that a certain degree of the priming effect was filtered out along with the variation due to individuals and that, as a consequence, the interaction no longer reached statistical significance in the mixed-effects model.

11.2.4 Stimulus order

The influence of token (i.e. the point in time the item was presented in the course of the experiment) on which answer was chosen is slightly more straightforward than the one of age for happy stimuli. The coefficient from the mixed-effects model (−0.011) implies a weak downward slope and this is visible in Figure 11.8.

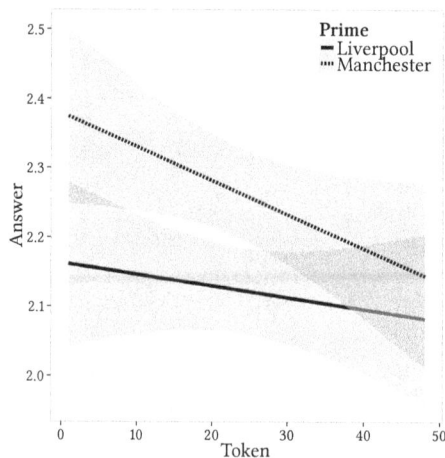

Figure 11.8: NURSE (perception) by token

Just as with age for happy there is a substantial amount of variation. Nevertheless, it seems clear that subjects are increasingly less likely to perceive the higher-numbered tokens and tend more and more towards the lower (hyper-)Mancunian end of the answer range the further they progress in the experiment. The dashed regression line for the "Manchester" priming condition is above the one for the "Liverpool" group (reflecting the fact that subjects primed for "Manchester" were more likely to respond with Liverpool-like tokens), but the distance between conditions tends to get smaller in the course of the test because the slope is steeper for the "Manchester" condition. That is to say participants primed for Manchester change their behaviour more drastically than the other group. In the last third of the experiment, the two conditions seem much more aligned: the lines are closer to each other than in the beginning and the standard error ranges start overlapping considerably. For the last ten items or so the regression lines are within the error range of the other group, indicating that the answers given in the two groups are not significantly different (anymore).

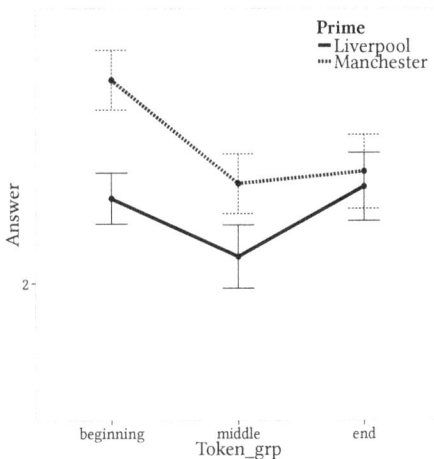

Figure 11.9: NURSE (perception) by token (grouped)

Figure 11.9 visualises the differences between priming groups when responses are grouped with respect to whether they were given at the beginning (items 1–18), in the middle (items 19–36), or towards the end (items 37–48) of the experiment. The dots mark the answer means in the respective phases of the test, priming conditions are coded by line type as usual (dashed for "Manchester", solid for "Liverpool"), and the error ranges are based on standard deviations. The graph tells much the same story as Figure 11.8: Answers in the two groups differ at the beginning of the test (the means are clearly distinguishable, error bars do not overlap, the regression lines in Figure 11.8 are far apart), then the difference grows smaller (means and error bars are closer, distance between regression lines decreases), and in the end the two groups are very close together (means and error bars in the two conditions are no longer distinguishable, regression lines lie within the dark grey area of overlapping standard deviations). χ^2-tests on the raw data at least partially tie in with this description, in that distributions of answers are significantly different at the beginning of the experiment (χ^2 = 9.551, df = 3; p = 0.023). The test for the tokens in the middle of the experiment yields a non-significant result (χ^2 = 4.964, df = 3; p = 0.174), but the p-value is still considerably lower than the one obtained when testing answers in the last third of the experiment (χ^2 = 1.541, df = 3; p = 0.673).

It is tempting to interpret this in the same way as the author has done in a previous study (cf. Juskan 2011): The priming effect is greater at the beginning of the experiment and then diminishes as subjects perceive more and more material that is (in the case of the "Liverpool" group) in conflict with the prime. This material activates exemplars that are acoustically similar (instead of indexed with the same social information as the prime) and shifts the basis of perception – the priming effect disappears. In the present case, however, this interpretation is difficult to uphold. For one thing, the development just described would only make sense in the condition where participants were primed for Liverpool. If people are correctly told the speaker is from Manchester there is no acoustic deviation from the exemplars that are activated through social indexation, so there is nothing that could be "corrected" by additional acoustic material. The line for "Manchester" in Figure 11.8 should therefore be flat, which it is not. Figure 11.9 and the χ^2-results do suggest that the priming effect seems to change in the course of the experiment, but it should be borne in mind that both are based on the raw data, whereas the mixed-effects model did not find a significant interaction of prime and stimulus order once variation due to individual properties of the subjects (and individual changes in behaviour during the test) had been taken out of the calculation. The differences between conditions that we are seeing in Figure 11.8 and Figure 11.9 could therefore be unduly amplified by random variation between subjects. As far as the regression model is concerned, the influence of stimulus order is the same in both conditions, *and* it is, after all, not a predictor which is significant at the 5%-level – in fact, it is not even a statistical trend. Both points should caution against overinterpretation of this factor.

11.3 /ŋ(g)/

11.3.1 Overview

Just as with the other variables, the first maximal mixed-effects ordinal model that was fit to the /ŋ(g)/ responses included the SUBTLEX frequency of the keyword as a fixed effect. The degree of collinearity was, again, not unacceptable in this model (κ = 12.35), but it *did* turn out that the Zipf scores of keywords strongly correlated with phonological environment of /ŋ(g)/. If we have another look at Table 10.1 on page 223, the problem becomes apparent. For the two consonantal variables velar nasal plus and lenition of /k/, the top three keywords have the variable in word-final position, while the bottom three contain the sound in question in an intervocalic context. For /ŋ(g)/, the frequencies of keywords are 2.13, 3.13, and 4.48 for 'intervocalic', and 4.39, 5.10, and 5.51 for 'word-final' respectively. Frequency of keyword and phonological context are therefore confounded because keywords where the variable occurs intervocalically are also on average less frequent than keywords that have the variable in final position.

This is unfortunate and should have been avoided, but it should be remembered that frequency is just a minor concern in this study anyway, that the selection of keywords was primarily based on other criteria, and that the overall experimental design was neither specifically intended nor particularly suited to investigate frequency in the first place (cf. §10.1.1). As a result of collinearity it becomes difficult to statistically tell the effect of one factor from that of the other. The easiest way to solve this problem is to drop one of the factors in question from the model. Since this study is more interested in a potential effect of environment,

Table 11.3: /ŋ(g)/ (perception): mixed-effects ordinal regression

Fixed effects:	Estimate	Std. Error	z value	Pr(>|z|)	
PRIMELiv	-0.250	0.145	-1.723	0.085	.
AGE	-0.025	0.015	-1.700	0.089	.
ENVIR_#	0.239	0.084	2.854	< 0.01	**

Random effects:			
Groups	Name	Variance	Std.Dev.
QUESTIONNAIRE	(Intercept)	0.653	0.808
QUESTIONNAIRE	TOKEN	<0.001	0.010
(number of obs: 534, groups: QUESTIONNAIRE, 55)			

frequency was eliminated from the set of predictors. Strictly speaking, this would not have been necessary as the collinearity in the original model did not reach a problematic level ($\kappa < 15$), but dropping frequency increased comparability with the model fit to the data for /k/ (cf. §11.4) while simultaneously decreasing collinearity in the /ŋ(g)/ model a bit further ($\kappa = 7.88$). The minimal adequate model for velar nasal plus is, once more, a rather simple one.[2]

Only three factors remain once all non-significant interactions and main effects have been eliminated from the model: Phonological environment, age (near-significant) and, somewhat surprisingly, prime, which almost reaches significance. The coefficient for priming condition "Liverpool" is negative (−0.250), indicating that, again, people who were led to believe the speaker was from Liverpool are actually *less* likely to choose one of the Liverpool tokens 3 or 4. The other significant main effect is environment, which, in this study, has two levels: intervocalic ("V_V") and word-final ("_#"). Let us start by looking at the predictor prime in the entire dataset, illustrated in Figure 11.10.

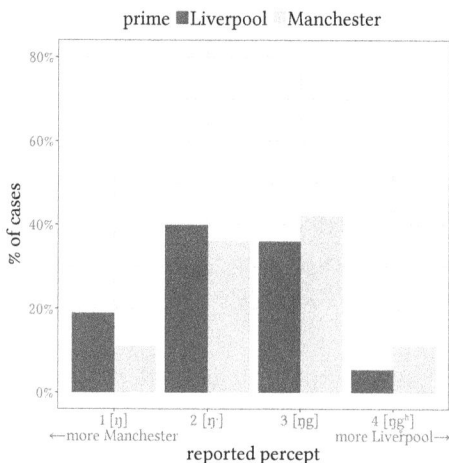

Figure 11.10: /ŋ(g)/ (perception) by prime

11.3.2 Prime

As far as the overall distribution of answers is concerned, Figure 11.10 looks quite similar to Figure 11.1. Tokens 2 (actual, long nasal) and 3 ("Liverpool", nasal plus

---

[2]Starting out from a maximal model that includes frequency as a fixed effect results in the same minimal adequate model, which is evidence that dropping Zipf scores as a predictor was justified and unproblematic.

burst) together account for almost 80% of all answers in both conditions. Participants who were in the "Manchester" condition then chose tokens 1 and 3 equally often, namely in around 10% of cases each. Subjects who thought the speaker was from Liverpool clearly preferred the hyper-standard token 1 (shortened nasal) to the hyper-Liverpudlian token 4 (nasal plus burst and aspiration). Apart from this difference, priming also manifests itself when we look at tokens 2 and 3: People primed for Liverpool reported having perceived the long nasal slightly more often than the nasal followed by a burst, whereas the opposite is true for participants who were correctly told the speaker was from Manchester. This graph thus looks very similar to those reported in Hay, Nolan, et al. 2006; Hay & Drager 2010, with the peak of the distribution falling on one token for the first condition ("Liverpool", token 2) and on another for the second condition ("Manchester", token 3). Subjects primed for Liverpool thus tend to perceive the /ŋ(g)/ stimuli more often as a long or shortened nasal than those in the control group who believed the speaker was from Manchester. The mixed-effects ordinal regression model did not find prime to be a significant predictor, but it does qualify as a statistical trend (p = 0.085) and a less conservative χ^2-test on the raw data actually finds this effect to be very significant (χ^2 = 12.876, df = 3; p = 0.005). While the effect is not as statistically robust as for NURSE, then, it seems as if there might at least be some priming going on for velar nasal plus as well. Intriguingly, the direction of the effect is, again, opposite to what was expected: Subjects are *less* likely to perceive Liverpool variants when they expect the speaker to be from Liverpool.

11.3.3 Phonological context

The only clearly significant predictor of answer tokens in the mixed ordinal regression model is the phonological context in which the variable is found in the keyword. The difference between the two environments analysed in this study is visualised in Figure 11.11a and Figure 11.11b. The overall distribution of answers seems to be roughly the same in both environments. Tokens 2 and 3 together account for around 70–80% of answers, in both priming conditions and in both intervocalic and word-final contexts. In the model we find a coefficient of 0.239 for word-final environments ('_#'), which indicates that people are more likely to answer with a higher-numbered token when the variable is word-final. This is visible in the graphs as well: In Figure 11.11b, the preference for tokens 2 and 3 is more pronounced, and the around 20% of answers that remain are relatively equally distributed among tokens 1 and 4 (if pooled across priming conditions). In Figure 11.11a, on the other hand, the proportion of '1' answers is much larger

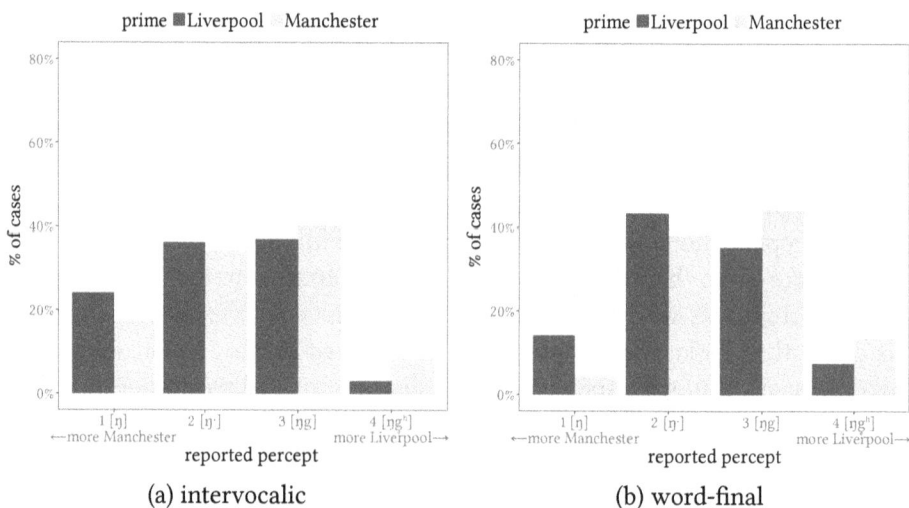

Figure 11.11: /ŋ(g)/ (perception) by environment

than that for token number 4, so people were more likely to report having perceived the ultra-standard shortened nasal than the fully realised Liverpudlian velar nasal plus. This preference of token 1 over token 4 then reduces the mean in this phonological context.

Another striking feature of Figure 11.11a and Figure 11.11b is that the differences between priming conditions do not seem to be identical. For word-final contexts we see essentially the same thing as for the pooled data (Figure 11.10: Clearly different peaks (token 2 for "Liverpool", token 3 for "Manchester") and distributions that are generally somewhat more skewed to the right ("Manchester") or to the left ("Liverpool"). Figure 11.11a looks more "messy" in this respect. Differences between priming conditions seem to exist, but they are less pronounced than in word-final contexts (cf. the small differences in height of the black and light grey bars for tokens 2 and 3 in particular). Again, it should be remembered, though, that this difference is not statistically significant once individual variation due to subjects has been eliminated: the mixed-effects ordinal regression model did not find a significant interaction of prime and phonological environment.

While a supposed difference in priming between contexts is not statistically solid, the difference between the contexts themselves (phonological environment as a main effect) is. Why then are subjects more likely to perceive a plosive if velar nasal plus occurs at the end of a word? I can only speculate at this point, but it might be to do with the fact that word-final /ŋ(g)/ is often not only realised with a plosive in the Liverpool (and Manchester) area, but also frequently devoiced and aspirated. These [ŋk] or [ŋkʰ] realisations might be more perceptible than the intervocalic variants where there is no change in voicing, which could mean that subjects "expect" a plosive more in word-final contexts.

11.3.4 Age

The last predictor that was found to be at least marginally significant (p = 0.089) in the mixed ordinal regression model for /ŋ(g)/ is age, the impact of which is visualised in Figure 11.12a, which shows age on the x-axis and estimated answer token on the y-axis, and codes priming condition by line type. Both regression lines have a downward slope, which was expected, given that the coefficient for age in the mixed-effects model was –0.025. At first glance, subjects in different priming conditions again seem to behave differently. There is hardly any movement in the "Liverpool" condition, the solid line is almost flat. The dashed regression line for participants in the "Manchester" condition, on the other hand, drops much more dramatically. One might be tempted to conclude that priming affected subjects of different ages in different ways. If we consider the error ranges, however, it becomes clear that this would be an unwarranted deduction. While it is true that the two regression lines are clearly separate for the youngest subjects in the sample (on the left hand side of the graph) and that they approach

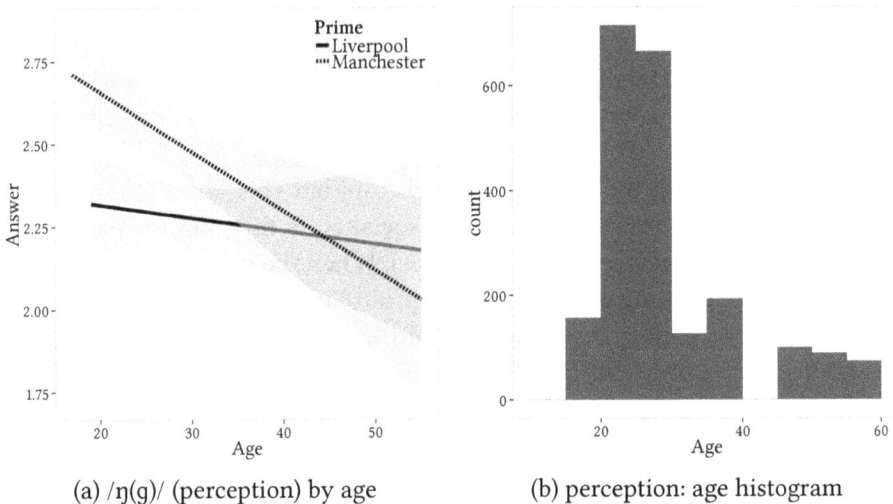

(a) /ŋ(g)/ (perception) by age   (b) perception: age histogram

Figure 11.12: Age in /ŋ(g)/ (perception) and overall

(and cross!) each other as we move along the age scale, it also has to be noted that both lines lie within a shared standard deviation once we reach participants aged around 37 and older. This could simply be due to the fact that the sample is heavily skewed towards subjects in their twenties (cf. Figure 11.12b, which shows that the vast majority of observations stems from subjects that are between 20 and 30 years of age), but in any case there seems to be far too much noise in the answers given by older subjects to meaningfully speculate about any differences that might exist. This is particularly true since the mixed-effects model does not contain a significant interaction of prime and age.

11.4 /k/

11.4.1 Overview

The condition number in the maximal model fit to responses relating to /k/ stimuli was slightly above the threshold for medium collinearity (κ = 15.94), and, just as for velar nasal plus, this was due to a strong correlation of frequency and phonological environment. Another look at Table 10.1 on page 223 reveals that if we compare keywords from the two phonological contexts in pairs (least frequent _# word and least frequent V_V word, medium frequency _# word and medium frequency V_V word, most frequent _# word and most frequent V_V word), the Zipf score of the keywords with the variable in word-final position is always higher. High frequency is thus, in this very limited sample, largely identical with word-final occurrence of the variable. Removing frequency as a fixed effect halved collinearity in the maximal model (κ = 7.9). Model selection based on AIC scores and F-tests comparing nested models resulted in the minimal adequate model printed below.

   Prime is not among the significant predictors but this is only because the model found an interaction of prime and social class that almost reached significance and was therefore kept in the model. When the interaction is removed prime turns into a significant main effect (p = 0.046). Social class, on the other hand, is (nearly) significant both as part of the interaction with prime and as a main effect of its own. The positive coefficient of 0.622 indicates that middle-class speakers tend to perceive higher-numbered tokens. With a p-value below 0.001, phonological environment is even more significant as a predictor than it was for /ŋ(g)/ answers. The coefficient (−0.391), however, is negative, which indicates that word-final /k/'s actually increase the likelihood of lower-numbered, i.e. more standard/Mancunian tokens. For velar nasal plus, the effect was in the

Table 11.4: /k/ (perception): mixed-effects ordinal regression

Fixed effects:	Estimate	Std. Error	z value	Pr(>|z|)	
PRIMELiv	0.048	0.199	0.240	0.810	
CLASSmc	0.622	0.200	3.110	< 0.01	**
ENVIR_#	-0.391	0.104	-3.764	< 0.001	***
DISTANCE	0.232	0.121	1.912	0.056	.
PRIMELiv:CLASSmc	-0.373	0.199	-1.870	0.061	.

Random effects:				
Groups	Name	Variance	Std.Dev.	
QUESTIONNAIRE	(Intercept)	0.227	0.477	
QUESTIONNAIRE	TOKEN	<0.001	<0.001	
(number of obs: 522, groups: QUESTIONNAIRE, 55)				

opposite direction. Geographical distance does not quite reach significance (p = 0.056), but the p-value is low enough to qualify as a statistical trend, so the factor was kept in the model.[3] I will now discuss these factors in more detail, starting once more with prime.

11.4.2 Prime and social class

Interestingly, there are a number of parallels in the pooled results for NURSE and lenition of /k/ as visualised in Figure 11.6 and Figure 11.13 (remember that the corresponding graphs for happY and /ŋ(g)/ also resembled each other): Again, the preference of subjects to choose the objectively most accurate token 2 is obvious in Figure 11.13: 70–75% of answers belong to this category. Token 1 (plosive with burst, but no aspiration) accounts for 20% of responses in the "Manchester" group, and 30% of answers for the participants who were primed for Liverpool. The affricate (token 3) and fricative (token 4) are rarely chosen across the board, but

---

[3]When Zipf scores are kept in the maximal model despite the collinearity with phonological environment, the minimal adequate model one arrives at is not too different from the one printed above. Social class and phonological environment remain significant predictors, but the interaction of prime and social class is eliminated from the model and, as a result, prime alone is found to be a significant fixed effect. The p-value for geographical distance is slightly greater than 0.1, so this factor gets eliminated. With a p-value of 0.113, the predictor frequency almost qualifies as a statistical trend. The impact of frequency will therefore be briefly analysed, too, in order to complete the picture.

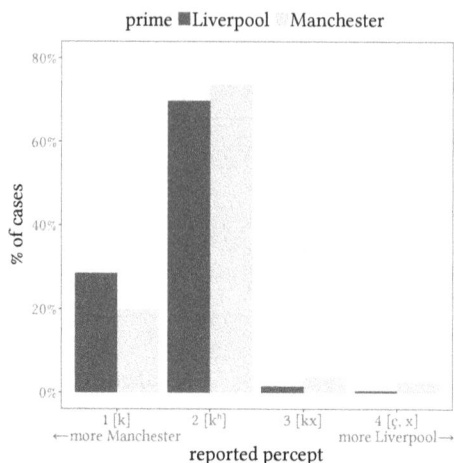

Figure 11.13: /k/ (perception) by prime

still clearly more often if people think the speaker is from Manchester (light grey bars). Once more, the priming effect is not in the expected direction: Subjects are *less* likely to perceive /k/-lenition if they are led to believe the speaker is actually from Liverpool.

In the NURSE results there was also a sizeable proportion of token 3 (mild Scouse) answers, which has "moved" to token 1 (hyper standard/Mancunian) in the responses to /k/ stimuli. Apart from that, pooled results for the two salient variables are remarkably similar: pronounced preference for the objectively most accurate token in both conditions, priming effect in the unexpected direction. This priming effect is subtle (people are not fooled most of the time and choose the "correct" token 2 in three out of four cases), but nevertheless clearly visible in the graph. While prime is not a significant main effect in the mixed ordinal regression model (due to the presence of the interaction with social class, see beginning of this section), the difference between conditions is found to be significant in a model not including this interaction (estimate = -0.256, se = 0.128, z value = -1.999, p = 0.046), which supports the interpretation of Figure 11.13 just presented. The interaction of prime and social class is what we will look at next.

Figure 11.14a shows the data for working-class subjects only, while Figure 11.14b visualises the responses given by middle-class participants. As outlined earlier, the correlation coefficient for middle class (0.622) suggests that middle-class participants were more likely to perceive higher-numbered tokens. The two subplots of Figure 11.14 illustrate this in an impressively (and unexpectedly) clear way.

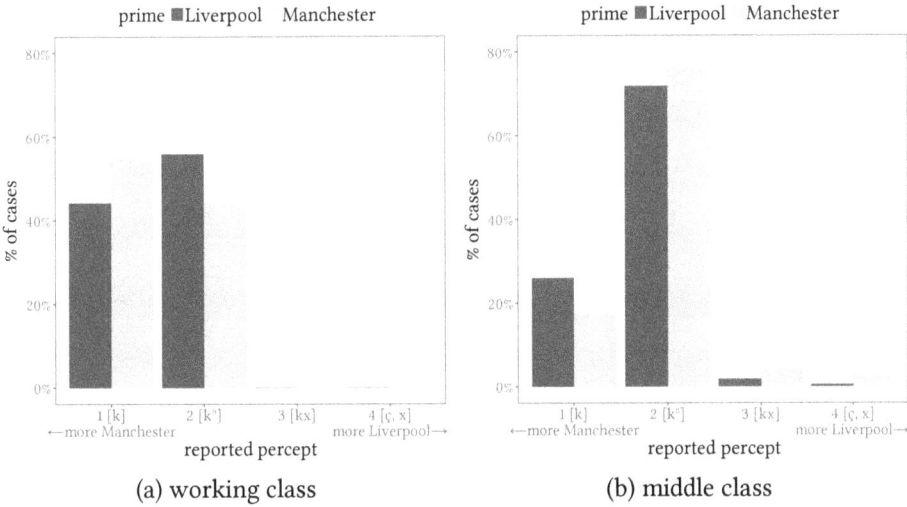

Figure 11.14: /k/ (perception) by social class

Working-class participants chose answer token 1 in around 45% and token 2 in about 55% of cases when they were in the "Liverpool" condition; the WC subjects in the "Manchester" condition reverse these figures. Two factors are responsible for the lower average of WC subjects: (a) Working-class participants never (!) chose tokens 3 or 4 (irrespective of priming condition), and (b) tokens 1 and 2 have an (almost, if conditions are considered separately) equal share of the total number of WC answers.

Middle-class subjects, on the other hand, show a distribution which is very similar to the one we find when results are pooled for social class (cf. Figure 11.13). This is not surprising, given that subjects with a middle-class background clearly dominate the sample in terms of numbers (cf. §10.3). Token 2 accounts for 70–75% of answers, depending on priming condition. Just as in Figure 11.13, the next most frequent answer is the hyper-standard/Mancunian token number 1 (plosive with burst, but no friction), which was chosen in around 25% ("Liverpool") and about 17% ("Manchester") of cases. The affricate (token 3) and fricative variants (token 4) were once more only chosen in a small minority of cases, but clearly more often when subjects were primed for Manchester. The interaction of prime and class that the mixed ordinal regression model found is thus also visible in the raw data.

In Figure 11.15 the interaction of these two factors is visualised. As with the other scatter/regression plots estimated answer token is to be found on the y-axis.

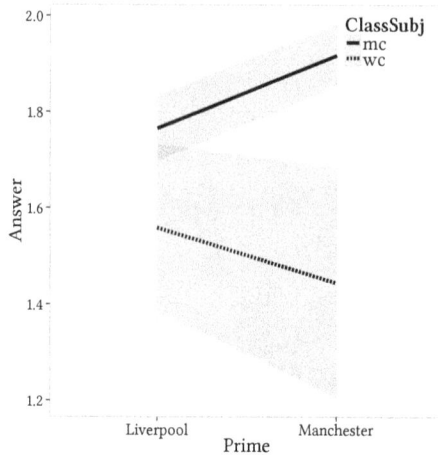

Figure 11.15: /k/ (perception) by prime and social class

On the x-axis we have the distinction into subjects primed for "Manchester" and "Liverpool". Social class, finally, is coded by line type: The solid line represents middle-class subjects, while the dashed line stands for working-class participants. The difference between the two social classes is quite obvious. For working-class subjects the regression line has a negative slope. Average answer token number is lower in the "Manchester" condition, so if there was a statistically significant priming effect in this sub-group it would actually be in the expected direction (more Liverpool-like percepts in the "Liverpool" condition, more Manchester-like percepts in the "Manchester" condition). In the middle-class group, this effect is reversed. The positive slope indicates that participants who were primed for Liverpool are *less* likely to perceive Liverpool variants of /k/. The increase in the middle-class group is also steeper than the decrease in the working-class subjects, which suggests that there is more of an effect in the former than in the latter. We also see that there seems to be much more variation in the answers given by working-class respondents (the standard error, marked by the grey area around the regression line, is much larger than the one for middle-class participants). This is probably mostly due to the small number of observations in this sub-sample (n(WC) = 69; n(MC) = 487), which might also be the main reason why the difference is not statistically significant.

Given this very pronounced middle-class bias in the sample of this experiment (48 middle-class and 7 working-class subjects; 3 participants did not give their social class), any conclusions drawn about social class differences should be taken with a grain of salt. Notwithstanding this caveat, it is highly interesting that a priming effect can only be found for middle-class subjects, but not for their working-class counterparts. Also, it remains striking, even if the small number of observations is taken into account, that WC subjects did not choose tokens 3 and 4 even once. 2.2% ("Liverpool") to 6.5% ("Manchester") of MC answers were token 3 or 4. If working-class participants had similar percentages, tokens 3 and 4 would have been chosen between 1 and 5 times. Furthermore, this result – statistically shaky as it may be – is in line with previous research. Hay, Nolan, et al. (2006) and Hay & Drager (2010) both found an interaction of social class and condition, and in both cases the priming effect was most pronounced for the highest social classes, less extreme in the middle range, and completely absent for participants situated towards the lower end of the socioeconomic scale.

For a socially salient variable, this should not really come as a surprise. Rather, a result like this is only to be expected, because speakers from higher socioeconomic classes are, on the whole, hypothesised to be much more sensitive to, and aware of, social differences in language use. It seems only logical that they would also be more susceptible to a manipulation that is based on these subtle differences. Another option is that due to differences in mobility and social networks, working-class subjects just do not have any exemplars indexed with "Liverpool" (the same would hold true for "Manchester"), so priming them cannot activate any exemplars that would bias their perception.

11.4.3 Phonological context

The last (highly) significant factor in the mixed ordinal regression model is phonological environment. We have the same two environments _# and V_V as for velar nasal plus. Results for V_V are visualised in Figure 11.16a, those for _# contexts are represented by Figure 11.16b. Similar to the results for /ŋ(g)/, where phonological context was also a significant factor, there do not seem to be huge differences between Figure 11.16a and Figure 11.16b. In both contexts, subjects show the clear preference for token 2 (released plosive with normal aspiration) that we have already seen for the pooled results. Token 1 (plosive with burst, but no aspiration) is the next most frequent choice in both environments. However, it accounts for between 15 and just above 20% of answers in the intervocalic stimuli, whereas for keywords that have the variable in word-final position, token 1 is chosen in around 27 to 35% of cases. Tokens 3 (affricate) and 4 (fricative) have about the same share in both phonological contexts. The fact that token 1 is a considerably more (and token 2 a considerably less) frequent response to word-final stimuli thus explains why the mixed-effects model found a lower likelihood of higher-numbered answer tokens in this sub-sample (the coefficient is −0.391).

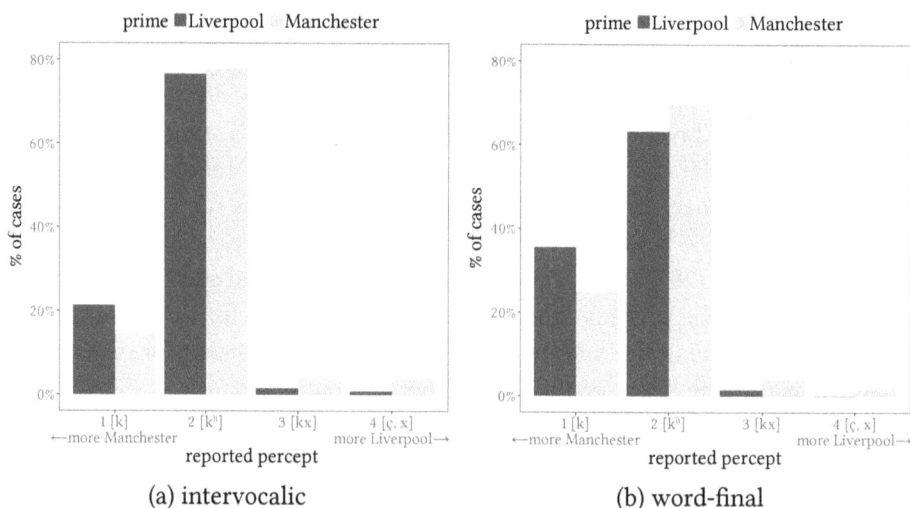

Figure 11.16: /k/ (perception) by environment

One might also suspect a different size of the priming effect when only looking at the two graphs. Differences between conditions appear to be more pronounced in Figure 11.16b, particularly for token 2. On the other hand, the potential influence of prime seems to be largely identical in size for tokens 3 and 4 in both phonological contexts, and the distance between conditions for token 1 *is* greater in word-final than in intervocalic environments, but not as much as it is for token 2. If phonological context does affect the degree of the priming effect, then the difference can only be a very subtle one. The raw data thus seem to support the fact that the mixed-effects model did not find a significant interaction of prime and phonological environment; the effect is largely the same.

Even though environments are not significantly different from each other, it is tempting to link the slightly more pronounced difference between priming conditions for the word-final stimuli to higher salience of /k/-lenition in this context. Remember that, in production, subjects used more lenition for /k/'s that appeared intervocalically compared to those that occurred word-finally (cf. §7.2.2). This was taken to be a hint that lenition of /k/ is more socially salient in the latter environment, or, rather, it is *less* salient in intervocalic contexts, possibly because leniting a stop in-between vowels can be "justified" phonetically (and is quite common typologically). It would tie in nicely with the main hypothesis of this study if a feature that has been shown to be more salient in a particular phonological environment in production also creates a larger priming effect in this context in perception. Unfortunately, however, there is only little statistical evidence to support this claim, as has been pointed out above.

With respect to the stronger preference for token 2 in intervocalic stimuli, there is a possible explanation that is more directly based on the phonological environment itself, and one that also works for the significant difference between phonological contexts as a whole – across priming conditions – that was revealed in the mixed ordinal regression. In RP, GA, and many other accents of English, the voiceless plosives /p, t, k/ have three main allophones which are in complement-ary distribution: Aspirated variants [pʰ, tʰ, kʰ] occur in simple onsets of syllables, unaspirated variants [p, t, k] are found in complex onsets, and unreleased real-isations [p̚, t̚, k̚] are common in coda position. For any word-final /k/ stimulus it is therefore possible that subjects sub-consciously expected a [k̚] realisation. In intervocalic, i.e. syllable-initial position, on the other hand, the expected variant would be [kʰ]. Token 2 (plosive with burst and aspiration, i.e. [kʰ]) thus fits ex-pectations based on allophonic distributions very well when /k/ is presented in inter-vocalic environments. If we assume that participants are somewhat biased to perceive a non-released [k̚] in word-final contexts, their best option to report this percept would be choosing token 1 (plosive with a short burst, but no aspira-tion) as it is phonetically most similar to [k̚], so we would expect a larger share of token 1 answers, and this is exactly what we are seeing in Figure 11.16a and Figure 11.16b. Explaining the larger proportion of token 1 answers for _# stim-uli with expectations based on well-known allophonic distributions is the same as saying subjects were primed by the phonological context. While there was no significant interaction of prime and phonological environment (differences between conditions are non-significant in both cases), then, we seem to have revealed an unintended priming effect of phonological context itself.

11.4.4 Geographical distance

Let us now turn to geographical distance from Liverpool, a fixed effect which was not found to be significant in the mixed ordinal regression model, but whose p-value was low enough ($p = 0.056$) to qualify as a statistical trend. The estimate found (0.232) suggests that higher-numbered answer tokens increase in parallel with growing distance from Liverpool. This trend is immediately obvious in Fig-ure 11.17. As usual, the estimated answer token is marked on the y-axis. On the x-axis we find Euclidean distance from Liverpool, and priming condition is once more coded by line type (dashed for "Manchester", solid for "Liverpool").

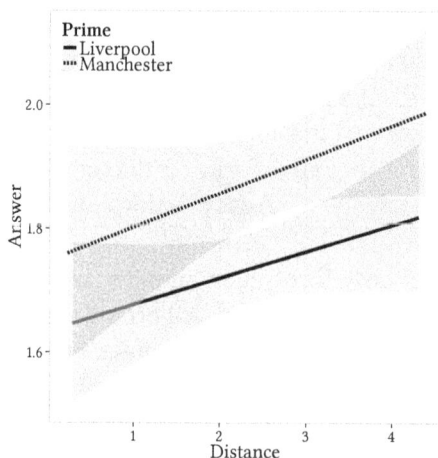

Figure 11.17: /k/ (perception) by geographical distance

Both regression lines have a clear upward slope, indicating that a higher-numbered response becomes ever more likely as the geographical distance of the participant from Liverpool increases. This effect seems to be the same in both conditions. While the two lines have different intercepts (this is the overall priming effect), they run almost perfectly in parallel, which means that the effect of distance is identical in both conditions. Since geographical distance does not reach significance as a predictor but only crosses the trend threshold, the meaning of this result should probably not be overestimated. All the same, it is interesting that Figure 11.17 looks comparable to Figure 11.3 (minus the priming effect). For both variables we might be seeing a (weak) proximity effect in the sense that people living further away are more prone to choosing one of the objectively less accurate, Liverpool-like tokens 3 or 4, whereas subjects living closer to Liverpool prefer the accurate and hyper-correct tokens 1 and 2. If this effect is more than a statistical artefact, it could be to do with familiarity. People who live closer to Liverpool (and Manchester, probably) might be reluctant to choose the Liverpool variants because they know comparatively well what these variants sound like and therefore feel rather confident in deciding that what they are hearing in the stimuli is not Liverpool English. As a consequence, Liverpool tokens 3 and 4 are largely out. Subjects who are less familiar with Scouse, because they live far away from Liverpool, might be less willing to rule out these answer options, simply because they have less experience with them. If there really is a proximity effect, however, it would have to be addressed why it is absent for (salient)

NURSE, but seems to be present for happy, where we would not expect it since the variable is non-salient.

11.4.5 Frequency

For the sake of completeness, we will also have a very brief look at frequency. Figure 11.18 is another regression plot, this time with frequency measured in Zipf scores on the x-axis. Again, the two lines are not too different in slope, although the decline in the "Liverpool" group is somewhat steeper. In both priming conditions, estimated answer token decreases slightly with increasing frequency. This is the exact opposite of what was found for happy responses, where there was a positive correlation of estimated answer and frequency (cf. Figure 11.4). For the /k/ responses we *might* argue that higher word frequencies could coincide with higher familiarity (i.e. more (recent) exemplars), which, in turn, may lead to higher accuracy in perception, and translate into lower-numbered answer tokens (see the discussion of the role of distance just above). With regard to the happy results, however, this would not work, since the direction of the effect is inverted. I have no explanation to offer at this point which would cover both results, but two things should be borne in mind: (a) The general problems of using frequency as a predictor in this study (cf. §10.1.1), and (b) the fact that frequency does not end up as a significant fixed effect in the regression model anyway. Chances are that what seems to be a (marginally significant) effect of frequency is really due to lexical effects of individual carrier words.

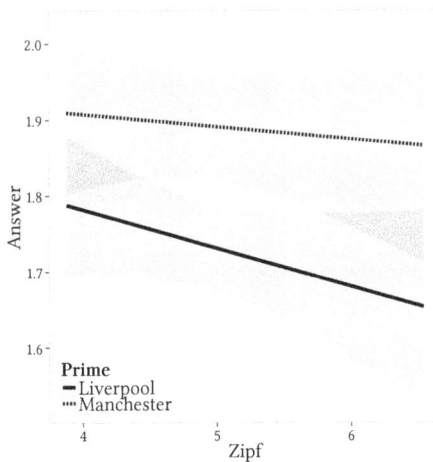

Figure 11.18: /k/ (perception) by Zipf score

12 Discussion (Perception)

12.1 Priming and salience

12.1.1 Salient vs. non-salient variables

The main hypothesis of this study is that priming effects in perception experiments depend on the salience of the variable that is investigated. This is largely corroborated. No priming effect could be identified for happy, the non-salient vocalic variable: priming condition did not surface as a significant predictor. This suggests that subjects were not influenced by social information relating to the speaker's regional origin. Rather, they perceived the stimuli in pretty much the same way, regardless of whether they had been told the speaker was from Manchester or Liverpool. In addition, answers were comparatively evenly distributed across all four synthesised tokens, the preference for tokens 2 and 3 was only weak. It seems thus that subjects were not too sure (or unanimous) about which token best matched the stimulus heard in the sentence.

Essentially the same remarks can be made about the responses to velar nasal plus stimuli. Overall, the distribution of answers looks very similar to those collected for happy. However, the dominance of tokens 2 and 3 answers has clearly increased compared to happy responses: These two tokens together now account for around 75% of answers (as opposed to about 65% for happy). In the mixed-effects ordinal regression model, which also took into account random variation due to individual characteristics of the participants, there was no significant difference between priming conditions. All the same it should be noted that even in this mixed-effects regression, the p-value for prime indicated a statistical trend. Both in terms of overall distribution and statistical significance it could therefore be said that the /ŋ(g)/ data occupy a sort of middle ground, which ties in quite nicely with the production results, where this variable also ended up in front of happy but behind both NURSE and /k/, as far as salience is concerned.

Towards the other end of the scale we have NURSE and lenition of /k/. When confronted with NURSE stimuli, people have a very clear preference: Token 2, the synthesised vowel that is closest to the one actually heard in the sentence, is chosen in around 2 out of 3 cases. The other options only account for a rather small minority of cases. In the case of NURSE stimuli, subjects were thus much better at identifying the best match, and responses were much more uniform. In addition, participants were more susceptible to the priming manipulation for NURSE than for both happy and velar nasal plus. Subjects perceived NURSE stimuli differently in the two priming conditions, and this difference was found to be significant in the mixed-effects regression, which identified prime as a main effect (but also showed that the effect was mostly driven by sentence-medial stimuli).

Results for lenition of /k/ are similar to those for NURSE in the same way that happy results are comparable to the ones found for /ŋ(g)/. We again find token 2 to be the dominant response, but the /k/ results differ from the NURSE data in that the dominance of the objectively most accurate answer option is even more pronounced here: Token 2 alone has a share of almost 75% of all answers (just above 65% in the case of NURSE). Subjects again behaved differently, depending on which city/accent they had been primed for: The priming effect was found to be significant in the regression model, provided the interaction of prime and social class was removed first. Judged against the background of the very strong preference for one particular token, the priming effect for lenition stimuli seems to be even more statistically robust than it was for NURSE.

12.1.2 Degree of priming and accuracy

So far, two criteria have been identified that can be used to place the four variables investigated on a scale: Objective accuracy of responses and degree of the priming effect. With respect to priming, we would have happy at the lower end of the scale, because this variable did not produce any priming effect at all. Next would be velar nasal plus, where a priming effect might be suspected when looking at the raw data, but becomes non-significant in the mixed-effects ordinal regression. This would be followed by NURSE, which produced a clear priming effect that was statistically robust. At the upper end of the scale, finally, we find /k/-lenition, the variable where a statistically robust priming effect could be found even though, overall, subjects were heavily focused on the objectively correct answer token. When we look at accuracy, the same picture emerges: Matching the synthesised tokens to the stimuli seems to have been most difficult for happy, where responses are very diverse, and the most accurate token accounts for less than 40% of answers. In the /ŋ(g)/ data, this percentage is slightly higher, and, more importantly, the share of token 4 (the one that is most unlike the vowel actually heard in the sentence) drops considerably. Perception of NURSE stimuli was then considerably more accurate ("correct" percept in 2 out of 3 cases) and in the case of lenition, finally, participants chose the objectively most similar option almost 75% of the time.

It is possible that the *task* participants had to perform was not always equally difficult, either because some of the four variables were *intrinsically* more "difficult" than others, or for reasons of experimental design and stimulus creation. I do not see any compelling evidence for this argument, though. For the two vowels in particular the extremes of the answer scale were very comparable: A rather central vowel on the lower end, and a fronted (and raised in the case of happy vs. lowered in the case of NURSE) one on the upper end. The parameters used in synthesis were also quite similar (cf. Table 10.2), so there should have been roughly equal phonetic distance between answer tokens of both variables. For the two consonants this kind of equivalence is harder to achieve, but remember that here, too, a comparable feature (proportion of frication/aspiration) was manipulated in both cases (cf. §5.4.1 and §10.1.3). In addition, the resulting tokens were not only checked auditorily by the author, but also subjected to the scrutiny of other linguists during a pilot test which did not reveal any problems with the stimuli or the synthesised answer tokens. We know from work about folk linguistics and perceptual dialectology that experts' judgements do not necessarily have to coincide with those of laypersons (Preston 1999; Niedzielski & Preston 2000). But while it cannot be ruled out that perceivers found the tokens of one variable to be less distinct than those of another, there is no evidence to actively support this idea (in the post-experiment comments of subjects, for instance).

I will therefore assume that there is another explanation, and one which is capable of explaining both the differences in terms of accuracy and in the priming effect. It is, after all, quite striking that these two criteria result in exactly the same ordering of variables. This parallelism suggests a common source or characteristic, and I believe this characteristic is social salience. If a variable is socially salient, i.e. more informative in social terms, this will have consequences for the perception, and, more importantly, the storage in long-term memory of exemplars pertaining to this variable. As explained earlier in this study, not everything we experience is memorised (cf. §4.2.3). In fact, we cannot even actively *process* every little detail present in the visual or acoustic input, let alone *store* all of it. Rather, we pay attention to certain things and not to others, and only the information that passes through this filter enters into long-term memory.

12.1.3 Salience as likelihood of remembrance

Whatever definition of salience one adheres to, the one common feature everyone usually can agree on is that salient features 'stick out' (cf. §4.1.1). Another way of putting this is to say that a salient feature attracts attention. Chapter 4 explained that, in an exemplar framework, salience should therefore have an impact on memory structure. Salient features (as well as the words and phrases containing them) will be more often remembered than non- or less salient ones. The result is that exemplar clouds of salient variables will be more detailed because they contain a greater number of slightly different variants due to the fact that realisations of this variable have a higher likelihood of being remembered. For the same reason (likelihood of remembrance) the most common realisations will also be more entrenched because these exemplars get strengthened more often by newly remembered, largely identical input, than the traces of non-salient variables do.

If we assume that features are at least in part salient because they are socially informative it is also conceivable that salience has an impact on indexation, in the sense that less additional information will be remembered if the variable is not salient. When a perceiver does not believe a feature to be socially diagnostic they will pay less attention to it. This will either mean that social information is remembered, but fades more quickly than for socially more meaningful exemplars, or the exemplar is not indexed with certain kinds of social information in the first place. After all, if some sort of acoustic input is not (thought to be) linked to a specific social group, why store information about it?

The priming differences found in my data are hard to account for in a non-episodic framework. After all, if, say, some general sort of social filter (cf. Niedzielski 1999) interfered with subjects' perception, why would this apply more to some variables than to others? If the prime 'Liverpool' triggererd expectations based on knowledge about Scouse segment realisation rules, then why do we find differences between the variables, and especially differences in degree. Presumably, a rule is either known (in which case it should trigger a priming effect) or unknown (in which case the prime should be ineffective), but not 'slightly more known' than the rule for another variable. It is not immediately obvious how a non-episodic explanation would account for the fact that not all parts of the input (i.e. the previous experience with Scouse) seem to enjoy equal prominence in long-term memory.

If, however, priming builds on remembered exemplar clouds and if these clouds are variably structured, differences in the priming effect are only to be expected. If social information is used to prime for a socially non-salient variable, either no exemplars are activated at all (because they are not indexed for this kind of information), or the activation will be comparatively weak (because there are only a limited number of relevant exemplars that have not faded yet). As a result the priming effect will be weak or even non-existent. In the case of a highly salient variable, on the other hand, priming can rely on a large cloud of exemplars which activate both easily and strongly since they have a higher baseline of activation to start with, given that they are strengthened rather frequently. The consequence is a statistically robust and comparatively strong priming effect. This is precisely what was observed: No or weak priming effects for the non-salient variables happy and velar nasal plus, stronger, more robust priming effects for the two stereotypes NURSE and lenition of /k/.

Accuracy and the lack thereof is a result of the size of the exemplar cloud, which, as has been explained above, is ultimately a product of salience, too. If subjects are not used to paying attention to a variable, they will only have a small number of memory traces to compare the input to, and it will be more difficult to match the synthesised tokens to the stimulus because the scale available in memory is not very fine-grained. When there *is* a very detailed memory cloud the likelihood that the input will activate a similar exemplar is higher, in which case the subject will feel more confident in making a choice in the experiment. In other words, if remembered exemplars are few and far between, there is a higher probability for the stimulus that needs to be classified to have no exact match in subjects' memory, but instead to be equally distant from a number of different exemplars – all of which are then an acceptable choice – and subjects may then categorise the same input as belonging to different categories on different occasions, without a clear preference for one category in particular. In a dense memory cloud, however, chances are that the stimulus will correspond very well to one remembered exemplar in particular, which means that it will be classified as belonging to that category in the majority of cases. The data collected for this study exhibit just the distributions that are to be expected if one embraces the explanation given above: From the least salient variable happy over velar nasal plus and NURSE to /k/ lenition (the most salient one) answers are less and less equally distributed across the four available tokens because the percentage of the objectively correct token increases steadily.

My data furthermore suggest that salience in exemplar priming experiments is not a categorical matter in the sense that a variable is either salient or non-salient, and therefore generates a priming effect or does not. Rather, the word *scale* was used deliberately when describing the ordering of the four test variables earlier. While the non-salient variables happy and /ŋ(g)/, and the salient ones NURSE and /k/-lenition, respectively, do to a certain extent behave as a group, it has also been outlined that there is evidence for a continuum: Perception of velar nasal plus is slightly more primeable (statistical trend) and accurate than it is for happy, and perception of /k/ seems slightly easier to prime than NURSE, given that, in the former case, the effect is robust *despite* an extremely strong preference for token 2. Further research on a larger set of variables is needed to see if this pattern can be replicated, but the fact that the same ordering also emerges from the production data (cf. §9.5) lends support to this interpretation. Furthermore, if we posit – as I have done above – that salience translates into attention paid to a variable in perception and that its effect can be operationalised as the likelihood of remembrance of an exemplar (or the likelihood of indexation with a certain type of information), then there is no reason *not* to assume that this phenomenon is gradual in nature. Since a likelihood can assume a theoretically infinite number of concrete values, there can also be an infinite number of exemplar clouds that differ in terms of size/detail and the number of exemplars that are indexed for a specific category.

12.2 Social factors

12.2.1 Social class

I would argue that the gradualness of salience also (indirectly) shows up in the social characteristics of the *perceiver* that play a role in priming. Hay, Nolan, et al. 2006 and Hay & Drager 2010, for instance, found an interaction of priming condition and social class of the participant in their experiments. Only subjects from higher social classes showed a priming effect, whereas those with lower socioeconomic status did not. This was true irrespective of whether priming was achieved with the help of explicit regional labels on the answer sheets or through the presence of stuffed toys that invoked the same concepts (cf. Hay & Drager 2010: 878). The authors explain this effect with the "amount of exposure that New Zealanders from different socioeconomic backgrounds would have to the speech of Australians" (Hay & Drager 2010: 878). They hypothesise (probably rightly so) that New Zealanders from higher social classes are "more able to travel to Australia" and therefore have "more stored exemplars indexed with "Australian" " which can be activated by a prime.

Amount of exposure is the only explanation Hay & Drager give for their social class interaction. They do not consider the option at all that there might not be the same degree of sensitivity (or attention) to a socially meaningful variable in the different social groups. This is somewhat surprising given that the authors do make reference to this idea when it comes to the influence of perceivers' gender, arguing that "females may be more aware of the relationship between variability in speech and social characteristics and may therefore index their exemplars with a larger amount of social detail and/or place more weight on this social detail"

(Hay & Drager 2010: 884). To be fair, they then go on to discard this explanation (which was first voiced by Drager 2005), because they believe it does not explain all their gender-related results.

The crucial result of the present study in this respect is now that a significant interaction of priming condition and social class of the participant could only be identified for one of the four variables, lenition of /k/. It does make sense to assume that middle-class subjects are more mobile than working-class participants, and might therefore have more exemplars that are indexed with "Liverpool" and can be activated by social priming. This interpretation works fine for /k/, but it fails to explain why it *only* works for /k/. Why is there no interaction of prime and social class in the NURSE data? It seems very unlikely indeed that middle-class speakers are more often exposed to Scouse variants of /k/ than their working-class counterparts, but have the same amount of experience with Liverpool NURSE variants. As an alternative explanation, I would like to argue once more for awareness, or, in the terminology used above, attention. It has been shown that NURSE – though undoubtedly a salient variable – still seems to be somewhat less salient than lenition of /k/, but this alone would not explain why there is a difference between social classes for the latter, but not for the former. Rather, it would have to be the case that the *difference* in salience between working-class and middle-class listeners is greater for /k/-lenition than it is for NURSE.

This is post hoc argumentation and in need of further support. All the same, this claim does make sense given that lenition of /k/ is arguably not only the most salient feature of Scouse, but also possibly the most stereotyped one which, in addition, is often very negatively evaluated even *within* Liverpool (cf. §8.2.3). It does not seem too far-fetched that middle-class attitudes would be particularly "extreme" for a feature which is even looked down on by some of its users. While this interpretation of the nearly-significant prime X social class interaction for /k/ ties in quite nicely with the explanation given above for the results pertaining to accuracy and robustness of the priming effect, I would like to stress once more that the sample of this study is heavily skewed towards middle-class participants and that the claims just made about social class differences can only be rather speculative in nature.

12.2.2 Gender

There is even less evidence for the impact of other social factors which are usually of interest in a sociolinguistic study. The perhaps most surprising result is that, in the present data set, gender of subject does not surface as a significant fixed effect in *any* regression model, irrespective of whether the dependent variable's salience is high or low. Previous research has produced heterogeneous evidence in this respect. Niedzielski (1999: 69 and 79–80) found in her study in Detroit that "there was essentially no difference between what male and female respondents selected in either the "Canadian" group or the "Michigan" group", despite the fact that only female subjects overtly commented on stereotypical features of Canadian English (but Niedzielski also provides some evidence why she still believes Detroit women and men hold essentially the same stereotypes about Canadian English). Hay and colleagues, on the other hand, consistently did find a gender effect when they replicated Niedzielski's experiment in New Zealand. Their results showed that only female participants behaved as expected, hearing Australian vowels when being primed for Australia, and perceiving more New Zealand vowels when the concept 'New Zealand' had been invoked. Men were also influenced by the prime, but the priming effect was in the opposite direction: Male subjects actually heard more *New Zealand* vowels when they had been led to expect a speaker from Australia (Hay, Nolan, et al. 2006; Hay & Drager 2010). The absence of a gender effect in the present study might be due to the fact that female and male participants share the same stereotypes about Liverpool (and possibly Manchester) English, as Niedzielski has argued, but there might actually be more to this. Both the lack of a gender difference and the direction of the priming effect in this study will be further discussed in §12.4.

12.2.3 Age

Another social factor besides class (which is only relevant for /k/) that comes at least close to statistical significance is age of participant. Both in the data for happy and for velar nasal plus there was a statistical trend for older subjects to choose lower number tokens (more Mancunian/standard) more often than younger participants did. As has been noted earlier, this could be explained by language change in the case of happy-tensing: The peripheral [i] is now the norm in standard British English, but up until the beginning of the 80s traditional RP speakers would have a lax [ɪ] realisation for this vowel (cf. Harrington 2006). Younger participants have not experienced this change and only know [i] as the standard pronunciation (although they could encounter [ɪ] when listening to very conservative speakers). It is nonetheless dubious whether this is enough to claim that the [ɪ]-[i] distinction in happy is more salient for older subjects or that younger speakers are more likely to expect [i] generally. After all, large parts of (northern) England still have a lax happy vowel, a variant which is even actively exploited as an identity marker by some younger speakers in Nottingham (cf. Flynn 2010), and, apparently, also in Liverpool (cf. §9.1.1).

In addition, slightly higher salience in the group of older participants would only explain why the distance between priming conditions seems to get a bit larger, but not why older subjects choose lower number tokens more often *across the board*, i.e. irrespective of priming condition. Hay & Drager (2010: 878–879) also found an effect of age in their data: Younger participants were more likely to perceive a tense [i] instead of more central variants. The authors explain this by suggesting that participants at least in part process the input using their own production as a point of reference. Since the younger participants in their study are thought to have more central /ɪ/ realisations than the speaker who produced the stimuli, they are therefore inclined to perceive these stimuli as more peripheral because they *are* relative to their own production. If we want to apply this explanation to the results of the present study, this would mean that older subjects would have to have tenser realisations of /ɪ/ than the younger participants, which would make the stimuli sound more central to the former than to the latter. While this is possible, the scenario does not seem likely. Participants came from all over Britain and as far as I am aware there is no evidence that happy is becoming more central in *all* younger speakers across the country. I cannot verify this at present because no production data were collected from participants. Further research would be needed to shed light on this matter.

The slight age effect in the responses to /ŋ(g)/ stimuli is just as difficult to explain. At least for Liverpool speakers, (non-)salience of this feature seems to be stable across age groups (cf. §9.3.3) I have no way of knowing whether this is true for the subjects from the rest of the country as well, but I am at least not aware of any evidence that would suggest anything to the contrary. Do older participants' realisations of <ng> contain voiced velar plosives more often than younger subjects', then? Since most participants are not from the area where velar nasal plus is commonly found this seems rather far-fetched, especially so when considering that the proportion of subjects who come from Trudgill's 1999 velar nasal plus area is actually higher among those aged 35 or younger than among older participants. I do not have a good explanation for the age effects in both happy and velar nasal plus results, but it should be noted that there is no call for over-interpretation anyway: (a) For velar nasal plus it is only a statistical trend, in the case of happy, age is only a significant predictor in a model that was eventually not even retained, and (b) the sample is heavily skewed towards participants in their twenties. The few older subjects I do have might not actually be representative of the group they have been assumed to be representative of, and their responses might be considerably overlaid by idiosyncracies, due to the small number of participants the answers can be averaged across. A much more balanced sample (and possibly relevant production data from participants) would be necessary for a more detailed analysis.

12.2.4 Geographical distance

When we look at where participants live (the other social predictor which did not quite reach statistical significance) the picture is also somewhat unclear, albeit for different reasons. Geographical distance from Liverpool is a near-significant fixed effect in the regression models estimating the responses to happʏ and /k/-lenition stimuli. In both cases there is a trend for subjects who live further away from Liverpool to choose higher number tokens somewhat more frequently. That is to say that the further a participant lives from Liverpool, the more likely they are to perceive a more Liverpool-like token. In §11.4 it has been suggested that familiarity might be a possible explanation for this effect. If we assume that people who live close to the Liverpool area are more familiar with the accent of this city (and I believe this makes sense) it could be the case that these subjects are less likely to perceive the stimuli as one of the Liverpool variants that are represented by tokens 3 and 4, simply because they know rather well what these realisations actually sound like (i.e. they have more stored exemplars of these variants), and, as a consequence, feel more secure in deciding that this is not what was presented in the stimuli. People who live far away from Liverpool and have little personal experience with Scouse, on the other hand, might be more tempted to select tokens 3 and 4 from time to time, feeling less confident to rule them out and possibly assuming that these answer options must be there 'for a reason'.

   This interpretation might seem rather speculative, but it would at least explain why there was no interaction of distance and prime: We are not seeing an effect only in the "Liverpool" group, but actually in both conditions. It would not have been surprising to see the priming effect change as a function of geographical distance from Liverpool. On the basis of how Hay & Drager (2010) explained their social class effect, it would have been expected that people who are less familiar with Scouse show less of a priming effect because they have fewer exemplars that can be activated by the prime. However, not only do we see an effect in the "Manchester" group (where subjects should not have been biased to hearing Liverpool variants no matter where they live), but also this effect is actually in the direction which does not tie in with Hay & Drager's exposure-activation account. The interpretation of the possible relationship between frequency of remembrance and accuracy in perception given above, on the other hand, would predict the results this study has actually produced: Higher distance comes with lower accuracy, only this time frequency of remembrance does not change due to lower salience, but to less frequent exposure to relevant variants. This account still does not explain why this effect is found for the *least* salient variable happy and the *most* salient one /k/-lenition, but not the other two. At this point, I have no good explanation for this strange pairing which seems rather random. The issue of distance and familiarity clearly warrants further research, possibly based on a larger sample – both in terms of variables and participants – to arrive at a clearer and more detailed picture.

12.3 Non-social factors

12.3.1 Time held in memory

Let us now turn to independent variables which are non-social in nature. Hay, Nolan, et al. (2006) had originally worked with two different types of stimuli sentences because they wanted to investigate whether the priming effect depended on the time the subject had to hold the relevant sound in memory before they heard the synthesised answer tokens. However, they confounded position of the keyword with sentence length (sentences where the keyword appeared in the middle were always longer than sentences where the keyword was in final position), so it was not possible to tease these two factors apart. In the present study, care was taken to ensure stimulus sentences at least roughly contained the same amount of phonetic material (cf. §10.1.1). Results were ambiguous. Position of the carrier word within the stimulus sentence was found to be a significant predictor for both vocalic variables, happy and NURSE, but not for the two consonants.

In the case of happy, the reason for this is probably rather trivial and related to inconsistency in the synthesis of the answer tokens. As has been explained in §10.1.2, it was not possible to re-synthesise a satisfying vowel continuum out of the sentence-final happy realisations. The continua synthesised for the corresponding sentence-medial stimuli were used instead. While the scale was the same and subjects always had a choice of options ranging from very central to very peripheral vowels, this had an unintended effect: For the sentence-medial stimuli (where happy was naturally realised as [ɪ] by the speaker) the objectively best match was token 2, but in the sentence-final stimuli (where the speaker had [ə]) token 1 was objectively closest to what participants had heard. This means that subjects did not really behave differently with respect to sentence-medial and sentence-final stimuli. Rather, they always perceived happy as slightly more fronted and raised than it actually was. In the case of sentence-medial stimuli there was thus a slight preference for token 3 ([i̞]), whereas participants chose token 2 most often ([ɪ]), because it was already slightly more peripheral than the actually occurring [ə]. This explanation is very similar to how Hay & Drager (2010: 878–879; see also above) interpreted their age-related differences; the only difference is that in the present study the reference point people select the token against is not their own production, but the vowel occurring in the stimulus. Why subjects consistently perceived a vowel that was slightly more peripheral remains an open question, as it is very unlikely that participants' own production was even more central (across the board) than that of the Manchester speaker who recorded the stimuli (cf. Hay & Drager 2010: 878–879).

No such technical issues complicate the interpretation of the answers given for NURSE stimuli. Participants produced a significantly lower average token number when the keyword containing the sound in question occurred in the middle of the sentence. The share of token 2 replies is also greater for these stimuli, so it can be said that subjects perceived sentence-medial stimuli slightly more accurately. This result is similar to what Hay, Nolan, et al. (2006) found. In their study, subjects had a tendency to answer with more New Zealand tokens when the keyword had been presented in the middle of the sentence. They are unsure about whether this is due to the fact that people have to hold the sound in memory (which might shift it towards their own production) or whether the shift is due to additional acoustic material that follows the keyword and provides further "phonetic cues which are associated with NZ" (Hay, Nolan, et al. 2006: 365). Priming did not have an impact on this effect. In the present study, there was also no significant interaction prime X position of keyword in the mixed-effects regression model, but if one looks at the raw data, the difference between priming conditions seems more pronounced for sentence-medial stimuli.

The author is tempted to accept Hay, Nolan, et al.'s (2006) explanation that following phonetic material (which was Mancunian in this study) shifts participants' perception towards the lower (Mancunian/standard) end of the scale. A shift towards subjects' own perception would also be possible, as it is very likely that the vast majority of perceivers had a central realisation of NURSE. However, this account struggles to explain why the difference between sentence-medial and sentence-final stimuli seems to be driven almost exclusively by perceivers in the "Liverpool" condition. It seems as if holding the sound in memory has the effect of making the stimulus sound even more Mancunian, but only to subjects who have been primed for Liverpool. What I think happens is that these participants were successfully primed to expect a Liverpool realisation of the

NURSE vowel. When they then get to the relevant vowel in the carrier word, this realisation does not agree with the expectation that was created. Against the backdrop of their expectation, the vowel then sounds even more Mancunian compared to what it was *supposed* to sound like (cf. §12.5). This effect can be seen for sentence-final stimuli, too (subjects primed for Liverpool seemed ever so slightly less likely to perceive Scouse variants), but it grows tremendously in size for sentence-medial stimuli, presumably because subjects are confronted with further material that is in conflict with their expectation.

The amount of conflicting material then does not seem to be as important as the question of whether it occurs before or after the sound that needs to be memorised and then categorised (remember that both sentence-medial and sentence-final stimuli contained roughly the same amount of phonetic material). I am still reluctant to generalise from this result to claiming that larger priming effects are to be expected if participants have to hold the relevant sound in memory. First of all, this is not corroborated by previous research in sociophonetics (Hay, Nolan, et al. 2006; Hay & Drager 2010). Secondly, it would also contradict findings in social psychology, where studies have shown that subjects are most likely to apply "automatic" processing (which relies on stereotypes) when they have to react very fast – "controlled" processing, which is more conscious and objective, can only occur when subjects are given enough time (cf. Petersen & Six 2008: 33–34). When the keyword appears in the middle of the sentence, participants should therefore have to rely less on their stereotypes as they have more time to process the stimulus. In any case, there does not seem to be a straightforward explanation why the present study only found such an effect for NURSE, but not for lenition of /k/. It is clear that there is something interesting going on here, but it remains to be seen whether the effect can be replicated in different contexts.

12.3.2 Stimulus order

Another effect which only surfaced in the responses pertaining to NURSE sentences is the impact of stimulus order. In these data there was almost a statistical trend for subjects to answer with a lower number token the further they progressed in the experiment. Answers thus became more Manchester-like towards the end of the test. There is at least some evidence that the priming effect is largest at the beginning and diminishes as people work their way through the stimuli, but it has also been pointed out that there are a number of things which caution against making too much of this. Most importantly, priming only has a significantly different effect in the raw data, whereas the mixed-effects regression did not find an interaction of prime and stimulus order. Both Hay, Nolan, et al. (2006) and Hay & Drager (2010) found a similar effect and provided a number of possible explanations: (1) The further they were into the experiment subjects "relied more on the most frequently activated exemplars", (2) they "relied more on exemplars representing their own speech", and (3) they were "getting increasingly used to the speaker's voice", arguing that the trend "may reflect an increase in accuracy" (Hay & Drager 2010: 881–882).

Especially the last point seems to be a reasonable interpretation of what might be going on: Participants just need a certain time to home in on token number 2. In an earlier study I have interpreted an impact of stimulus order in one (!) condition as evidence for a priming effect which is then corrected by acoustic material that is in conflict with the prime (Juskan 2011). This account would lead us to only expect such an effect for the "Liverpool" condition, because if participants are primed for Manchester there is no "wrong" expectation that could be corrected by diverging acoustic input. In the present study, however, there is an order effect in *both* conditions, even if it is slightly weaker in one of them (the fact that the effect is greater in the "Manchester" group is not necessarily a problem; cf. §12.5). An explanation based on 'getting used to the speaker', on the other hand, works fine for both conditions. Just as with position of the keyword the question remains as to why there is only an effect for NURSE, but not for the other three variables (or at least for /k/ as the other salient one). It should also be borne in mind that the effect is not even quite a statistical trend, and might, in fact, be nothing but an artefact that could disappear in a larger sample.

12.3.3 Phonological environment

For the two consonants there was an additional predictor because stimuli could be distinguished with respect to whether the variable occurred as the last sound of the carrier word or whether it was presented in an intervocalic context. Phonological environment was a (highly) significant predictor for both consonantal variables. The effects were also nearly equally strong, but the direction was different: While for velar nasal plus subjects were more likely to choose higher number tokens when the variable was at the end of the carrier word, they actually showed a preference for lower number tokens in the same context for /k/ stimuli. For word-final stimuli, participants were thus *more* inclined to perceive Liverpool variants of /ŋ(g)/ and *less* willing to hear lenited realisations of /k/. Mixed effects regression did not find an interaction of prime and phonological environment for either variable, but graphical inspection of the raw data at least suggests the priming effect to be slightly stronger when the sound in question occurs word-finally.

As far as velar nasal plus is concerned, I can only offer a very tentative explanation of the results. Earlier in this book (cf. §11.3.3) I have presented the idea that this variable might actually be slightly more salient in _# environments because of the variants that are often encountered there. Knowles (1973) already found that /ŋ(g)/ is often realised as [ŋk] at the end of words in Liverpool (cf. §3.3.1) and, while I did not code for this, these variants are also commonly found in my own data. When /ŋ(g)/ occurs in-between vowels, devoicing does not usually take place because switching voicing off between two voiced sounds would be uneconomical. The [ŋk] or even [ŋkʰ] variants in word-final position could be somewhat more salient because they are phonetically even more different from the standard realisation [ŋ] than [ŋg] is. For intervocalic [ŋg] realisations the only cue for the plosive is often a (sometimes very subtle) burst since there is frequently no real silence phase because voicing is maintained all throughout. Also, in this context, a burst that is low in amplitude might be "misinterpreted" as a somewhat too rapid release of the velar nasal and might therefore not attract as much attention.

In the case of /k/ lenition there is more evidence to base an interpretation on. Here, I think, it is a lot less controversial and speculative to claim that social salience is at least part of the explanation. This is because the perception data mirror quite nicely what was found in production. Liverpool speakers showed less style shifting for /k/-lenition in intervocalic contexts, presumably because these variants can be "justified" phonetically and are therefore potentially slightly less salient in this environment (which is why lenited variants are especially frequent, cf. §7.2.2). Going from a vowel (with no real obstruction of the airstream) to the closure of a plosive (complete blockage of the airstream in the oral cavity) and back to another vowel (no blockage again) is the most extreme phonetic difference possible between two linguistic sounds. Lenition (to fricatives) reduces this contrast (and the articulatory effort) considerably, and replacing a plosive with a fricative is thus an instantiation of the principle of economy and a "natural" thing to occur.

When /k/ appears in _# environments, on the other hand, participants show somewhat lower lenition rates (though still high in absolute terms) in production, which indicates that Liverpool variants are a bit *more* salient in these contexts. The fact that, in the same context, the priming effect in perception is also slightly greater is therefore highly interesting and relevant with respect to the main hypothesis of this study. Even though the statistical grounding is not too robust and conclusions will therefore have to be tentative, these results can be taken as evidence that the salience of a variable might not only be able to explain general trends in exemplar priming experiments, but can, in fact, serve as a (maybe *the*) crucial predictor that is also capable of shedding light on diverging results in sub-groups of stimuli (phonological environment) or subjects (social class).

While salience is a good explanation for different sizes of the priming effect in the two phonological environments, it does not straightforwardly predict why the average token number in word-final stimuli would be lower, i.e. why subjects were more likely to perceive the ultra-Mancunian/standard token 1 (plosive with burst but no aspiration) in this context. We can, in fact, apply the same explanation if we assume that higher salience in this context results in a (stronger) priming effect in the unexpected direction (cf. §12.5). Put simply, participants expect a lenited variant (even more so than in the other context), and the actual acoustic input therefore sounds even more standard/Mancunian than it actually is, because it is judged against a very 'Liverpool-like' baseline. Subjects could then be said to hyper-correct their perception more for word-final stimuli because the distance between the activated exemplars and the actual acoustic input is greater in this context due to stronger activation by the prime.

In this particular case, however, there is also an alternative explanation which has been hinted at earlier: The higher proportion of token 1 answers in word-final contexts might be to do with expectations based on common allophonic distributions. Word-final plosives in English are often unreleased, i.e. not articulated with an audible burst or friction. These unreleased realisations are much rarer in intervocalic position. If participants expected to hear a non-released /k/ at the end of a word because this variant is often encountered in natural language in this position then this might have biased them towards choosing token number 1 (which did have a release burst, but no aspiration) as this was the answer option which best corresponded to their expectation. When the /k/ occurs in the onset of syllables (as it does in intervocalic environments) unreleased realisations are less common and so subjects choose token 1 less often. In this framework, participants would actually have been primed, but not with social information regarding the speaker, but rather by the phonological context the variable was presented in. I will call this allophonic priming, because of its grounding in the language system and its largely regular, i.e. rule-based realisations.

Both accounts predict the results equally well, so it is not really possible to decide which one is preferable on the basis of the current dataset. In both cases, however, we are looking at another piece of evidence for an exemplar account since perceivers seem to be influenced by prior experiences that are different depending on the context, and which must have been stored separately. However, it is an important insight in its own right that these different results might have been brought about more directly by the phonological environment itself (via its typical allophonic /k/ realisations) instead of indirectly through social salience attached to it. This could in fact mean that a second, unintended level of (allophonic) priming was present in the research design. While it has just been outlined that, in this study, the two effects (social priming and allophonic priming) would produce a shift in the same direction, it is easily conceivable that this does not always have to be the case. In a scenario where these two factors are at odds, i.e. where the phonological environment biases participants towards other variants than the actual prime that is investigated, they might produce considerable noise in the dataset. As far as I am aware, the priming potential of allophonic distributions has not figured prominently in the sociophonetic literature up to this date, but it is certainly an interesting avenue for future research. In any case, researchers should take care to avoid any potential conflicts between allophonic and other sorts of priming to make sure they actually measure what they mean to measure and do not draw their conclusions on the basis of "corrupted" datasets.

12.4 Issues and limitations

12.4.1 The problem of velar nasal plus

This analysis, like any piece of research, comes with a number of short-comings and limitations, a few of which will be addressed in the following paragraphs. The aspect of this study which will probably strike the reader most as potentially problematic is the use of velar nasal plus as a variable in the perception test. This is because the realisation of <ng> clusters as [ŋg] is not restricted to Scouse, but is actually found in an area that is roughly delimited by the cities of Liverpool in the west, Manchester in the east, and Birmingham in the south (cf. §3.3.1). In retrospect, it might have been preferable to contrast lenition of /k/ with lenition of /t/, because these two phenomena are, in fact, both restricted to Liverpool, at least in their extent and particular patterning. In the interviews conducted for this study, lenition of /t/ turned out to be much less salient to Scousers than lenited variants of /k/ (for instance, lenition of /t/ was never explicitly commented on), but this information was not available until the perception experiment was well under way. In the literature, lenition of these two variables (and others) is most often treated as one single phenomenon and the label 'highly salient' is usually likewise extended to all lenited plosive realisations. However, lenition of /t/ would have posed another serious problem, even if it had been clear from the start that its salience is lower than that of /k/ lenition. This is because /t/ not only lenites to the affricate /ts/ or the fricative /s/, but also to [tθ], [θ], [h], and [Ø] (cf. §3.3.2), so direct comparison with /k/ (and the creation of equivalent stimuli) would have been challenging to say the least. When the perception experiment was planned and designed, velar nasal plus seemed to be the only Scouse variable that was consonantal, less salient, at least roughly comparable to /k/ in phonetic terms, and relatively restricted in geographical spread.

It has been mentioned in §10.1.1 that the speaker from Manchester who recorded the stimuli also naturally produced [ŋg] realisations in the relevant carrier words. Priming would therefore not have been necessary to "make" participants hear [ŋg] variants. Rather, it would have sufficed to let subjects perceive "objectively" since these pronunciations would actually have been present in the stimuli. This was not the case because the stimuli for velar nasal plus had been edited appropriately. The speaker recorded the sentences using her native [ŋg] realisation, but the plosive was cut from the material before it was used in the perception test (cf. §10.1.3). The point of departure was therefore the same as for the other three variables: If subjects reported having heard the Liverpool variants 3 or 4, they must have been biased in their perception, because the realisation that actually occurred in the stimuli was in fact (close to) the standard or Mancunian one. This does not solve the issue of the priming categories used. Since velar nasal plus is present both in the speech of Liverpudlians and Mancunians, priming subjects for Liverpool or Manchester should, in fact, produce the same results: Participants should be biased towards hearing [ŋg] in both cases.

I would like to argue that this is not, in fact, the outcome that should be expected, due to the general salience of the Scouse accent as a whole in the linguistic landscape of the United Kingdom. In his 2007a PhD thesis Montgomery investigated laypersons' perceptions of several northern English varieties. One of the tasks he asked participants to complete was to draw in dialect areas on a (largely) blank map. His results were that, with a rate of almost 58%, Scouse was the most often recognised dialect region in his sample, whereas only about one participant in four drew and labelled a Manc area (cf. Montgomery 2007a: 194). Participants in his study also provided more "characteristics" (evaluations, comments, stereotypes) of Scousers than they did for Manc speakers. The difference was particularly pronounced with respect to linguistic features, where the Manchester area received only a single comment overall (cf. Montgomery 2007a: 246–252). Given that Manchester was not even recognised as a dialect area "on its own" in previous linguistic studies, Montgomery (cf. 2007a: 214–215) rightly points out that Manchester has gained in cultural salience in the last 2–3 decades (to a large extent probably due to pop music), but it seems quite clear that

Scouse as the "most salient" (Montgomery 2007a: 216) accent area is still much more present in people's minds.

The argument for including velar nasal plus in this study was thus that if Scouse as an accent is so much more culturally salient (and also stigmatised, as can be deduced from the explicit comments of people) than Manchester English, then priming for Liverpool should also have a stronger effect than priming for Manchester. In other words, it was hypothesised that participants either had no stored exemplars indexed with "Manchester" at all (in which case priming them for Manchester would have had no effect at all), or, if they did, their number would be significantly smaller and/or activation of these exemplars would be weaker because the category is cognitively less present in general (in which case there would have been a priming effect for both "Liverpool" and "Manchester" in the same direction, but less strong in the latter case).

Remember that there almost *is* a priming effect in the velar nasal plus results (a statistical trend in the mixed-effects model), which is evidence that there is something going on between priming conditions. This constitutes post-hoc support for the reasoning presented above and shows that sticking to velar nasal plus as a variable in this experiment is justified. In fact, velar nasal plus shows more priming than was expected even when production data from Liverpool speakers (who showed some – slightly inconclusive – signs of salience) are taken into account. It seems as if velar nasal plus is more salient to outsiders than previously thought.

12.4.2 Comparability with previous research

As has been mentioned in several places already, this study owes a lot to previous research, especially Niedzielski 1999; Hay, Nolan, et al. 2006; Hay, Warren, et al. 2006; Hay & Drager 2010, whose results it was meant to replicate and contextualise. A number of characteristics of the present study, however, might reduce comparability with these papers.

For instance, most previous work has confronted subjects with resynthesised vowel tokens presented in isolation. This was deemed impractical for my own study, primarily because subjects were going to have to match consonants as well as vowels. In the case of /k/ in particular it would have been quite difficult to distinguish variants in perception as the tokens used in this experiment differ (not exclusively, but mostly) in the percentage of aspiration/friction in relation to the closure/silence phase. The duration of silence, in turn, can only be processed if there is acoustic material preceding said silence. Intriguingly, Hay & Drager (2010: 887–888) wonder about whether priming should even "be revealed in the task that [they] have employed" because "perception of the [answer] continuum should be affected in the same way" as perception of the stimuli words/sentences. They furthermore speculate that priming might affect perception of the synthesised tokens less only because they are not "word-embedded, natural stimuli", and can therefore be "processed for what they are". In the present study, this does not seem to have been a problem, though, maybe because the resynthesised tokens still sounded artificial enough, even when they occurred within a word.

The second important difference in methodology is the sex of the speaker who provided the stimuli. Hay, Nolan, et al. (2006) and Hay & Drager (2010) had a male speaker record their stimulus sentences, but in the present study the speaker was female. This might not appear to be a major issue at first glance, but it could actually make a difference in the specific framework of this particular analysis. The two variables where the most pronounced priming effects were found (NURSE and /k/-lenition) are not only very salient but also highly stigmatised. It is very well possible that subjects either do not actively associate women very strongly with stigmatised variants, or that they have less stored exemplars that contain these variants *and* are indexed with "female" (because these variants are, in fact, less frequent in the speech of female speakers in real life). It is therefore conceivable that stronger priming effects could have been found in this study if a male instead of a female speaker had recorded the stimuli. Further research replicating this study with a male speaker, or, perhaps preferably, an androgynous voice and a 2x2 priming scheme ('Liverpool female', 'Liverpool male', 'Manchester female', 'Manchester male') would be necessary to shed more light on this question.

12.4.3 The issue of frequency

The impact of frequency on the results of this study is rather unclear. An effect could only be found for happy and /k/-lenition (which seems to be a strange pairing, given that the former is the least and the latter the most salient variable in this sample), and even in these cases it was not very robust, statistically speaking. What is more, the effect was actually in different directions: For happy, percepts become *more* Liverpool-like, while, for /k/, stimuli they become *less* Liverpool-like with higher frequency of the keyword. Even weak frequency effects of this sort can be seen as general evidence for episodic accounts of language processing, but beyond that, I have no explanation to offer at this point that would account for these diametrically opposed results in a straightforward manner. It is likely that the potential impact of frequency is obscured in this analysis because the method employed was not primarily conceived to investigate frequency in the first place and is therefore only partially suited to do so. The issue will remain until this (or a similar) study is replicated with a larger set of carrier words that constitutes a more detailed and more representative sample of the frequency range actually encountered in naturalistic language. However, this hypothetical study will most likely have to focus on one phonological variable only in order to keep the expense of time manageable for participants.

12.4.4 Size of the priming effect

As a last caveat it should be noted that although many of the priming effects reported on in this analysis were found to be statistically robust the importance of these effects should not be exaggerated. In almost all cases, there was a preference for the acoustically most accurate token number 2, or it was at least a close runner-up for first place. For the two salient variables, token 2 accounted for at least 60% of answers. What this means is that people were not fooled in the majority of cases. While their perception can be manipulated, this manipulation has limits. We *can* create a sort of penchant, but this does not mean that perception disregards the actual speech signal completely. I would like to stress that this also holds true of previous research: In Hay & Drager's (2010) study, for instance, participants also show a clear preference for the acoustically closest or a very similar token, at least as far as the main variable of the study is concerned.

12.5 Direction of priming

The most important problem that the results of my perception experiment pose has so far been avoided, because it deserves a more detailed discussion and should therefore be treated separately. I am referring to the fact that whenever a statistically significant priming effect was found in the data, said effect was in the unexpected direction. Participants who had been led to believe the speaker they were going to listen to was from Liverpool were *less* likely to perceive variants that are typical of Scouse speech. This seems rather strange and calls for an explanation.

12.5.1 The problem of replicating priming experiments

First of all, I would like to point out that the present experiment is not the first sociolinguistic study that fails to closely replicate Niedzielski's, Hay, Nolan, et al.'s, and Hay & Drager's findings. In fact, at least two studies have looked at different variables in different locations and have not found a social priming effect at all.

Squires, for example, also looked at social priming in the context of language processing, but in contrast to most other studies in this area she did not focus on a phonological variable, but instead investigated the perception of subject-verb agreement. The two syntactic variables whose processing she analysed are NP+*don't* and *there's*+NP, both of which occur with singular and plural NPs (e.g. *the truck/trucks don't run* and *there's a truck/trucks in the driveway* (cf. Squires 2013: 206). For both features, usage of the non-standard variant can be linked to social class, but more so for invariant *don't*, the feature that is also more stigmat-ised in American English (cf. Squires 2013: 207–208). Participants were played recordings of ambiguous frames (___ *don't like it*; *there's* ___ *showing*) that oc-cur with both singular and plural NPs in actual speech. The NP was replaced by white noise in the audio stimuli and the subjects were asked to indicate what they had "heard" by selecting a visual representation of a singular or a plural NP (such as one bird vs. several birds). Participants were primed with the help of high- and low-status speaker photos that were shown while the audio stimulus was playing (cf. Squires 2013: 210–211). The hypothesis that high-status photos would favour standard responses, while low-status photos would decrease this rate was not borne out: "the social status of the target photo did not have an effect on sentence perception" (Squires 2013: 216).

It could well be that "social information simply does not affect morphological or syntactic perception in the same way that it does speech perception" as Squires (2013: 229) puts it. However, conflicting evidence also exists for phonological variables. Lawrence (2015), for instance, has looked at perceptions of BATH and STRUT. Both vowels are "widely acknowledged as highly salient markers of re-gional identity in British English", more specifically they divide England into a northern and a southern part: Southern speakers usually realise BATH as [ɑː] and STRUT as [ʌ], whereas speakers from northern England usually have [a] in BATH, and [ʊ] or [ə] in STRUT words (cf. Lawrence 2015: 1). Lawrence had his stimuli recorded by a speaker from Sheffield, resynthesised 6-step vowel continua and played these to listeners who were speakers of Southern Standard British Eng-lish. Half of them were told the speaker they were listening to was from 'Sheffield, Northern England', while the other half were told the speaker was from 'London, Southern England' (cf. Lawrence 2015: 2–3). No significant priming effects could be found, neither for BATH, nor for STRUT. Lawrence (cf. 2015: 4) concludes that "the influence of social information on linguistic perception may be more limited than has been previously suggested".

Note that, at this point in time, it is not completely uncontroversial whether we *should* expect priming effects to be identical or at least similar in different studies. Cesario (2014: 45), for example, claims that "the expectation of wide-spread invariance in priming effects is inappropriate". He argues that in order to replicate a study in the first place, we need to know which features "must be reproduced exactly for a replication attempt to be informative" and goes on to explain that we need to have "relevant theories that tell us that these features should matter" (Cesario 2014: 42). In his opinion, though, theories of priming are not yet advanced and sophisticated enough due to the "relatively young state of priming research". In consequence, researchers trying to replicate a study might unwillingly change "some critical feature of the experimental context" because it is – wrongly – "deemed irrelevant" (Cesario 2014: 43). This "error" could, for instance, simply consist in "sampling from a population that differs markedly (...) from the population sampled by the original researcher" (Cesario 2014: 43). This might well be the case if samples in the different studies are from the US, New Zealand, and Britain.

12.5.2 Hay et al.'s explanation for inverted effects

In this study, however, the problem is not the lack of a priming effect, but the fact that it is reversed. Interestingly, both Hay, Nolan, et al. (2006) and Hay & Drager (2010) had to face the same issue in a sub-sample of their data. While a robust priming effect was found for the entire dataset in both cases, closer inspection revealed that not only was the trend "most strongly carried by the female participants" (Hay & Drager 2010: 875), but it was also actually *reversed* for the males (cf. Hay & Drager 2010: 876–877).

The authors hypothesise that this gender difference could be due to "differences in attitude". They argue that (a) there is a "fierce sporting rivalry between New Zealand and Australia", (b) that sport is the most important "cultural marker of nationalism" in New Zealand, and that (c) this is primarily a male domain. Hay & Drager deduce that male New Zealanders are "more likely to have negative associations with Australia, whereas females may have more positive (or neutral) associations". In consequence, women behave as expected when the concept "Australia" is invoked and shift towards Australian exemplars (the authors liken this to accommodation in production). When men, on the other hand, are primed for "Australia" they not only activate their Australian exemplars but also their negative associations with that country. In an attempt to disassociate with Australia (comparable to speech divergence), they then shift towards New Zealand exemplars (cf. Hay & Drager 2010: 884–885).

This is an interesting explanation, and one which at first glance appears to be neatly transferable to my own results. After all, it has been pointed out repeatedly in this book that Liverpool English is one of the most heavily stereotyped varieties in Britain. Attitudes towards the city itself are also still widely negative, and dominated by concepts such as crime, poverty, deprivation, and decay. It makes perfect sense to assume that British listeners, when confronted with the category "Liverpool", do not only activate any Scouse exemplars that they may have stored, but also their negative attitudes towards Liverpool itself, and that they may then wish to disassociate from the city and activate their non-Scouse exemplars even more strongly. All the same, this account has one crucial shortcoming: It only works for the outsiders. Whenever we find a priming effect in the responses provided by subjects from Liverpool itself, however, the shift is *also* in the unexpected direction, i.e. towards *less* Liverpudlian variants when the prime was "Liverpool" (cf. the discussion at the beginning of Chapter 11). Liverpool speakers are clearly *not* disassociating from their city. Quite the opposite is true. Especially younger Scousers are rather happy to use Liverpool features to mark their local identity, as has been shown in the part of this book that is concerned with production data. Despite some linguistic insecurity, overt comments about Liverpool and its accent essentially tell the same story (cf. §8.3). Disassociation does therefore not seem to be a realistic option in explaining the reversed priming effect, at least not for Liverpool participants.

12.5.3 Assimilation and contrast effects

Research in social psychology provides an alternative explanation in the form of "assimilation" and "contrast" effects.[1] The priming effects we know from the literature on the integration of social information in language perception are instances of assimilation effects, where "[s]ubjects primed with exemplars of a particular category are more likely to use that category in evaluating a subsequently presented category-relevant stimulus" and to classify this stimulus "as an instance of that category" (Herr 1986: 1106–1107). Consider, for example, subjects primed with the concept "Australia" who are then more likely to perceive Australian vowels. Also possible, however, are so-called contrast effects, where the outcome of priming can be described as "judgments inconsistent with, and opposite in nature to, the primed category" (Herr 1986: 1107). I am going to argue that the results of the present study (participants primed for Liverpool perceive *less* Liverpool-like tokens) can be understood as an example of a contrast effect.

In Herr's opinion, the crucial factor that determines whether priming will result in an assimilation or a contrast effect is the extent to which the primed cat-

---

[1]Heartfelt thanks go to Andrew MacFarlane for pointing me to the relevant studies.

egory and the stimulus overlap. When the prime is a "moderate category" and the stimulus is "ambiguous", then the stimulus "should in fact be judged as an instance of that category". If, on the other hand, the category used for priming is "extreme", then the "ambiguous target should not be categorized within the primed category" because there is little or even no match between the stimulus and the prime. The prime *will*, however, act as sort of a cognitive "anchor" for evaluating the stimulus (cf. Herr 1986: 1107). In other words: When the stimulus is reasonably similar to the primed category, then subjects will classify the stimulus as an instance of the *same* category, priming thus results in an assimilation effect. If, on the other hand, the perceived distance between the prime and the stimulus is too great because there is (next to) no overlap, perceivers will not only not categorise the stimulus in the same cognitive bin, but they will use the primed category as the "standard" value and consequently shift the stimulus towards the other end of the scale because it is directly compared (or contrasted) with the prime.

Herr illustrates this principle quite impressively with an experiment manipulating subjects' expectations of "hostility". In this test Herr primed participants with the help of famous people that had, in pretests, been revealed as representing different levels of hostility. The primes fell into one of four categories: "extremely nonhostile" (e.g. *Pope John Paul* or *Santa Claus*), "moderately nonhostile" (*Robin Hood, Henry Kissinger*), "moderately hostile" (*Alice Cooper, Menachem Begin*), and "extremely hostile" (*Dracula, Adolf Hitler*). Each participant was confronted with one of the lists just mentioned (which consisted of four names each) in the form of a matrix of letters puzzle where the names from the list had to be identified. After priming, subjects were given a description of a fictitious person ("Donald") to rate, whose behaviour was ambiguous and could be classified as either hostile or non-hostile (cf. Herr 1986: 1108). Results of this experiment were pretty clear and as expected: There was an interaction of prime and its "extremeness". Participants primed with moderately non-hostile *or* extremely hostile exemplars rated "Donald" as less hostile, and more friendly and kind than did subjects who had been exposed to the moderately hostile *or* extremely non-hostile category (cf. Herr 1986: 1109). In other words, subjects rated the fictitious person as similar if the prime was moderate, but reversed the effect when priming used "extreme" categories; compared to, say, Adolf Hitler, Donald actually seems to be a pretty nice person. Obviously, this explanation only works in an episodic framework, as it necessarily requires the presence of stored exemplars that can act as reference points.

I believe the very same process is behind the results of my own perception test. The only assumption that needs to be accepted to explain the direction of priming as a contrast effect is that the prime used in this study was what Herr calls "extreme", and this does not seem too far-fetched. Actually, it is not at all implausible to think that trying to make listeners perceive a Manchester voice as a Liverpool one is pushing the whole affair too far. What seems to have happened is that the Manc variants of the two salient variables present in the recordings are phonetically too different for British listeners to categorise them in the same category as the Scouse variants, even if these exemplars *have* been activated. Priming does still have an effect, though: Perceivers use the primed category "Liverpool" as the baseline that the acoustic input is categorised against, so evaluations are shifted towards the other end of the scale. The result is the contrast effect that was identified time and again in this study: The "Liverpool" speaker sounds even more Mancunian than she would anyway.

The same reasoning might also explain why subjects chose the slightly-Scouse token 3 much more often for NURSE stimuli than for /k/ ones. It is true that, at least for English, vowels "on the whole carry more responsibility than consonants in determining differences between accents" (Foulkes & Docherty 1999: 12), which would make them more liable to carry social meaning, all other things being equal. However, they also form a natural continuum without clearly delimited borders (cf. Foulkes & Docherty 1999: 12), which could make it generally harder to unambiguously categorise a specific token as an instance of category A or B. Subjects might therefore be more tempted to at least occasionally categorise the perceived variants as Scouse, because vowel categories have more fuzzy boundaries per se, compared to the realisations of /k/ which are thought of as more categorical in articulatory terms (plosive, affricate, fricative) to start with. Herr's framework could also provide further explanation for the class X priming interaction in the results for /k/ lenition. Middle class subjects showed a contrast effect. Working class participants exhibited a trend in the other (i.e. expected) direction. This is rather speculative because there were very few observations for working-class perceivers, but if this trend solidifies and becomes a significant assimilation effect in a larger dataset it could well be because working-class subjects are less aware of and sensitive to social differences in language use, so the prime "Liverpool" might actually be less extreme for them than it is for middle-class perceivers.

Finally, assimilation and contrast effects can also offer an alternative explanation for Hay, Nolan, et al.'s (2006) and Hay & Drager's (2010) gender differences. The authors argue that women behaved as expected because their associations with Australia are positive or neutral, whereas men have more negative attitudes due to the sporting rivalry and wish to disassociate from the invoked concept "Australia". It is equally possible, however, that the gender differences that were found in these studies are ultimately caused by different levels of awareness of variation in the test variable, rather than different attitudes. Normally, we would expect women to be more aware of a socially salient variable, but in this case it might actually be the men because they are more invested in the national rivalry based on sport. If the difference between New Zealand English and Australian English is only moderately salient for women, they should show an assimilation effect (which they did). For men, on the other hand, the distinction is very (!) salient. If their categories are (felt to be) more distinct or distant from one another, then the prime "Australia" would actually be much more extreme for them than for the women. Possibly just as extreme as the prime "Liverpool" was for the British subjects in my study, which might explain why both my participants and the male perceivers in New Zealand show a very similar contrast effect.

12.6 Summary and implications

So, what do the results of this study mean for exemplar priming in sociolinguistics and how do they relate to previous research?

First of all, priming does indeed seem to be limited to (highly) salient variables. Less or non-salient variables do not generate a priming effect or, at most, a very weak one. Secondly, priming might, on the whole and all other things being equal, turn out to work better with vowels than with consonants, at least in cases where the consonantal variants cannot be placed on a vowel-like continuum without comparatively straightforward boundaries (as in, for example, the [s]-[ʃ] continuum, cf. Strand 1999). This would also be in line with research from social psychology, which has found that we are most likely to look for the "help" of stereotypes when making a certain decision (i.e. categorisation) is difficult (cf. Petersen & Six 2008: 28). Thirdly, the prime and the acoustic material to be categorised must not be too different, at least not if the "goal" is to generate an assimilation effect.

The existing research by Niedzielski and Hay and colleagues, might in fact, only have succeeded in finding a priming effect because their studies (possibly unknowingly) fulfilled all three criteria. Both US English and Canadian English, on the one hand, and New Zealand English and Australian English, on the other, are accents that are – compared to the range of variation present in the anglophone world – relatively similar to one another (cf. Halford 2002: 31 for

Canadian English, and Hay, Nolan, et al. 2006: 354 for New Zealand). What is more, the variables used for testing (Canadian Raising for Niedzielski 1999, raising/centralisation of [ɪ] for Hay, Nolan, et al. 2006; Hay & Drager 2010) are very salient to speakers of these varieties, possibly because it is one of the few features (or even *the* feature) that distinguishes these varieties. And finally, they both involve rather fine-grained phonetic differences between variants, so perceivers might be more susceptible to the influence of priming because the task of categorising these stimuli is a comparatively difficult one to start with.

In Britain, for instance, the situation is very different because accents differ much more drastically from each other. As a consequence, priming can easily fall into the trap of 'overdoing it' by trying to suggest something to perceivers which is just too incredible to swallow, given that the actual phonetic material is too different from what it is supposed to be. This can then result either in a contrast effect, such as in the present study, or, possibly, in subjects' ignoring the prime altogether (like in Lawrence 2015) when they (sub-consciously) realise that it is not "helping". The violation of principle three above could also be behind the fact that social factors play a less prominent role in this study than was previously expected (gender does not turn up as a significant predictor, social class is only relevant for /k/). Maybe the conflict between the prime and the stimuli was so drastic that a lot of the potential impact of social factors was "swamped" by the overwhelming contrast effect.

Finally, future research in this area should take care to avoid the pitfalls of adding noise or even a second and unintended priming effect to their data by not controlling for factors such as phonological environment and possibly also frequency of carrier words, although the evidence is less clear in the latter respect.

None of this is meant to imply that social priming in language perception is not real. It is now very well established that humans *do* store social information in long-term memory and later integrate it with acoustic data when they process linguistic input, and the present study has added further to the pile of evidence supporting this idea. After all, it did find a priming effect, even if it was not in the expected direction. What the results of this study might also be able to do is to put the whole priming paradigm into perspective: Priming works, but only in certain, very special contexts. While exemplar priming remains extremely interesting from a *theoretical* point of view, it is possibly a lot less important in *practical* terms than has previously been suggested.

13 Conclusion

Although this study primarily set out to explore the role of salience in exemplar priming it has also produced a number of related results, which are nonetheless interesting. The claim that younger Scousers' speech is noticeably more local (cf. Watson 2007a) could be confirmed, but only for the two salient variables in the sample (NURSE-SQUARE and lenition), which appear to carry considerable amounts of covert prestige. Local variants of non-salient variables, on the other hand, were actually found to be receding. Young Liverpudlians seem to be somewhat more willing to express a local identity linguistically than older ones, but they rely almost exclusively on highly salient and/or stigmatised features for doing so.

Linguistic norms and attitudes in the speech community have remained relatively stable. Speakers of all three generations investigated generally like "soft" or light Liverpool accents, but largely reject very strong ones, to a not inconsiderable degree because the latter are perceived as exaggerated and artificial. Despite these similarities the presence of hypercorrection particularly in the middle-aged speakers suggests that this group is most sensitive to the negative image of Liverpool and Scouse, probably because economic decline and stigmatisation of the city were at its historic height in the 1970's and 80's when these speakers were growing up.

The phonological variables investigated are not equally salient in all three age groups. For happy-tensing and velar nasal plus there is essentially no change, both variables are largely below the radar for all speakers in the sample. With respect to the NURSE-SQUARE merger, however, conscious and sub-conscious awareness declines from the middle to the young generation, while lenition of /k/ sees a steady and linear increase in salience from the oldest to the youngest speakers. Crucially, however, lenition of /k/ is the most salient feature in *all* age groups, and is universally followed by the NURSE-SQUARE merger, velar nasal plus, and happy-tensing. While speakers of different age groups have thus not the same level of awareness of the individual variables, the relative ordering is the same in all three generations.

This ordering is then mirrored in the perception data. Both accuracy of "correct" token selection and statistical robustness of the priming effect correlate with the social salience of the test variable. No effect at all is detectable for happy-tensing, and only a weak one for velar nasal plus (if participant as a random factor is not taken into account). The NURSE-SQUARE merger and /k/ lenition, on the other hand, both generate robust priming effects, and for the latter salience can even explain differences between sub-groups of stimuli (divided by phonological environment) or subjects (middle- vs. working-class background). The main hypothesis that this study was built on could thus be confirmed: The more socially salient a linguistic variable is, the more pronounced the resulting effect in an exemplar priming experiment will be; below a certain level of sub-conscious awareness no statistically significant priming effects are generated.

Intriguingly, all significant effects in the perception experiment are in the unexpected direction: Subjects who have been led to believe that the speaker is from Liverpool are *less* likely to perceive variants typical of Liverpool English. While it is seemingly at odds with existing priming research in sociolinguistics, this result is actually compatible with previous work in psychology and suggests that the phonetic distance between the prime and the actual speech signal is too great for perceivers to include the stimulus in the primed category. Priming works nevertheless, but the outcome is a contrast effect instead of the assimilation effects that were found in the studies conducted in Detroit and New Zealand.

Another unexpected outcome of the perception test is that frequency of the carrier word is not really a factor worth mentioning when it comes to predicting how subjects will perceive the stimulus. In Chapter 4 I did argue that frequency of *remembrance* and not frequency of *occurrence* should be most important, but it is still surprising that the latter should essentially play no role at all. It is possible that frequency is just not relevant in this particular context. The production data support this idea, because frequency turned out to be a (nearly) non-significant predictor in production as well. All the same, a different test design that is specifically aimed at investigating frequency effects in priming experiments might be able to yield further interesting insights.

For the perception test, it would also be desirable to have a less biased sample of participants than the one this study is based on. The dataset for perception is quite heavily skewed towards participants that are in their twenties and have a middle-class background. This is not due to a flaw in design, but something of an unfortunate coincidence linked to the difficulties of recruiting participants over the internet. A more balanced sample of subjects would, however, enable the researcher to conduct a much more thorough analysis of the impact of social characteristics of the perceivers than I have been able to do in this study. The tentative results and conclusions presented in this book, and, more importantly, the ones that can be found in previous research (cf. Hay, Nolan, et al. 2006; Hay & Drager 2010) strongly suggest that this is a fruitful area for future research that can help us to better understand how language perception works.

Turning back to the primary issue of this book, my analysis shows that exemplar priming in sociolinguistics not only needs a variable that comes with a high degree of social salience. In addition, two further requirements have to be met, at least when the goal is to create an assimilation effect: The phonetic distance between the primed variety and the one actually used in the stimuli must be comparatively small, and categorisation of the stimuli must be a comparatively difficult task to start with. So far, criteria defining contexts where "successful" exemplar priming is to be expected have been lacking. I hope that the ones I have suggested here can serve as a starting point for developing a more elaborate "theory of priming" (cf. Cesario 2014) in the realm of sociophonetics.

Appendix A: Questionnaire

Personal information

- How old are you?
- What is your level of education?
- What is your first language?
- Did you grow up speaking any other languages?
- What do you do for a living?
- Were you born in Liverpool?
- If yes, in which district?
- If not, where?
- How old were you when you came to Liverpool?
- In which district do you live now?
- In how many other places besides Liverpool have you lived?
- Was your mother born in Liverpool?
- If not, where?
- What's her profession?
- Was your father born in Liverpool?
- If not, where?
- What's his profession?
- Would you consider yourself WC or MC?
- What is your creed? If Christian, Protestant or Catholic?

Local knowledge

- Who is mayor of Liverpool?

- Who controls the City Council?

- Do you vote in local elections?

- Name as many districts of Liverpool as you can.

Sports and hobbies

- Are you a football fan? Liverpool FC or Everton FC?

- Does this matter a lot? Would you say the two clubs are different in character? Does that also hold for their supporters?

- What sports do people prefer here (apart from football)?

"Children's lore"

- Could you describe the district you grew up in?

- Do you still live there? If not, how about the new district?

- Can you tell me about some games you played, in the school yard for example?

- Do you know "conkers"? How does that work?

- Did you use any rhymes to make fun of people?

- Do you remember any counting out rhymes you used?

- Did you know any clapping games? What songs went with them?

- Did you ever get into fights when you were a kid?

- Did you have any rules about what was considered fair?

- Was your class ethnically mixed? How did you experience that?

- Was it a "close-knit" community in your district where everyone knew everyone? A good place to grow up?

- Do you remember what you wanted to do for a living when you were young?

Attachment to Liverpool

- Do you like living here? Are there places you would rather live?

- Do you think Liverpool is a good place to raise kids?

- Would you say most of your best friends are from Liverpool or from outside the city?

- What are the first things that come to mind when you think of Liverpool?

- What do you like about Liverpool? What don't you like about it?

- If someone came to visit the city what would you show them?

- Where can you experience the "real" Liverpool?

- Are there any festivals or traditions you can tell me about?

Identity

- What would you call yourself (British, English, Northerner, Merseysider, Liverpudlian, Scouser)? If several, in what order?

- How would you feel if someone called you a Scouser?

- What are Woolybacks? Where do they live? Plastic Scousers? Scally Scouser?

- "In the North, but not of it" – your opinion?

Recent developments

- Do you think Liverpool has changed in the last 20 years? For better or worse?

- What do you think of Liverpool ONE?

- Do you think urban restructuring is destroying Liverpool's character?

- What did you think of Liverpool as European Capital of Culture?

- Do you feel neglected by the central government? If yes, in what ways?

- More and more tourists seem to be visiting Liverpool. Is that a good thing?

- How do you feel about the Beatles cult?

Liverpool's image

- Are you familiar with the label "Livercool"? Do you think it is appropriate?

- Do you think Liverpool is stigmatised in England/the United Kingdom?

- Why do you think some people have rather negative attitudes towards Liverpool?

- Older subjects: Do you remember the Toxteth riots of 1981? How did you experience them? What exactly happened?

- Do you think the riots still form part of Liverpool's image in the rest of the country?

- "The world in one city" - would you say this is still true today?

- Would you say Liverpool is a dangerous place?

- Liverpool frequently "doubles" for other cities in films. Does that make you proud or rather angry?

Liverpool and Manchester

- There's an old rivalry between Liverpool and Manchester. Is that still alive today? Why do you think that is?

- Do you think Manchester is doing better than Liverpool? Why (not)?

- Do you sometimes go to Manchester? What for?

- What are the people there like? Can you characterise them?

Questions about Scouse

- Can you tell someone is from Liverpool by the way they talk? How?

- What are the most typical features of Liverpool English? Certain words or sounds?

- What do you think of the sound of Scouse?

- Do you think Scouse has changed in the last 20 years? How?

- If yes, how do you evaluate this change?

Appendix B: Reading passage

When you get older, your childhood often seems like the best time you ever had. We all remember little things that aren't really important but which still appear to have left their mark.

Me, my best mate John and a bunch of other kids used to meet in the little square next to the brick church. Except for the water fountain, there wasn't anything special about it, but for us it was the best place on earth, because no one cared what we did there.

Some of the other kids were already real characters at the time. Bill, for instance. We loved to play hide-and-seek, but Bill would always turn around early and peek. He used to say he had miscounted. It wasn't fair and we all knew it was a flimsy excuse, but he got very angry when we told him so. He could be a real trouble maker, so we just took to hiding a bit quicker when it was his turn. He was fun all the same: we once dared him to go home naked – and lost.

There were also a number of girls, but at the time we didn't consider them part of the gang. Susan was the bookish one, rather quiet though physically fitter than most of us, while Jenny, as a natural born public speaker, was giving speeches all the time.

Sometimes we just chatted. One day, we spent hours going on about what we wanted to become when we were grown-ups. Most of the girls either wanted to be a vet or dreamed of being a famous singer. John wanted nothing but to be a baker (he really did love cake), and Bill had his mind set on becoming a snooker champion. Later that day, Susan arrived carrying a cardboard box.

The box was full of kittens, a whole litter. "Oh look, baby cats!", Jenny squeaked, "take one, John!" "No, thanks. I don't like animals", John answered. "Well, I think you're just scared of that little fang", said Jenny. That was a bit of a clanger, because John had been hurt quite badly by a dog as a toddler and he was still rather touchy about the subject.

To take attention off the matter, I took one of the cats and held it close to my face. It started to purr immediately and licked my nose with its rough little tongue. When I got home, I kicked off my sneakers and found my mum brushing her hair in the bathroom.

She looked disapprovingly at my scruffy clothes (I had ruined my shirt again), but the cat quickly caught her attention. My parents weren't stingy but I knew room was scarce in our house. So I said: "Look, mummy, I found a kitty! Please, can I keep it as a pet? It could live in the cupboard under the stairs."

I felt rather canny at the time for coming up with that idea, although, in retrospect, I probably stole it from a children's book. She seemed reluctant at first, but then she stroked the cat's fluffy fur and, after a longish silence, she sighed: "Ok..., but you'll have to care for it yourself!"

Some stuff might indeed have been better in the days when I was young and strongish. Back then, that furry little thing was all it took to make me happy.

Appendix C: Word list

church	city	cracker
care	longish	latter
happy	book	shirt
singer	bet	wear
walk	bird	stingy
fat	bare	king
turn	lady	snooker
air	singable	motto
lazy	pack	work
swinger	sit	scare
like	girl	navy
lot	pair	gang
fur	baby	sneaker
fair	song	litter
pretty	hacker	term
hanger	matter	spare
look	stir	gravy
net	bear	young
blur	angry	speaker
hair	ring	bitter

Appendix D: Stimuli for perception test

NURSE

Final

1. People in that town almost never went to church.

2. It was best to hide fast when it was his turn.

3. The old cat still had quite a nice, soft fur.

4. There are hundreds of nice names for a girl.

5. He always managed to ruin his new shirt.

6. She wasn't sure this was the right word.

Medial

1. In that town church was not popular with people.

2. When it was his turn we often hid extra fast.

3. The cat's nice, soft fur now appeared rather sordid.

4. Mary was a nice girl, but not a smart one.

5. He wanted that shirt but couldn't pay for it.

6. She knew the word but pretended not to.

happy

Final

1. At the end of the day we all want to be happy.

2. He had always known that she was lazy.

3. She had never thought it important to be pretty.

4. There are lots of new hotels in the city.

5. For two years, they had tried for a baby.

6. No one in our street could be called stingy.

Medial

1. We all want to be happy, but not all in the same way.

2. He knew she was lazy, and mean as well.

3. She had never been pretty until about age fourteen.

4. Most hotels in the city are now located downtown.

5. Two toddlers and a baby required all their attention.

6. No one there was stingy, at least not in public.

Lenition of /k/

Final

1. She's just someone you have got to li<u>k</u>e.

2. The film's not half as good as the boo<u>k</u>.

3. Bill had never even been part of the pa<u>ck</u>.

4. He's good, but I wouldn't call him a ha<u>ck</u>er.

5. They used to meet quite often to play snoo<u>k</u>er.

6. The way he moved reminded us of a chi<u>ck</u>en.

Medial

1. She's just someone you li<u>k</u>e, regardless of unpleasant habits.

2. I quite enjoyed the boo<u>k</u>, but the film's terrible.

3. Well, there was the pa<u>ck</u>, but that was different.

4. He's not quite a ha<u>ck</u>er, at least not yet.

5. They used to play snoo<u>k</u>er in their favourite pub.

6. We had both ordered chi<u>ck</u>en and got beef instead.

Velar nasal plus

Final

1. As a child Heather wanted to be a si<u>ng</u>er.

2. Please put your coat on the free ha<u>ng</u>er.

3. I bet that speech will be rather lo<u>ng</u>ish.

4. This is by far my wife's favourite so<u>ng</u>.

5. None of us was a member of a ga<u>ng</u>.

6. At the time I was still quite you<u>ng</u>.

Medial

1. Often, a famous rock si<u>ng</u>er lives on the edge.

2. Put it on the ha<u>ng</u>er to your right, please.

3. It'll be rather lo<u>ng</u>ish, so don't fall asleep.

4. She adores this so<u>ng</u> because of its rhythm.

5. It was a notorious ga<u>ng</u> but she wasn't afraid.

6. Jake appeared quite you<u>ng</u>, which often annoyed him.

References

Adank, Patti, Roel Smits & Roeland van Hout. 2004. A comparison of vowel normalization procedures for language variation research. *Journal of the Acoustical Society of America* 116. 3099–3107.

Agha, Asif. 2003. The social life of cultural value. *Journal of Linguistic Anthropology* 23. 231–271.

Anon. 1812. *The stranger in Liverpool: Or, an historical and descriptive view of the town of Liverpool and its environs.* Liverpool: Kaye.

Auer, Peter. 2014. Anmerkungen zum Salienzbegriff in der Soziolinguistik. *Linguistik online* 66(4). 7–20.

Baayen, Rolf Harald, R. Piepenbrock & van H. Rijn. 1993. *The CELEX lexical data base on CD-ROM.* Philadelphia, PA: Linguistic Data Consortium.

Barr, Dale J., Roger Levy, Christoph Scheepers & Harry J. Tily. 2013. Random effects structure for confirmatory hypothesis testing: Keep it maximal. *Journal of Memory and Language* 68. 255–278.

Bates, Douglas, Martin Mächler, Ben Bolker & Steve Walker. 2015. Fitting linear mixed-effects models using lme4. *Journal of Statistical Software* 67(1). 1–48. DOI:10.18637/jss.v067.i01

Beal, Joan C. 2010. *An introduction to regional Englishes: Dialect variation in England.* Edinburgh: Edinburgh University Press.

Belchem, John. 2006a. 'An accent exceedingly rare': Scouse and the inflexion of class. In *Merseypride: Essays in Liverpool exceptionalism*, Second edition, 31–64. Liverpool: Liverpool University Press.

Belchem, John. 2006b. Celebrating Liverpool. In John Belchem (ed.), *Liverpool 800: Culture, character and history*, 9–57. Liverpool: Liverpool University Press.

Belchem, John. 2006c. Introduction: The new 'Livercool'. In *Merseypride: Essays in Liverpool exceptionalism*, Second edition, xi–xxix. Liverpool: Liverpool University Press.

Belchem, John. 2006d. *Merseypride: Essays in Liverpool exceptionalism.* Second edition. Liverpool: Liverpool University Press.

Belchem, John & Donald M. MacRaild. 2006. Cosmopolitan Liverpool. In John Belchem (ed.), *Liverpool 800: Culture, character and history*, 311–391. Liverpool: Liverpool University Press.

Boersma, Paul & David Weenink. 2015. *Praat: Doing phonetics by computer.* Version 5.4.08. http://www.praat.org/ (27 March, 2015). http://www.praat.org/, accessed 2015-3-27.

Cesario, Joseph. 2014. Priming, replication, and the hardest science. *Perspectives on Psychological Science* 9(1). 40–48.

Christensen, R. H. B. 2015. *Ordinal—regression models for ordinal data.* R package version 2015.6-28. http://www.cran.r-project.org/package=ordinal/.

Clopper, Cynthia G. 2009. Computational methods for normalizing acoustic vowel data for talker differences. *Language and Linguistics Compass* 3. 1430–1442.

Couch, Chris. 2003a. Economic and physical influences on urban regeneration in Europe. In Chris Couch, Charles Fraser & Susan Percy (eds.), *Urban regeneration in Europe*, 166–179. Oxford: Blackwell Science.

Couch, Chris. 2003b. Urban regeneration in Liverpool. In Chris Couch, Charles Fraser & Susan Percy (eds.), *Urban regeneration in Europe*, 34–55. Oxford: Blackwell Science.

Crowley, Tony. 2012. *Scouse: A social and cultural history.* Liverpool: Liverpool University Press.

De Lyon, Hilary. 1981. *A sociolinguistic study of aspects of the Liverpool accent.* University of Liverpool M.Phil. dissertation.

Disner, Sandra Ferrari. 1980. Evaluation of vowel normalization procedures. *Journal of the Acoustical Society of America* 67. 253–261.

Drager, Katie. 2005. *Social effects on the perception of dress and trap in New Zealand English.* University of Canterbury Unpublished Master thesis.

Ellis, Alexander John. 1889. *Early English pronunciation. part 5.* London: Trübner.

Fabricius, Anne, Dominic Watt & Daniel Ezra Johnson. 2009. A comparison of three speaker-intrinsic vowel formant frequency normalization algorithms for sociophonetics. *Language Variation and Change* 21. 413–435.

Flynn, Nicholas. 2010. Gender-based variation of word-final unstressed vowels by Nottingham adolescents. In Miriam Meyerhoff, Chie Adachi, Agata Daleszynska & Anna Strycharz (eds.), *Proceedings of the second summer school of sociolinguistics.*

Foulkes, Paul & Gerard J. Docherty. 1999. Urban voices — overview. In Paul Foulkes & Gerard J. Docherty (eds.), *Urban voices: Accent studies in the British Isles*, 1–24. London: Arnold.

Fraser, Charles. 2003a. Change in the European industrial city. In Chris Couch, Charles Fraser & Susan Percy (eds.), *Urban regeneration in Europe*, 17–33. Oxford: Blackwell Science.

Fraser, Charles. 2003b. The institutional and financial conditions of urban regeneration in Europe. In Chris Couch, Charles Fraser & Susan Percy (eds.), *Urban regeneration in Europe*, 180–199. Oxford: Blackwell Science.

Garcia, Beatriz, Ruth Melville & Tamsin Cox. 2010. *Creating an impact: Liverpool's experience as European Capital of Culture.* http://www.liv.ac.uk/impacts08/, accessed 2013-9-3.

GB Historical GIS. 2009–2014. *A Vision of Britain through Time.* University of Portsmouth (ed.). http://www.visionofbritain.org.uk (19 January, 2016). http://www.visionofbritain.org.uk, accessed 2016-1-19.

Goldinger, Stephen D. 1996. Words and voices: Episodic traces in spoken word identification and recognition memory. *Journal of Experimental Psychology* 22. 1166–1183.

Halford, Brigitte K. 2002. Canadian English: Distinct in North America? In David John Allerton (ed.), *Perspectives on English as a world language*, 31–44. Basel: Schwabe.

Hall-Lew, Lauren. 2010. Improved representation of variance in measures of vowel merger. *Proceedings of Meetings on Acoustics (POMA)* 9(1). 1–10.

Harrington, Jonathan. 2006. An acoustic analysis of 'happy-tensing' in the Queen's Christmas broadcasts. *Journal of Phonetics* 34. 439–457.

Harris, John. 1985. *Phonological variation and change: Studies in Hiberno-English.* Cambridge: Cambridge University Press.

Hay, Jennifer & Katie Drager. 2010. Stuffed toys and speech perception. *Linguistics* 48. 865–892.

Hay, Jennifer, Aaron Nolan & Katie Drager. 2006. From fush to feesh: Exemplar priming in speech perception. *The Linguistic Review* 23. 351–379.

Hay, Jennifer, Paul Warren & Katie Drager. 2006. Factors influencing speech perception in the context of a merger-in-progress. *Journal of Phonetics* 34. 458–484.

Herr, Paul M. 1986. Consequences of priming: Judgment and behavior. *Journal of Personality and Social Psychology* 51(6). 1106–1115.

Hickey, Raymond. 1996. Lenition in Irish English. *Working Papers in Linguistics* 13. 173–193.

Hickey, Raymond. 1999. Dublin English: Current changes and their motivation. In Paul Foulkes & Gerard J. Docherty (eds.), *Urban voices: Accent studies in the British Isles*, 265–281. London: Arnold.

Hindle, Donald. 1978. Approaches to vowel normalization in the study of natural speech. In David Sankoff (ed.), *Linguistic variation models and methods*, 161–171. New York: Academic Press.

Hogan, John T. & Anton J. Rozsypal. 1980. Evaluation of vowel duration as a cue for the voicing distinction in the following word-final consonant. *Journal of the Acoustical Society of America* 67. 1764–1771.

Hohenberg, Paul M. & Lynn Hollen Lees. 1985. *The making of urban Europe 1000–1950* (Harvard Studies in Urban History). Cambridge, MA & London, England: Harvard University Press.

Honeybone, Patrick. 2001. Lenition inhibition in Liverpool English. *English Language and Linguistics* 5(2). 213–249.

Honeybone, Patrick. 2007. New-dialect formation in nineteenth century Liverpool: A brief history of Scouse. In Anthony Grant & Clive Grey (eds.), *The Mersey sound: Liverpool's language, people and places*, 106–140. Liverpool: Open House Press.

Honeybone, Patrick & Kevin Watson. 2013. Salience and the sociolinguistics of Scouse spelling: Exploring the phonology of the Contemporary Humorous Localised Dialect Literature of Liverpool. *English World-Wide* 34(3). 305–340.

House, S. A. & K. N. Stevens. 1956. Analog studies of the nasalization of vowels. *Journal of Speech and Hearing Disorders* 21. 218–232.

Jaeger, T. Florian & Kodi Weatherholtz. 2017. What the heck is salience? How predictive language processing contributes to sociolinguistic perception. In Alice Blumenthal-Dramé, Adriana Hanulíková & Bernd Kortmann (eds.), *Perceptual linguistic salience: Modeling causes and consequences*, 36–40. Lausanne: Frontiers Media.

Jannedy, Stefanie, Melanie Weirich & Jana Brunner. 2011. The effect of inferences on the perceptual categorization of Berlin German fricatives. In *Proceedings of the International Congress of Phonetic Sciences*, 962–965. Hong Kong.

Johnson, Keith. 1997. Speech perception without speaker normalization. In Keith Johnson & John W. Mullennix (eds.), *Talker variability in speech processing*, 145–166. San Diego: Academic Press.

Johnson, Keith. 2005. Speaker normalization in speech perception. In David B. Pisoni & Robert E. Remez (eds.), *The handbook of speech perception*, 363–389. Oxford: Blackwell.

Johnstone, Barbara, Jennifer Andrus & Andrew Danielson. 2006. Mobility, indexicality and the enregisterment of 'Pittsburghese'. *Journal of English Linguistics* 34(2). 77–104.

Judd, Dennis & Michael Parkinson. 1990. Urban leadership and regeneration. In Dennis Judd & Michael Parkinson (eds.), *Leadership and urban regeneration*, vol. 37 (Urban Affairs Annual Reviews), 13–30. Newbury Park, CA, London, England & New Delhi, India: Sage Publications.

Juskan, Marten. 2011. *National stereotypes in speech perception and speaker evaluation*. University of Freiburg, English Department Unpublished Master thesis.

Juskan, Marten. 2015. Selective accent revival in Liverpool. *JournaLIPP* 4. 1–12. http://lipp.ub.lmu.de/article/download/4839/2721, accessed 2015-10-9.

Kendall, Tyler & Valerie Fridland. 2017. Regional relationships among the low vowels of U.S. English: Evidence from production and perception. *Language Variation and Change* 29. 245–271.

Kendall, Tyler & Erik R. Thomas. 2009–2014. *Vowels: Vowel Manipulation, Normalization, and Plotting in R: R package*. Version 1.2-1. http://ncslaap.lib.ncsu.edu/tools/norm/ (10 March, 2015). http://ncslaap.lib.ncsu.edu/tools/norm/, accessed 2015-3-10.

Kermode, Jenny, Janet Hollinshead & Malcolm Gratton. 2006. Small beginnings: Liverpool 1207–1680. In John Belchem (ed.), *Liverpool 800: Culture, character and history*, 59–111. Liverpool: Liverpool University Press.

Kerswill, Paul. 2003. Dialect levelling and geographical diffusion in British English. In David Britain & Jenny Cheshire (eds.), *Social dialectology: In honour of Peter Trudgill*, 223–243. Amsterdam: Benjamins.

Kerswill, Paul & Ann Williams. 2002. Salience as an explanatory factor in language change: Evidence from dialect levelling in urban England. In Mari C. Jones (ed.), *Language change: The interplay of internal, external and extra-linguistic factors*, 81–110. Berlin: Mouton de Gruyter.

Knowles, Gerald O. 1973. *Scouse: The urban dialect of Liverpool*. University of Leeds. Department of English Language & Medieval English Literature dissertation.

Knowles, Gerald O. 1978. The nature of phonological variables in Scouse. In Peter Trudgill (ed.), *Sociolinguistic patterns in British English*, 80–90. London: Arnold.

Knowles, Gerald O. 1997. *A cultural history of the English language*. London: Arnold.

Kuznetsova, Alexandra, Per Bruun Brockhoff & Rune Haubo Bojesen Christensen. 2015. *lmerTest: Tests in Linear Mixed Effects Models*. http ://CRAN.R-project.org/package=lmerTest. R package version 2.0-29.

Labov, William. 1972. *Sociolinguistic patterns*. Philadelphia: University of Philadelphia Press. Chap. On the mechanism of linguistic change, 160–182.

References

Labov, William. 1994. *Principles of linguistic change: Volume 1: Internal factors.* Oxford, UK & Cambridge, MA: Blackwell.

Labov, William. 2001. *Principles of linguistic change: Volume 2: Social factors.* Oxford, UK & Cambridge, MA: Blackwell.

Labov, William. 2006. A sociolinguistic perspective on sociophonetic research. *Journal of Phonetics* 34. 500–515.

Labov, William, Sharon Ash & Charles Boberg. 2006. *The Atlas of North American English: Phonology, phonetics, and sound change. A multimedia reference tool.* Berlin: Mouton de Gruyter.

Langstrof, Christian. 2006. *Vowel change in New Zealand English—patterns and implications.* University of Canterbury dissertation. http://christianlangstrof. org/publications/langstrofthesis.pdf, accessed 2015-6-15.

Lawrence, Daniel. 2015. Limited evidence for social priming in the perception of the BATH and STRUT vowels. In The Scottish Consortium for ICPhS 2015 (ed.), *Proceedings of the 18th International Congress of Phonetic Sciences*, 1–5. Glasgow: University of Glasgow. http://icphs2015.info/pdfs/Papers/ICPHS0244.pdf, accessed 2015-10-9. Paper number 244.

Lehiste, Ilse. 1964. *Acoustical characteristics of selected English consonants.* Bloomington, IN: Indiana University.

Liverpool City Council. 2010. *The Index of Multiple Deprivation 2010: A Liverpool analysis.* Liverpool. http://liverpool.gov.uk/media/1448371/2-imd-2010-final-document-compressed-with-links.pdf, accessed 2014-3-11.

Liverpool City Council. 2016. *Liverpool Economic Briefing 2016: A monitor of jobs, business and economic growth.* Liverpool. http://liverpool.gov.uk/council/key-statistics-and-data/liverpool-economic-briefing/, accessed 2016-1-23.

Llamas, Carmen, Dominic Watt & Andrew E. MacFarlane. 2017. Estimating the relative sociolinguistic salience of segmental variables in a dialect boundary zone. In Alice Blumenthal-Dramé, Adriana Hanulíková & Bernd Kortmann (eds.), *Perceptual linguistic salience: Modeling causes and consequences*, 41–58. Lausanne: Frontiers Media.

Lobanov, Boris M. 1971. Classification of Russian vowels spoken by different speakers. *Journal of the Acoustical Society of America* 49. 606–608.

Longmore, Jane. 2006. Civic Liverpool: 1680–1800. In John Belchem (ed.), *Liverpool 800: Culture, character and history*, 113–169. Liverpool: Liverpool University Press.

Medin, Douglas L. & Marguerite M. Schaffer. 1978. Context theory of classification learning. *Psychological Review* 85. 207–238.

Milne, Graeme J. 2006. Maritime Liverpool. In John Belchem (ed.), *Liverpool 800: Culture, character and history*, 257–309. Liverpool: Liverpool University Press.

Montgomery, Chris. 2007a. *Northern English dialects: A perceptual approach*. University of Sheffield dissertation. http://etheses.whiterose.ac.uk/1203/.

Montgomery, Chris. 2007b. Perceptions of Liverpool English. In Anthony Grant & Clive Grey (eds.), *The Mersey sound: Liverpool's language, people and places*, 164–188. Liverpool: Open House Press.

Murden, Jon. 2006. 'City of change and challenge': Liverpool since 1945. In John Belchem (ed.), *Liverpool 800: Culture, character and history*, 393–485. Liverpool: Liverpool University Press.

Newbrook, Mark. 1999. West Wirral: Norms, self reports and usage. In Paul Foulkes & Gerard J. Docherty (eds.), *Urban voices: Accent studies in the British Isles*, 90–106. London: Arnold.

Niedzielski, Nancy. 1999. The effect of social information on the perception of sociolinguistic variables. *Journal of Language and Social Psychology* 18. 62–85.

Niedzielski, Nancy & Dennis R. Preston. 2000. *Folk linguistics*. Berlin/New York: Mouton de Gruyter.

Office for National Statistics. 2016. *Nomis. Official Labour Market Statistics*. http://www.nomisweb.co.uk/ (19 January, 2016). http://www.nomisweb.co.uk/, accessed 2016-1-19.

Parkinson, Michael. 1990. Leadership and regeneration in Liverpool: Confusion, confrontation, or coalition? In Dennis Judd & Michael Parkinson (eds.), *Leadership and urban regeneration*, vol. 37 (Urban Affairs Annual Reviews), 241–257. Newbury Park, CA, London, England & New Delhi, India: Sage Publications.

Percy, Susan. 2003. New agendas. In Chris Couch, Charles Fraser & Susan Percy (eds.), *Urban regeneration in Europe*, 200–209. Oxford: Blackwell Science.

Petersen, Lars-Eric & Bernd Six (eds.). 2008. *Stereotype, Vorurteile und soziale Diskriminierung. Theorien, Befunde und Interventionen*. Basel: Beltz.

Pierrehumbert, Janet. 2002. Word-specific phonetics. In Carlos Gussenhoven & Natasha Warner (eds.), *Laboratory phonology*, vol. VII, 101–139. Berlin: Mouton de Gruyter. http://faculty.wcas.northwestern.edu/~jbp/publications/word_specific.pdf, accessed 2015-12-15.

Pierrehumbert, Janet. 2006. The next toolkit. *Journal of Phonetics* 34. 516–530.

Pooley, Colin G. 2006. Living in Liverpool: The modern city. In John Belchem (ed.), *Liverpool 800: Culture, character and history*, 171–255. Liverpool: Liverpool University Press.

Preston, Dennis R. (ed.). 1999. *Handbook of perceptual dialectology*. Amsterdam: Benjamins.

References

QGIS Development Team. 2016. *QGIS Geographic Information System.* Open Source Geospatial Foundation. http://qgis.osgeo.org.

R Core Team. 2015. *R: A Language and Environment for Statistical Computing.* R Foundation for Statistical Computing. Vienna, Austria. https://www.R-project.org/.

r-sig-mixed-models mailing list. 2015. *GLMM for ecologists and evolutionary biologists: FAQ.* http://glmm.wikidot.com/faq (10 March, 2015). http://glmm.wikidot.com/faq, accessed 2015-3-10.

Rácz, Péter. 2013. *Salience in sociolinguistics: A quantitative approach.* Berlin/Boston: De Gruyter.

Rampton, Ben. 1995. *Crossing: Language and ethnicity among adolescents.* London: Longman.

Sangster, Catherine M. 2001. Lenition of alveolar stops in Liverpool English. *Journal of Sociolinguistics* 5(3). 401–412.

Scott, Dixon Walter. 1907. *Liverpool 1907.* London: Adam & Charles Black.

Silverstein, Michael. 2003. Indexical order and the dialectics of sociolinguistic life. *Language and Communication* 23. 193–229.

SoSciSurvey.de. 2015. https://www.soscisurvey.de/index.php?page=home&l=eng (24 March, 2015). https://www.soscisurvey.de/index.php?page=home&l=eng, accessed 2015-3-24.

Squires, Lauren. 2013. It don't go both ways: Limited bidirectionality in sociolinguistic perception. *Journal of Sociolinguistics* 17(2). 200–237.

Stoddart, Jana, Clive Upton & J. D. A. Widdowson. 1999. Sheffield dialect in the 1990s: Revisiting the concept of NORMs. In Paul Foulkes & Gerard J. Docherty (eds.), *Urban voices: Accent studies in the British Isles*, 72–89. London: Arnold.

Strand, Elizabeth. 1999. Uncovering the role of gender stereotypes in speech perception. *Journal of Language and Social Psychology* 18. 86–99.

Strand, Elizabeth & Keith Johnson. 1996. Gradient and visual speaker normalization in the perception of fricatives. In Dafydd Gibbon (ed.), *Natural language processing and speech technology: Results of the 3rd KONVENS conference, Bielefeld, October 1996*, 14–26. Berlin: Mouton.

Styler, William F. 2008. *Establishing the nature of context in speaker vowel space normalization.* University of Colorado, Department of Linguistics Unpublished Master thesis.

Syrdal, Ann K. & H. S. Gopal. 1986. A perceptual model of vowel recognition based on the auditory representation of American English vowels. *Journal of the Acoustical Society of America* 79. 1086–1100.

Thomas, Erik R. 2002. Instrumental phonetics. In Jack K. Chambers, Peter Trudgill & Natalie Schilling-Estes (eds.), *The handbook of language variation and change*, 168–200. Oxford/Malden, MA: Blackwell.

Traunmüller, Hartmut. 1990. Analytical expressions for the tonotopic sensory scale. *Journal of the Acoustical Society of America* 88. 97–100.

Troughton, Thomas. 1810. *History of Liverpool: From the earliest authenticated period down to the present time.* Liverpool: Robinson.

Trudgill, Peter. 1986. *Dialects in contact.* Oxford: Blackwell.

Trudgill, Peter. 1999. *The dialects of England.* Second edition. Oxford: Blackwell.

Trudgill, Peter. 2004. *New-dialect formation: The inevitability of colonial Englishes.* Edinburgh: Edinburgh University Press.

Van Heuven, W.J.B., P. Mandera, E. Keuleers & M. Brysbaert. 2014. Subtlex-uk: A new and improved word frequency database for British English. *Quarterly Journal of Experimental Psychology* 67. 1176–1190.

Wales, Katie. 2006. *Northern English: A cultural and social history.* Cambridge: CUP.

Watson, Kevin. 2002. The realization of final /t/ in Liverpool English. *Durham Working Papers in Linguistics* 8. 195–205.

Watson, Kevin. 2006. Phonological resistance and innovation in the North-West of England. *English Today* 22(2). 55–61.

Watson, Kevin. 2007a. Is Scouse getting Scouser? Phonological change in contemporary Liverpool English. In Anthony Grant & Clive Grey (eds.), *The Mersey sound: Liverpool's language, people and places*, 215–241. Liverpool: Open House Press.

Watson, Kevin. 2007b. Liverpool English. *Journal of the International Phonetic Association* 37(3). 351–360.

Watson, Kevin & Lynn Clark. 2013. How salient is the NURSE SQUARE merger? *English Language and Linguistics* 17(2). 297–323.

Watson, Kevin & Lynn Clark. 2015. Exploring listeners' real-time reactions to regional accents. *Language Awareness* 24(1). 38–59.

Watt, Dominic & Anne Fabricius. 2002. Evaluation of a technique for improving the mapping of multiple speakers' vowel spaces in the F1~F2 plane. *Leeds Working Papers in Linguistics and Phonetics* 9. 159–173.

Watts, Emma L. 2006. *Mobility-induced dialect contact: A sociolinguistic investigation of speech variation in Wilmslow, Cheshire* dissertation.

Wells, John Christopher. 1982. *Accents of English.* Cambridge: Cambridge University Press.

Wells, John Christopher. 1997. Whatever happened to received pronunciation? *Il Jornadas de Estudios Ingleses* 2. 19–28.

West, Helen Faye. 2015. Language attitudes and divergence on the Merseyside/Lancashire border. In Raymond Hickey (ed.), *Researching Northern English*, 317–341. Amsterdam: Benjamins.

Wickham, Hadley. 2009. *Ggplot2: Elegant graphics for data analysis*. New York: Springer. http://had.co.nz/ggplot2/book.

Wickham, Hadley. 2011. The split-apply-combine strategy for data analysis. *Journal of Statistical Software* 40(1). 1–29. http://www.jstatsoft.org/v40/i01/.

Xie, Yihui. 2015. *knitr: A General-Purpose Package for Dynamic Report Generation in R*. http://yihui.name/knitr/. R package version 1.11.

Zarcone, Alessandra, Marten van Schijndel, Jorrig Vogels & Vera Demberg. 2017. Salience and attention in surprisal-based accounts of language processing. In Alice Blumenthal-Dramé, Adriana Hanulíková & Bernd Kortmann (eds.), *Perceptual linguistic salience: Modeling causes and consequences*, 7–23. Lausanne: Frontiers Media.

Name index

Subject index

www.ingramcontent.com/pod-product-compliance
Lightning Source LLC
Chambersburg PA
CBHW080917100426
42812CB00007B/2301